AF725573

THE RULE OF LAW IN THE REAL WORLD

In *The Rule of Law in the Real World*, Paul Gowder defends a new conception of the rule of law as the coordinated control of power, and demonstrates that the rule of law, thus understood, creates and preserves social equality in a state. In a highly engaging, interdisciplinary text that moves seamlessly from theory to reality, using examples ranging from ancient Greece through the present, Gowder sheds light on how societies have achieved the rule of law, how they have sustained it in the face of political upheaval, and how it may be measured and developed in the future. *The Rule of Law in the Real World* is an essential work for scholars, students, policy makers, and anyone else who believes the rule of law is critical to the proper functioning of society. For more information, visit http://rulelaw.net. This title is also available as Open Access on Cambridge Core.

Paul Gowder is an associate professor of law and of political science at the University of Iowa, researching constitutional law, ethics, normative and conceptual jurisprudence, political philosophy, computational and empirical legal studies, and game theory. Before joining academia, he worked as a public interest litigator practicing poverty and civil rights law.

The Rule of Law in the Real World

PAUL GOWDER
University of Iowa

CAMBRIDGE
UNIVERSITY PRESS

CAMBRIDGE
UNIVERSITY PRESS

Shaftesbury Road, Cambridge CB2 8EA, United Kingdom

One Liberty Plaza, 20th Floor, New York, NY 10006, USA

477 Williamstown Road, Port Melbourne, VIC 3207, Australia

314–321, 3rd Floor, Plot 3, Splendor Forum, Jasola District Centre, New Delhi – 110025, India

103 Penang Road, #05–06/07, Visioncrest Commercial, Singapore 238467

Cambridge University Press is part of Cambridge University Press & Assessment, a department of the University of Cambridge.

We share the University's mission to contribute to society through the pursuit of education, learning and research at the highest international levels of excellence.

www.cambridge.org
Information on this title: www.cambridge.org/9781316502020

© Paul Gowder 2016

This work is in copyright. It is subject to statutory exceptions and to the provisions of relevant licensing agreements; with the exception of the Creative Commons version the link for which is provided below, no reproduction of any part of this work may take place without the written permission of Cambridge University Press.

An online version of this work is published at doi.org/10.1017/9781316480182 under a Creative Commons Open Access license CC-BY-NC-ND 4.0 which permits re-use, distribution and reproduction in any medium for non-commercial purposes providing appropriate credit to the original work is given. You may not distribute derivative works without permission. To view a copy of this license, visit Creative Commons – Attribution-NonCommercial-NoDerivatives 4.0 International – CC BY-NC-ND 4.0

All versions of this work may contain content reproduced under license from third parties. Permission to reproduce this third-party content must be obtained from these third-parties directly.

When citing this work, please include a reference to the DOI 10.1017/9781316480182

First published 2016

A catalog record for this publication is available from the British Library.

Library of Congress Cataloging in Publication Data
Gowder, Paul, author.
The rule of law in the real world / Paul Gowder.
New York : Cambridge University Press, 2016.
LCCN 2015038101 | ISBN 9781107136892 (hardback)
LCSH: Rule of law.
LCC K3171 .G69 2016 | DDC 340/.11–dc23
LC record available at http://lccn.loc.gov/2015038101

ISBN 978-1-107-13689-2 Hardback
ISBN 978-1-316-50202-0 Paperback

Cambridge University Press & Assessment has no responsibility for the persistence or accuracy of URLs for external or third-party internet websites referred to in this publication and does not guarantee that any content on such websites is, or will remain, accurate or appropriate.

For Vero

Contents

Acknowledgments

Part of this book is derived from my prior publications, although all have been heavily revised and no chapter has previously appeared elsewhere in its entirety. Parts of Chapter 1 and Chapter 2 have previously appeared in part in Paul Gowder, 2013, "The Rule of Law and Equality," *Law and Philosophy* 32(5): 565–618 (reproduced by permission per Springer copyright transfer agreement). Parts of Chapter 2 and Chapter 3 have previously appeared in part in Paul Gowder, 2014, "Equal Law in an Unequal World," *Iowa Law Review* 99(3): 1021–81 (copyright retained and republication rights reserved by the undersigned). Parts of Chapter 5 and Chapter 6 have previously appeared in part in Paul Gowder, 2014, "Democracy, Solidarity, and the Rule of Law: Lessons from Athens," *Buffalo Law Review* 62(1): 1–67 (copyright retained and republication rights reserved by the undersigned). Finally, part of Chapter 6 has appeared in part in Paul Gowder, 2015, "Trust and Commitment: How Athens Rebuilt the Rule of Law," in Claudio Corradetti, Nir Eisikovits, and Jack Volpe Rotondi, eds., *Theorizing Transitional Justice* (Ashgate, 2015) (copyright retained and republication rights reserved by the undersigned). In addition, parts of "The Rule of Law and Equality" and "Democracy, Solidarity, and the Rule of Law: Lessons from Athens" as well as parts of Chapter 1 and Chapter 4 were previously part of my (unpublished, and not otherwise available) Stanford University PhD dissertation (2012) (during which process I received financial support from the Gerhard Casper Stanford Graduate Fellowship and the Geballe Dissertation Prize Fellowship). The final months of the writing of this book were supported by the Institute for Advanced Study, School of Social Science.

So many people have offered kind feedback that the only possible way to acknowledge them all is in a soulless alphabetical list (and many are unfortunately forgotten), to wit: Arash Abizadeh, Danielle Allen, Elizabeth Anderson, Marcus Arvan, Kristen Bell, Patricia Broussard, Rachel Brule, Dustin Buehler, Steven Burton, Joshua Cohen, Charlton Copeland, David Dyzenhaus, James Fearon, Gary Fine, Evan Fox-Decent, Tom Gallanis, Robert Gordon, Avner Greif, Enrique Guerra, Peter Halewood, Herb Hovenkamp, John Inazu, Patti Lenard,

Jacob Levy, Catherine Lu, Dan Markel (late and greatly missed), Candace McCoy, Hudson Meadwell, Frank Michelman, Ebrahim Moosa, Muriel Morisey, Victor Muñiz-Fraticelli, Michael Nafi, Josiah Ober, Angela Onwuachi-Willig, Mark Osiel, Andrew Rehfeld, John Reitz, Tobey Scharding, Micah Schwartzman, Ahmed Souaiaia, Natalie Stoljar, Brian Tamanaha, Alexander Tsesis, Eli Wald, Daniel Weinstock, and Adrian Wing, as well as those others who helped out in the many workshops noted below. Joshua Cohen and Josiah Ober in particular provided endless support and inspiration, both intensively during the writing of the PhD dissertation that suggested the skeleton for this book and with wise advice thereafter.

I would also like to thank the University of Iowa research assistants who have contributed to the preparation of this book, Brett Holubeck, Shawn McCullough, Malvika Rawal, Estiven Rojo, and Eric Schmitt, as well as Seth Jones, a professional copy editor who rescued my references after a technological catastrophe, and Rhonda DeCook and her students in a University of Iowa statistical consulting seminar, Stephanie Kriewall and Laura Hosch, who provided invaluable assistance with early modeling attempts. Alejandro Ponce of the World Justice Project very kindly provided the raw data on which the analyses in Chapter 9 were carried out, and Margaret Levi kindly connected us. Corey Yanofsky and Joe Foley provided kind advice for writing the R code that made up the simulation in Chapter 8. The assistance of Brenna Miller and Benjamin Rogers at the University of Iowa High Performance Computing cluster has been invaluable in actually getting that simulation running. Mandy Keifetz miraculously conjured an index out of thin air (and experience, and skill, and training).

Various parts of this book have been presented in numerous workshops and conferences, including the Sharing Scholarship, Building Teachers Workshop at Albany Law School; Arizona State University Legal Scholars Workshop; ClassCrits V, Culp Colloquium at Duke University; Big Ten Untenured Faculty Conference at Indiana University Maurer School of Law; the workshop on egalitarianism at the Institute for Advanced Study, School of Social Science; Iowa Legal Studies Workshop; Mid-Atlantic People of Color Legal Scholarship Conference; Midwest Junior Scholars Workshop at Washington University, St. Louis; Montreal Political Theory Manuscript Workshop of the Groupe de Recherche Interuniversitaire en Philosophie Politique de Montréal; Southeast/Southwest People of Color Legal Scholarship Conference; Stanford Humanities Center Workshop, Stanford Political Theory Workshop, a classics/political science seminar at Stanford, a Stanford Law School workshop, and a joint workshop between the Freeman Spogli Institute for International Studies and Stanford Law School; and faculty job talks in 2011 and 2012 at the University of California (Hastings), University of Iowa, University of Virginia, and Washington University (St. Louis); I have benefited greatly from feedback from the participants therein, some, but not all, of whom are individually mentioned above.

Introduction

Everyone seems to care about the rule of law. The rich and powerful governments of the world judge others by it; the poor and weak insist that they have it, and thus are entitled to the respect and commercial opportunities offered by the developed world; the United Nations, the World Bank, and nongovernmental organizations galore try to promote it, and philosophers praise it. But what is it? And should we really care? Is it just another form of neocolonial cultural hegemony, an excuse for state-building that just means making the governments of the world safer for multinational corporations ("economic development")? Or can it have meaning to the masses as well as the elite, to Afghanistan as well as the United States? These are the questions that this book explores. Ultimately, I will suggest that the rule of law really is valuable for all, but not for the reasons most academics and policy makers have traditionally thought, and that this yields important insights on how it is achieved and how policy makers should promote it.

Most of us know the rule of law in the form of buzzwords: "A government of laws, not of men." "Nobody is above the law." We can more or less reliably pick out the countries that have it – the Western democracies are the usual suspects – and we have a pretty good clue of the countries that don't: in recent history, the classic examples are tyrannies like the Soviet Union and Haiti under the Duvaliers; today we think of countries like Afghanistan, in the grip of chaos and violence thanks, in Afghanistan's case, to foreign invasion. Pressed to explain what it means for those countries to lack the rule of law, most of us would start to talk about show trials and disappearances, Tonton Macoutes in Haiti and KGB agents terrorizing the Russian public, bribe-taking, and police running amok. On the brighter side, we might talk about fair trials and public laws, about neutral judges and police who read you your rights as they take you to the lockup. But do we have anything more than a list of good things to strive for and bad things to avoid?

Scholars in a variety of academic disciplines think that they do. Philosophers and lawyers, often following leading accounts by Lon Fuller and Friedrich Hayek, have collected a cluster of ideas under the rubric of the rule of law: the law is to be predictable, stable, public, general, and (to some scholars) more or less actually obeyed within the societies it purports to regulate. But within these loose boundaries, there is no agreement as to the details of what it means to satisfy these broad ideals, and many even deny that all are important – the leading legal philosopher Joseph Raz, for example, has argued that the law need not be general. On the other hand, some, such as Ronald Dworkin, have argued that the rule of law makes much more extensive demands on political communities, perhaps amounting to an entire theory of justice.[1]

Nor do the philosophers and lawyers agree on the importance of the rule of law in a general theory of law and politics: among the many areas of disagreement are whether a state has to have the rule of law to have something that might be described as "law" at all, whether the rule of law requires anything of ordinary citizens or just of government officials, and whether the rule of law is part of a theory of democracy or independent from it – or, on the other end, whether the rule of law is flat out inconsistent with democracy. All of this chaos has led some scholars, such as Jeremy Waldron, to call the rule of law an "essentially contested concept."[2]

At the same time that philosophers and lawyers are unable to agree on what the rule of law is, social scientists are busily making use of their interpretations of the concept in empirical studies. Unfortunately, they appear to have next to nothing to do with what the philosophers and lawyers say the rule of law is. Some of the measures the empirical social scientists use turn out to be downright bizarre. For example, the World Bank's "governance indicator" for the rule of law combines data about, among other things, the strength of intellectual property protection, how much crime there is, the prevalence of illegal donations to political parties, how quickly disputes get resolved, and, my personal favorite, "access to water for agriculture."[3] Similarly, the World Justice Project's (generally much superior) rule of law index concatenates variables about the control of crime, religious freedom, labor rights, and freedom of opinion, with more conventional rule of law ideas like public laws and government powers specified by law.[4]

Often those in the social sciences and the policy community essentially assimilate the rule of law to the protection of property rights.[5] This notion, however, does little to help us think about possibilities like a socialist state that nonetheless regulates its citizens under a well-organized legal system, or, in the other direction, a capitalist tyranny that protects the property rights of the elite and promotes economic development while conducting a reign of terror featuring disappearances, show trials, and similar markers of a twentieth-century failed legal system.[6]

Even though academics can't come up with a consistent story of what the rule of law is, states in the developed world, and the international organizations that they dominate, offer the rule of law as a panacea to the developing countries.[7] The entities that concern themselves with promoting the rule of law include the United Nations, the European Union, the North Atlantic Treaty Organization, the World Bank, the Organisation for Economic Co-operation and Development, the Organization for Security and Cooperation in Europe, the American Bar

Association, the Carnegie Endowment, the Open Society Foundations, Human Rights Watch, and many others, and the Government Accountability Office reports that the United States had spent upwards of $970 million on promoting the rule of law from 1993 to 1998.

In the face of the widespread disagreements that I've already noted, each of the two distinct academic communities has some areas of consensus. Among philosophers and lawyers, there seems to be a near universal belief that the rule of law promotes individual liberty. This should seem odd, since there are so many different conceptions of what the rule of law is (and even more different conceptions of what liberty is). Similarly, political scientists and economists generally seem to think that the rule of law promotes economic growth.[8] This too is odd, since they lack a consensus definition of what it is that they're measuring.

By way of armchair diagnosis, I suspect the disconnection between the law/philosophy conversations about the rule of law and the political science/economics conversations is attributable to faults on both sides. From the philosophers and lawyers, the standard normative theory accounts of the concept of the rule of law are quite abstract and difficult to connect to observable phenomena of the sorts that can be tested by social scientists, yet simultaneously extensive and demanding, generating lengthy laundry lists of requirements that states must satisfy.[9] Moreover, it is often not obvious how to conceive of differences in the degree to which states satisfy the rule of law, and some theorists go so far as to deny that achievement of the rule of law can be a matter of degree.[10] Both of those features make it difficult for social scientists to generate testable hypotheses in which the rule of law is either a dependent or an independent variable, and thus naturally leads them to turn to other ways of conceiving the idea. And from the political science and economics side, much of the conversation seems to be distorted (not to say corrupted) by the needs of the "development community" (i.e., the World Bank, the International Monetary Fund, and the like) and the foreign policies of the richest countries, which in turn are substantially focused on exporting capitalism and a safe investment environment for multinational business, in accordance with the privatization agenda often labeled the "Washington consensus"), in which the rule of law in its guise as the protection of property rights can be found.[11]

Yet the different conversations on the rule of law must not be separate. A normative and conceptual account of an "essentially contested concept" like the rule of law cannot be given wholly from the armchair – especially not when its practical extensions are so closely tied to our perceptions of specific states and institutions of the contemporary world and a particular course of history. Rather, such an account must prove itself by its ability to make sense of those real-world institutions, which requires delving into history, law, and political science to find its place in those domains. Similarly, political scientists and economists cannot measure the rule of law unless they have some clue what it is and why it matters to study the things that are being observed – that is, unless a philosophical foundation is first built for the object of measurement. And development professionals will not be able to promote the rule of law unless they have both adequately conceptualized measurement tools in order to determine its presence and effects, as well as an account of why it is worth having – both to make sense themselves of why they are involved in the enterprise in the first place and to understand what might motivate the people in the countries they are trying to aid to care.

Accordingly, this book aims to heal the breaches between law and philosophy, political science and economics, and the development community. It first makes an argument about what the rule of law is (emphatically *not* capitalism or private property rights): a normative principle regulating political states, according to which coercive power – in the first, weaker, version of the rule of law – must be used under rules that give those over whom that power is exercised the opportunity to call the users of the power to account on the basis of reasons; in the second (stronger) version, those rules must be actually justifiable to all on the basis of reasons that are consistent with the equality of all. It then argues that understanding the rule of law this way can help us understand what has motivated those who have defended the rule of law in the past – an attempt to sustain the equal standing of those with a stake in legal systems. And it can help us understand what will help build and sustain the rule of law in the future – legal systems that, by treating their people as equals, give those people reasons to commit to their defense in the face of threat and instability. In that way, the social scientific account of the rule of law directly incorporates the normative value that the rule of law serves as an explanatory factor in its development and persistence as well as the basis for policy initiatives to bring it about in the real world.

The first task is to give a consistent and convincing account of what the rule of law is, using the normative/conceptual tools of lawyers and philosophers. The normative and conceptual account is designed from the start to span the divide between the philosophy/law community and the economics/political science community. It is parsimonious and relatively concrete, so that social scientists can measure it, and the defense of the account against other competing accounts of what the rule of law is and why we should care about it incorporates the criterion that the correct account of the rule of law should have something to do with the real world: it should help us understand actual states, and the many ways in which the rule of law appears to function in the world around us. The egalitarian theory in the first four chapters represents a sharp break from the traditional theorizing about the rule of law, associated with scholars ranging from Friedrich Hayek to John Rawls, who have connected the rule of law to individual liberty.

Supporting this account, chapters on classical Athens (Chapters 5 and 6) and Britain (Chapter 7) show how this egalitarian conception of the rule of law helps us understand actual societies through history and how they need not be connected with distinctively American institutions like the separation of powers, binding judicial review, and the like. The last several chapters then draw on those case studies of Athens and Britain, as well as the American legal system, and deploy strategic modeling tools commonly used in the new institutional economics to shed new light on what leads rule of law societies into existence and what holds them together. I argue that the key mechanism is commitment: the rule of law will exist and persist only if the members of a political community can see how it preserves their equal status, and are able to commit to coordinated enforcement of the law against the powerful. Thus, this book gives evidence that the masses in Athens defended the rule of law in order to protect their collective strength and status against the threats of oligarchic elites. It also gives evidence that the parliamentarians in England saw the rule of law as an important element of their status as equal citizens, against the overweening aspirations of the king. And it gives a strategic account of how these beliefs were right, and how these peoples managed to successfully control the abuse of power in the aid of community-wide equality.

The book concludes by turning from the past to the future, and argues that, ultimately, the reason we should promote the rule of law in the real world is based on that commitment to equality. Following on Chapter 6, Chapters 8 and 9 push the ideas developed in the previous chapters to their limits, by making broad claims about the arc of the development of the rule of law over centuries, and about what this suggests for contemporary efforts to bring it about in the short term. Thus, Chapter 8 develops and defends bold claims about the rule of law's teleology of equality: how the formal legal constraints on power of the weak version of the rule of law create long-term pressure to make the law more substantively equal over time.

Chapter 9 directly addresses the development community. It draws out the implications of the normative, historical, and strategic claims developed in the rest of the book to provide a case for the strategy broadly known as "bottom-up rule of law development," and suggests a focus, within that strategy, on promoting equal law that wins the commitment of the people living under it, and the institutions necessary to support mass coordination in order to implement that commitment. It then develops a novel measurement strategy for the rule of law. Unlike previous measurement attempts, this book offers a proof-of-concept unidimensional rule of law scale that is directly drawn from a conceptual account of the nature of the rule of law, and built in conjunction with it. It demonstrates that a preliminary implementation of a measurement based on these techniques behaves much as we would, theoretically, expect it to behave. This final chapter merely maps a preliminary outline for future efforts: I have neither access to the extensive cross-national data to fully implement the measurement technique described, nor the local expertise to offer specific counsel to rule of law development practitioners on the ground. Nonetheless, I hope that it will give development practitioners and social scientists strong reason to take the ideas it offers seriously, and to bring them to local expertise and more comprehensive data.

This book concludes by turning inward. Much rule of law scholarship and policy making are concerned with the promotion of the rule of law in economically, politically, and militarily weak or unstable countries that are presumed to lack it, in initiatives led by powerful and stable countries that are presumed to have it. In reality, however, those powerful countries – particularly the United States – are subject to serious criticism from a rule of law perspective. The actions of the federal government in conjunction with the war on terror suggest that law on the books is not fully public and regular; more alarmingly still, the unchecked actions of police across the nation suggest that neither American officials nor the American public are fully committed to defending equal legal rights for African-Americans. This book thus concludes by calling for rule of law development at home as well as abroad.

Three themes – *equality, commitment, and realism* – run through the book. The rule of law gives flesh to the ideal of legal equality, and, in doing so, expresses an important kind of social equality, is necessary for political equality, and generates a demand for material equality. It achieves these ends through commitment, in both the philosophical sense and the strategic sense: the rule of law makes it possible for citizens to become committed to the legal order in which they live, and demands that commitment in order to permit the law to be used as a tool to coordinate their behavior in order to preserve their equal standing. When a state achieves the rule of law, it achieves a commitment to equality among its citizens. And it does so in the real world.

Chapter 1

The rule of law: a basic account

In this chapter and the next, I present a novel account of what the rule of law demands and why we should care. The account brings together pretheoretical evaluations of rule of law institutions in real states, functional generalizations of those institutions, and an account of their moral worth.

Together, Chapters 1 and 2 defend two key theses. First, the rule of law is morally valuable because it is required for the state to treat subjects of law as equals ("the equality thesis"). Specifically, the rule of law fosters *vertical equality* between officials and nonofficials and *horizontal equality* among nonofficials.

Second, states comply with the rule of law to the extent that they satisfy the following three conditions ("the three principles"):

Regularity: Officials are reliably constrained to use the state's coercive power only when authorized by good faith and reasonable interpretations of preexisting, reasonably specific, legal rules.

Publicity: The rules on which officials rely to authorize coercion are available for subjects of law to learn; officials give an explanation, on reasonable demand, of their application of the rules to authorize coercion in individual cases; and officials offer those who are the objects of state coercion the opportunity to make arguments about the application of legal rules to their circumstances; the public at large may observe these reasons and the arguments about them.

Generality: Neither the rules under which officials exercise coercion nor officials' use of discretion under those rules make irrelevant distinctions between subjects of law; a distinction is irrelevant if it is not justifiable by public reasons to all concerned.

Each condition presupposes the satisfaction of those before it. (It is possible, however, to combine the partial satisfaction of a later principle with only a partial satisfaction of an earlier principle – for example, to have a state that is partly general, but excludes some discrete class of individuals from the protection of the laws, and hence is also only partly regular and public.) Regularity and publicity together lead to vertical equality. A state that has achieved them has achieved a weak version of the rule of law: its officials cannot easily abuse their power, and individuals can be fairly secure in their legal rights against the state. Generality leads to horizontal equality. A state that has achieved it has achieved a strong version of the rule of law: in it, individuals are genuinely equal under the law.

When states achieve vertical equality, their legal institutions guard against *hubris*, officials' use of their powers to claim superior status. They also guard against *terror*, the use of the state's power to cow individuals into submissiveness.

When states achieve horizontal equality, their legal institutions prevent *legal caste*, the state's support of hierarchies among individuals, particularly along ascriptive group lines. They serve the obligation of *reciprocity* that individuals have to one another to share alike the cost to produce the public good of law and order. Finally, they ensure that everyone is *counted* – the interests of no one in the community are treated by the law with complete disregard.

The heart of this conception of the rule of law is responsiveness to reasons. The weak version of the rule of law treats people with respect, as minimally capable of responding to reasons given them by preexisting rules that govern their behavior, while also restricting those officials who wield coercive power to acting in accordance with those reasons, rather than simply their own wills. Moreover, they directly recruit the capacity of ordinary people to reason about reasons by making the use of state force against them conditional on their having an opportunity to publicly contest and deploy the reasons given by law.

The reasons at play in the weak version are artificial (or artifactual) in that they are creations of an act of rule making: by saying that they are "reasons," I simply mean that they take the form of reasons: externally specified normative standards for behavior that can form the basis for better or worse rational arguments, and that can be deployed effectively to criticize people for failing to comply with them. The form of a reason is the opposite of arbitrariness, which is disconnection from reasons: the arbitrary official, when asked why she or he coerced some citizen, can just say "Because," whereas the official who is bound to legal reasons at least has to be able to say something that is comprehensible to the person over whom power is exercised. In doing so, that official treats the other like an adult, and an equal.

The reasons at play in the strong version are real reasons, in that someone whom the state orders about on the authority of general laws will able to understand the laws as actually meaningful to her (at least in a constructive sense if not a subjective one). The law will recognize her as a stakeholder in the society, and recognize that she ought not to be ordered about at gunpoint unless the orders can be understood to capture something that she has reason to do independent of the unadulterated will of some lawmaker.

This chapter explicates the weak version of the rule of law. Chapter 2 will cover the strong version.

I OPENING TECHNICALITIES

Mindful of the fact that the audience for this book includes not only philosophers and lawyers, but also political scientists, economists, and development experts, most of the technical philosophical groundwork has been deferred to the end of this chapter; some has been published elsewhere.[1] In particular, many clarifications, fine points, and answers to objections appear in an article entitled "The Rule of Law and Equality"; the reader who thinks I have missed something obvious is advised to double-check there.[2] However, three points are important enough to highlight at the beginning of the main argument.

First, the rule of law has institutional (or what I have previously called "descriptive") and evaluative components. To see what I mean, compare an idea like democracy to an idea like justice. Justice covers a multitude of normative principles and concrete social practices; there are innumerable uses of the term that bear at most a family resemblance to one another. One's favored conception of justice might be instantiated in anything from a tax-and-transfer system of redistribution to a society ruled by Platonic guardians. By contrast, while there are numerous theories of democracy, they all occupy pretty much the same territory: all have *something* to do with will or opinion aggregation, hearing minority views, removing disobedient officials, and so forth. The rule of law is more like democracy than justice: it has a relatively concrete set of practical extensions. This has important methodological implications: it suggests a coherentist account of the rule of law that draws together normative ideas about the value it serves and observations about the social practices that we ordinarily associate with it.[3] It also suggests that the best account of the rule of law will have the property that I have elsewhere called "verisimilitude" – it will describe actual societies in the real world better than alternative, equally coherent, conceptions.[4]

Second, the rule of law regulates *states* when they exercise their power over individuals. It does not regulate the private use of coercion or violence.[5] Particularly, it does not give us a reason to object to anarchy, nor does it oblige nonofficials to obey the law. However, as will be seen in Chapters 6 and 8, the rule of law does require nonofficials to be sufficiently committed to its preservation to be willing to collectively defend it against officials who might abuse their power. That is, in the first instance, a practical rather than a conceptual requirement, although, in view of the goal of this book to state a conception of the rule of law that bridges philosophical and social scientific approaches to the topic, it will soon become clear that such strong practical constraints feature in the concept of the rule of law as well.

While there are many regulative principles for both private and state violence, the unique significance of state violence generates a unique principle, the rule of law, to guard against its abuse. States are distinguished from all other entities by their expressive and practical significance. By "expressive significance," I refer to the facts identified by Weber and legal philosopher Joseph Raz: states ordinarily claim a monopoly over the legitimate use of violence in their territories, and ordinarily claim that those in the territory are obliged to obey their commands.[6] With that, they typically forbid individuals from resisting the force that they wield; often they also claim to be acting in the name of the citizenry as a whole or some constitutive social, national, or ethnic group.[7]

By "practical significance," I refer to the fact identified by Thomas Hobbes: states have overwhelming force within their territories. In ordinary political life, in a modern state, it's impossible or staggeringly costly for individuals to resist its power; moreover, there's ordinarily no external power to which individuals can turn to protect them from it.

These features (which I will henceforth call the "Weberian and Hobbesian properties") make state power different in kind from the private use of force. Its expressive significance confers upon it more morally relevant dimensions than private power: a mugger who assaults you on the street doesn't claim you're obliged to quietly submit to the violence, or that it's done in your name. The state does. Its practical significance makes it more fearsome and influential: you might have a chance to fight back against the mugger, or at least call upon the state to defend you. There's no one to defend you from the state.

However, in some societies, there can be forms of nonstate power that sufficiently resemble state power, particularly in its practical significance, so that their control too becomes a matter for the rule of law. For example, in Classical Athens, as will be seen in Chapters 5 and 6, the rich and powerful had an interest in undermining the state, and were capable of overwhelming ordinary citizens on a one-to-one basis. There, the rule of law required their nonstate power be regulated, too, just because it threatened to take on the Hobbesian and Weberian properties. At the end of Chapter 3, I explain more precisely where the rule of law requires private power be regulated.

Finally, I claim that the egalitarian account of the rule of law and its moral value is factually and normatively robust. By "factually robust," I mean that the arguments offered do not depend on strong assumptions about facts about social arrangements, human motivations, or the like that differ from society to society. This is a weaker criterion than necessary truth: the arguments might not be true in every possible social world, but they are true for a substantial range of reasonably common social worlds. By "normatively robust," I mean that these arguments are, as far as possible, nonsectarian. They are meant to be acceptable without taking on overly controversial normative commitments. This argument for the moral value of the rule of law relies on the ecumenical core of the ideal of equality: if nothing else, those who value equality object to hierarchies of status and esteem, and demand that the state treat individuals with equal respect and take each of their interests into account.

The robustness criteria respond to concerns with the scientific and the political usefulness of a conception of the rule of law. First, a conception of the rule of law ought to be compatible with a social scientific explanation of its appearance in societies characterized by different political institutions and ethical ideals. Thus, we ought not to say that the rule of law responds to institutions and motivations that have appeared in few rule of law societies, or to values their citizens have rejected. In

Chapters 5 and 7, I show that a variety of societies have accepted egalitarian values as the basis of their rule of law, or at least have been influenced by them; in Chapter 9, I put the robustness of this conception of the rule of law to immediate use, by developing a proof of concept scale to aid social scientists in measuring the rule of law.

Second, an account of the rule of law ought to be able to motivate citizens and officials to act in accordance with it in the real world. Explaining the moral value of the rule of law is a political task as well as a justificatory one. Not everyone supports the rule of law, and political leaders may think they have good reason to ignore its constraints in the pursuit of their vision of the public good. Those who think that the rule of law generates normative obligations should be able to offer their arguments to those leaders. For those arguments to be persuasive, they should not appeal to sectarian values that may not be shared by those addressed, and they should be applicable across the broad range of human societies in which we may wish to offer them.[8]

Normative robustness is important for a second reason. As Chapter 6 will show, the rule of law depends (practically) on a commitment to its preservation on the part of those whom the law protects. A conception of the rule of law that is normatively robust is more likely to be able to sustain that commitment – those who would encourage their fellows to defend it will have moral as well as pragmatic arguments to offer for it. In Chapter 8, I will argue that the egalitarian value of the rule of law helps us understand how rule of law states actually hold on to it; this explanatory insight depends on the normative robustness of the egalitarian account. In Chapter 9, I explain how the egalitarian values underlying the rule of law can actually be used by development specialists and others to promote it across the world.

Finally, throughout this book, I speak of "subjects of law," or, more informally, "individuals" or "citizens" as those whose equal standing the rule of law protects. Sometimes, I say "nonofficials" to highlight the distinction between ordinary individuals and those who wield official power. By all of these terms, I mean those whom the state claims the authority to command. This category is not limited to those who count as members of the political community ("citizens" in the conventional sense), and includes, for example, aliens stopped at the border, transients incidentally in the territory, and those whom the state has disenfranchised or enslaved. I cannot here reach any conclusions about the scope of the protections of the rule of law as applied to aliens found outside the territory (e.g., in military conflicts). Also, by the use of the term "individuals," I do not mean to deny that groups, corporate entities, and the like can claim the protection of the rule of law; this question, too, is beyond the scope of the present work.

Having gotten the technical hurdles out of this way, I now turn to defend the principles of regularity and publicity, and the conception of equality that they serve. They respond to our experience, throughout history, of societies in which the rule of law catastrophically fails – societies such as Haiti under the Duvaliers, or the Soviet Union, in which individuals live in constant fear of officials and officials behave arrogantly toward nonofficials. First, I will elaborate publicity and regularity, their scope, and how they are derived from the specific practices of rule of law states. Then I will show that publicity and regularity are necessary to free states from hubris and terror, and sufficient to at least greatly circumscribe them.

II THE WEAK VERSION OF THE RULE OF LAW IN TWO PRINCIPLES

We begin with the core concept: the rule of law imposes the twin demands on the state to control the use of its monopoly over violence with rules and to make those rules accessible to those over whom that monopoly is used.

A *Regularity*

If the rule of law means anything, it must mean that those who control the power of the state may not use it whenever and however they want, bound only by their untrammeled whims – their power must be bound by law in some meaningful sense. I express this fundamental idea in the principle of regularity, the minimum condition for a state to have even a rudimentary version of the rule of law. A state satisfies it if officials are reliably constrained to use the state's coercive power only when authorized by good faith and reasonable interpretations of preexisting, reasonably specific rules.[9]

Regularity defines the line between states that control official violence and those that are run at the will of executive officials, or in which soldiers and police use violence willy-nilly against individuals who have something they want or who anger them. Because this is the most fundamental function of the rule of law, most conceptions contain something like it.

Another way to express the ambition of the principle of regularity is that it requires the state's coercive power be exercised *impersonally*. Regularity is violated when officials are permitted to treat the power with which they're entrusted as part of their personal endowments, suitable for use in their private relations with members of the community; it's respected when they are constrained to treat their power as the instrument of an agency relationship between themselves and the state, usable only for the purposes and under the conditions given by the terms of their legal authority.[10] This is an ideal of *role separation*.

The heart of the idea of role separation is captured in a 1916 short story by Munshi Premchand, "Panch Parmeshwar."[11] The two main characters, Jumman Sheikh and Alagu Chaudhuri, begin as close friends, but Jumman mistreats his aunt, and when she convenes the local council (*panchayat*) to resolve the ensuing dispute, Alagu is nominated as the chair. Thanks to their friendship, Jumman expects an easy victory.

However, moved by his official responsibilities, Alagu chooses justice over friendship, and rules in favor of the aunt.

After the judgment, Jumman, feeling betrayed, becomes Alagu's enemy, and casts about looking for revenge. An opportunity comes a few months later: Alagu convenes the council to get payment on a disputed debt, and this time Jumman is named chair. Alagu is dejected, sure that he has lost his money. Here's what happens next:

> As soon as he accepted the headship of the panchayat, a new awareness of his duties dawned on him. He said to himself: "I am now the arbiter of justice and dharma. What I say will be accepted as a divine fiat, and I cannot allow my private prejudices to influence the sanctity of the divine word. I must not depart by a hair's-breadth from the truth."

After hearing the case, Jumman surprises everyone by ruling in Alagu's favor. Explaining himself later, he says: "Today I have discovered a great truth – I have seen that when you become one of the panchayat, you are no one's friend and no one's enemy. You are only there to dispense justice. Today I have realized that God speaks through the panchayat." Moved by the realization, the men again become friends.

This story captures the central idea of role separation through its most familiar exemplar, the impartial judge. Upon assuming the judicial role, each of the protagonists not only surrenders his personal attachments of friendship and enmity, but also surrenders his identity altogether, becoming the voice of God. This, in ideal form, is the principle of regularity. When an official (not just a judge) puts on her public role, she becomes the voice of the law. While the rules may leave her with some discretion, that discretion isn't exercised *as her*; it's exercised *as the voice of the law*, for the law's ends.

I will argue that regularity and publicity together protect individuals from being subjected to official terror – from the specter of officials with open-ended threats who can use their power to make individuals live in fear and behave submissively. (By "open-ended threats" or "open threats," I just mean a capacity to do harm to a citizen that an official can use substantially at a whim.) Just as Alagu feared the *panchayat* under his enemy, subjects will fear the power wielded by officials in irregular states. Unless official coercion is rule-bound, officials will be able to use their power to avenge themselves against their enemies, to expropriate property, and to extort deferential treatment from the population at large – to behave like the Tonton Macoutes or the KGB.

Numerous standard practices of rule of law societies serve the principle of regularity.[12] Rule of law societies tend to forbid vague laws. They tend to use tools like the independent judiciary, appellate review, and the jury trial to impose checks on officials' actually conforming their behavior to rules. They tend to require that the law be prospective and forbid bills of attainder. Each of these practices helps to protect individuals from living in fear of open-ended threats from unconstrained officials. For example, regularity forbids vague laws because officials can manipulate them to punish individuals whenever they want. Similarly, regularity forbids retroactive laws and bills of attainder because they can be enacted to retaliate against individuals who cross officials.[13]

The reader may understandably hesitate at the fairly vague requirement that the rules be "reasonably specific." Unfortunately, this is a feature of the normative terrain. More specific rules leave officials less discretion in applying them, but there is no perfect specificity: all rules must leave officials some discretion, because no text can perfectly specify all situations to which it will apply.[14] For want of a plausible formal way to specify how much that discretion must be constrained, I turn to context-dependent and pragmatic judgments to pick out the rules that are too open-ended.

We can give some content to reasonable specificity by appealing to the goals of the principle of regularity. A given power may pose more or less of a risk of generating open-ended threats; we can often determine how serious this risk is, and thus how much control is required for a particular power, with intuition and common sense. For example, the scrutiny of independent judges over the power of eminent domain in the United States is arguably sufficient to render it consistent with the rule of law despite its only being constrained by vague standards like public purposes and just compensation. By contrast, a state whose police arrested individuals under the similarly vague standard "whenever it is just" would confer open-ended threats on those police to an unacceptable degree. The power to arrest is much easier to abuse: it's easy for an individual officer to deploy, and causes a serious short-term harm to the one arrested. By contrast, eminent domain is typically carried out by cumbersome elected or administrative bodies, and requires a further lengthy bureaucratic process before anyone is actually removed from the condemned property. The greater immediate harm the arrest power can cause gives officials who wield it more potential for open-ended threats, and thus gives us good reason to keep it on a tighter leash.

Further difficulty arises from the fact that all rules are open to different interpretations. It would be too demanding to insist that officials only ever use coercive power pursuant to accurate interpretations of the rules, for officials can make reasonable mistakes in applying them, and we do not ordinarily think that a state in which officials make mistakes offends the rule of law on those grounds. At the same time, it is too undemanding to adopt a fully subjective standard, which would permit unreasonable interpretations of law. Separately, it seems too demanding to say that officials be *only motivated* by the rules: certain kinds of reasons can fairly guide officials' choices within the domain permitted by preexisting rules; a police officer, for example, may decide that drunk driving is a particularly dangerous crime and spend more of his efforts catching drunk drivers and less catching speeders without offending the rule of law.

I propose to resolve these difficulties by saying that officials must follow the rules in good faith. By this, I mean that they must act as if they take the rules as generating reasons to act in compliance with them and forbidding their violation (the rule of law does not propose to examine the psychological motivations of officials, just their behavior). This forbids uses of power that officials ought to know that the rules do not permit (e.g., it would be bad faith for the officer of the previous paragraph to decide that driving in the rain is too dangerous and to arrest people for that) while permitting officials to use reasons fairly implied by the law (like drunk driving being more dangerous than speeding) to guide their application of the rules within the domain of discretion the law gives them.[15] It also forbids unreasonable interpretations of the rules yet accommodates (the inevitable) disagreement.

In practice, this is perhaps a worryingly ambiguous criterion. However, the principle of publicity, to be addressed next, will help draw some boundaries around the idea of good faith. It will be seen in the course of discussing that principle that officials must be able to explain how their uses of power are permitted by the rules, and those explanations must be able to survive exposure to counterarguments offered by those over whom power is to be exercised. In a context in which officials listen to those counterarguments and take them seriously, as required by the principle of publicity, the process of external scrutiny will set an upper bound on the extent to which they can sustain exercises of power that are premised on unreasonable interpretations of the rules.

One might have the opposite worry, that regularity is too rigid. Some scholars, most notably Dworkin, deny that law is primarily a matter of specific rules.[16] Instead, according to Dworkin, much of our legal practice involves the application of "principles" – normative standards that are to be weighed against one another in reaching decisions, and that require the extensive use of case-by-case judgment.

Regular legal systems may contain principles. What matters for regularity is that officials be constrained, not how they are constrained. Officials might be constrained by strict de jure rules, where their failure to do so subjects them to legal, social, or political sanction, or they might be constrained by looser de jure rules – open-ended principles leaving them a substantial amount of discretion – where that discretion is itself constrained by unwritten standards that fill out the content of the rules, by social norms that sanction officials for abusing their discretion, by political competition, by checks and balances from other officials, or by something else. Where the written rules constrain less, other tools must take up the slack to constrain more.[17]

B Publicity

The principle of publicity requires that the rules under which officials use power be accessible to nonofficials. It presupposes that there are such (effective) rules – that is, that regularity is satisfied to a significant extent. Specifically, publicity requires that

(a) the laws that authorize official coercion be available for nonofficials to learn (i.e., not secret or unreasonably obscure); (b) officials publicly explain, on demand, their application of the law to authorize coercion in an individual case, where that law itself must meet the principle of regularity; and (c) officials offer those whom they coerce some opportunity to participate in the application of legal rules to their circumstances (i.e., by having an opportunity to make arguments for a particular interpretation of those rules). (The third requirement depends on the second: if officials do not say how the rules authorize their behavior, individuals will find it much more difficult to dispute official decisions.)

The principle of publicity is essentially a reason-giving requirement. Officials must be prepared to give the reasons for their uses of coercion over individual citizens, and those reasons must be statements of how the law, correctly interpreted and applied, permits their actions. Ordinarily this giving of reasons must happen *in public*: the community at large must be able to observe that officials are following the law and come to independent judgments about the extent of official faithfulness.

A state can run afoul of publicity, but not regularity, if officials' power is actually constrained by preexisting rules, but nonofficials have no access to those rules or influence over what befalls them under their auspices. In such societies, the law is the exclusive domain of an elite class of officials, and nonofficials must rely on those elites to protect them.[18]

If regularity is the official-centered side of the rule of law, publicity is the subject-centered side. It responds to the concern not only that officials' use of the state's coercive power actually be constrained, but that subjects of law be able to *know* and to *subjectively rely on* the constraints. Thus, many of the same practices that serve regularity also serve publicity by involving individuals in the mechanisms to control official power. However, some standard practices of rule of law states serve publicity in particular: these include the prohibition against secret law, the requirement that subjects of law have notice and an opportunity to be heard before being coerced, the right to be represented by counsel, the right to be confronted by the evidence against oneself, and similar practices that allow subjects to observe that officials are constrained by rules and participate in the application of those constraints.[19]

Publicity allows nonofficials to verify for themselves that the state satisfies regularity. From a nonofficial's perspective, a state that satisfies regularity but not publicity might not look very different from a state that satisfies neither.

Because publicity allows subjects to figure out whether officials are obeying the law, it also allows them to participate in its enforcement. Institutions (whether courts or otherwise) that force officials to give reasons for their uses of coercion in public permit the population in general to evaluate those reasons. Those that give subjects a forum to claim that officials have ignored the law also give the public a tool to come to consensus evaluations of officials' actions, and thereby to collectively hold them to the law. This reveals how publicity and regularity come together in the weak version of the rule of law: although it might be possible in principle for officials to be constrained to obey the law absent coordinated enforcement by those who benefit (e.g., by some kind of game-theoretic equilibrium among officials with diverse interests who are motivated to hold one another to the law in order to maintain a political compromise), this is practically unlikely to be stable. In most realistic states, we should expect that dispersed power to observe and sanction official rule violations, whether held by relatively elite or relatively nonelite subjects, will be instrumental in the enterprise of controlling official power. (There will be much more on coordinated enforcement in subsequent chapters.)

If we look more closely at the matter, publicity and regularity begin to appear to dissolve into one another. For we may recast the notions of discretion and specificity, so central to the concept of regularity, into epistemic ideas.[20] A minimally specific law, one that grants maximal discretion to the official implementing it, is one in which the meaning (in a nontechnical sense of "practical implications") of its words is known only to that official. For example, if King Rex writes a law in a private language (Rexish), he has maximum discretion in applying it, simply because nobody else can tell him he is wrong. Put differently, the law may have a specific meaning in Rexish, but Rex cannot be constrained to apply the law only consistent with that meaning, for there is nobody with the capacity to constrain him – all the independent judges and well-armed nobles and engaged populaces in the world might have the power to force Rex to obey a law they can understand, but if they cannot observe when Rex has broken the law, then he is totally unconstrained.

Scaling that idea up, a law is more specific, in the sense that it grants less discretion to an individual official, if it is written in a language that only officials know (Officialish). If the police officer on the street badly enforces a law written in Officialish, she is constrained by other officials, but not the public. Practically speaking, this means that, if all the other officials do not care about the law being obeyed, it will not constrain the individual police officer. Equivalently, we may say that the law written in Officialish has the power to constrain an individual police officer relative to all officials, but does not have the power to constrain the class of all officials relative to everyone else.[21]

Now consider a law written in a language everyone speaks. Individual words in that language may be more or less penetrable to the public, but are necessarily penetrable to those with final decision-making authority about them. For example, the law may say "No one may drive at an unreasonable speed." This word "unreasonable" may be quite unclear to ordinary people, but it crystalizes into clarity in particular cases at the moment a judge applies the rule to decide whether someone is guilty or not guilty of speeding, because the judge has the legal authority to finalize the case-by-case meaning of the word. Should she do so without giving any explanation, she is unconstrained (except by any appellate court), and the police are constrained only by the judge, for the judge is the only one with certain knowledge about what the word (legally speaking) means. It begins to appear like an instance of Judgish.

But the procedural demands of the principle of publicity expand that constraint. By allowing the one on trial to make arguments about the word "unreasonable," the judge's interpretation of it is opened to the influence from the linguistic and legal understandings of ordinary subjects. Moreover, the process of giving reasons to explain her ruling allows the judge to expand her epistemic power of making the ultimate judgment to the public at large: by making it possible for the public more generally to argue with judges as well as with police about the word, and to use political power to constrain them, she translates "unreasonable" from Judgish to Publicish.[22]

What this line of argument has suggested is that regularity and publicity refer to the same broad idea. Without publicity, regularity is also lacking, because the notion of being constrained by rules depends on the broad accessibility of both the meaning of the rules doing the constraining and the practical tools for constraint. Separating them is useful for heuristic purposes, to track the historical differences between societies that have not bound the powerful with rules at all and those that have ostensibly bound them with secret or obscure rules. For that reason, I shall continue to do so, but we must keep in mind that the distinction is artificial. There is a difference between the chaos of Caligula and the secrecy of the bureaucratized standards for getting on the Transportation Security Administration no-fly list, but we appeal to the same underlying idea in describing both as offenses to the rule of law.

The requirement that officials explain themselves to those whom they coerce has received less attention in the academic literature than the other elements of publicity, but is quite important in the legal culture of rule of law states. This is particularly visible in the requirements we impose on judges, whom we expect not only to have but to utter reasons for their decisions – a judge who fails to offer written opinions on serious controversies, or who issues significant rulings from the bench without any explanation, has seriously violated legal norms.[23] Such a judge will be seen as high-handed, dismissive of the interests of the parties and of the fact that it might matter to them that they understand what is being done to them and have the opportunity to respond to the reasons given them with their own reasons. As I will argue shortly, such a judge is indulging in an act of antiegalitarian hubris: by declining to explain herself, she is expressing the idea that she doesn't *have* to explain herself – that she is of sufficiently higher status than those appearing before her that she can give imperious commands and those coming before her should just shut up and do what they're told.[24]

I now proceed to the details of that very point.

III VERTICAL EQUALITY

There are two major vices of a state in which publicity and regularity fail: first, officials treat nonofficials with *hubris*: they behave as if they are a superior class in a status hierarchy. Second, officials inflict *terror* on nonofficials: they force nonofficials to fear their power and make it rational for individuals to behave submissively in the face of it.

A *Respect and hubris*

When officials use coercive power without offering reasons, drawn from preexisting law (legal reasons), to the objects of that power, they deliver the message that the one using the power is superior to the one over whom the power is used, and actually constitute a relationship of subordination between themselves and subjects.[25] I call this idea "hubris" to acknowledge its derivation from the classical Athenian hubris law, which forbade the striking of fellow citizens (and even slaves) because such striking expressed a disrespectful attitude of superiority toward its victims – it was a figurative as well as a literal slap in the face (see Chapter 5). By contrast, when a state complies with regularity and publicity, officials express respect toward nonofficials and the political community as a whole, and actually constitute a relationship of equality between them.[26]

By offering reasons for their use of power at all, officials express three distinct forms of respect toward those over whom power is to be used. First, they express the recognition that they actually have to have reasons, and hence that subjects of law are immune from the casual use of official power.[27] Superiors do not need reasons to use their power over inferiors: masters need not have any particular reason to beat their slaves; bosses need not have any particular reason to fire their employees. Second, they express the idea that they are accountable to the particular individuals over whom power is used. Equals are accountable to one another; superiors are not accountable to inferiors: even if the master or boss has some coherent reason for his behavior, he need not explain it to his slave or employee. Third, they express respect for individuals' powers of reasoning – they express that nonofficials are capable of understanding why they are to be coerced, and that it matters that they be given the opportunity to so understand. To be given reasons is to be treated like an adult.

So far, this doesn't require very much respect. When the defendant asks why she's going to jail, the judge might just say "Because I don't like you." That's a reason, to be sure, and it's perhaps a little better than "Shut up or I'll double your sentence," but it still clearly expresses an attitude of superiority.

It is slightly more respectful to offer a reason drawn from something other than the official's personal will. Rather than saying "Because I don't like you," or "Because I felt like it," she might say "Because your conduct posed a danger to the community." This suggests that she doesn't get to use her power just because she wants to – it implies that if the individual's conduct hadn't posed a danger to the community she wouldn't have been entitled to punish him. However, this still falls short of the respect an official ought to offer a subject of law. For offering "Because your conduct posed a danger to the community," standing alone, suggests that the official is the sole judge of what reasons suffice to use her power. She could have just as well said "Because you're a jerk" or "Because the moon is in Virgo."

If an official offers legal reasons for her use of coercive power, matters are different. Even if the law just authorizes the defendant's imprisonment based on the same reasons that our judge would otherwise have offered on her own (e.g., "Anyone whose conduct poses a danger to the community is liable to imprisonment"), legal reasons are embedded in a network of other people's judgments; depending on the precise details of the legal system in question, a legislature or prior judges will have decided that there should be a law about the conduct in question, appellate judges will review the trial judge's decision to ensure that it's actually authorized by the law, prior cases will have filled out the legal rule and given the one over whom power is to be used some idea of what sort of evidence he might offer to defend himself, and so forth. An official who offers legal reasons treats individuals respectfully by showing that her use of power isn't just a matter of her own judgment, but responds to the judgment of all those other people, too. When an official listens to an individual's arguments about how the law is to be applied in a particular case, she also expresses respect for that individual's judgment.[28]

A judge who offers legal reasons for her use of power also treats the political community as a whole respectfully in two ways. First, she acknowledges that it's not ultimately her judgment about the rightful use of that power that matters, but the judgment of the political community. Her judgment is involved in applying the legal rules, but only within bounds specified by the collective judgment.[29] Second, she acknowledges the agency relationship between herself and the state. The judge who uses her official power without appealing to legal reasons is like an employee who disrespectfully uses her employer's property as her own, commingling them and not distinguishing between her purposes and her employer's purposes.

Officials avoid hubris by maintaining a separation of role and personal identity.[30] When an official acts in an official role, she is bound by rules and to the practice of explaining her acts in terms of those rules; the rules and the practice of reason-giving constitute the role. By contrast, an official who is not so constrained communicates that her right to exercise coercive power over another individual is a personal property, rather than a property of her role. The explanation "Because the rules say so" attributes authority and status to the law, whereas the explanation "Because I say so," like no explanation at all, attributes authority and status to the official. Even an official who exercises discretion, when he acts in good faith by doing so on the basis of legal reasons, again attributes authority and status to the rules; by incorporating reasons drawn from his personal preferences or beliefs, he attributes authority and status to himself.

B Terror

Nonofficials in states that do not comport with regularity and publicity, whether or not they are actually targeted by official violence, have good reason to fear officials.

For they know that their well-being is at the whim of a class of people who can wield overwhelming force at will, and those over whose heads that threat is held have no means of defense.

Those who are subject to such terror are rendered unequal twice. First, they are subjected to the experience of relative powerlessness and fear.[31] Second, they are forced to act out their own subordination by behaving submissively toward powerful officials. When an ordinary citizen passed by a member of the Tonton Macoutes or the KGB, he must have felt a pang of alarm, an urge to cringe away and avoid the attention of the wielder of fearsome powers. He must have been obsequiously polite if he was forced to interact with them, and would have been inclined to submit to any "request" the official made.[32] Note that this is also true in a society that has achieved regularity, but not publicity. Even if the KGB officer is constrained by rules, if an ordinary individual doesn't know what those rules are, or will have no say in their application, he still has reason to fear the officer's power. The individual doesn't know the circumstances under which the officer will be able to do him harm, and will not be able to participate in his own defense if he does come into conflict with the officer, instead having to trust other officials to protect his legal rights. He is likely to feel powerless and fearful even if he believes that there really are background rules regulating the officer's behavior. By contrast, a nonofficial who can help herself to the power of rules that constrain the power of officials need not bow and scrape, because she can rely on those rules to keep the officer from retaliating against her for failing to do so.

The asymmetry confronted by an ordinary person facing the might of the state is an essential feature of inegalitarian terror. In a Hobbesian state of nature, we may have unconstrained power over one another, but it doesn't make us unequal. Defenselessness in the face of overwhelming power creates the pervasive fear characteristic of systems of state terror. This is one reason that the rule of law is a regulative principle for state violence, not private violence.

Before moving on, consider the following objection. The law might actually authorize officials to terrorize; for example, it may permit judges to issue a torture warrant.[33] Under such circumstances, this objection goes, the rule of law would not prevent terror: officials with the power to torture are terrorizing regardless of whether their power to do so is regularized by the procedural apparatus of a rule of law legal system.

However, regularized torture is different in kind from the terror that is inflicted in the sort of states where one is always subject to the knock on the door in the middle of the night from some KGB officer. We already have regularized torture in the contemporary Western liberal democracies: think of the horror of a US prison, pervaded by rampant violence, the punitive use of solitary confinement, extraordinarily negligent medical care, and too many other forms of torture to list. Yet the prospect of being put in one of those prisons does not ordinarily cast a pall over day-to-day life in the United States because, at least in those privileged (e.g., white, upper-income) communities where officials comport with the rule of law, ordinary people know that they aren't likely to be put in prison unless they commit an actual crime, that they'll have a chance to defend themselves beforehand, and so forth.

If officials wished to adopt regularized procedures to create full-fledged terror, they doubtless could do so. They could, for example, create a system of secret ex parte torture warrants, and thus replicate the knock on the door in the night under the aegis of procedural propriety. But this would manifestly violate the principle of publicity, as would any system in which officials were authorized to inflict brutal treatment on subjects without notice and an opportunity to defend themselves. By guaranteeing a minimum of warning, by guaranteeing that those subject to brutal treatment at least have an opportunity to put up a defense in a forum where their objections will be listened to and taken seriously, and by making it possible for people to minimize their risk of being subjected to official brutality by complying with public rules, the rule of law puts a strong upper bound on the extent to which any legal system can inflict terror.

Note the further important point that this entails: the weak version of the rule of law not only does not require liberal democracy, but can even be morally valuable in states other than liberal democracies. The case of the torture warrant shows that the weak version of the rule of law is morally valuable in a state that does not respect basic human rights. For another example, the weak version of the rule of law can be morally valuable in a state that does not respect political freedoms, and punishes dissidents, in virtue of the fact that it at least does not allow dissidents to be terrorized: at least they will get trials before they are punished, and the punishment will not come as a terrifying surprise. It follows that nonliberal states and nondemocracies are at least potentially blameworthy for not complying with the rule of law, and praiseworthy for complying with it, independent of their blameworthiness for not being liberal or democratic.[34]

C *Normative robustness*

I have said that an account of the evaluative side of the rule of law should be factually robust, in that it is likely to be true of a broad range of human societies, and normatively robust, in that it avoids controversial normative claims as much as possible. The case for factual robustness is primarily made over the following chapters, where the egalitarian conception of the rule of law is shown to match both history and the strategic structure of rule of law states.[35]

As for normative robustness, although equality is often a highly controversial ideal, some egalitarian ideas are uncontroversial: the claim that the state ought not to create a group of citizens (officials) who can engage in arrogant hubris over others or terrorize them into submission is unlikely to draw objections. The avoidance of hubris and terror is compatible with a very broad range of ways of thinking about equality and overall normative standpoints. Those, for example, who value treating the subjects of law with equal dignity can recognize that hubris and terror are wrong because of the way they create a status hierarchy between officials and ordinary people.[36] Egalitarian democrats, who are concerned primarily with the distribution of political power, may note that the failure of the rule of law is inconsistent with the participation of ordinary citizens as equals in the political process, because officials could use terrorizing power to prop up their own rule against citizens' wills.[37] Those who are concerned with the egalitarian distribution of economic resources can note that terrorizing power enables rent seeking and exploitation. Welfarist egalitarians can note that the lives of those subjected to hubris and terror go dramatically less well than the lives of those who inflict it. Egalitarians concerned with capabilities can note that terror drastically reduces one's functional opportunities.[38] Even those who do not think of themselves as egalitarians, such as libertarians, can agree that the state ought not actually create hierarchies between individuals. Moreover, since the weak version of the rule of law does not require liberal democracy and its moral value is independent of liberal democracy, it does not require one to endorse liberalism or democracy in order to endorse its demands.

So much for the contemporary reason-giving power of hubris and terror, but one might object that the same cannot be said of the past. I advanced the normative robustness desideratum on the basis, in part, that it is necessary to make the philosophical/legal conception of the rule of law compatible with historical and social scientific explanations that take into account the actual motivations of those in rule of law states. However, the rule of law has been around, in various forms, much longer than the general consensus that the state should treat the subjects of law as equals. Pseudo-Xenophon, for example, criticized Athens for protecting slaves from hubris and terror.[39]

However, for determining whether a conception of the rule of law is normatively robust, the relevant motivations are those of officials and ordinary people who take the internal point of view in societies that already have the rule of law, as well as those who are fighting for the rule of law in societies without it. It is not relevant that Pseudo-Xenophon saw fit to criticize elements of the rule of law in the pursuit of his own oligarchic interests, interests naturally leading him to be opposed to the egalitarian institutions of democratic Athens, or that feudal states without the rule of law have been built on an ideology of natural inequality. (Chapter 5 will show that Athenian supporters of the rule of law indeed saw it as valuable for egalitarian reasons.)

Actually, Pseudo-Xenophon himself recognized the way that the rule of law promoted equality (although for him, being an aristocrat, this was a bug, not a feature). His account of the role of law in preventing hubris and terror provided much of the inspiration for mine:

> Now amongst the slaves and metics at Athens there is the greatest uncontrolled wantonness; you can't hit them there, and a slave will not stand aside for you. I shall

> point out why this is their native practice: if it were customary for a slave (or metic or freedman) to be struck by one who is free, you would often hit an Athenian citizen by mistake on the assumption that he was a slave. For the people there are no better dressed than the slaves and metics, nor are they any more handsome. If anyone is also startled by the fact that they let the slaves live luxuriously there and some of them sumptuously, it would be clear that even this they do for a reason. For where there is naval power, it is necessary from financial considerations to be slaves to the slaves in order to take a portion of their earnings, and it is then necessary to let them go free. And where there are rich slaves, it is no longer profitable in such a place for my slave to fear you. In Sparta my slave would fear you; but if your slave fears me, there will be the chance that he will give over his money so as not to have to worry anymore. For this reason we have set up equality between slaves and free men, and between metics and citizens.[40]

Pseudo-Xenophon invites us to compare two sorts of political community, represented by Athens and Sparta. In Sparta, citizens are more beautiful and richer than slaves, and express their superiority by striking their inferiors at will. Accordingly, slaves fear citizens and stand aside for them. By contrast, in Athens, slaves are immune from casual violence and, consequently, have no fear of citizens. Thus, slaves in Athens feel no need to stand aside. All of this entails that slaves and citizens are equal in Athens and unequal in Sparta.

The parallel between Pseudo-Xenophon's insights and my argument is clear. First, Pseudo-Xenophon recognizes that unconstrained violence can be an expression of social status – consistent with the Athenian law against hubris, which recognized the insulting power of violence, to be discussed further in Chapter 5. Second, he recognizes the power of unconstrained violence to inflict terror on its victims and lead them to "stand aside" – to fear and behave submissively toward those who wield it. Regardless of whether any individual citizen actually strikes any individual slave, all slaves fear all citizens in Sparta, just by virtue of the fact that any citizen has the power to strike any slave. By contrast, in Athens, citizens and slaves, in Pseudo-Xenophon's hyperbole, are *equals*, at least in respect of their immunity from casual violence.[41] Pseudo-Xenophon shows us that the egalitarian significance of controlling arbitrary violence has been known for quite a long time.

IV CLOSING TECHNICALITIES

Thus far I have assumed, but not defended, a variety of ideas about the sort of normative principle the rule of law is. Here, I list them. Most of these propositions either are uncontroversial, if often implicit, positions in the existing literature or are closely integrated into the conception as a whole such that they can be unproblematically accepted given the argument I've already made. However, before we move from the weak to the strong version, we need to have a clearer fix on the properties of the idea.

As I argued, the rule of law in the first instance governs states (or other discrete political communities), not individuals; we say that a state, not an individual official, comports with or violates the rule of law. However, to see whether the state comports with the rule of law, we must inspect officials' use of the state's coercive power. By "officials," I simply mean those who wield the violent resources ordinarily associated with the state; this includes not only duly appointed officials of ordinarily legitimate states but usurpers, warlords in failed states, and the like. And by "coercive power," I mean violence and commands backed up by the threat of violence.[42]

An official uses the state's coercive power when she applies it to a specific person or known group of people. Ordinarily, officials who wield the state's coercive power will be those exercising executive or judicial functions. The rule of law regulates the behavior of legislators indirectly: it commands that officials use the state's coercive power only in accordance with laws holding certain properties; legislators can help bring it about that the state does or does not comport with the rule of law by enacting laws that do or do not hold those properties. Legislators may directly apply coercion to citizens in special cases, such as when passing bills of attainder.

The rule of law is observed or violated only by *general patterns of behavior* in a political community. If a single judge misuses his power in a way that is inconsistent with the three principles of the rule of law (by, for example, putting people in prison "just because I say so"), we don't say the rule of law has failed; we say that particular judge is violating the law.[43] If judges regularly do so, the rule of law has failed.

The rule of law's constraints must be met *reliably*. It does not require any particular method of enactment or enforcement. For example, the United Kingdom has no written constitution, and adheres to the doctrine of parliamentary supremacy such that Parliament could, in principle, enact laws authorizing officials to violate the strictures of the rule of law at will. It nonetheless comports with the weak version of the rule of law to the extent that its constraints are a stable legal norm with which officials reliably comply, and to the extent that British officials who fail to do so can ordinarily anticipate social and political sanctions. (I discuss the extent to which these claims can and do correspond to British reality in Chapter 7.) However, a state will not count as adhering to the rule of law if its officials exercise their power in ways consistent with its demands out of mere benevolence, with no social, cultural, legal, political, or strategic constraints keeping them from violating it whenever they want.

The last two propositions – that the rule of law is about general patterns of behavior and norms, and that these patterns must be reliable – can be summed up in the claim that the rule of law is observed or violated only by a state's *institutions*. I hesitate to say this, because the term "institution" pervades the academic literature and seems to have a different meaning every time.[44] Here, I use the term "institution" to mean just the object of those last two propositions – reliable general patterns of behavior and norms. "Institutions" differ from the specific "practices" of a state, which are the sorts of things that are closer to a pretheoretic understanding of the word "institution," such as the trial by jury, or the independent judiciary, or the writ of habeas corpus.[45] Practices are nonexclusive ways of instantiating the three (institutional) principles; the independent judiciary, for example, is one way to bring it about that officials more reliably use coercion only pursuant to preexisting law. But the independent judiciary is not necessary for the rule of law – we can have the rule of law without it (for more, see Chapter 8). However, when people use the word "institutions," they usually mean what I call "practices"; for ease of comprehension, I adopt this terminology toward the end of the book, particularly in the last few chapters, where I argue that no particular institutions (read: "practices") are necessary components of the rule of law, though there must be some "institutions" that serve a given set of functions in each rule of law society. We only need the linguistic distinction between institutions and practices for a moment in order to get at the underlying conceptual idea.

The rule of law is (relatively) formal. By this, I do not mean that the rule of law does not regulate the substantive content of law – obviously it does, and when we reach the principle of generality it does so fairly pervasively. Instead, I mean to reject thicker conceptions of the rule of law, such as Dworkin's "rights conception,"[46] in which the rule of law basically requires liberal democracy, or the familiar notion that the rule of law requires an extensive system of private property rights. On the contrary, the rule of law does not require citizens to have any specific rights at all (other than the procedural rights to have access to the law and be heard in their own cases, as given by the principle of publicity), except insofar as those rights are necessary to constrain officials to use their power only consistent with the three principles. It is possible to have the rule of law without any private property, as in a state in which all property is held collectively but officials do not abuse their power.[47] I will not defend this thin conception of the rule of law here (except to note that we already have perfectly good normative arguments for liberal democracy and private property rights).[48]

The rule of law is a continuum, not a binary: states can satisfy it to a greater or lesser extent.[49] It is a continuum along three dimensions. First, a state can satisfy some of the principles but not others. Second, a state can satisfy a principle to a greater or lesser extent. Third, a state can satisfy its principles with respect to some citizens but not others – it could, for example, comport with publicity, regularity, and generality with respect to the elites but not the masses.

Finally, I will not say that the rule of law is necessary for a state to have law in the first place. There can be legal systems (Ancien Régime France, the Soviet Union) that radically fail to meet the standards of the rule of law, and still count as having law nonetheless. This is a controversial position.[50] An alternative approach would follow Simmonds in understanding the concept of law to refer both to an ideal and to real-world practices. On Simmonds's view, there is an "archetype" of law, which is "intrinsically moral," and which tracks ideals like those typically captured under the notion of the rule of law; we understand real-world laws as such in virtue of their partaking, in very much a Platonic sense, of the ideal concept (however imperfectly).[51]

However, nothing important is at stake in this dispute. Both sides admit of the possibility of saying that even tyrannical states have law, even if the Simmonds position would call it law that is extremely flawed in virtue of its failure to conform to the Form of Law. We might then describe a continuum from Law_0 to Law_1, where the latter is Simmonds's archetype, and the former is (say) the legalistic Soviet or Nazi bureaucracies. Similarly, all agree that there is a point along that continuum where we can find morally valuable properties. These points of agreement between those who would attach the rule of law to the concept of law and those who do not are enough for the argument of this book.

Likewise, all agree (following Fuller) that the morally valuable properties of rule of law systems have some connection to the technology of law itself.[52] A core function of law is to give authoritative commands, and commands must at least be epistemically available to those who are supposed to obey them, and must be reliably backed by enforcement to get that obedience.[53] This entails that the law must be minimally public, and officials must be minimally constrained.[54]

But here, too, we seem to be working with a continuum where moral value appears in the middle, not at the beginning. $RuleofLaw_0$, a minimally regular and minimally public law that serves only to make it cheaper for an otherwise unconstrained top-level official to hold lower-level officials to her program and give commands to the rest, is unlikely to have moral value. Caligula could enact a (minimally public and regular) law when he wanted obedience, and just order people executed when he wanted amusement.[55] Somewhere on the way to $RuleofLaw_1$, the fully general and egalitarian state that will be described in the next two chapters, the rule of law begins to acquire moral value – when, for example, it begins to forbid Caligula's amusement-executions.

The weak version of the rule of law is something like $RuleofLaw_{0.5}$; I now turn to $RuleofLaw_1$, and the principle of generality. The next two chapters are devoted to expressing the ideal of the rule of law in its most demanding form.

Chapter 2

The strong version of the rule of law

It is widely accepted among rule of law scholars, as well as lawyers and philosophers at large, that the law must be general – that it must treat all in the community equally, or as equals (as will be seen, those two phrases mean different things). This ideal appears in more familiar forms in the demands of activists and the provisions of constitutions worldwide, such as the Equal Protection and the Privileges and Immunities Clauses of the US Constitution. It's surprisingly hard, however, to sort out what that abstract ideal should actually require of our political communities.

I have said that achieving regularity and publicity rules out hubris and terror, but this is only partially true: a state can be regular and public with respect to only some of the subjects of law, while still inflicting hubris and terror on others (e.g., slaves). To be wholly free from hubris and terror, a state's laws must be minimally general in that official coercion of *all* subjects of law satisfies regularity and publicity.

However, even if the state achieves publicity and regularity with respect to all subjects of law, its legal system still might not treat the subjects of law as equals, if there is one (public and regular) law for some individuals (i.e., elites) and another for the masses. Generality, the third and strongest principle of the rule of law, forbids this. For the state to comply with the principle of generality, officials must substantially satisfy the principles of publicity and regularity *and* only use the state's coercive power in accordance with laws that do not draw irrelevant distinctions between individuals (that is, general laws). They must also use the discretion given to them consistently with the same principle: in a standard formulation, they must treat like cases and individuals alike, treating them differently only if there is a relevant distinction between them.

Most of the argument in this chapter will be devoted to filling out the idea of a "relevant distinction." This, I argue, means that when a law or exercise of official discretion treats people differently from one another, there must be public reasons to justify the different treatment. I also add some more flesh to the notion that generality is about equality. However, since the claim that generality is an egalitarian principle is neither novel nor controversial, the main work of this chapter is to answer the far more vexed question of what generality demands.[1]

I GENERALITY AND THE IDEA OF A RELEVANT DISTINCTION

After describing the existing accounts of generality, this section defends the argument that we must have a substantive, not formal, conception of what it means for law to be general. The extent to which a law is general cannot be determined from abstract properties of its text alone.

A *Many conceptions of generality*

The literature reveals no consistent account of what generality requires. Hayek alone has four different conceptions of generality within a few pages of one another: (1) general law applies to everyone, particularly those who make and enforce it; (2) general law can pick out particular classes of application so long as the distinction so made is equally justifiable to those within and without the classes to which it applies; (3) law is general when legislators cannot know the particular cases to which it will apply; and (4) generality is an "aspect" of a feature of law called "abstractness," which appears to refer to law that does not give overly detailed directions to its subjects or too closely specify its circumstances of application.[2] The relationship between those four versions of generality is obscure. For Rawls, generality is the requirement that like cases be treated alike, but he acknowledges that specifying a rule to determine which cases are like is a major difficulty with this formulation.[3] Hart also suggested that the principle of generality means "treating like cases alike," but added that "the criteria of when cases are alike will be, so far, only the general elements specified in the rules," which simply reduces generality to regularity.[4]

Some commentators would more or less strip generality from our conception of the rule of law. Most notable among these is Raz, who limits the principle of generality to only the constitutional basics of government – the secondary rules governing how primary rules are to be made – and flatly denies that the rule of law forbids systematic discrimination.[5] Unsurprisingly, Raz also denies that the rule of law has anything to do with equality. Others have taken less extreme, but still minimalist, positions – most notable is Rousseau, who argues that general law is law that does not have a specific object, by which he appears to primarily mean law that does not pick out particular individuals by name.[6]

B *Against the formal conception of generality*

We can start to understand the problems posed by generality by thinking about one of its more prominent loci of application, the principle of judicial impartiality. Certain applications of this idea are easy: no rule of law scholar would disagree with Locke's principle that no one may be a judge in his own case, or the stronger demands of contemporary legal ethics that require judges to not share interests with the parties to a case and to resist pressure by the powerful. But many things other than their personal interests can bias judges. For example, a judge may rule from racial animus. A racist judge manifestly violates generality. He treats like individuals differently because he distinguishes between them on the basis of irrelevant personal properties. But a judge is allowed to take some kinds of distinctions into account. She must not give one defendant a harsher sentence than another for the same crime because one is black and the other is white, but she may give a defendant a harsher sentence because, for example, he held a position of trust with respect to the victim. It's surprisingly difficult to give an abstract principle that captures both the impermissibility of the first distinction and the permissibility of the second.

Similarly, we can consider how difficult is the job of lawyers in a common-law jurisdiction. They are paid to consider a mass of cases – all of which are like in some respects and not like in others – and demonstrate that the instant case is relevantly like some, and not relevantly like others ("distinguishing" those others, in legal jargon).

The same point applies to legislation. Consider that the law "No vehicles in the park" makes a distinction between inside the park and outside the park. We think that's general, as we do the law "No motorbikes in the park." But we don't think the laws "Black people may not ride motorbikes in the park" or "Tim Smith may not ride a motorbike in the park" are general. One candidate for a formal principle to distinguish between those cases is that the latter cases single out specific classes of *people* – but that's permissible sometimes, too. It doesn't, for example, offend the rule of law to decree that "Two parking spaces in each lot shall be reserved for disabled people" or "Convicted felons may not own firearms."

In all these applications, we see that "treat like cases alike" does not provide enough information to guide officials.[7] We must have some account of what makes the cases like or unlike – a relevance criterion governing the reasons under which officials may treat cases and individuals differently. The search is for some principle to capture the twin intuitions that disability is a relevant criterion for allocating parking spaces and race is not a relevant criterion for allocating the right to ride motorbikes in the park.[8]

This point can be broadened and made more abstract. The idea of general law can be conceived as either formal or substantive. Define a formal conception of generality as one according to which an observer can determine whether a law is general purely by examining properties of a law itself, including its text, and/or the process by which it was enacted, including the actions and motivations of legislators. By contrast, a substantive conception requires an observer to examine nonlegal social facts and/or appeal to normative values (such as "liberty" or "equality") in order to determine whether a law is general.

I defend a substantive conception of generality, and argue that the formal conception of generality is necessarily incoherent. In order to do so, I distinguish, and reject, three different subtypes of the formal conception.

On the *minimal* conception of generality, the law is not allowed to pick out particular people. This conception forbids things like the bill of attainder, or the law with a proper name in it.[9] In addition to proper names, this minimal version of the principle must (on pain of absurdity) also forbid laws that incorporate other rigid designators that refer to people, such as indexicals used in the right context. For example, it would prohibit a king from pointing at someone and saying, "You are hereby outlawed."

On the *epistemic* conception of generality, laws are forbidden to the extent that those who enact them know (can pick out) to whom they are to apply. This conception is distinctively associated with Hayek.[10]

Finally, on the *similarity* conception of generality, law must be cast in general (or abstract) terms, or treat every citizen the same. These conceptions propose to police the extent to which the law classifies citizens into different groups in order to ensure that it "treats like cases (and citizens) alike."[11]

The minimal conception fails because it is unstable along the dimensions of both *uniqueness* and *rigidity*, which are the only two plausible criteria by which we might distinguish the laws it forbids from the laws it permits. First: if the law may not contain rigid designators referring to one person, it would be irrational to permit it to contain rigid designators referring to multiple people. That is, if the rule of law forbids the legislature from enacting "Thomas Wentworth may not work as a lawyer," it must also forbid "Thomas and Margaret Wentworth may not work as lawyers," and if it forbids that, it must also forbid "Thomas, Margaret, Sarah, John, Phillip … [etc.] Wentworth may not work as lawyers," or "None of you people whom I am addressing right now may work as a lawyer."

Second, if the law forbids rigid designators, it must also forbid at least *some* nonrigid designators that, in the actual world, are extensionally equivalent to rigid designators. This is clearest in the individual case: if the legislature may not enact "Thomas Wentworth may not work as a lawyer," it also may not enact "The person who lives at 1640 Attainder Lane on July 30, 2012, may not work as a lawyer." Otherwise, the prohibition against rigid designators would be practically meaningless, since the legislature could always find a sufficiently precise nonrigid designator that would pick out exactly those whom the legislature wished to attaint.

The instability of the minimal conception along the dimension of number and its instability along the dimension of rigidity can combine: from the preceding, it follows quite naturally that the rule of law forbids the legislature from enacting "Nobody in the family of the person who lives at 1640 Attainder Lane on July 30, 2012, may work as a lawyer." And after taking that step, we've lost both of the candidate principles by which we might distinguish those descriptions the minimal formal conception of generality forbids and those it permits. If the state can't pick out the class of people who live at a given address for special (mis)treatment, can it pick out nobles as a class, or the class of people in a given city, or the disabled, or even natives (as opposed to foreigners) as a class? The minimal conception of generality offers us no answer.[12]

To see that the epistemic conception fails, simply ask: "Knows under what description?" If the legislature passes a law that "All redheads must serve in the army," each legislator knows exactly to whom the law will apply, under the description "redheads," even if none know each individual by name. The same is true if the legislature enacts "Everyone who lives at 1640 Attainder Lane is to be shot," just in case legislators aren't quite sure of the names of the residents. Either the epistemic formal conception just reduces to the minimal formal conception (and collapses for the same reason) – that is, to the demand that the legislature must not know those to whom a law can apply *by name* (or other rigid designator) – or it fails to constrain laws, because legislatures always know to whom a law applies under the description written into the law.

The failure of the minimal and epistemic conceptions should have been predictable, for any conception of the principle of generality worthy of the name must surely forbid "the Jews are barred from England" and must surely permit "only those over 21 may buy alcohol." Neither version of the principle has the capacity to distinguish between those two examples. Unsurprisingly, then, the best contemporary liberal legal theorists have endorsed the similarity conception, in the form of the command that the law "treat like cases alike." The problem with the similarity conception is that, on it, all legislative acts are formally nongeneral, for some conceptions of what it means for cases to be "like," because all laws include conditions for their application, which will only be met by some people and cases. On the other side, all legislative acts except for those that actually contain rigid designators are also formally general, relative to some other conception of "likeness," in that they specify in abstract terms (for some level of abstractness) the criteria for their application. The same point put differently: all cases, and people, are like in some respects and different in some respects.[13] The demand to "treat like cases alike" requires a nonformal criterion by which we may pick out the features of the cases that are relevant for determining whether they are "like," for generality purposes, or not.[14]

People with disabilities are dissimilar from people without disabilities; black people are also dissimilar from white people. Yet, taken in a formal sense, the command "treat like cases alike" cannot help us understand why it is permissible to enact the law "The seats at the front of the bus are reserved for people with disabilities," but impermissible to enact the law "Black people must sit at the back of the bus." Intuitively, we know that disability is relevant to bus seating in a way that race is not, but that relevance judgment comes not from some formal idea of what it means to treat like cases alike but from our deeper moral and political commitments to making the world accessible for the disabled and to avoiding racial segregation.

Ultimately, the judgment of generality is ineluctably substantive and normative: when we say a law is general, we mean that it doesn't pick out its classes of application in a way that offends the value that lies behind imposing the requirement of generality in the first place.[15] I will say that this value is a "relevance criterion": it is what allows us to treat like cases alike by defining those properties of cases and treatment that are relevant for judging likeness.[16]

C Public reason as relevance criterion

Since we ordinarily say that the principle of generality captures the idea of equality under law, and since the rule of law as a whole is an egalitarian ideal, the relevance criterion that allows us to apply the requirement of generality should capture the idea that the subjects of law are to be treated as equals.[17] Thus, I propose that we say that the relevance of a legal distinction is picked out by its justifiability by public reasons. The idea of public reason is ready-made for this kind of problem, because it ensures that we treat our fellow subjects of law as equals by offering them reasons for the things we require of them that we can reasonably expect them to accept.[18] If all subjects of law know that distinctions between them are justified by public reasons, those who get the short end of the stick in some distinction are at least spared the insult of being disregarded or treated as inferiors, and comforted by the existence of some general reason, which counts as a reason for everyone, for their treatment.[19] Put differently, coercing someone based on reasons that at least have the potential to count as reasons *for her*, rather than simply determining her fate based on the idiosyncratic reasons of the decision maker, expresses respect for her status as an agent to whom justification is owed for what is done to her.

This reinterpretation of the idea of general law as law that is justifiable by public reasons captures a high-level similarity between the two ideas. Public reasons are reasons that can be addressed to all citizens.[20] The law, in turn, is general when it genuinely is addressed to all. And this mode of address comes in the form of reasons that express respect for the subjects of the law as the kinds of beings to whom reasons must be offered. In doing so, we express their inclusion in the political and legal community on equal terms.[21]

II HOW TO APPLY THE PUBLIC REASON CONCEPTION OF GENERALITY

To say that the principle of generality imports the idea of public reason may seem unhelpful. It might be worried that, for many commentators, "public reason" will just mean "reason I agree with." In this section, I argue that we can more precisely spell out the notion, at least as an evaluative criterion for law in particular.

A Public reason: expressive

The requirement of public reason as it applies in the rule of law context is helpfully understood as expressive, in the sense given by Anderson and Pildes.[22] To see this, consider that the standard formulation, given by Rawls, is that a public reason is "at least reasonable for others to accept . . ., as free and equal citizens, and not as dominated or manipulated, or under the pressure of an inferior political or social position."[23] However, it is unclear what it might mean for it to be "reasonable" to so accept.

This reasonableness requirement might be understood in the first-person sense, from the point of view of the person offering the reason (the sovereign or a representative). However, this is underdemanding: it would entail that a law is general whenever those who enact it think that those whom they regulate ought to agree, without regard to what the regulated think.[24] Alternatively, it might be understood in the second-person sense, from the point of view of those to whom the reason is offered. But this is overdemanding. It would amount to giving those regulated by a law a veto over that law, since if they reject the reasons for it they will naturally think that it's not reasonable to demand they accept those reasons.[25] Nor is there likely to be some kind of objective "view from nowhere" third-person source of the judgment about whether it is reasonable to demand that someone accept the reasons for a law.[26]

Instead, we should understand these reasonableness judgments as conventional, drawn from the understandings shared by the members of a legal community. It is unreasonable to demand that someone accept a reason if, in the community shared by the reason-giver and the reason-taker, demanding that reason be accepted is not something one does to a free and equal citizen, and accepting that reason is not something one does when one sees oneself as a free and equal citizen. That is, to fail to offer public reasons is one way in which one might fail to treat the one to whom reasons ought to be offered with the respect owed to a free and equal citizen, as that status is understood in the community in question.

This is an expressive standard of behavior in Anderson's sense: it begins with an evaluative attitude toward an object ("equal" attached to the reason-taker), and generates the demand that one behave in the way appropriate to that attitude (by giving only reasons consistent with it). The match of appropriate reasons to attitudes is given by the social meaning of those reasons and that attitude. And as Anderson explains, to take an appropriate evaluative attitude to something is, in part, to act in the way that, in one's social world, one acts when one holds that attitude.[27]

As I will argue in a moment, this exercise amounts to finding the social meaning of a law: Does it express the equality of the citizens it regulates, or does it not? To determine the social (or expressive – I use the terms interchangeably) meaning of a law is to determine the attitudes about those regulated that members of the relevant community must attribute to the relevant agent in order to rationalize that law. The remainder of this section gives an account of how to identify those attitudes.[28]

B Finding the expressive content of a law

Law is (a) susceptible to purposive interpretation, (b) authority-claiming, and (c) legitimacy-claiming. Those properties render it distinctively susceptible to expressive interpretation.

1 Reasons and meanings

In the rule of law context, we need to use the expressive content of a law not only to figure out whether the reasons under which a law is justified are consistent with conceiving of all members of the community as free and equal, but also to determine what those reasons are in the first place.

We are not engaged in a mind-reading exercise in which the object is to sort out what the legislature was thinking. We are engaged in a justificatory exercise in which the object is to sort out whether a law can be justified in the right sort of way to each member of the community. The inquiry is about whether a law could, in principle, be publicly justified, not about whether some legislators said the right magic words or subjectively held an attitude of respect toward those regulated. If a public reason for a law is available, even if not actually in anyone's brain, then that law is general.[29]

I claim that the inquiry into the expressive meaning of a law is rationalistic, in that it amounts to an inquiry into reasons associated with a law, and constructive, in that it *attributes* those reasons to the occupiers of several standpoints with respect to the law, based on the reasons that apply to people in those standpoints. To attribute to all relevant agents the reasons they might endorse a given law is both to exhaust the logical space for expressive meanings of that law and to exhaust the possible public reasons for that law. For that reason, the public reason inquiry and the expressive meaning inquiry are the same.

Such a method, which positively invites skepticism, is possible with respect to law, because laws, unlike other expressive acts, implicitly make claims about the particular ways in which (1) legislators, (2) those called upon to obey the law, and (3) the community at large are supposed to relate to the law. By attending to these special properties of laws from those particular standpoints, we can fill out their expressive content in a way that we cannot so easily accomplish for other acts.[30]

Specifically, legislators are supposed to enact laws for rational, purposive, and collectively oriented reasons: a law, to not be arbitrary, has to be rationally directed at some ostensibly public end. We can understand the expressive content of a law from the first-person perspective of the legislature enacting it in terms of the end at which it implicitly claims to be directed.

As to those whom a law commands, the law demands it be taken as authoritative, that is, as giving exclusionary reasons for actions. And that claim to authority in turn depends on the claim that the law helps them act according to reasons that already apply to them.[31] We can understand the meaning of the law from the second-person perspective of the one called upon to obey a law in terms of the reasons that it implicitly claims to help those who are asked to obey to apply.

Finally, as to the general members of a community for which a law is enacted, the law claims to be enacted in their names.[32] As such, it claims to be consistent with their self-understanding as a political community and the relationships with one another that self-understanding instantiates. We can understand the meaning of the law from the third-person perspective of the general member of the community in terms of the self-understanding with which it implicitly claims to be consistent.[33]

Moreover, the language of law is the language of reasons; those who participate in legislation and law obedience do so with the presupposition that there is a rational connection between the reasons for a law and the law itself.[34] Accordingly, interpreting a law is analogous to interpreting a linguistic act in the rationalistic approach associated with Donald Davidson and his concept of "radical interpretation."[35] Davidson elucidates a "principle of charity" that assumes that the speaker holds true beliefs and speaks honestly, including a "principle of coherence," which requires us to take the utterances of the speaker as logically consistent, and a "principle of correspondence," which requires us to attribute to the speaker beliefs that we take to be true. Taking those principles together entails, in Davidson's words – which are even more compelling when applied to legal enactments rather than to ordinary linguistic acts – that "[s]uccessful interpretation necessarily invests the person interpreted with basic rationality."[36]

In sum, the expressive content of a law can be found by bringing four theses together:

Expressive meanings are conventional. The expressive content(s) of a law is the content that it has in the community in which it is enacted, from the standpoint of that community, and cannot be determined apart from the social facts of that community, including its history and the way its members currently relate to one another. The inquiry is about social facts, not psychological facts about legislators or anyone else.

Laws have meaning from three points of view. Laws have expressive content from the first-person, second-person, and third-person standpoints, corresponding to the points of view of the legislator, person regulated, and ordinary member of the community. However, the content of each of these standpoints is to be interpreted in light of the first thesis; that is, we understand the expressive content of a law as the meaning that the community at large can attribute to the law from the first-, second-, and third-person standpoints – not the subjective content of the brains of the legislators, people who are called upon to obey, and ordinary citizens.

Law makes distinctive claims. The expressive content of a law is distinct from the expressive content of any other act, because laws make special demands on those who interact with them.

Expressive meanings of laws are rationalistic. This act of interpretation must be carried out, per Davidson's principle of charity, by attributing true, rational beliefs to the occupiers of each standpoint, where those beliefs are the reasons for the occupier of each standpoint to interact with the law in the way appropriate to each standpoint (enact it for that reason, obey it for that reason, etc.).

Using those principles, I can specify the expressive content of a law from each of the three standpoints. From the first-person standpoint, the members of a community may attribute expressive content to a given law by answering this question: "What attitudes must a legislator in our community hold in order to rationally enact this law for some public purpose?"[37]

From the second-person standpoint, the members of a community may attribute expressive content to a given law by answering this question: "What attitudes must those whom the law commands hold in order to rationally take this law as helping them to act according to reasons that already apply to them?"

From the third-person standpoint, the members of a community may attribute expressive content to a given law by answering this question: "What attitudes must we hold in order to rationally take this law as enacted in our names and expressing our self-understanding as a political community?"

This account borrows techniques from ethical constructivism to give the content of expressive values. Constructivist views idealize (to a greater or lesser degree) human interests and reasons, from standpoints specified by the view and/or by people's actual positions in the world, and derive moral claims from them.[38] This theory of law's expressive meaning takes idealized interpretations of the reasons that apply to people, from the three sorts of standpoints relative to the law that they may occupy, plus the claim that laws must be rational to people in each of those standpoints, and uses those building blocks to make claims about what law must mean, expressively, to the occupiers of each standpoint.

There are two distinct idealizing steps. The first is to attribute reasons to legislators, those called upon to obey a law, and those in the political community in whose name the law is enacted. The second is to attribute beliefs about those reasons (the reasons discovered in the first idealization) to members of the community at large. The point is that those meanings need not correspond to actual thoughts held by any of those people. A law can have (say) insulting meaning even if, empirically, nobody in the community actually thinks the law is insulting, just so long as the interpretation of the law according to which it is insulting is the correct way to interpret it in its social context.[39] We don't take an opinion poll to find out the expressive meaning of a law; we reason (from an external standpoint) about what community members should think.

Nonetheless, expressive meanings are social facts – observers don't get to just make them up. Rather, the reasons that observers may attribute to a law depend on the obligations and interests of, and constraints on, those in a given community at a given time. Moreover, while the expressive meaning of a law does not depend on how people in the community actually interpret it, ordinarily the best evidence for the expressive meaning of a law will be the interpretation that actual people in the community give to a law. If the constructed interpretation of a law differs from the actual interpretation in the community, that's a reason to worry that the constructed interpretation is wrong, and to investigate it further with additional evidence or argument. There are some situations where the expressive meaning of a law depends (in a nonevidentiary sense) on the actual interpretations given it in the community. This is particularly likely where the law commands some symbolic or communicative behavior with a preexisting meaning.[40]

A law may have multiple expressive meanings. This is not a problem for the account. If there is any public reason available for a law, then that public reason should correspond to an expressive meaning for that law that incorporates reasons consistent with the equality of each citizen. If any such meaning is available from each standpoint, the law is general.

Finally, the expressive meaning of a law may change over time, because the social facts underlying that meaning may change. This entails that the correct rule of law evaluation of a law may also change over time: a law may be general at one moment and nongeneral at another. That's not a problem: there are many acts and institutions whose moral evaluation may change over time, as understood by ordinary moral and political theory. For example, a utilitarian will accept or reject a law depending on the extent to which that law maximizes well-being or preference satisfaction; this evaluation may change over time as people's preferences or needs change.[41]

2 Proof of concept

Consider a concrete example: the law "Black people must sit at the back of the bus." This is a very easy case: de jure racial segregation is nongeneral if anything is, but the analysis will help clarify how generality works. The law will satisfy the principle of generality if and only if some public reason can plausibly be offered for it from each of the three standpoints. Each standpoint is necessary, because all laws serve a triple function – as purposive public policy (corresponding to the first-person standpoint), obligation-generating legal command (the second-person standpoint), and expression of the community's self-understanding (the third-person standpoint) – and if a law cannot serve each of those functions without making use of the idea that some members of the community are of superior or inferior status, the law as a whole expresses the inequality that the principle of generality forbids.[42]

Considering the first-person standpoint, those in a racialized society such as the United States would attribute expressive content to it as follows: "There's no obvious public purpose for this law, except to express something about how black people and white people are to relate to one another. In our social world, black people are ordinarily treated as inferiors, so a rational legislator, in the world in which we live, must accept that black people are indeed inferiors and intend to reinforce that existing hierarchical treatment in order to enact this law."[43]

Considering the second-person standpoint, those regulated would attribute expressive content as follows: "Why should a black person sit at the back of the bus? There's no obvious reason that applies to black people except for reasons about their relative status and some duty to behave in accordance with it. Given our social environment, in which black people are understood as inferiors, the only reason that could be being served by such a law is a supposed duty on behalf of black people to act in accordance with this inferior status. Therefore, to rationally take this law as authoritative, a black person must accept his or her own social inferiority."

Considering the third-person standpoint, community members would attribute expressive content as follows: "Why would we, as a political community, have a stake in bringing it about that black people sit at the back of the bus? What matters, for our relationships with one another, that gives us reason to rationally endorse the social arrangements that this law brings about? Since the only effects of the law are to separate the subordinate caste from the dominant caste and to physically manifest underlying social relations, we must believe that it is right for black people to be subordinate in order to endorse this law."

Unsurprisingly, the law "Black people must sit at the back of the bus" expressed the inferior social status of black people from all three standpoints. Since the inferiority of black people is not a public reason, and, within the social context of mid-twentieth-century America no other reasons could plausibly be assigned to such a law, the law was not justifiable by public reasons.

It will be helpful to again compare the bus segregation law to a law such as "The seats at the front of the bus are reserved for disabled people." Such a law is susceptible to rationalistic interpretations that do not presuppose the inferiority of the disabled: from the first-person and third-person standpoints, the law can represent an egalitarian concern for the physical accessibility of public services for all citizens, while from the second-person standpoint, those ordered to move to the back can understand it as helping them to follow their general duties of care toward their fellow humans. Even though other, more pernicious, interpretations may be available (the law may be seen as representing a paternalistic or patronizing attitude toward the disabled), the existence, in the actual social world, of a highly plausible interpretation of the law that renders it consistent with the equal standing of the disabled from all three standpoints allows us to see the reserved seating for the disabled law, unlike the bus segregation law, as general.

To clarify, although the expressive meaning of the bus segregation law was set by the way that those in the community should have understood it, our moral evaluation of that meaning is set by universalistic standards. That is, the law "Black people must sit at the back of the bus" can only be said to express the inferiority of black people in the social context in which it was enacted. In a different social context, it might have a different meaning. (We might imagine a culture in which the rear of a seating area is a symbolic position of esteem.) But the moral evaluation of a given socially determined expressive meaning does not itself depend on social facts. Once we determine that some law expresses the inferiority of some members of the community, that law is to be condemned on rule of law grounds whether or not anyone (or, indeed, everyone) in that community endorses this message. Even if both black and white people agreed that black people were inferior and that it was appropriate to express this inferiority through segregation, that would not make the laws acceptable from the standpoint of the rule of law.[44]

However, because the meaning itself depends on social facts, public reason as used here exercises a weaker constraint than Rawls's version. For example, in a nonhierarchical religious society, one in which nonmembers of the dominant religion are still seen as equals, laws might prefer the dominant religion without expressing disrespect to nonadherents; in such a society, those laws will be consistent with the version of public reason used here. They would not be consistent with Rawls's version, which excludes religious reasons – but Rawls's version is the public reason of a liberal democracy, and the rule of law is compatible (see Chapter 1) with states other than liberal democracies. Accordingly, Islamic states (for example) can be compatible with the rule of law.

III GENERALITY AS EGALITARIAN PRINCIPLE

The principle of generality captures the idea that subjects of law are to be treated as equals under the law. This is, as I've noted, largely uncontroversial. Hence, it doesn't require very much defense, just a few notes to make the conventional wisdom a little more precise. The literature does not contain much detail on the conception of equality being invoked. I suggest that generality is necessary and sufficient for the state to satisfy three uncontroversial egalitarian demands.

First, generality satisfies the demand that the state be *free from legal caste*.[45] Few forms of inequality are more pernicious than those running along ascriptive group lines – the creation of superior and inferior groups of people based on race, gender, sexual orientation, parentage, and the like. Many of history's greatest evils – numerous genocides, the centuries of discrimination against Jews, the mass enslavement of Africans – have been made possible by ascriptive caste. And while ascriptive castes can be created or maintained purely by private initiative, the state historically has propped these systems up with its laws by, inter alia, denying political representation to members of lower-caste groups, prohibiting them from owning property or participating in certain professions, and imposing badges of inequality on them. Sometimes the state even invents the ascriptive groups on which castes are based, or warps the meaning of preexisting ascriptive groups, as the Belgians did in Rwanda.[46] Every reasonable person endorses the view that the state is forbidden to create or support such castes.

Second, generality is necessary and sufficient to satisfy the demand that the costs of legal public goods be *reciprocally borne*. Subjects of any legal system share an interest in the benefits of law – benefits like security against violence, property rights, the power to make enforceable contracts, and so forth. But for there to be law, there must be some constraints on the choices of community members. Since each of us receives the benefits of those constraints, each should suffer from them on equal terms. It's just unfair for me to demand that others produce the public good of law by subjecting their behavior to social control unless I'm willing to pay the same price, or unless I can offer them some reason that I can reasonably expect them to accept to justify my special treatment.[47] Otherwise, I exploit them to serve my own interests.[48]

Third, generality is necessary to satisfy the egalitarian demand that the interests of all subjects of law be *counted*. A state that does not satisfy the principle of generality has laws that are not justifiable to some subjects, that is, that treat those subjects' interests as dispensable, as not worthy of consideration in making public policy. This is essentially a restatement of the fundamental idea of the expressive conception of generality, and is thus an appropriate way to end this chapter. Making a general law is a way of respecting the right that each has to have his or her interests matter for the community that proposes to command his or her behavior.

Chapter 3

Generality and hierarchy

In this chapter, I will use the conception of generality from the previous chapter to make sense of the way that the rule of law helps us understand hierarchical subordination in the real world. As will be seen, the principle of generality makes demands not only of legal systems, but of the entire basic structure of a state that organizes itself through law. Establishing true legal equality is not easy, but it turns out to be of more than merely formal value.

I THE LITERACY TESTS: A MODEL OF NONGENERAL LAW

I will flesh out the demands of the principle of generality through an examination of the Jim Crow literacy tests that were used to exclude African Americans from the ballot box. For analytic purposes, we may assume, counterfactually, that they were evenhandedly implemented across races. Nonetheless, I claim that the public reason conception of generality would have condemned even fairly administered literacy tests in the social context of the Jim Crow South.

Begin with some intuition. As we today interpret our history, the literacy tests could only be understood as insults to the freed slaves and their descendants, whose equal citizenship had supposedly been acknowledged by the Reconstruction amendments. By making this acknowledgment into a lie, the literacy tests implied that no matter what the Constitution said, they would never be full members of the political community.[1]

Because the enactment of the literacy tests unavoidably carried that message, the distinctions they drew between the literate and the illiterate were unjustifiable by public reasons. Consequently, the laws were not general.

Thus, at least, is the intuition. Someone might object and deny that the literacy tests carried any such message. While unfortunate, our objector might suggest that the literacy tests just so happened to pick out freed slaves for disenfranchisement; they need not carry any social meaning about their less than full citizenship.

Further pressing this objection, one might point out that we could imagine all kinds of benign literacy tests. Were a public reason available for the literacy tests from each of the first-, second-, and third-person standpoints, then they would not have *unavoidably* carried the inegalitarian expressive content.

Indeed, in the abstract, there are many plausible arguments that lead to the conclusion that one ought to have literacy tests for the exercise of the franchise. For example, there are some epistemic arguments for democracy in which democratic institutions are justified by their propensity to reach better decisions, along the lines of the Condorcet jury theorem. But for the Condorcet jury theorem to entail that democracies make better decisions than plausible alternatives, individual voters must tend, on the whole, to have a greater than .5 probability of coming to the right answer. A literacy test could usefully eliminate the voters with the lowest probability of correctness, since voting well may depend on access to complex (written) information about public policy.

This sort of argument isn't limited to those who think democracy is justified by its alleged decision-improving properties. Anyone who thinks it matters, morally, whether political decisions lead to nonfoolish policy has at least prima facie reason to want the least competent citizens to stay home, even if that reason is ultimately outweighed by countervailing considerations relating to, for example, autonomy, pluralism, the civic educational value of political participation, or the like. Take an easy example: I imagine that many readers will agree with me that it would be simply better if the members of the Ku Klux Klan kept out of the voting booth, not just because they are evil, but also because they are incompetent: they hold culpably false beliefs about race, and voting based on those beliefs does harm to the community as a whole. More generally, Jason Brennan has plausibly argued that those unwilling to put in the effort to become educated about public policy have a moral duty not to vote.[2] Literacy is a plausible proxy for minimal effort and competence.

Moreover, literacy tests may have useful indirect effects. Mill made the basic case for some kind of educational qualification for the exercise of the franchise, based on three considerations: (1) the franchise "is power over others," and ought to be exercised only by those who are qualified; (2) it would provide an incentive to acquire an education; and (3) it would communicate to the public at large that the vote is a trust to be used not for the voter's self-interest, but in the interest of the community at large.[3]

Mill's argument, in addition to being plausible, is at least apparently consistent with public reason: all three reasons could be offered to every citizen, even those thus excluded from the franchise, consistent with understanding them as equal citizens.

Importantly, Mill was clear that the state may impose only such educational qualifications as "can be fairly regarded as within the reach of every one."[4] By offering citizens the means to acquire the education necessary to the franchise (or at least conditioning disenfranchisement on their access to it), a Millian state recognizes their legitimate stake in the polity, and attaches disenfranchisement only to choices (a) in which the public as a whole has a stake and (b) that are in the control of the disenfranchised.

By contrast, the American states that implemented literacy tests did not recognize the freed slaves' and their descendants' stakes in it by offering them the means to become qualified to vote. Quite the contrary: freed slaves had been denied an education.[5] And their descendants continued to be given inferior educations in segregated schools.

The literacy test, in the context of gross educational inequality, expressed not the civic responsibility of those denied the franchise but the state's opinion about their innate inferiority. We find this expressive content from the second-person standpoint, by following the method described in the previous chapter. Because they had been denied literacy, freed slaves and their descendants could not understand the literacy test as helping them fulfill their duty to be competent voters. And the community at large could not attribute any such understanding to them. This is so thanks to the basic normative principle of "ought implies can" (with a qualification to be described in a moment). They had been deprived of the means of becoming literate, therefore they had no such duty. In a world in which they could not be charged with a duty to be literate, African-American citizens could only have taken the laws as helping them act in accordance with reasons that already applied to them if those reasons were derived from some intrinsic duty to not vote – not because of their contingent failures to satisfy a duty of literacy but because of their inherent unsuitability for the franchise – a belief that, of course, was already manifestly present in the political culture.

Before moving on, I pause to describe the qualification to "ought implies can" promised a couple paragraphs ago. A law forbidding the blind from driving is obviously justifiable by public reasons: driving is a dangerous activity, and the blind do not (with current technology) have the capacity to do it safely; not killing people on the roads is a reason that counts for everyone.

But we might worry that a similar argument applies to the literacy tests. Voting is also a dangerous activity. Those who vote badly can contribute to immense human suffering by permitting ruinous wars, environmental destruction, economic collapse, and many other evils; those who lack the capacity to do it safely have reason to stay away from the polls. Notwithstanding the injustice they had suffered, someone might argue that the freed slaves simply lacked the capacity to vote safely.

The difference between the freed slave and the blind driver, however, is that the inability of the blind driver is the result (*ex hypothesi*) of nothing more than bad luck. By contrast, the state and the society at large were attributively responsible for the illiteracy of the freed slaves and their educationally deprived descendants. And this matters, in turn, for the reasons that applied to them. A citizen might have a compelling reason to sacrifice her own interests (e.g., in driving) to spare the rest of society from the ill effects of her bad luck of being blind, but it's much less fair to demand that she sacrifice her interests to spare the rest of society from the ill effects of a disability that society has imposed on her in the first place.[6]

II THE RULE OF LAW AND SOCIAL FACTS

The foregoing reveals that we can't read a state's compliance with the principle of generality off of the face of its legal texts, or even from observing the relationship between its legal texts and the practices of its officials. In the most abstract statement of this point, because generality is an expressive ideal, and because the expressive content of any legal act is conventional and depends on social meanings that themselves depend on social facts, our evaluation of whether a law is subject to criticism will depend in part on prevailing social conditions when it is in effect.

Moreover, because the correct evaluation of a law depends on social conditions, it can change when those social conditions change. Imagine that the states after the civil war had suddenly become much more liberal, and had begun to offer a decent education to freed slaves. No longer being denied literacy, the freed slaves would no longer have had reason to object to the literacy tests (to repeat, this all assumes, counterfactually, that they were administered honestly and fairly). Ultimately, the principle of generality is an evaluative standard for a relationship between laws and an array of social facts that determine the meanings of those laws.

A *The disjunctive character of rule of law commands*

The rule of law, as a regulative principle for political states, has the power to generate at least defeasible (if not absolute) demands for its obedience. The discussion thus far has revealed a perhaps unintuitive property of this demand: it need not be a demand for the state to change anything about its legal system. Rather, it might be a demand for the state to remedy the unequal social circumstances that make its laws objectionable from the standpoint of the rule of law.

More formally, since a law is criticizable for violating the rule of law requirement that the laws be general when that law, in the social circumstances in which it is found, is not justifiable by public reasons, it follows that in order for a state to make an objectionable law comply with the rule of law, either it can abolish the law in question or it can remedy the social circumstances (usually injustices, social hierarchies) that make it objectionable. Thus, the rule of law issued a disjunctive demand to the Jim Crow South: get rid of the literacy tests, or provide African Americans with a decent education.

III THE RULE OF LAW AND THE CRIMINALIZATION OF POVERTY

Now let us move from race to class and consider Anatole France's sarcastic jibe against the law's vain pretense of equality: "The law, in its majestic equality, forbids the rich and the poor alike to sleep under bridges, to beg in the streets, and to steal bread."[7] France's point seems to be that the laws forbidding vagrancy, begging, and theft are not general.

It's easy to agree with France. In the context of extreme poverty, those laws leave some citizens no realistic choice but to commit the very acts that have been made criminal. Hence the contemporary critique of "the criminalization of poverty,"[8] a phrase that accurately expresses the fact that a law that forbids the very poor from sleeping on the street, in a community in which some are unable to acquire anywhere else to sleep and a species in which one must sleep, is really the same thing as a law making it a crime to be poor – much like the literacy tests were really laws making blackness a disqualification for citizenship. Under such circumstances, the connection between criminal punishment and responsibility is broken, and the state expresses the scolding disapproval that goes along with criminal punishment against those citizens for something that is wholly out of their control. *No matter what you do, you're a criminal just for being alive* is the message sent to the very poor. This is a "status crime" in two senses: it criminalizes the status of poverty, and it uses criminalization to reinforce the subordinated status of those who are poor.

This insult is reaffirmed in the minute daily interactions of the poor with the state. The case of the homeless is instructive. If one is homeless and there are vagrancy laws, then merely to go to sleep is to be in constant danger of being turfed out of the "bed" one has made in some public space and chased away like a stray dog or a disobedient child. Being, of necessity, always engaged in lawbreaking, the homeless are constantly subject to state coercion at the will of any official who comes along and wishes to wield it. The homeless are perhaps exceeded only by those in total institutions like prisons and military barracks in the extent to which they can be ordered about.[9] And every such interaction is a further blow to the dignity of the citizen who is constantly told that his very presence in a public place and his satisfaction of the basic needs of human existence are objectionable to his fellows.

The structures of the second-person expressive content of the laws criminalizing poverty are identical to those of the literacy tests. In each case, an otherwise potentially permissible law becomes nongeneral because the regulated citizen cannot understand it as authoritative without accepting his or her own inferiority. And in each case, this failure of authority comes as a result of the fact that the reasons to which the law would ordinarily respond have become unavailable to that citizen. Thus, in the case of the criminalization of poverty, in a society in which some citizens were not reduced to destitution, one could understand the law against sleeping on the street as directed at a preexisting duty not to inconvenience one's fellow citizens in public places by doing so. But "ought implies can" again arises, where some citizens are destitute, to vitiate the preexisting duty not to sleep on the street. Everyone must sleep to exist; if destitute citizens are to sleep at all, it must be on the street. Or, evidently, in jail.

Consequently, the only way that a destitute citizen can understand the vagrancy laws as helping her satisfy reasons that already apply to her is if she assumes that her existence itself violates a duty toward her fellow citizens – that is, if she believes that she is contemptible and unfit to be a member of the community. That is the belief the community at large must attribute to her in order to understand the expressive meaning of the vagrancy law in a social context where extreme poverty exists.

Not only does the criminalization of poverty violate the rule of law on the grounds that it is not general, but it violates perhaps the most uncontroversial and fundamental rule of law requirement as well: the law's commands must be capable of being followed. That requirement is an implication of the principle of regularity, because officials have open threats against any citizen who is unable to follow the law.

Earlier, I argued that the illiteracy of freed slaves gave them no reason not to vote, because society at large was responsible for their illiteracy, not the freed slaves. Likewise, here, the argument depends on the proposition that society at large bears responsibility for extreme poverty in virtue of the way it shapes the economic constraints under which citizens live (the "basic structure," in Rawls's terms), and could do something to alleviate extreme poverty. Those are empirical questions; we need only note for present purposes that they are fairly debatable. The point is that *if* the economy gives some members of the community no practical choice but to sleep under bridges, beg in the streets, and steal bread, and *if* these conditions are in the state's control, then the laws against vagrancy, begging, and theft violate the rule of law.

A *The rule of law critique of economic injustice*

This confers a new dimension on our economic justice discourse. Recall the disjunctive character of rule of law judgments. If Anatole France and I are right that the rule of law prohibits vagrancy and theft laws in the social context of extreme poverty, then it demands an end to one or the other.[10]

States probably ought to have laws against theft. On many accounts, the definition and protection of private property is a defining purpose of political states, and this is one of the chief lines of argument against the anarchist who denies that states are justifiable in the first place.[11] Even a socialist society, though it will not have private property rights in the means of production, might defensibly have private property rights in personal goods – like food.[12] And laws against theft are constitutive of private property rights – without a law forbidding everyone else from taking away my belongings, it would be silly to say that I have a private property right in them in the first place.[13] A state with no law against theft of food may fail so completely in doing what states ought to do that it cannot defend itself against the anarchist critique. There is also a case – albeit significantly weaker – for vagrancy laws, to the extent those sleeping on the street impose unjustifiable costs on their fellow citizens (a question on which I take no position).

The final step now presents itself. If the rule of law is inconsistent with a law against stealing food in a society in which some must steal in order to eat, and if in consequence the rule of law generates a disjunctive demand to either repeal the law against theft of food or correct the unequal social conditions in which some are starving, and if it would be impermissible for independent reasons to repeal the law against theft of food, then one fork in the disjunctive road must be blocked off. The rule of law generates the demand to put a stop to extreme poverty or abolish the laws against theft. Similar points may be made with respect to vagrancy, and to any other laws that states arguably ought to make, where such laws impose legal condemnation or boundless susceptibility to official coercion on the poor. To the extent we cannot abolish such laws, the rule of law generates the demand to put a stop to extreme poverty.

Kant, of all people, made a very similar argument. As Ripstein explains Kant's analysis, a network of private property rights can deprive one with no access to land of "[t]he innate right to occupy space"; "[i]f private owners are entitled to exclude from their land, and nobody is allowed to live on public highways, the poor could find themselves with no place to go, in the sense that they would do wrong simply by being wherever they happened to be" – that is, the law is impossible to obey.[14] This makes the poor dependent on those with wealth. The legal system is responsible for that dependence: by creating property rights in land and other resources not in the physical possession of their owners, it makes it possible for some to be deprived of the basics of existence, and accordingly to be subject to the unfettered choice of other people, inconsistent with the "rightful honor" (which I would call equal status) of those so subjected.[15] A legal system that permits this is inconsistent with what Ripstein calls the "omnilateral will" that, for Kant, is a prerequisite of sovereign legitimacy. Accordingly, on Kant's argument, the state has a duty to support the poor.

IV IS THIS STILL THE RULE OF LAW?

At this point, it will be helpful to pause to consider an objection, the answer to which will help flesh out the egalitarian conception of the rule of law. I want to claim that those who think themselves committed to the rule of law have also committed themselves to the strong ideas about social equality developed here, but perhaps those who want to resist that argument may simply deny that the strong version of the rule of law is part of what they are committed to. Why not reject generality altogether, or at least treat the strong and the weak versions of the rule of law as two independent principles that need not be accepted or rejected together?

Typically, commentators have thought that the requirement that the law be general is a demand of the rule of law. But, as discussed in the previous chapter, they have thought that this was a formal requirement, involving ideas like law being written in abstract terms or not containing proper names. And there seems to be a natural affinity between the formal conception of generality and the rest of the rule of law, which I have described as the "weak version": the weak version is distinctively concerned with keeping state officials from abusing their power over citizens, such as by using it to retaliate against those who cross them, and hence force citizens to live in fear; the formal conception of generality can contribute to that end. For example, the rule against proper names can help keep officials from being able to legislate against their enemies. The demand that officials be subject to the same law as everyone else forbids them from giving themselves the right to ignore the personal and property rights of their fellows.

I have argued that the formal conception of generality is incoherent. However, in light of the substantial demands of the substantive conception, and its apparent lack of such a close connection with the weak version, one might think that the appropriate response to the failure of the formal conception isn't to thicken it but to drop the generality principle altogether.

That would be too hasty. There is also a close connection between the substantive principle of generality and the weak version of the rule of law. I have already pointed out one dimension of this connection: the criminalization of poverty not only violates the principle of generality, but also violates the principle traditionally associated with the weak version of the rule of law that the law must be capable of being followed. This isn't a coincidence: all law that creates status crimes will be impossible to follow and will express the social inferiority of those who are subject to it, since none will be able to understand such law as corresponding to reasons that apply to them except insofar as they see themselves as inherently criminal. Put in terms of the weak version of the rule of law, a status crime grants officials open threats against those who are thus criminalized, and such open threats cannot be reconciled with public reason, precisely for the reasons given in Chapter 1: to grant one person such arbitrary coercive power over another is to construct a relationship of hierarchy and subordination between them.

More broadly, the weak version also partially answers a question that the strong version asks. The strong version demands that we give public reasons for all legal distinctions, including the fact that officials have special powers that nonofficials don't have.[16] And the weak version constrains those powers to ensure that public reasons are, in fact, available for them. There are obvious public reasons to create officials with the power to do things like adjudicate civil disputes and put lawbreakers in jail; there are no public reasons to create officials with the power to coerce at whim. As discussed in Chapter 1, such unconstrained power carries with it a message that the one who has it is of hierarchically superior status to those who do not have it. It carries this message in part because it is not justifiable by public reasons, such that those subject to unconstrained power cannot attribute anything other than hierarchical superiority to those who hold it. Anything that violates the weak version also violates the strong version; we can conceive of the weak version as a special case of the strong version. (This is also part of why a state cannot be general unless it is also regular and public.)

Another point of contact between the strong and the weak versions of the rule of law goes through the idea of arbitrariness. What it means for a decision, or decision maker, to be arbitrary is quite undertheorized. However, one promising candidate for an interpretation of the concept is as a failure of decisions to be independent of decision makers (i.e., judges).[17] If nothing about a case changes except the identity of the decision maker, and the result changes, we could call the result arbitrary; we would also suspect that it is a failure of generality.[18]

I have suggested that the principle of public reason gives us a test for generality of decisions within and across judges as well as for generality as applied to decisions. The worry about a ruling that varies with the identity of the judge is that the judge is importing some inappropriate reasons, independent of the law, into her decision-making process. Accordingly, the quintessential judicial violation of the principle of generality is the judge who hands out higher sentences to a criminal because of his race, or who throws out a case because she and her spouse had a fight that morning. However, this is also an act of hubris: such a judge expresses that her power is a personal possession, which she is entitled to use to carry out her idiosyncratic preferences or prejudices without regard to her obligation to have reasons for her decisions consistent with the equality of those over whom she holds power. From this, it can be seen that a judge who issues arbitrary rulings offends both the strong and the weak versions of the rule of law.

There is also a historical connection between the strong and the weak versions. One of the earliest demands for substantive legal equality came from the Levellers of seventeenth-century England.[19] The Levellers demanded substantive legal equality in the sense of the principle of generality together with the procedural protections that fall under the weak version of the rule of law. The connection between these two ideas at the time was obvious: substantive legal inequality operated through procedural inequality, as, for example, when commoners were prohibited from prosecuting nobles. Equal access to judicial resolution of disputes can be seen as the most basic form of legal equality. Not incidentally, the Levellers also went further, in the direction I go in this chapter, to include demands for socioeconomic justice, such as free schooling and access to subsistence resources in the commons.

Finally, the weak and the strong versions of the rule of law appeal to the same higher-level normative idea of respect for equals through reason-giving. The weak version demands that officials give legal reasons – that is, reasons that can be found in the law – for their use of state power. And I have argued that the giving of legal reasons amounts to a kind of respect for the general public. The strong version requires the law itself to be consistent with giving reasons that respectfully address the public at large. Both the strong and the weak versions of the rule of law in this way express the same basic idea, in its most abstract form: no use of state coercive power without giving the right (respectful) kinds of reasons for that use.[20]

It is wrong – inconsistent with the value of equality – to use the state's monopoly of force to coerce someone without being able to offer reasons for that coercion that are consistent with nonetheless treating the one coerced with respect. Both the weak and the strong versions of the rule of law denote the set of principles that tell states what they have to do to avoid that wrongness. Similarly, it's wrong, because inconsistent with the value of freedom, to coerce people without giving them some say in the matter; "democracy" denotes the set of principles that tell states what they have to do to avoid that. "Distributive justice" denotes the set of principles that tell states how to run a system of economic cooperation for mutual benefit consistent with equality. And so forth.

These considerations suggest that when we discuss the weak and the strong versions of the rule of law, we are discussing one thing, not two things. They are the same principle applied to different chronological stages of the law: the strong version to the enactment of law and the use of discretion in its interpretation; the weak version to its execution.

Before closing this chapter, we must consider one more objection to the egalitarian conception, which requires us to return to Jim Crow.

V PRIVATE POWER AND ORDINARY CITIZENS

In the preceding pages, I have set out a conception of the rule of law as a shield against the use of coercive force to create or maintain social hierarchy. However, expressed in those terms, one might fairly wonder why the coercive force under scrutiny is limited to that of states. In this section, I aim to head off that worry.

A *Does the rule of law require ordinary citizens to obey the law?*

It is popular among legal philosophers and constitutional theorists to suggest that the rule of law requires everyone, not just officials, to obey the law;[21] for they rightly suppose that there are many forms of power other than state power, and much of that power can be more significant in the day-to-day lives of ordinary citizens than that which comes with a flag and a badge. Gerald Postema, for example, reminds us that the Jim Crow South relied on not only officials but also ordinary people ignoring the law and exercising private as well as state power over black Americans.[22] To this we might add worries about the contemporary power of multinational corporations (or just domestic employers), the power of informal social norms, and the like.

I said, in Chapter 1, that the rule of law does not require private obedience to the law. Here, I further defend that position with reference to the Jim Crow South. This section will further clarify the full power of the principle of generality to combat private inequality facilitated by the state.

To start, however, a discussion of the philosophical question in the abstract is in order. For it seems silly to suggest that the rule of law – this majestic guardian against tyranny – requires citizens of the United States to refrain from smoking marijuana and drive within the speed limit.

There are two strong objections to that position, an objection external to the rule of law and an objection internal to it. First (the external objection), many philosophers of law have argued – and those arguments seem convincing – that there is no general moral obligation for ordinary citizens to obey the law.[23] But the following three claims are incompatible: (1) there is no moral obligation for ordinary citizens to obey the law, (2) the rule of law imposes moral obligations, and (3) the rule of law requires ordinary citizens to obey the law. Abandoning the first runs against those convincing arguments just mentioned.[24] Abandoning the second makes talk about the rule of law rather pointless. We must abandon the third.[25]

Second (the internal objection), partial satisfaction of the rule of law is possible (it is a continuum, not a binary), and partial satisfaction of the rule of law is better than no satisfaction of it. For example, the Jim Crow South, while evil partly because the law was radically not general, was morally better than the antebellum slave South, in virtue of the fact that the law was *somewhat* more equal with respect to blacks. Nonetheless, as in the Jim Crow South, a partially satisfied rule of law may be compatible with profoundly unjust laws, even if the full satisfaction of the strong version would preclude them. And those unjust laws may, and in the Jim Crow era did, attempt to recruit ordinary citizens into their implementation. For example, a racist law may forbid private citizens from offering unsegregated public accommodations – again, this happened in the South, even over the objections of, for example, railroad companies that did not wish to segregate their passengers.[26] Or it may simply command ordinary citizens to quietly acquiesce in gross injustices against themselves, rather than defiantly resist them.

If the rule of law requires ordinary citizens to obey the laws, it would require – or at least offer some defeasible reason in favor of – citizens to obey even such evil laws. In doing so, it would perpetrate injustice, and might in fact bring it about that partial satisfaction of the rule of law is worse than no satisfaction of it. While this may simply be a moral truth – perhaps the rule of law has the potential for great wickedness in its partial implementation, so we ought to consider denying the second claim in the external objection after all – in view of the fact that we ordinarily think that the rule of law is a moral good, it is worthwhile to strive to find a version of the concept that does not have these objectionable properties.[27]

That being said, rule of law does impose some obligations, pragmatic if not theoretical, on ordinary citizens. Once we leave pure philosophy and enter the domains of history and social science, this will be seen quite clearly: the only thing that keeps the rule of law going in many (perhaps all) societies is the commitment of ordinary citizens to use the law to coordinate their resistance to the illegal use of coercive power (see Chapters 6 and 8).

Moreover, the boundary between ordinary citizens and the state can sometimes be quite porous. This will be clearest in Chapter 5, when the Athenian case is discussed. It does not overmuch compromise the position defended here and in Chapter 1 to suppose that the rule of law regulates the coercion not only of those who actually have the power of the state, but also of those who pose a real prospect of forcibly seizing it, or who, more generally, have such power that they genuinely compete with the existing government for monopoly control over the use of force in the jurisdiction – that is, have a real prospect of assuming the Hobbesian and Weberian properties.

I shall say, then, that the rule of law requires ordinary citizens – and officials – to exercise any major, state-level coercive power that they happen to hold over one another only in ways permitted by law, and to refrain from seizing such unregulated power. Its requirements apply in the first instance to officials simply because officials by definition have major coercive power over ordinary citizens. And it requires that ordinary citizens as well as officials be willing to coordinate their actions to hold other ordinary citizens and officials responsible for not using or acquiring major, state-level coercive power except as permitted by law. But that's it. It doesn't require a general obedience to the law, or a society regulated by some kind of legal ethos. Moreover, the rule of law not only permits citizens as well as officials to sometimes disobey the law, but, when the law calls for gross injustices, a full understanding of the rule of law requires it. By obeying the law's command to discriminate against and ultimately murder the Jews, for example, the Nazi officials flouted the rule of law.

In short, the state is something like the core application of the rule of law, while other kinds of arbitrary power are on a periphery, instances of which nonetheless might be subject to critique on rule of law grounds in virtue of their taking on some of the properties that we usually apply to the state. Even once we step far enough away from the state to admit of the prospect that democratic Athens can be praised under the rubric of the rule of law for restraining the power of rich would-be oligarchs, we can't step far enough away to say, for example, that a street gang, even a powerful one, represents the failure of the rule of law. A street gang typically does not exercise power under a claim of right, the way states typically do and the way the Athenian oligarchs tried to do, and this is a morally critical feature. Even in Athens, as we shall see in a couple of chapters, much of the heart of the opposition of the masses to the oligarchs was that their exercises of power came packaged as hubris, a claim of high status, and with it, the entitlement to use power to act out that status.

B *The Jim Crow challenge*

The case of the Jim Crow South remains a critical challenge to the proposition that the rule of law only demands that the state's violence, or private violence that assumes the attributes of statehood, be controlled. In the Jim Crow South, organizations such as the Ku Klux Klan, as well as unorganized bands of white citizens, frequently inflicted violent terror on black citizens, and, in doing so, reinforced the grossly subordinate status that blacks held in these communities. In particular, the practice of lynching not just blacks who were accused of crimes against whites, but also blacks who had simply offended whites, brutally solidified the racial hierarchy in the South.[28] Yet, at the same time, the Klan probably didn't have major coercive power to the same extent as, for example, a local warlord in a failed state or the oligarchic elites in Athens. It was an organized mob, not a serious competitor for the monopoly of force in the jurisdiction.

Still, perhaps that claim is too fast. The white power structure as a whole may have similar properties to those of the oligarchic elite in Athens: they had quite a lot of power, and may have achieved a de facto monopoly of force insofar as they came to use violence against others in the community with near-total impunity. And they certainly exercised that violence based on a claim of right, rooted in a narrative of racial superiority.

According to the Tuskegee Institute, through 1968, there were 4,742 reported lynchings, 3,445 of which were of blacks.[29] If the egalitarian conception of the rule of law cannot tell us something about what went wrong with such a reign of inegalitarian terror under the eye of the authorities, then something is seriously amiss with the conception.

Here is a sense of the stakes. Willie James Howard, a 15-year-old black boy who worked at a soda stand, sent a love letter to a white coworker on New Year's Day, 1944. In response, her father and two of his friends seized him from his home at gunpoint, tied him up, and forced him to jump to his death in a river, all in front of his father, who was later forced to sign an affidavit saying the boy jumped voluntarily.[30] Howard's killers were never prosecuted, and even his grave – his hasty burial without a death certificate having been ordered by the white sheriff – went unmarked until 2005.[31] Surely the rule of law has *something* to say about this?

But Howard's case illustrates the instrumental complicity of state authorities in private racial terror. Local law enforcement allowed lynch mobs to take blacks accused of crimes against whites from jail and kill them; declined to identify, let alone prosecute, the perpetrators; and sometimes, as was apparently true in Howard's case, actively impeded any chance that anyone else would have to prosecute the killers. Sometimes, law enforcement officials were actually among the gangs carrying out the lynchings.[32] And the complicity of law enforcement was instrumental in the prevalence of the phenomenon: at those rare moments where local officials actually tried to put a stop to the lynchings, they largely succeeded.[33] Moreover, consistent with the egalitarian theory of the rule of law, the lynchings were part of a conscious state attempt to enforce the subordinate status of blacks. Thus, Dixiecrats in Congress fought an antilynching law specifically on the grounds that it would embolden blacks to demand "the social equality long promised them by ignorant northern do-gooders," and the lynchings would no longer be necessary "when the white race asserts its supremacy to all races."[34]

What this reveals is that the lynchings were enabled largely by a failure of the rule of law on the egalitarian conception: had officials complied with the principle of generality, and used their official powers to punish whites who committed crimes against blacks to the same extent they did to punish blacks who were accused of committing crimes against whites, the Klan's reign of terror would probably have been dramatically curtailed.[35] The rule of law provides ample grounds to critique their behavior, and if the rule of law had been established in the South, the lynchings would have been brought to an end, or at least would not have been nearly such a pervasive phenomenon.[36] Jim Crow was a case of "state-sponsored terrorism."

By contrast, we don't need a rule of law critique of the behavior of the private citizens who made up the white mobs. Murder is wrong no matter who does it. There are ample moral principles available to criticize their evil behavior. The rule of law is a condition to be established by and through the state, and by limiting the rule of law to a critique of the state's behavior, we enable ourselves to see what the state did distinctively wrong in handling the lynchings: it withdrew its protections unequally from black citizens.

Indeed, supposing that the rule of law requires private obedience to the law other than in the case where private power approaches the Hobbesian and Weberian properties is to pose the danger that we might actually assimilate lynchings to the rule of law more generally. Carr makes just such an argument: because the history of lynching suggests that it was typically defended as a way to preserve or impose law and order against supposed uncontrollable criminality by marginal groups, he argues that lynching is inextricably linked to the rule of law, and that a critique of lynching is also a critique of the rule of law.[37] Carr's argument is compelling – but only if we allow him to assimilate "the rule of law" to "law enforcement."

Such a version of the rule of law is normatively quite unappealing just because, as Carr identifies, it comes wrapped up with all kinds of pernicious social control strategies. But we can recover the rule of law from Carr's critique by holding on to the position that the rule of law, like satire, punches up: we simply cannot describe mob violence by the powerful against the powerless, even in the name of law and order, as action in support of the rule of law. By contrast, mob violence directed against the powerful *can* support the rule of law in the right conditions – a riot against police brutality or a rebellion against a tyrant can be effective ways of constraining the powerful. But that constraint must be applied to the powerful. Indeed, with the conception of the rule of law as fundamentally egalitarian in hand, this seems obvious. Of course it sometimes licenses violent action by the weak and subordinated against the powerful, but not the other way around. That is what an egalitarian political ideal must do, where the modifier "political" serves as a reminder that violence is always on the table.

Against the objection that I have said that the rule of law is a principle guarding against the use of state coercive power, and that the complaint against officials' complicity in lynchings is about the *failure* to use state coercive power against homicidal racist whites, I have two responses. First, it's not true that officials merely declined to use their official power to protect blacks. In many cases, they actively used their official power to aid lynch mobs, as by turning over blacks who were in the jails to the mobs and participating in cover-ups and intimidation of witnesses and those who would seek justice for victims. Second, the principle of generality is about the use of coercive power, not individual acts of coercion: choosing to use coercion against some citizens but not others with no public reasons to justify the distinction is still a violation. (Imagine, for example, a state that enacted the following law: "No one shall be prosecuted for stealing from redheads." That law would obviously be nongeneral, even though its effect is to reduce the absolute number of instances of state coercion, because the state uses its power unequally.)

It might be further objected that the South could simply have complied with the rule of law, on this argument, by abandoning law enforcement altogether. Had it disbanded the police and sheriffs in toto and simply abandoned the territory to the white mobs, lynchings would still have happened (indeed, they probably would have increased), and, we may safely assume, the disparity in social and economic power would have kept blacks from successfully fighting back in the lawless world. Does the rule of law license this result?

To answer that objection, I again note that the rule of law need not give us a reason to criticize anarchy. If the Southern states had been so eager to permit racial violence that they surrendered their monopoly over violence altogether, then we have ample normative principles with which to criticize them. One reason to have a state is that it can protect the weak against the strong, and Hobbes gives us a perfectly adequate reason to say that a supposed state that makes no effort to control private violence at all loses any entitlement to the name. We do not need the rule of law to reach this result.

In reality, the Southern states would never have surrendered their monopoly over violence just to avoid being required to enforce the laws equally. We saw this when the civil rights movement finally began to win: the Southerners kicked and screamed and fought in the courts and in the streets, but ultimately acquiesced rather than allowing their territory to descend into anarchy. They did, occasionally, shut down some nonessential services – the city of Jackson, for example, notoriously closed some swimming pools in order to keep them from being integrated. But even Jackson kept a number of other public recreational facilities open, involuntarily integrating them rather than closing them down.[38] In Arkansas and Virginia, segregationists managed to shut down the public schools, but that attempt at defiance lasted only a year.[39]

The rule of law gives those who would deprive some subjects of the protection of the laws in order to reinforce the subordinate status of those subjects a choice:

surrender to anarchy altogether, or protect all within the territory equally. This is the true power of the ideal of general law: it strongly forbids what some have called "rule by law," or the practice of imposing laws on those whom one would subordinate but not on the subordinators. And that is enough to command an end to hierarchical structures like Jim Crow, even when much of the active work in enforcing the hierarchy is left to private citizens.

For these reasons, ultimately, the state was so complicit in the racial terror of the Jim Crow South that it may be justifiable to say that the Klan and other "private" white racists really were part of the state. By working together, private racists and public officials subjected blacks to a regime of unconstrained violence that reinforced the claimed high status of all whites (hubris, the Weberian property) through the use of unanswerable violent threats (terror, open threats, the Hobbesian property). It is that combination of public and private power that made Jim Crow racial terror so menacing and so evil; it is what generates rule of law objections to it.

To close this chapter, we may note two important implications of this argument. First, it also applies to further explain the rule of law objections to economic inequality with which this chapter began. Property rights, as Cohen has pointed out, are licenses to use the state's coercive power to interfere in the choices of others.[40] Consequently, property rights can generate open-ended threats because officials and other private citizens working together can wield the state's coercion at will over the one who is, for example, homeless.[41] This kind of combined private–state action depends on the active participation of officials wielding the state's coercive power, and ought, for that reason, to count against a state's regularity for much the same reason that the US Supreme Court, in *Shelley v. Kraemer*, attributed the private racist covenants of a seller of land to the action of the court called upon to enforce them.

Second, the state remains complicit in the unconstrained uses of power over African-Americans, through (inter alia) the practices of racist policing that have rocked America's cities in recent years. I take up this point again in the Conclusion, but it is important to see that what Michelle Alexander has rightly called "The New Jim Crow"[42] – the pattern of unequal criminalization as well as official violence directed at African-Americans – genuinely is a story of continuation, not difference. The abuse of the institutions of the state to deploy a field of unconstrained susceptibility to violence around the bodies of African-Americans, and thereby to enforce racial status hierarchies, has been a constant factor in American history from slavery to Jim Crow to mass criminalization, and it is vital to understand how and why it must be resisted, not *just* as racism or as violence but as a warping of the ideals expressed by the notion of government under law, based on public reasoning among equals, and the institutions meant to manifest those ideals in the world.

Chapter 4

Egalitarian liberty and reciprocity in strategic context

In this chapter, I consider the chief alternative to the normative account of the preceding three chapters. Most philosophers and lawyers have thought that the rule of law is closely associated with an ideal of liberty. I have some skepticism about this claim ("the liberty thesis"), and aim with this chapter to subject the multiplicity of arguments for it to closer examination. To do so, this chapter introduces the transition between the purely normative and conceptual analysis of the rule of law and a strategic analysis. The full account of this book integrates the two analytic strategies, arguing that both give us reason to expect a strong association between the rule of law and equality. Here, this integration is begun.

This chapter begins (section I) by arguing – using an elementary game theoretic model – that the rule of law actually may facilitate the control by officials over nonofficials, and thus may impair rather than advance individual liberty. This strategic argument foreshadows the later chapters of this book (especially Chapter 6), which center on the claim that the rule of law will be maintainable only in an environment in which coordinated nonofficial action holds officials to account. This tool for holding officials to the limits of the law, I argue, also can be a tool to allow officials to credibly commit to costly punishment, and hence to reliably get their orders carried out.

This chapter then considers several arguments that have been offered in the philosophical and legal literature for the liberty thesis. Although, as noted, I approach them with substantial skepticism, the goal is not to refute them – all have their merits – but to find their boundaries and to consider the extent to which they apply to real-world states. In examining these arguments, the focus remains largely on the strategic context – that is, on the incentives that the rule of law and its institutional supports create, and the extent to which those incentives either facilitate or inhibit interferences with the choices of nonofficials.

The chapter closes by returning to the equality thesis of the previous chapters, and to the expressive approach to interpreting value claims that those chapters emphasize. It turns out, I argue, that we can helpfully interpret compelling arguments in the domain of liberty as egalitarian appeals to the ideal of equal respect for people as autonomous decision makers.

I THE RULE OF LAW AS A TECHNOLOGY OF CONSTRAINT

To begin, let us consider a very conventional problem in the strategic analysis of questions in political science: the credible threat. This is a highly general problem, relating to the fact that using force is typically costly. If I want to order you around on pain of violence, and you disobey my orders, I have to decide whether to expend the cost to punish you. In many strategic circumstances (which may vary depending, for example, on whether we're embedded in a system of repeated interactions with sufficiently low discounting, whether my punishing you may send useful signals to other players, etc.), it becomes hard to see my punishing you as rational. In the simplest case, your disobedience has already occurred and is irrevocable: punishing you is simply a costly act of spite that cannot change your behavior. As a result, looking down the game tree, if you think I'm rational, you need not obey my initial command, for you know it is not rational for me to punish you for disobedience.

As I said, this is a very general problem in political science, which is, after all, the discipline about understanding when people can successfully deploy force against one another to achieve their ends. It is particularly prominent in the international context, where political scientists have long studied the strategy of deterrence.[1] It is also a very old problem: to my knowledge, the first person to see it was Niccolò Machiavelli, who counseled rulers to be careful about punishing the powerful (i.e., those as to whom punishment is particularly costly).[2] Let us consider it in the law enforcement context.

Suppose an absolute ruler (Louis), completely unconstrained by the rule of law, wishes to forbid some behavior. He announces that he will interfere with citizens' choices to do so by violently punishing those choices. However, Louis knows that punishment is costly: even an absolute ruler must pay his soldiers in order to keep his job, and he has only a limited budget for doing so; that is, to punish someone, violent resources must be diverted from other uses at an opportunity cost. Moreover, the fact of punishment itself can be damaging: to punish someone might invite distrust and potential retaliation, or simply may undermine Louis's propaganda campaign, which has maintained that nobody would dare think of disobeying him.

So Louis issues the following decree: "No one may put a pink flamingo on his or her lawn, on pain of imprisonment." In order to figure out whether it will be obeyed, we must go through some basic game theory.

Start with a straightforward two-stage punishment game, in which a citizen first chooses either to obey or to disobey the ruler's command, and the ruler then chooses to punish or not. Citizen's payoff for obeying is F, for disobeying G. Ruler's payoff for obedience is Q, for disobedience D. $G > F$, and $Q > D$. Ruler can punish at cost M, which inflicts cost P on the citizen (see Figure 4A).

Trivially, where $M > 0$, the only pure strategy subgame perfect equilibrium of the one-round version of this game has the citizen disobeying and the ruler refraining from punishment.[3]

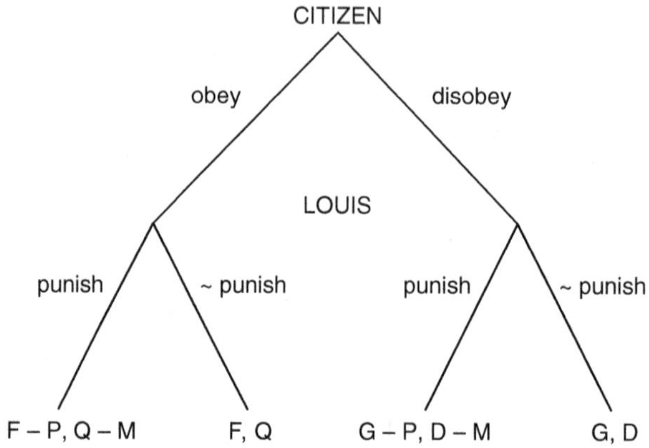

FIGURE 4A: A credible commitment game

Let us consider a finitely repeated version of the same game with N rounds. By backward induction, where M > 0 the only pure strategy pair that is in subgame perfect equilibrium is [always disobey, never punish]. In round N, regardless of the previous play, we're back in the one-round game such that citizen disobeys and ruler declines to punish. Given that, neither can make credible threats about one's behavior in round N to influence the choice about round N – 1, so in round N – 1, again citizen disobeys and ruler declines to punish, and so on. In this simple model, it looks like we may festoon our lawns with pink flamingos with impunity.

There are many ways to solve this model and give Louis the power to punish us. If, for example, we are in an indefinitely repeated game with sufficiently low discounting (if we might obey or disobey Louis again and again and again), then there are folk theorem equilibriums according to which we obey. (However, there are also folk theorem equilibriums according to which we disobey. Equilibrium selection in these contexts is a thorny problem.) There are also reputation-based mechanisms for solving these problems; it may be worthwhile for Louis to punish me in order to communicate his willingness to punish you (signal that punishment is not all that costly to him).[4] The political science literature is rich with such models.

However, if Louis is particularly clever, he may recruit us to punish ourselves. Here's how. Suppose he can off-load the decision whether or not to inflict punishment for his decrees to an independent punisher, like a bureaucracy, judge, mass jury, or even a computer program. Call the independent punisher "Richelieu." If Richelieu does not personally incur the cost of punishment, then she is not inhibited by that cost from imposing it; if she is embedded in an institutional context in which there is a positive incentive to actually impose the punishment (such as one in which she is trained and rewarded for following the decrees or laws Louis enacts), then we would expect it to actually occur. Well, in truth, we would expect it never to actually occur, because disobedience, and thus punishment, would be off the equilibrium path: now that Louis can credibly threaten punishment, nobody will ever disobey, and Richelieu need never carry it out.[5]

Now Louis has a new problem: how can Richelieu be independent? After all, Louis still pays for Richelieu's punishments. Accordingly, even if he decrees that Richelieu's decisions are immune from his control, that decree itself is not credible. The moment Richelieu orders a costly punishment, Louis ought to countermand that order.

Suppose, however, that Louis can make a deal with the masses (or the nobility, or anyone else with the power to act in concert against him). Here are the terms of the bargain: "I will write down a list of my rules, announce them in advance, and give them to Richelieu to enforce. Richelieu will be trained to really care about these rules, and paid to obey them. You backstop Richelieu's power, and make sure that I don't interfere with her judgments. In exchange, I won't try to punish you for anything that isn't on the list." Political scientists know this technique as creating "audience costs": finding someone who will sanction Louis for not doing the thing he wants to commit to do.[6] As I will argue in Chapter 6, that is a very good deal for the people: if they have a common-knowledge set of rules governing the use of Louis's power against them, and a consensus method of resolving disputes about the application of those rules (i.e., Richelieu), then they can develop the capacity to collectively hold Louis to those rules. That chapter will argue that the rule of law is actually built and sustained by establishing means by which people know the conditions under which their fellows will act against their government.[7]

The catch is that by doing so, they empower Richelieu, and if the law motivates Richelieu, and if Louis writes the law, then the very means by which the people can hold Louis to only using violence against them pursuant to the law is also the means by which Louis can off-load the cost of punishment and hence make the commands he writes into the law enforceable.[8]

Used this way, the weak version of the rule of law is partly a tool of freedom, partly a tool of unfreedom. It allows rulers or officials – at least in nondemocratic societies, or imperfectly democratic societies – to inflict a specified list of unfreedoms on the people, in exchange for the guarantee that those are the only unfreedoms that will be so inflicted (or at least that there will be some kind of public announcement before adding to the list, and the list won't be retroactively supplemented).[9] The bargain is to recruit the people (or those with power) to help create an alternative source of power that can bind all; doing so both holds rulers to the law they have set out and helps rulers enforce those laws over the people.

This separation between enforcement power and enforcement costs is a general-purpose technology of law enforcement, which works both for and against officials. That technology explains regimes like that of Singapore, a wealthy, capitalist, efficient state with high levels of property rights protection, low levels of corruption, effective and fair police and courts, and an incredibly restrictive and harsh criminal law featuring extensive surveillance, bans on chewing gum, floggings, and bold red letters on the immigration forms one must fill out to enter the country reminding visitors that it levies the death penalty for drug trafficking.[10] Singapore has aimed its extraordinarily effective technologies of law enforcement at citizens and officials alike.[11]

Of course, the bargain to create audience costs will not work unless the people inflicting those audience costs get something out of the deal. Depending on the configuration of power relationships in the populace, this might actually mean substantive guarantees of individual liberty, or it might mean economic development (as in Singapore), or even just rents attached to a powerful aristocracy. These issues will be taken up further in Chapter 8. For now, suffice it to say that the rule of law appears to be a general-purpose technology of constraint that may allow officials to constrain people, as well as allow people to constrain officials; it is not obvious that it facilitates individual liberty.

With that initial skepticism established, let us now move to the affirmative case for the liberty thesis.

II SOME ARGUMENTS FOR THE LIBERTY THESIS

In this section, I run through some arguments for the liberty thesis and their associated conceptions of liberty. We may begin with mainline liberal arguments for the claim that the rule of law facilitates what is often known as "negative liberty," or the ability of people to be free from interferences in their choices (including increases in the costs imposed on their choices by others).

A *The incentives argument*

From the liberal standpoint, I consider two major lines of argument. The first, which appears in Hayek as well as in *Federalist* No. 57, I call the "incentives argument":[12] the rule of law requires officials to apply the laws to their own behavior; this encourages them to minimize their interference with subjects' choices in order to avoid interfering with their own.[13]

This argument, though stated in abstract form, might lead to actual claims about real-world societies. Consider a religious state in which restrictive regulations are enforced against ordinary citizens, but not against the ruling elite. Reputedly, for example, in Saudi Arabia, sharia is enforced against ordinary citizens, but the elite who control the state's institutions violate it with impunity.[14] Were elites constrained to obey the laws they apply to the masses, it would at least become more likely that they would adopt a less restrictive interpretation of Islamic law in order to preserve as many of their own pleasures as possible.

The incentives argument is plausible with respect to states with a substantial degree of similarity between officials' preferences and ordinary subjects', particularly with respect to the desirable domain of noninterference. This suggests that it will not be plausible in two types of societies. First, in societies governed by officials who subscribe to strong comprehensive doctrines (e.g., theocracies), officials may not particularly care about restrictions on their own liberty.[15] Second, in highly diverse societies, the things that officials count as restrictions on their liberty may not be the same as those that ordinary subjects (or cultural minorities) count as restrictions on their liberty.[16]

A potentially stronger variation on the incentives argument appears in a concurring opinion by US Supreme Court Justice Robert Jackson. There, he argues that a state that is bound to apply the same law to political majorities as to political minorities (that is, a state with general law, on a formal conception) will protect the people from "arbitrary and unreasonable government," because it will subject officials to "political retribution" from the affected majority if the laws are oppressive.[17]

However, the same point about pluralism applies to Jackson's version of the argument. A wide variety of illiberal laws might be enacted that majorities are happy to suffer, but that are experienced as oppressive by cultural or religious minorities, or just those with idiosyncratic preferences.

That being said, the incentives argument may still give us good reason to suppose that the rule of law facilitates individual freedom, for even fanatical officials or bigoted majorities may prefer some level of individual freedom for themselves. There might be some laws that not even Savonarola would be willing to apply to himself – perhaps he's willing to apply the sumptuary laws to himself, but he really likes eating meat on Friday, so in a rule of law society he finds himself forced to restrain his regulatory zeal to at least that minimal extent. The incentives argument gives us some reason to believe that the rule of law will facilitate individual liberty, but it is unclear how far that reason goes.

B The chilling effects argument

The second argument comes from Rawls, who argues that where citizens' liberties are uncertain, they will be deterred from actually exercising them in virtue of the risk that they might be punished for something that they had thought was within their domain of choice.[18] This closely resembles an argument often deployed in US free speech law, in which vague restrictions on speech are said to cause a "chilling effect," leading to self-censorship.

The force of the chilling effects argument is not limited to vague law. Potentially, any failures of regularity and publicity risk a chilling effect. If official power is inadequately controlled by legal rules, or citizens have no way of knowing what those rules are or participating in their enforcement, then they may have reason to fear that official power will be used against them unexpectedly, and this may, in turn, give them reason to keep their heads down and restrict their activities to avoid drawing the attention of the powerful.

Let us note, however, that all law creates some chilling effect regardless of whether the rule of law is satisfied. Legal theorists have long recognized that there is room for disagreement about the application of laws in marginal cases (in what Hart called the "penumbra" of a legal rule). This indeterminacy creates a chilling risk: a citizen whose behavior is on those margins may have good reason to avoid choices that she believes to be lawful out of the fear that officials may disagree and punish her – if the law is "No vehicles are allowed in the park," a sensibly cautious citizen might refrain from skateboarding in the park even if she thinks that skateboards don't count as vehicles.

For the chilling effects argument to count as a defense of the liberty thesis, citizens' choices must be chilled to a greater extent in a state that does not comport with the rule of law (and hence just enforces officials' unvarnished preferences, if those officials can find a way to credibly commit to punishing those who violate them) than in a state that does. Alternatively, we may create a version of the chilling effects argument according to which subjects don't constrain their own choices, but they sometimes get punished for acts they thought would go unpunished – experiencing interferences in their liberty in virtue of that cost imposed on their choices, even if they make their most preferred choices anyway. Either version of the argument, however, depends on the proposition that officials' preferences are unknown or unstable, or that the practical consequences of those preferences are less knowable than the practical implications of public and preexisting law in rule of law states.[19]

To see this, compare two societies: in one society, the law bans pink flamingo lawn ornaments and requires garden gnomes. The first society comports with the rule of law, so citizens know they won't be punished for any other lawn ornament choices. In the second society, there is an absolute and unconstrained, but rational, dictator (Claudius). Citizens who anger Claudius are punished regardless of the content of the law (if any). It so happens that Claudius hates pink flamingos and loves garden gnomes.

If Claudius's preferences with respect to lawn ornaments are known and stable, citizens will know to never have pink flamingos and always have garden gnomes, and they will know that Claudius won't bother them for any other lawn ornaments. Claudius's subjects will behave exactly as do citizens of the first society, and experience exactly the same amount of interference with their choices.[20]

However, if they are ruled not by Claudius but by Caligula, whose preferences are unknown and unstable, they will have reason to fear. "Does Caligula hate birdbaths this week? Or does he love them?" Citizens under Caligula will experience all their choices as more costly, in view of the uncertainty about for what Caligula will choose to punish them.[21]

Linz suggests a useful distinction between an "authoritarian" regime, in which the ruler "exercises power within formally ill-defined limits but actually quite predictable ones," and a "sultanistic-authoritarian" regime, which features the "arbitrary and unpredictable use of power."[22] The discussion thus far suggests that subjects of sultanistic-authoritarian regimes will be less free than rule of law states, but subjects of merely authoritarian regimes need not be. It seems to me that, for several reasons, we ought to expect the non-rule of law world to be dominated by authoritarian rather than by sultanistic-authoritatian regimes, and thus that even unconstrained officials will be sufficiently predictable in their uses of power that they will not create much more of a chilling effect than will the penumbra of ordinary law.

First, the motives of unconstrained officials have often been fairly transparent. Some are in it for the money, and tend to concentrate their abuse of power on plundering wealthy citizens. Citizens can fairly reliably avoid punishment in their states by not accumulating or displaying riches. Unconstrained officials also tend to persecute their political opponents. Except in those cases where officials are paranoid (Stalin), citizens in their states can fairly reliably avoid punishment by not getting involved in politics and not becoming powerful enough to pose a threat to the existing rulers.[23] Many officials have a taste for markers of status; citizens in their states can fairly reliably avoid punishment by treating officials with great deference. Finally, some officials subscribe to religious or secular comprehensive doctrines, and use their powers to enforce them; examples include numerous religious governments as well as the Chinese Cultural Revolution. Citizens in their states can fairly reliably avoid punishment by complying with the official doctrine.

In addition to these generally understood historical motives, officials have some strategic reason to make their preferences known. We may safely suppose that those with political power in non-rule of law states, whether top-level rulers or intermediate officials, have at least four basic self-interested motives. First, each official wants to hold on to her position. Second, each official wants to maximize the rents she receives from power. Third, each official wants to maximize the extent to which citizens comply with her wishes. Fourth, each official wants to maximize her personal freedom of action; that is, if she decides to use her power against someone, she doesn't want anyone else to intervene and put a stop to it. Officials may have other motives as well, but it does not seem controversial to suggest that they will generally have at least those four.

There is some tension between those motives – particularly, officials who maximize their freedom of action may reduce the rents their societies can generate.[24] Nonetheless, some official choices are clearly better than others in respect of all four motives. I submit that an official typically does better to make her preferences known than to conceal them. Whether or not an official makes her preferences known has no effect on her satisfaction of the first or fourth motives – there's no obvious way in which doing so threatens her hold on power or flexibility in its use. Doing so, however, makes her better off with respect to the second and third motives.

An official must make her preferences known for citizens to comply with them. Claudius is much more likely to never have his sight offended by the presence of pink flamingos if he tells the citizenry just how much he hates them. If his preferences change (suddenly he loves pink flamingos and hates garden gnomes), he again is more likely to be obeyed if he announces the change.[25] Announcing his preferences will also make it much easier for subordinate officials to accurately enforce them.[26] And announcing his preferences will allow him to economize on the cost of violence: once again, soldiers must be paid, and Claudius may not wish to hire more of them to lop off the heads of pink flamingo offenders when, should he announce his preferences in advance, he may simply threaten to do so and remove disobedience as well as costly violence off the equilibrium path (assuming he has found some way other than the rule of law to make those threats credible).

Moreover, officials who make their preferences known can expect, ceteris paribus, to receive more economic rents from power. This point goes to the heart of the problem with the chilling effects argument: a rational official should strive to avoid chilling citizens' choices so long as those choices don't actually conflict with the official's desires, because citizens with greater practical freedom of choice will be able to engage in more economically productive activity, thus generating more rents for officials to capture.

It might be objected that some officials may prefer citizens to be cautious. Suppose a temperamental ruler systematically overreacts to offense: whatever pleases him pleases him only a little, but whatever offends him offends him mightily. Such a ruler might want all citizens to be walking on eggshells, and might want officials to aggressively punish doubtful behavior in order to shield himself from the slightest possibility of offense. Such a ruler does have some incentive to create a chilling effect, but it's an open empirical question whether such personalities predominate among rulers (or lower-level officials). At the very least, we do know that some autocratic rulers have created or tried to create fairly explicit and detailed law codes, giving us reason to think that they wanted citizens to know at least some of their preferences.[27] For these reasons, I am skeptical of the broad impact of the chilling effects argument.

1 The problem of complexity

More troublingly, modern rule of law societies have very complex laws, which are knowable by citizens in principle, but often only at some cost. It will not always be the case that the cost of learning the law (including expending time in legal research, hiring professional legal counsel, etc.) will be lower than the potential cost of risking breaking it. Those of us in the United States who file our tax returns without professional assistance, for example, seem to have implicitly made the judgment that the risk of making a mistake is worth taking. It is not clear that divining what one must do to avoid violating the Internal Revenue Code is any easier than divining what one must do to avoid angering Claudius (or even Caligula!).

Of course, there is some rule of law ground for criticizing overly complex laws under the principle of publicity. At a certain level of complexity, even fully disclosed laws begin to feel Kafkaesque; it is easy to imagine that someone living under very complex laws may experience her world as one in which those who have studied those laws more extensively (including, obviously, officials) have open threats against her.

Complexity is a troubling problem. It may be that there is a trade-off between legal complexity and discretion in economically advanced societies: as the activities in which people engage and the organizational structures in which they engage in them become more diverse, the number of ways in which the legal system must regulate those activities multiplies; it may do so either through multiplying rules or through making the rules less specific, and hence less constraining over officials.[28] If that is true, and if legal complexity really is a problem from the standpoint of publicity, then it would follow both that (1) there is an upper bound on the extent to which we can achieve the rule of law in a complex society, and that (2) there is an indirect tension between the rule of law and a conception of freedom that attends to subjects' practical scope of behavior: the more organizational and behavioral options people actually have, the less rule of law they can have.

Moreover, the creation of the rule of law not only may be a general-purpose technology of constraint, but it may also go along with general-purpose technologies of complexity. Consider that many economists and political scientists believe that the rule of law facilitates economic development, which in turn creates more scope for complex activities that require complex regulation. It may also be part of a package of institutional changes leading to overall social and legal complexity. North, Wallis, and Weingast, for example, argue that there are three "doorstep conditions" facilitating the transition to "open access" (i.e., vaguely liberal-democratic type) states, two of which are the rule of law (as applied to elites), and (complex) "perpetually lived organizations," such as the corporate form.[29]

Furthermore, many Richelieu-like institutional supports for the rule of law (as discussed at the beginning of this chapter, and at greater length in Chapters 6 and 8) may promote the professionalization and bureaucratization of law. Particularly when Richelieu is a judge or an administrative agency (rather than, say, a mass jury), creating institutions with a legal culture that is oriented to making and enforcing rules, and that operates rule-based systems at relatively lower cost, may encourage the creation of more complex legal rules.

For these reasons, modern rule of law societies are likely to be accompanied by a substantial degree of day-to-day citizen legal uncertainty. This is how lawyers stay in business. It follows that for those who do not have access to lawyers, the world may be full of chilling effects, even in a rule of law state. Of course, lack of lawyers is itself a problem from the standpoint of publicity – but a state can get pretty far along the rule of law path (much further than Claudius) without having free universal legal aid, and in doing so risk a bevy of chilling effects. It is not obvious that such a state is any more free, on the chilling effects argument, than many plausible state models that altogether lack the rule of law.

C *The planning argument*

Consider another argument. The rule of law is often said to protect citizens' ability to make and carry out plans to achieve their ends.[30] This idea has some intuitive grip, particularly on the conventional conception of the rule of law, which requires that official coercion be predictable. Though I argued against this conception elsewhere,[31] I will assume it in this section as necessary to cast the planning argument in its strongest form.

The intuition behind the planning argument is that citizens' liberty depends on their ability to plan and pursue complex and long-term goals, which in turn depends on the predictability of their environment; the rule of law protects that predictability. This is not merely the chilling effects argument under another name. For even if citizens know officials' preferences, the mere fact that their plans are subject to future disruption if officials' preferences change may count against their liberty, regardless of whether the prospect of future disruption counts as a cost imposed on their choices in the present.

This argument requires a conception of liberty in which citizens' abilities to make plans are important independent of the extent to which their choices are interfered with. It's most natural to turn for this to that family of conceptions of liberty based on the idea of autonomy associated with, inter alia, Kant and Spinoza.[32] On such conceptions, an agent is more free to the extent she is self-directed – able to run her own life and make her own rational decisions. An agent is less free to the extent her choices are heteronomous, that is, controlled (or influenced, or caused) by external circumstances or nonrational drives.[33] Since making plans is an important rational function by which we may run our lives, it is essential for liberty as autonomy. On the autonomy conception, a citizen whose long-term plans might be disrupted is less free because she is less in control of her own life.

My skepticism about the planning argument is rooted in the intuition that interfering with a citizen's long-term plans need not keep her from being in control of her own life. For many contingencies may disrupt an individual's long-term plans, including contingencies rooted in the arbitrary discretion of other people. One might start a business and find that one's employees all quit to work for a competitor; one might plan a family and turn out to have an unfaithful spouse. Ordinarily, when people make long-term plans, they take into account the possibility that other people might disrupt those plans (e.g., by making contingency plans); for that reason the risk of external intervention does not count against their general ability to plan.[34] This is true even when the interventions of others include the use of state coercive force:

consider that property rights themselves (and hence others' uses of them to frustrate our plans) are nothing more than licenses to use state coercion.[35]

The prospect of outside interventions due to the unconstrained power of state officials may be more disruptive to subjects' planning capacities than those other interventions, because such power has a tendency to be unbounded and uncertain, sometimes even secret. Caligula, unlike a property owner or an employee, may interfere with one's plans in unknown and surprising ways that are difficult to plan around, and may recursively interfere in the contingency plans built to account for that interference.[36] Such radical uncertainty may undermine subjects' long-term planning capacities altogether. On the other hand, as noted before with respect to the chilling effects argument, officials have good reason to make their preferences known, such that in many states that lack the rule of law we would nonetheless expect subjects to more or less be able to plan around official interventions. The planning argument may still be persuasive to the extent that subjects in states without the rule of law are unable to make contingency plans on the basis of the prospect of such officials' preferences changing, but this seems like a fairly narrow range of situations.

There are two interesting variations on the planning argument. The first has not, to my knowledge, been raised in the literature but may appear tempting.[37] It might go as follows. The rule of law, by making the legal restrictions on our own behavior and on the behavior of our fellow citizens more or less certain, allows us to make credible commitments to one another, and to carry out complex plans that rely on coordinated action with our fellow citizens. For example, my knowledge that the state will reliably enforce contracts against me as well as against others allows me to precommit to performing my agreements as well as rely on the performance of others, and thus makes those agreements (practically, strategically) possible. This, in turn, is advantageous from a liberty standpoint (i.e., in terms of a positive conception of liberty that attends to the scope of the choices available to me, or from a Kantian autonomy conception of liberty).

The flaw with the credible commitment argument is that the rule of law is neither necessary nor sufficient for the law to create stable expectations between ordinary citizens. As a counterexample to its necessity, consider a state that enforces contracts and property rights between ordinary citizens, but reserves a royal prerogative to imprison or plunder citizens at will – Leviathan, perhaps, or Pinochet. And suppose Leviathan's intrusions on citizens' persons and property are relatively minimal, either because he prudently establishes a reputation for restraint just in order to increase economic activity and thus maximize his rents from power,[38] or simply due to insufficient administrative resources to interfere with all but the biggest targets. In such a state, citizens will still be able to make plans that rely on contracts with one another.[39] As a counterexample to its sufficiency, consider a state that fully comports with the rule of law but whose law provides few or no tools for coordination among citizens; only those contracts specified on a very short statutory list are enforced, no corporations or partnerships are permitted, no private property is permitted in the means of production, and so forth. In such a state, citizens will not have the legal tools to make complex plans that rely on mutual coordination.[40]

The second variation on the planning argument is another of Hayek's contributions. In *Law, Legislation and Liberty*, Hayek argues that liberty-preservingness is a property of common-law systems in which judges state legal rules by attempting to give effect to the preexisting expectations of the parties before them.[41] Those expectations, in turn, are structured both by previous statements of legal rules and by the underlying norms and customs of the community.[42] This argument is similar to the original planning argument, in that it is premised on the claim that the object of adjudication is to satisfy citizens' preexisting expectations about their legal rights and obligations. However, it differs in that Hayek argues that a predictable (expectation-satisfying) legal system necessarily has the property of protecting some sphere of individual action independent of citizens' plans.

For the purposes of argument, we may grant the claim that common law systems track citizens' preexisting expectations (although that seems to require a fairly idealized view of the epistemic powers of both judges and citizens). Still, Hayek's argument doesn't go through.

Hayek argues that expectation satisfaction (that is, predictability) is maximized by a system of rules that carves out a protected domain of activity (that is, negative liberty) for each individual.[43] It is meant to follow, I take it, that expectation-satisfying legal systems will be liberty-preserving just in virtue of their conferring protected domains of activity on citizens.

However, even if the relationship between expectation satisfaction and the existence of protected domains of negative liberty holds as a general principle, in any given legal system that protected domain can be large or small, and there is no reason to believe that larger domains will be more expectation-satisfying than smaller domains. As a counterexample to any such notion, consider usury. Most would argue that a legal system that enforces contracts for interest is preferable, from the standpoint of liberal freedom, to an otherwise identical legal system that does not do so. Yet each of those legal systems should be equally expectation-satisfying: in the no-interest legal system, all citizens will expect that usurious contracts will not be enforced and that expectation will be satisfied, and vice versa in the other.

D *Neorepublican liberty*

Let us now turn to a conception of liberty that is particularly suitable to the rule of law. For neorepublicans such as Philip Pettit, Quentin Skinner, and Frank Lovett, an agent is unfree not when someone actually interferes with her choices, but when someone has the power to arbitrarily interfere with her choices, regardless of whether that power is actually exercised. Unsurprisingly, neorepublicans have said that the rule of law is necessary to prevent the state's dominating its citizens,[44] and aptly so: in states that fail to comport with the principle of regularity, officials have open threats against citizens. An official who has an open threat against a citizen may interfere with her choices at will by threatening to exercise that threat. Such an official dominates the citizens over whom he has open threats.

With this claim, I have no quarrel. It is also wholly compatible with the egalitarian theory of the rule of law, for essential to the idea of domination is a profound inequality. Pettit has repeatedly emphasized that domination is a relational, hierarchical idea, connected to behaviors like bowing and cringing and flattery.[45] He has gone so far as to describe domination as "a matter, essentially, of social standing or status" that "involves being able to walk tall, to look others in the eye, to be frank and forthright."[46]

Although neorepublicans are right that subjects are dominated in the absence of the rule of law, I am skeptical of the claim that the notion of domination maps to the higher-level concept of liberty, rather than that of equality. This is, however, a debate for another place:[47] here we may simply note that the equality thesis fits nicely with neorepublican theory.

Nigel Simmonds offers an interesting variation on the liberty thesis, drawing on both neorepublican and liberal conceptions of liberty.[48] According to Simmonds, the mere fact of prespecified and more or less stable rules that guide official coercion (i.e., regularity) preserves a formal domain of individual choice. Even if the law specifies everything I must do with every moment of my life in painful detail ("at 6:03 AM, you must eat exactly one hard-boiled egg . . ."), the mere fact that the rules must be specified, as opposing to leaving scrutiny of my choices to the post hoc discretion of some arbitrary authority, means that it must leave me some area of choice, however tiny, about how I carry out those commands. (Simmonds: "Should I wear a hat whilst doing so?") Moreover, the Weberian idea of the state as monopolist on violence implies the further limitation that the law must also forbid private violent interference with that reserved space of choice.

However, approaching the question from a strategic perspective shows that Simmonds's argument is not robust to a world in which officials' preferences change, or in which officials respond to incentives given by the prospect of behavioral innovation among the ruled. With respect to preference change, while it is true that having to think up and specify the restraints one wishes to impose on people in advance limits the extent to which one can coerce them, it also means those coercions can persist through preference change (either within one official or across officials), especially in a robust rule of law state in which officials enforce the law because they support lawfulness for its own sake (i.e., one in which Richelieu has been created and empowered). Thus, we may see archaic laws enforced through bureaucratic inertia by or in the name of officials who do not actually care whether the conduct commanded is carried out; by contrast, in a state without the rule of law, the preferences of prior generations of officials have no institutional means to perpetuate themselves: if the new king no longer cares about 6:03 AM egg eating, he may stop forcing people to do so.

With respect to behavioral innovation, a ruler or legislator who is uncertain about how people might offend her preferences has an incentive, in a world in which she must rule only by *ex ante* law, to regulate more broadly than she might otherwise choose. Taking Simmonds's hat example, suppose that our ruler is not currently offended by any of the hats people wear right now. However, she knows that people are endlessly creative, and worries that, in the future, people may make hat choices that she considers ugly. In order to forestall this prospect, she has an incentive, when enacting the law, to attempt to specify a complete list of permissible headgear, and, in doing so, forestall not only potential offense from future hat innovations, but also perfectly inoffensive hat innovations. By contrast, in a world in which she coerces people purely by case-by-case discretion, she is capable of punishing only the ugly future hats, not the attractive ones as well, and of hence leaving citizens more long-run hat-wearing freedom.

The two problems are merely an aspect of one well-known bug in legal rules: legal philosophers have long pointed out that rules are both underinclusive and over-inclusive; Simmonds's argument for the proposition that ruling by law preserves a space of freedom focuses all the attention on the underinclusiveness wing. But although a legislator may choose to make legal rules underinclusive with respect to the expected impact of future behavioral innovations on her anticipated future preferences – in scientific terms, prefer type II errors to type I errors – she may instead choose to make them overinclusive, that is, to prefer type I errors.

Simmonds's second point – that the formal protection of legal rules against type II errors has to be backed up by the state's monopoly over force, and thus carves out a space of freedom from private domination – is also incorrect. It is simply untrue that, as Simmonds claims, "[t]o make its governance effective, and to retain a substantive monopoly over the use of force, a regime must prohibit potentially coercive inter-ferences." To the contrary, a regime may not care about coercive interferences except insofar as those interferences themselves interfere with its commands.

Simmonds wants to derive antidomination from the Weberian notion of a state. Yet in a footnote, he acknowledges that such a state may have a "formal" monopoly of force, insofar as it allows the domination of some citizens by others "while pointing out that the conduct derives its legitimacy from the regime's will." In order to foreclose this possibility, and thus retain the claim that the state must restrain private violence, Simmonds mysteriously claims that "the Weberian analysis derives its plausibility from the way in which the monopoly of force is one facet of the state's instrumentalization of force in the service of its goals," which "requires a substantive monopoly, not a formal one." As far as I can comprehend this argument, I take it to mean that a Weberian state must actually direct the force it permits in pursuit of its goals; it may not simply allow private force to run amok and then claim that the private violence occurred with its permission. But this is not accurate. The state's goals may include economizing on law enforcement in order to pursue other priorities; in such an event, it may well allow private violence to occur in furtherance of its goals, although not, as with the case of Jim Crow as discussed in the previous chapter, to withdraw the protections of law unequally, from some rather than others.[49]

E Democratic liberty

To close this section, let us consider a family of arguments that connect the rule of law to a family of democratic conceptions of liberty as collective self-rule. These arguments tend to rest on the principle of generality, and suppose that democratic liberty requires the state to produce only laws that treat citizens as equals. Thus, for example, Dworkin suggests that democratic legitimacy requires the laws to treat each citizen with "equal concern."[50] Rousseau claims that the general will can only generate laws that are themselves general.[51] Hayek claims that "so far as men's actions toward other persons are concerned, freedom can never mean more than that they are restricted only by general rules."[52]

On a formal conception of generality, the claim that general law has anything to do with freedom seems implausible on its face. It's counterintuitive to think that the law "Joe Smith may not criticize the government" is more freedom-infringing than the law "No one may criticize the government" just because the former law has a proper name in it. On any conception of liberty discussed so far, everyone, even Joe Smith, is as unfree under the second law as under the first, and everyone but Joe Smith is less free under the second.

However, on the public reason conception of generality, Rousseau's claim that the general will can only issue general laws is quite plausible. If a law makes distinctions between citizens that are unjustified by public reasons, that law will disregard some citizens' legitimate interests; if that's the case, it cannot be a product of a general will, which is directed only at the general interest. And since, on a Rousseauian conception of democracy, the general will is what preserves the freedom of citizens within a state, nongeneral laws are not consistent with freedom. It would follow that the rule of law is necessary for freedom.

This argument is unsatisfactory as a general normative grounding of the rule of law, because it has nothing to say in defense of the rule of law in a nondemocratic state. By contrast, the egalitarian arguments in Chapters 1 through 3 are at least partially compatible with nondemocracies: an absolute monarchy that restricts itself to using violence against its people pursuant to public law, or that treats its subjects as equals rather than establishing legal hierarchies among them, is surely more morally valuable than the alternative. A Rousseauian democratic conception of liberty may give us additional reason to suppose that the rule of law is morally worthwhile in democracies (I say more about the relationship between the rule of law and democracy in Chapter 8), but still needs the egalitarian conception of the rule of law for the general case.

III LIBERTARIAN EQUALITY

The conventional claim that the rule of law supports individual liberty can actually be pressed into service in support of the equality thesis of the first three chapters. This potential appears in sharp relief when we consider Raz's discussion of the relationship between the rule of law and autonomy. While he gives lip service to the conventional claim that unpredictable or nonprospective law is a *threat* to citizens' autonomy, his actual argument for that proposition relies on the idea that it *insults* their autonomy.[53]

The insult claim is quite plausible for many ways in which the rule of law may be violated. Raz frames his version of the argument in the context of the planning conception of the relationship between the rule of law and liberty that I discussed earlier, and which is particularly amenable to the notion of an insult to autonomy. To ignore previously established legal entitlements is to disrespectfully disregard the likelihood that subjects have made plans in reliance on those entitlements; to take property without legal process is to disrespectfully disregard the likelihood that the property in question is instrumental in subjects' plans. Although Raz doesn't flesh out the claim in any detail, it's easy to believe that arbitrarily frustrating subjects' plans is to express disrespect for their capacity to plan in the first place.[54]

Raz distinguishes "insult, enslavement, and manipulation" as the three ways in which one might achieve "an offence to the dignity or a violation of the autonomy" of another. Enslavement and manipulation are, obviously, violations of autonomy. Equally obviously, insult is an offense to dignity (as are enslavement and manipulation). But we ought to understand this as a core egalitarian claim. Delivering an insult is a characteristic behavior of someone who thinks himself better than the one insulted. Similarly, respect is the characteristic attitude one displays to an equal, in contrast to the condescension and subservience displayed to, respectively, an inferior and a superior. The idea that violations of the rule of law insult the autonomous planning capacity of their victims is rooted in the ideal of equality.

Similarly, in a passage entitled "The View of Man Implicit in Legal Morality," Lon Fuller explains that the normative criteria that he applies to law (which track a plausible conception of the rule of law) imply claims about the kind of beings over whom a legal system operates.[55] The rule of law "involves of necessity a commitment to the view that man is, or can become, a responsible agent." Accordingly, violating it "is an affront to man's dignity as a responsible agent," and to do so with respect to a specific person "is to convey to him your indifference to his powers of self-determination."

In those arguments we can see a strong isomorphism with the expressive theory of this book. An official who chooses to respect or to disregard the rule of law engages in conduct that is susceptible to interpretation on the basis of the attitudes with which those choices are most consistent. Rephrased in my terms: to comply with the rule of law is to express the attitude that one's fellows are capable of self-determination; to decline to do so is to express the opposite.

Moreover, to insult someone's autonomy in that way is to act with hubris toward him or her, as I described in Chapter 1. Hubris in the rule of law context is the assertion of authority over someone based not on the responsiveness of that authority to the right kinds of reasons, but based on a gap in personal qualities between oneself and the other: because of one's superiority or the other's inferiority – a kind of assertion that, when made in the context of giving orders backed up with force, amounts to the assertion that the other is not entitled to make his or her own decisions.

We can understand the Raz and Fuller arguments as a kind of equality about liberty.[56] That is, they are plausible arguments for the notion that to coerce people unbound by the rule of law is to treat those people as inferiors. The connection (the mapping rule, if you will) between the violation of the rule of law and the expression of an attitude about inferiority incorporates a conception of people as free. Yet, the rule of law can respect people's free nature even as the law undermines their enjoyment of freedom.

I will explain further. A free person is one who has the power to make self-determining, autonomous choices. When we order such a person about, if we offer her the right kinds of reasons (drawn from law that meets the principle of generality, implemented in a way consistent with allowing her to argue back, etc.), then we hold out the possibility that she might obey those orders autonomously, as an act of free choice, rather than simply as a response to brute force – and this is so even though brute force is omnipresent in the background, and she is not genuinely free to disobey the command. In that way, (rule-of-law-compliant) law possesses, as Habermas has suggested, both "facticity" and "normativity": it is presented to people both as a brute reality – "Do this or you will be shot" – and as something that offers genuine reasons that can be complied with by an autonomous agent.[57]

The implicit utterance underneath every general law, "Do these things for the following good reasons, and also, if you don't, I'll hit you with this stick," thus expresses respect for the status of those addressed as beings capable of following the law for the good reasons, that is, as free in a Kantian sense. But we cannot ignore the stick. Ultimately, that utterance is still a threat that forces the one threatened to do what is required on pain of violence. For that reason, there will always be a threat to freedom implicit in the law, prefaced with a "rule of" or otherwise.

But we are not yet done with Fuller. Kristen Rundle offers an important reading of Fuller's "View of Man" passage.[58] On her argument, the dignity that Fuller sees the law respecting is not merely that of an adult who can voluntarily choose to follow the good reasons that apply to her, and that are expressed in the law. Rather, the legal conception of the agent is of one on whom the rules themselves depend, in Rundle's words, "akin to the Greek conception of the citizen . . . an active participant in the legal order." The subject is not just running her own life; she's also running the life of the *polis*. For Rundle, this is meant to capture two forms of participation: first, directly in the procedures of the legal system – as litigant or juror, perhaps – and second, participation through giving or withholding consent to that system.

For Rundle's Fuller, these kinds of participation make up a conception of reciprocity inherent in a well-ordered legal state. As I understand it, this is meant to be a moral relationship: citizen and official co-create the legal order by acting in accordance with the agency of the one and the reasons represented by the other, as well as the shared expectation that the rules will be respected by all.[59]

However, as I shall suggest in Chapter 6, the two forms of participation are interdependent. By making use of the participatory institutions of a legal system, citizens have the capacity to signal their commitment to or rejection of it – even in nondemocracies – and the stability of the system depends on that signaling. This is consistent with Fuller's conception of reciprocity, but gives it a new dimension: as we saw at the beginning of this chapter, in addition to the normative relationship, there is also a strategic relationship of reciprocity between official and subject: the rule of law allows subjects to control officials, and, by doing so, also allows officials to control subjects.

This idea of reciprocity also suggests a point that I will develop further in Chapter 8: if, as I have been arguing, the rule of law essentially captures the idea of coercing people only under the color of reasons that you have addressed to them, then participating in the rule of law – either as an official or perhaps even as a citizen – will tend to train one to think of those with whom one interacts through legal institutions as agents capable of responding to reasons, and to whom reasons are owed. As I will argue further in Chapter 8, this may suggest that the rule of law has the capacity to generate as well as express the understanding of citizens as of equal status. Moreover, Chapter 8 argues that the rule of law will be more stable to the extent that the substance of law is genuinely general, in the sense that it reflects the equal status of all through public reasons.

Having foreshadowed those claims (and with the hope that the reader will suspend disbelief in them until they can be defended in a few chapters), we can accept Fuller's argument, as elucidated by Rundle, and take it still further. The rule of law both expresses respect for and depends on subjects of law who respond to public reasons that treat them as equals. Such subjects will be responsible agents in fact – the legal system will depend on their responding to such reasons – and will be treated as such in an expressive sense. Such agents are free, in the sense that it is their exercise of agency that permits the legal system to exist, and they are equal in the further sense that their exercise of system-supporting agency is a response to being treated as equals.

In sum, to treat subjects as equals for rule of law purposes is to treat them as agents who are responsive to public reasons both with respect to their individual lives – in terms of the substance of the law that is uttered in their names and that they are asked to obey – and with respect to their collective lives, capable of and in fact choosing to act in public to uphold a legal system that so treats them.

At this point, the core case for the egalitarian conception of the rule of law has been built and reconciled with the arguments for the more traditional idea that the rule of law preserves individual liberty. Subsequent chapters move from construction to application, recognizing (a) that normative and conceptual work in political philosophy can and should be useful to social scientists as well as political actors in the real world, and (b) that a conception of an "essentially contested concept" such as the rule of law ought to be able to prove its worth outside the armchair. In order to do so, we shall immediately begin with the historical home of Rundle's "Greek conception of the citizen," and see that in Athens, the citizen was indeed "an active participant in the legal order," understood as the linchpin of a network of trust and commitment that protected the equal standing of all citizens.

Chapter 5

Isonomia: The dawn of legal equality

Democratic Athens was very different from contemporary liberal democracies.[1] Among many other differences, it was dramatically smaller (estimates vary, but for present purposes, there were, say, perhaps 30,000 full-fledged citizens and substantially more noncitizens);[2] it had an underclass of slaves, operated as a direct democracy in which all important decisions were made by the assembled citizenry, and operated mass popular courts. Nonetheless, it managed to have a surprisingly robust version of the rule of law.

This chapter serves several purposes. First, it supports the overall argument of this book that the rule of law does not subsist in particular institutional configurations – it can exist in societies as different as the contemporary United States and Athens of 400 BCE. Second, it shows that the identification of the rule of law with equality can help us understand an extraordinarily diverse set of societies. For that reason, it supports the factual and normative robustness of the account of the rule of law given in the first four chapters. Third, by abstracting away from contemporary institutional and social facts, it allows us to see some of the abstract dynamics of the rule of law – a point that will be developed in the next chapter.

This chapter defends several key claims. First, contrary to the arguments of some classicists and legal historians, classical Athens substantially satisfied the demands of the rule of law throughout the democratic period.[3] Second, Athenians saw further than many contemporary rule of law theorists: they recognized that the rule of law served the equality of mass and elite; and there was no contradiction (again contra some classicists) between the democratic power of the masses and the rule of law. It sets the groundwork for a third claim, developed in the next chapter: this connection between equality and the rule of law explains the most striking fact about Athenian legality: to wit, the otherwise puzzling effectiveness of a postconflict amnesty after a short-lived oligarchic tyranny at the end of the fifth century BCE.

I HOW WAS THE RULE OF LAW IMPLEMENTED IN ATHENS?

In this section, I first review the Athenian legal system, then argue for the proposition that it comported fairly well with the rule of law, except for its failures in the domain of generality with respect to women, foreigners, and slaves.

A An overview of the Athenian legal system

The period under consideration begins around 462 BCE, when the *Areopagus*, an elite council of former archons (high magistrates), lost almost all of its legal power to the democratic council, assembly, and courts.[4] From then onward, the Athenian legal system revolved around those three mass institutions. The assembly (*ekklesia*) was the chief legislative body, comprised of the entire male citizen population. It occasionally served a judicial role. The 500-member council (*boule*), whose members were selected by lot, set the agenda for the assembly and occasionally served a judicial function.

The courts (*dikasteria*) comprised, ordinarily, between 200 and 500 jurors, carefully selected at random through an elaborate procedure. Juries heard cases brought before them by private litigants, ordinarily in either a public suit (*graphe*) or a private suit (*dike*), though other specialized procedures existed.[5] There was nothing resembling the contemporary US distinction between questions of law for judges and questions of fact for juries: the Athenian jury decided the whole dispute, and was not subject to appeal.

Two legal procedures were of particular importance for rule of law purposes:

Graphe paranomon was a public suit against one who allegedly made an illegal proposal, either because the proposal was substantively illegal (such as a proposal to execute citizens without trial), or because it was offered by one not entitled to do so (i.e., if the proposer had been judicially deprived of his civic rights). Essentially *graphe paranomon* was a process by which the *ekklesia* could be subject to judicial review.[6] Both oligarchic coups at the end of the fourth century (as described in the next chapter) promptly abolished it.

Graphe hubreos was the prosecution for the crime of hubris, an ill-defined but important offense that included, at a minimum, physical assaults. Hubris (also transliterated as *hybris*) was seen as an insult against the dignity of the victim, rooted in the arrogance of the malefactor.[7]

In 403, in the wake of the oligarchic coups and a democratic restoration, Athens revised its procedure for enacting legislation. Until 403, the assembly made all the laws. Thereafter, it established a distinction resembling that in contemporary constitutional thought between entrenched "higher laws" and ordinary legislation. The former were just denoted laws (*nomoi*), and were to be enacted only pursuant to an elaborate procedure spanning several institutions, including newly created boards of lawmakers (*nomothetai*). The latter were called decrees (*psephismata*), and could be enacted by the assembly acting alone, but were not permitted to contradict *nomoi*.

B The rule of law and the oligarchy

As Ober recounts, the story of democratic Athens is one of a gradual shift in political power from a class of aristocratic elites to the citizenry as a whole.[8] Many aristocrats were dissatisfied with these developments. Throughout the democratic period there was the fear that the aristocrats would seize power. And this fear was justified, since they did so twice, establishing the oligarchies of 411 and 404, and ruling (as will be recounted shortly) with little regard to legal niceties.

We can only understand the rule of law in Athens with regard to this ever-present threat of oligarchic tyranny. A major function of the rule of law was to guard against the capture of the state by elites who would then abuse their newly acquired official power, or their subversion of legal constraints on their wealth and power within the democracy. The law had to constrain private as well as official power, because of the potential of unconstrained private power to assume the Weberian and Hobbesian properties by taking over the state.

At the same time, Athens had actual officials to control. There was no separate official class, but there were official institutions, particularly the *boule*, *ekklesia*, and *dikasteria*, and magistracies like the Eleven, through which ordinary citizens could put on official roles. The Athenian rule of law should be judged by how well it controlled both the abuse of public power by ordinary citizens while they were participating in official institutions, and the abuse of private power or seizure of public power by elite oligarchs in potentia.

In the following sections, I'll argue that the Athenian legal system successfully kept both kinds of power more or less in control.

C The Athenian rule of law

The Athenians certainly claimed that their legal system met the standards that today would be called "the rule of law." One catalog of these claims runs as follows:

> [O]rators affirmed that the law must consist of general principles equally applied, that laws should not be enacted against individuals, that no citizen should be punished without a proper trial, tried twice for the same offense, or prosecuted except according to a statute, and that statutes should be clear, comprehensible, and not contradict other provisions.[9]

Perhaps the most straightforward declaration of the rule of law at the time comes from Andocides. He describes the legal reforms enacted after the overthrow of the Thirty Tyrants as the following:

> In no circumstances shall magistrates enforce a law which has not been inscribed. No decree, whether of the Council or Assembly, shall override a law. No law shall be directed against an individual without applying to all citizens alike, unless an Assembly of six thousand so resolve by secret ballot.[10]

In this section, I will compare what we know about the Athenian legal system to the conception of the rule of law developed in the previous chapters in order to judge whether Andocides and the other orators are to be believed.

1 Regularity

It is difficult to confidently assess the extent to which democratic Athens satisfied the principle of regularity. However, the existing evidence offers some support for the proposition that it did.[11]

There are several prominent cases where the citizens occupying Athenian legal institutions seem to have disregarded the law: most notable among these is the trial of the generals (discussed at length later). But their very prominence suggests that they were exceptional circumstances, deviances from the ordinary lawful business of governance. For example, Xenophon emphasized the regret and recriminations that followed shortly after the trial of the generals. And even Pseudo-Xenophon, an aristocratic critic of the democracy, had to acknowledge in the *Constitution of the Athenians* that "there are some who have been unjustly disenfranchised, but very few indeed" and that "it is from failing to be a just magistrate or failing to say or do what is right that people are disenfranchised at Athens."[12]

Athens's institutional structure likely made it very difficult for those citizens who held magistracies under the democracy to abuse their power. Most officials held office for only a year, and were forbidden from holding the same office (except generalships) twice.[13] After leaving office, each official was subject to a *euthyna* at which accusations of misconduct could be heard and referred for prosecution. This probably greatly narrowed the scope for illegal uses of official coercion: an official who wished to seriously abuse his office would have been subject to trial no less than a year from the act, and would no longer have his official powers to protect him. With such short timescales, even a magistrate who discounted the future very heavily would have reason to fear punishment for his crimes.

Perhaps the most striking evidence for the regularity of the Athenian legal system is the post-civil war amnesty, discussed at length in the next chapter. After the Thirty Tyrants were removed, the vast majority of those implicated were granted amnesty for all of their crimes under the oligarchy. Despite the incentives democrats must have had for revenge as well as to remove those who had proven their disloyalty, the amnesty was successfully upheld.[14] The democratic *boule* went so far as to violate the rule of law in *maintaining* it, summarily executing one citizen for attempting self-help vengeance. The democrats even enacted a new judicial procedure, *paragraphe*, in order to prevent illegal prosecutions.

Also to be considered under the rubric of regularity is the extent to which the legal system succeeded in avoiding the danger, mentioned earlier, of oligarchic coups. The elites were mostly prevented from seizing control of the state, with the exception of the two fifth-century oligarchies, and I will argue in the next chapter that both of these oligarchies were occasioned by exogenous shocks – extraordinary military losses that the democracy could not withstand. And both oligarchies were quickly overthrown. In the next chapter, I will also suggest that failures of the rule of law contributed to these coups, but that the Athenians learned from their mistakes.

With respect to the abuse of elite power short of coup, there is also evidence that the legal system worked. The crime of hubris is often associated with aggressive display of superiority by the wealthy.[15] The extent to which this law actually restrained such violence is not clear, but there is at least evidence that hubris cases were sometimes brought, that in ordinary assault cases the accusation of hubris was also raised, and that threats to bring hubris prosecutions were sometimes made.[16] Carawan argues that the *graphe paranomon* served a similar function as hubris – preventing the powerful from abusing their power against the common interest, in this case by enacting illegal decrees.[17] These provisions offer us at least some reason to believe that the legal system as a whole contributed to regulating the potential for elites' day-to-day abuse of wealth and status.[18]

One worry, leading to a potential objection, with respect to regularity in Athens arises from the extent of the discretion that juries had to convict defendants. While the jurors were required to take an oath to follow the law, some scholars have argued that extralegal evidence was often taken into consideration, such that jurors often didn't act as if they were bound to convict or acquit defendants on legal grounds alone.[19] I am not equipped to intervene on the debate about the actual amount of discretion juries exercised, but I will submit that even if juries exceeded the written law, it does not necessarily follow that their decision-making power was sufficiently unconstrained to violate regularity.

Thus, although scholars such as Lanni argue that the Athenians disregarded the rule of law because juries made rulings on the basis of informal norms,[20] that does not warrant the conclusion that the Athenian legal system was irregular. Lanni was able to discern six clear categories of social norms enforced in the Athenian courts;[21] the mere fact that she can identify them is evidence that they were determinate enough to provide limits on the discretionary coercive power of juries.[22] Here, the immense size of the juries may have helped: no individual juror or small group of jurors could have punished a litigant for idiosyncratic reasons, absent some generally acceptable reason (i.e., rooted in the written law or a strong social norm) to bring along enough votes. Moreover, as Lanni points out elsewhere, the Athenian courts were conducted in a glare of publicity, and this helped hold jurors accountable to the opinion of the community.[23]

Lanni's work thus warrants the conclusion not that the Athenian juries ignored the law, but that the law in Athens included both written enactments of the assembly and those unwritten social norms that were widely accepted about citizens' public and private conduct.[24] In support of this interpretation, note that Thucydides' rendition of Pericles' funeral oration credits Athens with both written and unwritten laws, and Aristotle's *Politics* makes clear that both categories count as law.[25] The Athenian legal practice may have been similar to that of modern common-law states, which incorporate social custom into the law and still comply with the rule of law.[26] Indeed, even the very word νόμος, which meant law, also meant custom.

Carugati suggests that the real problem is that the existence of parallel legal and customary norm/rule systems "mak[es] outcomes unpredictable and *ad hoc* [and] defies [rule of law] standards of predictability and consistency."[27] That point, however, depends on the factual supposition that customary norms and legal norms commanded different outcomes. But in a direct democracy, the most plausible assumption in the absence of evidence is that the people wrote their customs into the formal law. The assembly and the jury were both mass institutions; there is scant reason to believe that the norms enforced by the latter would diverge too greatly from the norms enacted by the former, or from those endorsed (and understood) by the public at large. All these entities are made up of the same people. In general, where the formal law is enforced by the people, law that diverges too greatly from social norms is likely to be brought into line, but that pattern alone is not necessarily in tension with the rule of law.[28]

2 Publicity

The principle of publicity requires that citizens have access to adequate information about the law and an opportunity to defend their interests in fair judicial processes. As far as can be determined, Athens satisfied the publicity principle quite well.

Citizens were given extensive opportunities to participate in the legal process. Any citizen could initiate legal action before the popular courts, on the basis of injury done not only to themselves, but in many cases to anyone else as well (including the polis itself).[29] In addition, officials were held to account after the expiration of their terms in routine judicial procedures (*euthynai*) to which ordinary citizens had access,[30] as well as a special procedure (*eisangelia*) to challenge a magistrate's actions while still in office.[31] There was even a legal procedure (*graphe paranomon*) available to citizens to challenge unlawful decrees of the assembly. Moreover, trials were conducted in a glare of publicity; citizens would know what happened there.[32]

Once legal process was invoked against a citizen, there was ample opportunity to mount a full defense.[33] The seriousness with which a defendant's right to put up a defense was taken can be seen by the outrage Xenophon reports at the failure of the assembly to respect that right in the illegal trial of the generals (discussed later). There were also protections against frivolous or extortionate litigation: in many types of procedure, prosecutors who failed to get a fifth of the votes or who abandoned the cases after bringing them were subject to fine.[34] For illegal prosecutions after the 403 reforms, defendants could bring their own preemptive suit (*paragraphe*), victory in which led to a penalty for the prosecutor and the barring of the original litigation.

Information about the content of the law was more or less readily available, depending on the time under consideration. In 410, an attempt was made to collect the many uncodified laws and publish them in one place; in 404 the code was inscribed on a wall, and in 399 the final postoligarchical revision of the laws was completed.[35] Around the same period, a centralized location was created for paper copies of the laws.[36] Until that period, laws were published essentially wherever it seemed appropriate, and it may have been difficult for ordinary Athenians to know the laws that applied.[37] The change from scattered and hard-to-discover laws to a centralized law code was a clear improvement from the standpoint of publicity.[38] Generally, however, even before the reforms, Athens's small population, its cultural and religious homogeneity, the public nature of its procedures, and the extent of citizen participation in juries all give us good reason to suppose that ordinary citizens were familiar, in their capacities as subjects, with the law that they enforced in their capacities as jurors.

3 Generality

Athens failed to comport with the principle of generality with respect to women, foreigners, and slaves, each of whom was a subordinate legal class with dramatically inferior rights. However, the rule of law is a continuum, not a binary, and Athens did manage to achieve substantial strides toward generality along the dimension of socioeconomic class.

Eligibility for membership in all political institutions was determined by citizenship, a hereditary status: all people whose parents were both Athenian citizens had the status of citizens (subject to its loss by judicial process); all male citizens ordinarily had equal legal rights relating to, for example, property ownership, protection from violence, and the like, as well as equal rights to participate in the assembly and in the courts both as litigants and as jurors.[39] Metics (resident foreigners), women, and slaves had lesser legal rights, though none were completely devoid of rights.

Fundamental to the idea of Athenian democracy was *isonomia*, or political equality through legal equality. I discuss *isonomia* later; for present purposes it's worth noting only that orators routinely raised the ideology of class equality under law in their arguments, usually to urge the punishment of their rich opponents on the same terms as the poor would be punished. Even the diversity of legal procedures by which citizens could resolve their disputes was thought to accommodate class equality, allowing poorer and more vulnerable citizens to choose procedures that subjected them to less danger, though at the cost of being able to deploy less severe punishments, thus balancing the need to deter frivolous litigation with the need to guarantee equal access to justice.[40]

Even with respect to slaves, Athens did better than its peer cities. Sparta, to take the most striking contrast, allegedly went so far as to subject helots to a minimum number of blows per year to remind them of their inferiority.[41] In Athens, they were protected from private violence, and thus from pervasive terror of citizens and from the need to behave submissively to them.[42] Even if the Spartan story is apocryphal (and it has always sounded, to me, a little too hyperbolic to be true), it surely captures a real contrast in the extent to which the two leading cities of Greece were shot through with hierarchical organization.

II EQUALITY AND THE ATHENIAN RULE OF LAW

Not only Pseudo-Xenophon (see the end of Chapter 1) recognized that the rule of law led to equality in Athens. Numerous other historical sources reflect an understanding of the rule of law such that faithful enforcement of the laws protects the power and status of the masses against the inegalitarian ambitions of the elites; that is, the rule of law was the guardian of political equality, in the form of two *topoi*, which I call "the respect *topos*" and "the strength *topos*."

According to the respect *topos*, to break the law was to reveal one's character as an oligarch, one who has an arrogant (hubristic) disdain for the masses, as expressed in their distinctively democratic laws. To punish such oligarchs is to protect ordinary people from their hubris as well as to protect the democracy from their urge to overthrow it.[43] Even when citizens ignore the law in their private lives, this is seen as evidence of their oligarchic character and contempt for the masses.

According to the strength *topos*, to defend the law is to defend the democracy itself. Each individual citizen (particularly, each nonelite citizen) in the democracy is made strong when the laws are enforced and weak when they are not, and the relationship is reciprocal: the laws are strong when citizens defend them and are weak when they do not. When the laws are strong, nobody need live in fear, because the laws give the masses the tools to protect themselves against the elites.

The first subsection offers the evidence; the second addresses some objections to this section as well as to the previous one.

Before moving into the evidence proper, however, a linguistic note is in order. Several words can be translated as "equality" in the Athenian corpus, but the most significant is *isonomia*. There has been some debate among classicists about what the term means. According to Vlastos, *isonomia* captured the relationship between legal and political equality.[44] He contrasts the idea of "equality before the law" and "equality maintained through law," and argues that *isonomia* meant the latter, and in particular that the laws "should be equal in the wholly different sense of defining the equal share of all the citizens in the control of the state."[45] Ober suggests that *isonomia* could have meant "equality of participation in making the decisions (laws) that will maintain and promote equality and that will bind all citizens equally."[46] Ostwald interprets *isonomia* as meaning political equality, or "equality of rights and power."[47] For Ostwald, too, political and legal equality are two sides of the same coin in *isonomia*: "what is recognized as valid and binding is so regarded by and for all classes of society."[48] By contrast, Hansen distinguishes the rule of law, and equality under law, from *isonomia*. According to Hansen, "equality before the law" is "sometimes overlooked by historians, or only briefly described, perhaps because no slogan was coined for it as in the case of *isegoria* and *isonomia*."[49] For Hansen, *isonomia* only meant political equality (i.e., to participate in democratic governance).[50]

The classics literature has developed some of the themes in this section via an interpretation of the concept of *isonomia*. Particularly, Rosivach elucidates the relationship of political equality to hubristic disrespect.[51] On Rosivach's account, in Athens, *isonomia* was understood as the opposite of tyranny: the tyrant, qua feared figure in Athenian political culture, is guilty of *hubris* by virtue of his status-grabbing seizure of power, and can get away with further *hubris* because he is above the law and not subject to judicial control. Of course, such a tyrant could be oligarchic, at least after 399, when the term began to be applied to the regime of the Thirty Tyrants, and tyranny came to be identified less with one-person rule than with undemocratic rule.[52] Lewis argues that Solon established the superiority of law over personal whim in Athens just to solve the problem of widespread *hubris* that led Athenians to forcibly take one another as slaves.[53]

Regardless of these disagreements, it seems clear that there is a close connection between the three ideas of political equality, legal equality, and the avoidance of hubris. This connection will inform the interpretation of the evidence presented in the following subsections.

A *A catalog of Athenian evidence*

I offer evidence from contemporaneous forensic speeches, theater, historians, and philosophers for the relationship between the rule of law and equality. Classical scholars generally accept that forensic speeches are good evidence for Athenian political beliefs. The standard argument is that the speeches, being meant to convince a mass jury, would reflect arguments that talented orators and politicians would expect that jury to accept, so we can reliably use them to approximate mass opinion.[54] Matters are less clear with the theater, history, and philosophy. Theatrical performances, at least, would have been given in order to win popular support and prizes at festivals, so a similar argument could apply, albeit with lower stakes than forensic speeches (since nobody was executed for putting on a bad play). Philosophers' arguments and historians' explanations of events, of course, need be nothing more than the opinions of the individuals writing. Consequently, we should take the forensic speeches offered next as the strongest evidence, and the other materials as somewhat weaker.

1 Forensic evidence for the Athenian equality thesis

A THE RESPECT TOPOS

The first sort of forensic evidence for the egalitarian meaning of the rule of law in Athens is in a series of passages associating lawbreaking with oligarchic character. On this recurrent theme, lawbreaking was an indication that the lawbreaker aspired to be an oligarch. His arrogance and lawlessness on an individual basis were taken to suggest that, given the chance, he would carry those habits over into arrogant and lawless political power. This claim was sometimes elaborated by the notion that the populace had good reason to thus fear the lawbreaker.

Thus Isocrates, in "Against Lochites," argues that Lochites should be punished for assaulting a fellow citizen (the crime of hubris), because his crime reveals his oligarchic character.[55] To punish him, Isocrates argues, is to protect the public against those who wish to overthrow the democracy.

Similarly, Demosthenes, in "On the False Embassy,"[56] equates being superior to the laws to being superior to the people, and distinguishes between the acceptable greatness and power that a politician might achieve in the popular assembly and the unacceptable greatness and power that might be achieved in (that is, over) the courts; equality before the law is "the democratic way." Demosthenes warns that Aeschines is in danger of becoming superior to the courts in this undemocratic fashion, if the jury fails to convict him "merely because this man or that so desires."

Later in the speech, the oligarchic connection to all of this becomes clearer: having "perpetrated wrongs without number," Aeschines wishes to set himself up as an oligarch.[57] It's striking that in this latter passage Demonsthenes credits Aeschines' lawbreaking behavior for his turn toward oligarchic sentiments. There was a more natural supposition available to him: Demosthenes had been accusing Aeschines of taking Philip of Macedon's bribes; why didn't Demosthenes complete that theme and accuse him of becoming an oligarch because of his increase in wealth? The supposition seems to be that losing respect for the laws and losing respect for the democracy, and thus the equality of mass and elite, go together.

[Pseudo-?]Andocides expresses shock that Alcibiades is seen as a supporter of democracy, "that form of government which more than any other would seem to make equality its end," and cites as evidence for the contrary position Alcibiades' flouting of the laws in his private life, as well as his use of force to defend himself against the laws when called to account for his private profligacy.[58]

Finally, Isocrates, again in "Against Lochites," directly recognizes the relationship between equality under law and social status.[59] He argues that the penalty for hubris should be the same for a poor plaintiff as for a rich plaintiff, on the grounds that to treat them differently would amount to claiming that the poor have inferior civic status. To do so would "teach the young men to have contempt for the mass of citizens."[60] We can read this claim one of two ways. First, failing to enforce the law might lead the young (elite) men to have contempt for the masses just by virtue of the latter's having de facto inferior legal rights; that is, the inferior legal status of the masses might induce the elites to see the masses as inferior. Alternatively, failing to enforce the law against hubris might encourage young (elite) men to commit hubris, since they wouldn't be punished, and, by doing so, express contempt for the masses.

Either way, the failure of the law against hubris encourages unequal status between mass and elite.

B THE STRENGTH TOPOS

The second repeated theme in the forensic orations is that defending the law amounts to defending the power of the democracy, and, consequently, the individual strength and security of each citizen. According to Demosthenes in "Against Medias," the faithful enforcement of the law against hubris, particularly against rich men like Medias, allows citizens to live in security against casual violence and insult, regardless of how powerful their hubristic enemies are.[61] The relationship is reciprocal: the faithful enforcement of the laws by the masses makes the laws strong, and the laws, in turn, make each individual member of the masses strong against the depredations of the powerful.[62]

The strength *topos* helps fill out [Pseudo?-]Andocides' account of why Alcibiades is such a threat to the community: when Alcibiades wanted a painting, he threatened the painter with imprisonment unless he did the work. He then carried out this threat, treating the painter "like any acknowledged slave,"[63] and, when the polis failed to punish him for this, it "increased the awe and fear in which [Alcibiades] is held."[64] He then goes on to relate still another story, in which Alcibiades beat up a competing chorus leader, and the judges ruled in his favor out of fear.[65] And why all this fear? Well: "The blame lies with you. You refuse to punish insolence [hubris]." That is, Alcibiades' past hubris, and his demonstrated ability to get away with it, allows him to intimidate his fellow citizens into letting him get away with more hubris in the future. The jurors have failed to uphold the laws; consequently, the laws have lost their power to bind Alcibiades, and each of them is now in danger from his hubris. (This argument fits particularly well with the strategic account laid out in the next chapter, according to which the Athenian rule of law depended on citizens consistently signaling their willingness to enforce the law in the courts.[66])

Aeschines, at the beginning of "Against Ctesiphon," claims that the difference between a tyranny or oligarchy and a democracy is that the first two are ruled by the arbitrary will of the rulers, while the latter is ruled by the law (not, as one might otherwise suspect, the arbitrary will of the masses).[67] Consequently, absent enforcement of the law against illegal motions (*graphe paranomon*), the democracy is under threat: no law, no democracy. Thus, he equates ruling according to the law to serving in battle: each is necessary to defend the polis.[68]

Toward the end of the same speech, he argues that the power of the individual citizen in a democracy depends on the faithful enforcement of the laws, and to let lawbreakers off is to deliver that power into the hands of the scofflaw *rhetor*.[69] He goes on to suggest that politicians who would create oligarchy first must make themselves immune to law ("stronger than the courts"), and that this was the pattern displayed by the Thirty Tyrants. Since both oligarchic revolutions in fifth-century

Athens started off by abolishing the *graphe paranomon* in order to shield their actions from the courts, this claim stood on solid ground.

He makes a similar claim in another speech, "Against Timarchus," where he again says that democracies are distinct from oligarchies and autocracies in that democracies are ruled by the law, and further claims that the laws provide security to the citizens and the state, while oligarchs and tyrants must defend themselves by force of arms.[70] He then again urges the jury to follow the laws, because they have a government "based upon equality and law" and their strength depends on the vigilant enforcement of the laws.[71] The security claim is similar to a claim made in Hyperides' funeral oration, in which he echoes the idea of terror in alleging that the happiness and freedom of men depend on the supremacy of "the voice of law, and not a ruler's threats," and says that the safety of the citizenry must "depend on . . . the force of law alone."[72]

2 Evidence from poets, philosophers, and historians

There are nonforensic sources that also attest to the relationship between the rule of law and equality.[73] The most interesting evidence comes from Aristotle. In the *Politics*, he argues that "the law courts [are] an institution favoring the people," and that Solon "established popular power by opening membership in the law courts to all."[74] Ostwald further elaborates on this passage and similar passages in the *Constitution of the Athenians* to argue that (a) Solon's creation of jurisdiction in the popular courts and (b) his allowing anyone to bring a *graphe* regardless of individual injury together gave the public a check on the arbitrary use of power by elites.[75] That is, by making the courts widely participatory, they became more reliable in enforcing the laws against the elite, and reinforcing the strength of the masses.

Elsewhere in the *Politics*, Aristotle claims that the rule of law is necessary for those who are equals.[76] The argument proceeds as follows. He first claims that equal participation in government is the appropriate form of rule for people who are naturally equal. Next, he argues (in what seems to be an inference from the previous claim) that giving (discretionary) power to magistrates is inconsistent with the equality of all citizens, and, consequently, that the magistrates should be nothing more than "guardians and ministers of the law," for if the law rules, no individual rules.

Thucydides agrees with Aristotle. In his version of Pericles' funeral speech, we learn that Athens is a democracy in part because "[i]n private disputes all are equal before the law."[77]

Thucydides also echoes the respect *topos*. The masses feared Alcibiades, he says, because of his lawlessness: "Alarmed at the greatness of the license in his own life and habits, and at the ambition which he showed in all things whatsoever that he undertook, the mass of the people marked him as an aspirant to the tyranny and became his enemies."[78] That is, the rich and powerful, when they ignore the laws in their personal lives, are seen as tending toward oligarchic or tyrannical sentiments, and consequently inspire fear in the populace.

Euripides suggests that written laws, by enabling the weak to resist oppression by the strong, create legal and political equality:

> Nothing is more hostile to a city than a despot; where he is, there are first no laws common to all, but one man is tyrant, in whose keeping and in his alone the law resides, and in that case equality is at an end. But when the laws are written down, rich and weak alike have equal justice, and it is open to the weaker to use the same language to the prosperous when he is reviled by him, and the weaker prevails over the stronger if he has justice on his side. Freedom's mark is also seen in this: "Who has wholesome counsel to declare unto the state?" And he who chooses to do so gains renown, while he, who has no wish, remains silent. What greater equality can there be in a city?[79]

Aeschylus puts the strength *topos* in the mouth of Athena, explaining to the Athenians that she has established the court on the *Areopagus* as a "guardian of the land," and that if the Athenians respect and do not pollute the law, they will have "a defense for your land and salvation of your city." The court is "awake on behalf of those who sleep," Athena explains, and with the support of the citizens with their ballots, contrasts both with anarchy and tyranny.[80]

Pseudo-Xenophon, as discussed in Chapter 1, also transposes the strength and respect *topoi* to the relationship not between elite and mass citizens but between citizens and slaves. Likewise, Plato, in *Crito*, repeats a version of the strength topos. Socrates imagines the laws criticizing him on the grounds that to use bribery to procure impunity from jury verdicts will destroy the city: "Or do you think it possible for a city not to be destroyed if the verdicts of its courts have no force but are nullified and set at naught by private individuals?"[81]

In Herodotus's *History*, Otanes echoes the respect *topos*.[82] Monarchs become "outrageously arrogant" and "insolent," and this hubris is a consequence of their unconstrained power: "Even the best of men, if placed in this position of power, would lose his normal mental balance, for arrogance will grow within him." Otanes, like Pseudo-Xenophon, also suggests that the failure of the rule of law gives the weak reason to performatively affirm their lower status with subservient behavior: "if you admire him to a moderate degree, he is vexed that he is not being treated with sufficient deference, but if you treat him subserviently, then he becomes annoyed by your obsequiousness." He closes with a contrast between monarchy, characterized by lawlessness, and democracy, characterized by equality:

> And the worst of all his traits is that he overturns ancestral customs; he uses brute force on women, and he kills men without trial. The rule of the majority, however, not only has the most beautiful and powerful name of all, equality [*isonomia*], but in

practice, the majority does not act at all like a monarch ... it holds all of these officials accountable to an audit.[83]

III BUT IS THE RULE OF LAW REALLY CONSISTENT WITH EGALITARIAN DEMOCRACY?

The Athenian orators evidently thought (or expected the masses to think) that the rule of law was an integral part of the power of the masses, and thus of democratic equality. But they may have been mistaken. In particular, there's a potential tension between radical sorts of democracy characterized by the supremacy of popular or representative legislative institutions and the rule of law: what happens if the legislature uses its supreme power to rule by decree? This is not just a problem for the ancient Athenian *ekklesia*, but also for the contemporary British Parliament. The United Kingdom, today, is widely recognized as a rule of law state, but how is this to be reconciled with the doctrine of parliamentary supremacy? The standard answer for the British case is Dicey's: Parliament is constrained by strong constitutional norms, or "conventions"; even though it has the nominal legal power to overthrow the law, these norms provide a political check preventing it from doing so.[84] Does Dicey's argument also apply to Athens?

In this section, I will suggest that it does, by way of addressing two objections. Each objection centers on the notion that the democratic assembly exercised such broad powers that it was inconsistent with the rule of law. Both objections thus pose a threat to both arguments of this chapter, suggesting that Athens did not, in fact, have the rule of law, and that even if Athenians thought the rule of law was related to democratic equality, in fact, democratic equality as they conceived of it (as political equality, instantiated in strong mass legislative institutions) was inconsistent with the rule of law.

The first, which I will call the "conceptual objection," asserts that the broad legislative discretion of the assembly until the post-Thirty reforms was inconsistent with the rule of law. The second, which I will call the "practical objection," asserts that the assembly and courts did in fact ignore the constraints of rule of law by exercising unconstrained power, and were enabled to do so by their radical democratic structure.

A *The conceptual objection: constitutionalism as the rule of law*

The first objection to the notion that Athens satisfied the rule of law, at least until 403, is suggested by Ostwald's characterization of the "principle of popular sovereignty" as a contrast to the "principle of the sovereignty of the law."[85] On this account, Athens was under the "sovereignty of law" only after the post-Thirty reforms to the legislative process forbade the assembly from ruling by decree and required new laws to pass an elaborate process of scrutiny by boards of independent lawmakers as well as the courts.

Accepting this dichotomy seems to commit Ostwald to the proposition that "the sovereignty of law" – which I take to mean something equivalent to the rule of law – requires denying a legislative body like the *ekklesia* full control over the law.[86] But that proposition is mistaken.

To see why, we should make a distinction between the rule of law (or the "sovereignty of law") and a related concept that currently goes by the name "constitutionalism." For political scientists and theorists, a major function of constitutions is to permit political/legal actors to coordinate on widely shared values, and, by doing so, promote political stability in the face of pluralism by lowering the stakes of day-to-day politics – entrenching some basic values into a fundamental law code that is more difficult to change than day-to-day legislation.[87]

The changes in Athens after the Thirty nicely fit that conception of constitutionalism. By constitutionalizing the basic laws of Athens, identified with the ancestral laws of Solon and Draco, Athens entrenched the fundamental values of the democracy.[88] Its doing so immediately on the heels of devastating internal conflict that had been riddled with radical changes to the law suggests that the purpose was in fact to lower the stakes of politics – to make it more difficult for the polis to make the sorts of fundamental changes in political organization that contributed to political conflict and supported oligarchic tyranny.[89]

But these constitutional changes bear no direct relationship to the rule of law. In a stable political community, the rule of law can exist with or without constitutional entrenchment. This is just Dicey's point: as long as officials are constrained to conform to the law, the mere fact that some of it isn't entrenched won't keep them from doing so. And the converse is also true: no matter how entrenched the constitution is, coordinated action by some section of the population (e.g., a sufficient supermajority to change the constitution) can toss aside the laws, or those in control of military force can just ignore the laws, no matter what those laws say about how they are to be changed. Constitutionalism and the rule of law are distinct concepts. In fact, logically, the rule of law is necessary for (effectively enforced) constitutionalism, not the other way around. The rules that provide for things like supermajorities to amend the constitution are themselves legal rules, and will be obeyed only if the rule of law is respected in a state. A constitutional state without the rule of law is just a fraud – consider the Soviet constitution.

Consequently, contra Ostwald, I argue that Athens had the "sovereignty of law" long before it adopted a practice of constitutional entrenchment. While several of the post-Thirty law reforms did improve matters from a rule of law standpoint, depriving the assembly of absolute legislative power was not necessary for the rule of law.[90]

B The practical objection: arbitrary democracy and the trial of the generals

While there is significant evidence that the laws were respected, and that there was a strong norm of ruling the state under law, the assembly was also seen (at least by radical Athenian democrats) as supreme, and possessing, in principle, the capacity to rule by decree.[91] In fact, sometimes the assembly did so. The most prominent example of its law-ignoring rule by decree is the infamous trial of the Arginusae generals.

Xenophon is the standard source for these matters. I begin with some background. Eight generals together won a naval victory at Arginusae; in the process some ships were disabled, and the generals were unable to rescue their crews. On their return to Athens, several were put on trial in the assembly for the botched rescue, and were given very little opportunity to put up a defense. Perhaps most infamously, when one citizen by the name of Euryptolemus attempted to indict the prosecutor (presumably by *graphe paranomon*) for proposing the illegal summary mass trial, he was shouted down with cries that "it was a terrible thing if someone prevented the people from doing whatever they wished."[92] Making matters worse, the assembly loudly supported another citizen's threat to prosecute Euryptolemus along with the generals. The assembly then illegally sentenced all of the generals to death on a single vote.[93]

This highlights the evident dangers of radical democracy for the rule of law. It also calls into question the closeness of the relationship between the rule of law and equality in Athens: if the Athenians understood equality to consist in radical democratic institutions, and if those institutions posed a threat to the rule of law, *isonomia*, political and legal equality together, starts to seem like a contradiction in terms.

Yet this tension is easy to overstate. First, the trial of the generals was an extraordinary and aberrant incident.[94] Accordingly, Xenophon reports that the polis immediately regretted the rash decision and punished those who incited it.[95]

Second, there is evidence that the Athenians recognized that their political equality depended on some legal restraints on the assembly, and that the democracy required such restraints. As Hansen shows, in the fourth century, it was widely accepted that the *graphe paranomon* was necessary for democracy, and, consistent with this belief, both of the fifth-century oligarchical coups were accompanied or preceded by an abolition of the action.[96] On Hansen's account, radical democrats saw an unfettered assembly as the appropriate locus of political equality; moderate democrats found this in the popular courts and their law-enforcing role.[97] On the moderate democratic position, legal restraints on the assembly's power are not only compatible with, but necessary for, political equality as democracy.[98]

There are three other classic examples of miscarriages of Athenian justice. The first is the trial of Socrates. The second is the hysteria, with various excessive punishments meted out, on the eve of the Sicilian expedition, when a number of people were believed to have profaned the mysteries and/or mutilated statutes of

Hermes.[99] The third is the stoning of a Council member and his family for proposing to put a Persian peace proposal before the assembly.[100] The affair of the Herms/Mysteries was a particular disaster for Athens, leading to numerous arbitrary persecutions, seriously undermining civic unity in the midst of a massive (and ill-fated) military expedition, and pushing Alcibiades into one of his many treasons. Still, the argument in this section covers those cases, too. With the exception of the trial of Socrates (which seems to me to have been merely unjust, not illegal), all were the acts of a citizenry swept up in wartime hysteria.

C *The problem of informality*

Athens is both a fruitful and a difficult case for understanding the rule of law in modern states – fruitful because its institutional differences allow us to see the dynamics of the rule of law at a very general level, yet difficult because those same differences make it challenging to see the Athenian rule of law and the rule of law in modern states as genuine versions of the same kind of thing. For example, one key difference between Athens and later rule of law states is that Athens lacked the concept of "equity," a formal method for relaxing legal rules in cases where the strict application of those rules would lead to injustice – and to do so on the basis of explicitly stated reasons.[101] Quite the contrary: adjudication in Athens involved no reason-giving on the part of decision makers at all (and how could it, with hundreds-strong juries?) and we can understand legal rules and considerations of justice as continuous rather than separate in the Athenian legal system.[102]

Yet for all that, the Athenian legal system largely appears to have managed to carry out the core function and chief ethical mandate of the rule of law: holding power to be accountable to public reasons, in the interest of the equal status of all (always remembering the unjust cultural framework that excluded women and slaves from "all"). And it did so by ensuring that the use of power would be accountable to norms that were understood by the people as a whole and enforced by their committed collective action – which, I shall suggest in the next several chapters, is the key institutional feature of the rule of law.

Moreover, although Athens had no notion of equity or of a judicial opinion, those who used power – not perhaps the sovereign demos as a whole, acting through the assembly or the courts, but individuals, both wealthy and aristocratic private citizens and those who were entrusted with magistracies, as well as those who appeared before the demos qua court to request the use of its power – were required to state reasons for their uses of power, and quite directly subject those reasons to the scrutiny of the whole community by defending their actions in person in the jury room.

Athens varies from our standard picture of modern formal legal systems primarily in the unique feature of direct mass rule. Normally, the rule of law constrains the exercise of core organs of the state, as well as day-to-day officials and (where necessary) powerful private citizens, in the interest of the people as a whole. In Athens, the people as a whole directly held the reins of those core organs, and used them to constrain the power of officials and private elites. The tool to constrain power, a chief entity to be constrained, and the intended beneficiary of the constraint were different descriptions of the same collective agent (the jury/those who controlled the power of the polis/the demos).

Under such an arrangement, it should not be surprising that it sometimes becomes hard to distinguish between formal legal rules, overarching ethical norms, and the will of the masses. Still, Athens typically managed to achieve formality when it mattered: the trial of the generals was such a failure of the rule of law just because it represented an abandonment of the normal structured procedure of reason-giving by which prosecutor and defendant would stand before the jury and explain themselves as well as justify prospectively the use of power that they proposed for the demos as a whole. And even that dramatic failure, like the others, came in the context of the people as a whole lashing out at some of their elites, not, as in the twentieth-century tyrannies such as the Soviet Union, Maoist China, Papa Doc's Haiti, Pinochet's Chile, and Nazi Germany, top-level officials and elites rampantly running amok and wielding the power of the state willy-nilly against the weak. (When that was tried in Athens, it was quickly overthrown, twice.) Even the major Athenian legal failures, that is, remained consistent with the core idea of power bound to be accountable to the community as a whole, including its weakest members.

IV LAW CONTRA OLIGARCHY

Law, in classical Athens, was the distinctive possession of the masses. They served en masse in their juries – for which they were paid, to ensure access to the lowest classes – and the law was written to protect their equal status, to the point that the law against hubris directly forbade the arrogance of the rich and powerful. No surprise, then, that when before the courts the elite orators appealed directly to the interest of the masses in preserving the protections of the law. And, as we'll see in the next chapter, when the rule of law failed, the Athenians quickly reestablished it, and made it stronger, and with it their democracy recovered. Athens knew the egalitarian rule of law.

V APPENDIX: A BRIEF TIME LINE OF THE LATE-FIFTH-CENTURY ATHENIAN UPHEAVALS

This time line covers the relevant events at the end of the fifth and beginning of the fourth centuries, and will provide useful context for the next chapter.[103]

415	Affair of the Herms/Mysteries
415–413	Sicilian expedition
411–410	Democracy falls, short-lived oligarchic rule of the Four Hundred, then of the Five Thousand
410	Restoration of democracy
406–405	Trial of the Arginusae generals
404	Athenian defeat in the Peloponnesian War
404–403	Rule of the Thirty Tyrants, civil war
403	Peace and amnesty imposed by Pausanias (Spartan king), second restoration of democracy
401–400	Reconquest of Eleusis from the oligarchic party
400–399	Reform of the legal system completed
399	Trial of Socrates
395	Athens joins Corinthian War against Sparta

Chapter 6

The logic of coordination

Let us stay in Athens for a while. After the fall of the blood-soaked regime of the Thirty Tyrants, an amnesty was enacted for them and their collaborators. Why did it succeed? The Athenians had not managed to restrain themselves from judicially eliminating suspected oligarchs in the past; what changed after 403?

The amnesty was a stunning success for the rule of law; understanding how it worked despite all the seemingly compelling political reasons to disregard it will help us understand how the rule of law is brought about and maintained in general. Thus, the first section of this chapter reviews the history of the two late-fifth-century oligarchic coups, and then argues that a commitment to the rule of law, in virtue of their recognition of the strength *topos*, gave the Athenians strong reason to respect the amnesty. It then backs out and asks how the Athenians could have successfully coordinated to carry out their commitment to the rule of law, even though they would have had reason to worry about one another's actual recognition of the strength *topos*, or susceptibility to the temptation to remove oligarchs for short-term political advantage. I argue that the institution of the mass jury gave the Athenian democrats the ability to send costly signals of commitment to the rule of law, allowing them to learn to trust one another, and thereby to build common knowledge of that shared commitment.

The second section generalizes the Athenian case into a strategic model (very lightly formalized with some game theory) of the commitment problem facing states that wish to establish a rule of law backed up by coordinated enforcement from the public.[1] From that, I develop some general claims about the sorts of legal systems that are consistent with the rule of law, which, in Chapter 9, I will offer as potentially helpful for the task of promoting it abroad (and at home). I conclude by offering a couple of thoughts for how the general model helps us understand contemporary problems of transitional justice.

I THE STRENGTH TOPOS AND THE AMNESTY

I shall argue, in this section, that Athens managed to sustain the amnesty because the democrats learned, at the end of the fifth century, that the rule of law was necessary for the collective defense of their democratic system.

A The struggle between oligarchs and democrats, an overview

The Athenian democracy collapsed twice at the close of the fifth century. In both cases, it was replaced by an oligarchy that promptly ignored legal rules on a wide scale. Strikingly, both collapses immediately followed an exogenous military shock.

The first happened right after Athens's notoriously ill-advised invasion of Sicily.[2] After the military adventure collapsed, Alcibiades, from exile (thanks to the affair of the Herms/Mysteries), attempted to provoke a coup. Conspiring with Alcibiades, Peisander convinced the assembly to accept unspecified restrictions on the democratic franchise, negotiate with Alcibiades for his potential recall, and appoint a commission (the *syngrapheis*) to investigate the state of the city. This, on his argument, would convince the Persian king to lend financial support to the continued prosecution of the war against Sparta, the Sicilian adventure having put the city into serious financial straits. On Peisander's instructions, oligarchic clubs (*hetaireiai*) within the city began a campaign of terror and intimidation, carrying out several assassinations, including at least one democrat prominent enough for Thucydides to describe him as "the chief leader of the people."[3]

According to Thucydides, this campaign of terror worked: fear of hidden conspirators inhibited democrats from speaking up at the assembly or trusting one another enough to carry out collective action.[4] The *syngrapheis* proposed the abolition of the *graphe paranomon* and the transfer of authority into the hands of 5,000 citizens. Meanwhile, Peisander claimed that the Persians demanded a still smaller oligarchy (actually, he knew that Persian support was not forthcoming), then proposed the Four Hundred. The assembly was intimidated into compliance, and the Four Hundred took office, drove out the democratic council by force, and assumed power.

Perhaps predictably, the Four Hundred promptly began to ignore the rule of law. According to Thucydides, they "ruled the city by force; putting to death some men though not many, whom they thought it convenient to remove, and imprisoning and banishing others."[5]

The Four Hundred didn't last long. They had a big problem: the Athenian navy was at Samos, and it was "dominated by the lower classes."[6] In order to shore up their position, they repeatedly tried negotiating with Sparta, and also reendorsed their earlier promise to extend citizenship to 5,000 citizens. The promise was not enough to satisfy the mass opposition, and the Spartans, rightly mistrusting the stability of the regime, preferred to take advantage of the chaos and launch an invasion rather than make a deal with the oligarchs.[7] With a Spartan fleet at the door, the oligarchy promptly collapsed, being first replaced by the promised rule of the Five Thousand, then, shortly thereafter, a restored democracy. Under the latter, a number of oligarchs were tried and convicted of treason and subverting the democracy.[8]

The Thirty, despite its extensive overlapping personnel with the Four Hundred, originated and operated very differently.[9] It was imposed by Sparta after the final

Athenian defeat in the Peloponnesian War, and was, on Xenophon's account, initially welcomed.[10] However, the Thirty quickly went bad. They started by surrounding themselves with whip-bearing guards (always a bad sign). They reallocated the function of the people's courts to a puppet council. They carved out 3,000 elites to remain full-fledged citizens, and enacted a law permitting the Thirty to kill any of the rest at will. They disarmed the non-3,000 and forbade them from remaining in the city limits. They stole a lot of property.[11] The Thirty are generally credited with about 1,500 murders.[12]

Thrasybulus, an exiled Athenian general, led a revolution. The Thirty called for Spartan aid, but the Spartan king commanding the relief troops grew tired of the trouble and imposed a peace on the warring parties.

The terms of the peace, in summary, were as follows: the democracy was restored, but all of the oligarchic party except the actual Thirty (and a couple of other small, irrelevant groups) were to be given amnesty for all their crimes except personal murders. The Thirty themselves were to be subjected to *euthynai*, with a small thumb on the scale in their favor (the jurors were limited to property owners), and would be rehabilitated after accepting whatever punishment the court imposed. (At least one member of the Thirty passed this examination, and returned to citizen life.[13]) Unsold expropriated property was to be returned to its rightful owners. And those oligarchs who wished to do so were to be allowed to exile themselves to Eleusis instead. The amnesty was, on the whole, obeyed.[14]

B The puzzle of the amnesty

The Four Hundred, according to Thucydides, extradjudicially killed "not many" people.[15] Taylor has argued that the role of violence and terror in their coming to power has also been exaggerated.[16] Compared to the Thirty, the rule of the Four Hundred seems to have been characterized by a remarkable restraint in the murder, robbery, imprisoning, and exiling departments.[17] Yet, the Thirty received the benefits of an amnesty, while the Four Hundred were prosecuted. The amnesty was imposed by Spartan swords, but not enforced by them. Why did the democrats, dominating the assembly and courts, not promptly repudiate the amnesty and then execute the oligarchs (with or without trial)?

Two strategic hypotheses come immediately to mind, but neither is convincing. First, the democrats may have feared the return of Sparta to protect their oligarchic political allies. However, Athens joined the Corinthian war against Sparta less than 10 years after the Thirty were deposed.[18] Executing a few oligarchs doubtless would have annoyed the Spartans less than going to war against them did.[19]

Second, the establishment of an oligarchic state-in-exile in Eleusis may have been meant to provide the oligarchic party with enough resources to credibly threaten retaliation should the amnesty be violated. However, oligarchic Eleusis did not last very long: it was swiftly reconquered and reintegrated into Athens proper.[20]

David Teegarden argues that the actual oath taken to uphold the amnesty made it possible for the community to avoid private violence against former oligarchic collaborators, because it generated common knowledge of, in his words, citizens' "(at least apparent[ ]) credible commitment" not to retaliate against collaborators.[21] By doing so, it gave individual Athenians who might otherwise want to retaliate some reason to think that their fellow citizens would not support them. Since retaliating against collaborators was individually risky, they would not be willing to do so if they believed they would be unable to count on the support of their fellows.

However, Teegarden's argument makes the oath do too much work. As a general principle (albeit with a number of exceptions), mere costless words cannot establish a credible commitment; instead, they often are nothing more than cheap talk that does not change the underlying strategic dynamics of a situation.[22] In the Athenian context, the cheap talk interpretation of the oath seems most plausible. The amnesty and oath were imposed at sword point by the Spartan army. Under such circumstances, vindictive democrats would have had little reason to believe that the oath represented their fellow citizens' true intentions or preferences.

The traditional explanation for the success of the amnesty has been nonstrategic. Ostwald summarizes classical opinion as varying between "the patriotism of the Athenians as a whole" and "the forbearance and decency" of the democrats.[23]

The "forbearance and decency" argument ignores the fact that Athenian democrats did retaliate (in the courts) against the less grievous crimes of the Four Hundred only a few years beforehand. It is unlikely that the Athenian democrats experienced a collective cultural or ethical change between 411 and 403. Moreover, it is inconsistent with the fact that the democrats even retaliated against collaborators with the Thirty, *just not in ways forbidden by the amnesty*. The cavalry, for example, was a military role occupied in Athens by relatively wealthy citizens, and whose members largely supported the Thirty. After the Thirty, the democrats lashed out at the cavalry twice: first, by cutting their pay in order to raise the pay of the lower-class archers, and second, by deliberately sending 300 of them off to die in a foreign war.[24]

With the "forbearance and decency" argument ruled out, the most plausible explanation for the success of the amnesty in the existing literature is Lanni's, which comprises four elements.[25] First, she argues that there was a postwar process of whitewashing in the courts that focused blame for the tyranny on the Thirty themselves rather than on their many collaborators. On her account, litigants adopted this strategy on an individual basis, presumably because it would be most palatable to the jurors, many of whom would have been collaborators themselves. Despite that history of collaboration, Lanni points out that the forensic speeches often addressed the jurors as if each member had been a part of the resistance. The ultimate effect of this strategy was to construct a false "collective memory" in which most ordinary citizens were innocent of crimes under the Thirty.

Second, Lanni notes that litigants often used the amnesty as an example to illustrate the mild and virtuous democratic character of the Athenian people.

Consequently, she argues, the Athenians came to collectively identify as the sort of people who offer amnesty to their enemies, and to become motivated to continue doing so.

Third, Lanni points out that the amnesty contained a "safety valve" for individual cases: because crimes under the Thirty could be raised as character evidence in unrelated cases and in *dokimasiai* for incoming magistrates, limited-scope accountability was allowed. This satisfied some of the desire for revenge before it could spill over into a movement for broad-brush retaliation.

Finally, Lanni suggests that Athens's participatory political institutions may have, by forcing former oligarchs and democrats to work together, given them reason to repair their relationship after the oligarchy.

Lanni's account is partially convincing. But the material given thus far allows us to supplement it with an additional explanatory factor. The development of the law through and after the time of the oligarchic revolutions is consistent with the increasing recognition of the importance of law for the stability of the democratic state – the strength *topos*. The law reforms of the postconflict period suggest that the consciousness shown in the evidence for the strength *topos* was growing at that time. An effort had already begun to collect and codify the laws at the time of the Four Hundred, and after the Thirty, as noted, the democrats further strengthened their legal system by creating the quasi-constitutional difference between laws and decrees, requiring all acts of the assembly to be scrutinized against the existing law code and similar reforms.

Moreover, as Cohen cogently argues, the Thirty came to stand for grievous violations of the law in Athenian political culture. Democratic politicians, by contrast, laid claim to institutions of the rule of law in order to "bind the community together in opposition to its oligarchic opponents who sought to undermine its institutions to create *stasis* [factional conflict]."[26] The institutions of the democracy, including those legal institutions that the Thirty disregarded, became, on Cohen's account, identified with the democracy in part because the democracy identified itself in opposition to the Thirty, and the Thirty saliently disregarded the laws.

I submit, then, that the democratic obedience to the amnesty reflected a developing respect for the law among the Athenian people. The Athenians came to identify the law with the democracy and the equality that it represented (collectively, as *isonomia*), at the same time as they came to the belief that careful compliance with the laws was necessary to their political strength and stability.[27]

And the Athenians were correct to see it that way. The law could preserve the strength of each individual Athenian in the face of elite power by coordinating resistance to elite hubris as well as to outright threats to undermine democratic institutions. Athenians essentially were in a game-theoretic coordination equilibrium in which each knew that his fellow citizens would resist any illegal acts; this gave nonelite citizens the ability to rely on the law, embodied by their fellow citizens on the jury, to defend them from the elites. However, for the law to serve this function, each citizen must have believed that his fellow citizens would enforce the law. Since disregarding the amnesty would indicate jurors' willingness to throw aside the law in favor of political expediency, it would have vitiated this coordination function: no longer could citizens trust in the strength of the law to defend themselves from oligarchic hubris. And this is why moderate democrats were correct to see the jury, rather than the assembly, as the chief institution of democracy.

To anticipate an objection: Athenians had to rely on law to serve this function, rather than simply sharing a commitment to resist oligarchic acts, legal or illegal, because of the potential for uncertainty as to whether any given act posed oligarchic dangers. Frequently in the forensic speeches we see elites accusing one another of oligarchic sentiments and identifying themselves with the masses; this suggests that both sides of a legal dispute could often be plausibly characterized as oligarchic. But if someone were caught breaking the law, this could serve as an objective sign that the malefactor held an inadequate regard for the democracy. Moreover, a jury verdict could serve as a consensus signal of guilt on which citizens could rely to coordinate their opposition to an overweening potential oligarch. If a majority of a large and socially representative jury working in the glare of publicity was willing to condemn someone, each individual in the city could infer that the community at large would be similarly willing.[28] Thus, the law allowed citizens to infer oligarchic threats from a verdict, and provided common knowledge that each democratically inclined citizen would be willing to resist that threat: it was the vital keystone for civic trust.

In short, the amnesty worked because the Athenians developed a public commitment to the rule of law, in their official capacities as magistrates, jurors, prosecutors, and assemblymen.[29] If this is right, then Lanni errs in asserting that "the absence of the rule of law is a feature of the system [for promoting Athenian reconciliation after the Thirty] rather than a bug."[30] On the contrary, the Athenian rule of law, rooted as it was in citizens' recognition that the control of power by law was a precondition of an equal state, was a vital part of the success of the amnesty. Moreover, the commitment to law was useful not only to the masses, but also to the elites. Even those with oligarchic sympathies, who had committed crimes under the Thirty, would have reason to uphold the law – even to the extent of prosecuting their political allies for future oligarchic crimes – because if the law collapsed, the amnesty would cease to hold, and there would be nothing protecting them from mass vengeance. This is quite a trick: the law could reconcile the elites to the legal system by protecting them from punishment for their past misconduct, and at the very same time, to the extent the masses actually extended that legal protection to elites, it strengthened their own power to prevent future elite misconduct.

The democrats exactly recognized Sir Thomas More's worry, in *A Man for All Seasons*, that should they chop down all the laws to get at the oligarchic devil, there would be nowhere for them to hide when the oligarchs turned around and went after them.[31] If any doubt remains on this point, consider that none other than Thucydides himself originated that particular insight:

> Indeed men too often take upon themselves in the prosecution of their revenge to set the example of doing away with those general laws to which all alike can look for salvation in adversity, instead of allowing them to subsist against the day of danger when their aid may be required.[32]

For this reason, the democrats were concerned to preserve the Athenian rule of law, and were willing even to sacrifice their revenge against the Thirty Tyrants to do it.

C Did the Athenians learn from experience?

There is some reason to believe that the strength *topos* and its invocation in defense of the amnesty reflected the Athenian democrats' experience in the periods leading up to the two oligarchic coups. The material given thus far suggests the hypothesis that previous failures of the rule of law may have contributed to the initial success of both coups.

It's striking that the two major collapses of the democracy happened not only after major military defeats, but also after major lapses of the rule of law. The affair of the Herms/Mysteries, in which many citizens were executed or fled into exile on very scanty (and later discredited) evidence, happened at the beginning of the Sicilian expedition. That expedition precipitated the coup of the Four Hundred, and Alcibiades was one of the targets of the Herms/Mysteries witch hunt. Similarly, the coup of the Thirty was preceded by the trial of the Arginusae generals. These correlations may result from causation: if the affair of the Herms/Mysteries and the trial of the generals sufficiently undermined citizens' confidence in their fellows' willingness to follow the law under exigent circumstances, that may have contributed to their failure to do so at the time of the coups.[33]

This hypothesis draws some support from Thucydides' description of how the terror tactics leading up to the coup of the Four Hundred worked:

> People were afraid when they saw their numbers, and no one now dared to speak in opposition to them. If anyone did venture to do so, some appropriate method was soon found for having him killed, and no one tried to investigate such crimes or take action against those suspected of them. Instead the people kept quiet … They imagined that the revolutionary party was much bigger than it really was, and they lost all confidence in themselves, being unable to find out the facts because of the size of the city and because they had insufficient knowledge of each other … Throughout the democratic party people approached each other suspiciously, everyone thinking that the next man had something to do with what was going on.[34]

That is, on Thucydides' account, the rise of the Four Hundred was attributable in large part to the decline of civic trust among the Athenians, and that decline in civic trust made them unable to use the legal system to put a stop to oligarchic threats. This fits nicely into the causal hypothesis I've suggested: perhaps the Athenians ceased to trust their legal system (at least in part) because they recognized that their fellow citizens couldn't be relied upon to enforce the law in times of crisis, and that recognition was in turn based (at least in part) on their shameful behavior four years before in the affair of the Herms/Mysteries. It also fits the origin of the Four Hundred – in a council ostensibly called at first to restore the traditional laws.[35]

Moreover, Thucydides seems to be suggesting a broader decline in civic trust – not just that citizens failed to trust the legal system, but that they failed to trust one another in general. Contemporary empirical evidence exists to support the hypothesis that such a broader decline in civic trust, or "social capital," could be due to the flaws of the legal system: a recent study has suggested that regions that had the advantages of impartial and reliable legal institutions, in the form of the Napoleonic Code through the nineteenth century, show greater social capital even today.[36] Thucydides appears to be describing the contrapositive of that effect: with the failure of the legal system, the Athenian democrats lost the social capital that could have helped them collectively resist the Four Hundred.[37]

Contemporaneous sources confirm my supposition with respect to the rise of the Thirty Tyrants. On Xenophon's account, one of the first acts of the Thirty was to summarily execute those who were alleged to be "sycophants" – the equivalent of modern professional frivolous litigators, the Athenian "ambulance chaser."[38] This first bloodletting met with universal approval.[39] Regardless of whether sycophants were actually a problem, Xenophon clearly expected his readers to believe that the Athenian public thought the legal system was being routinely abused.

At least one scholar has further suggested that the alleged sycophantic problem at the time of the Thirty arose out of attempts to retaliate against those who were attached to the Four Hundred.[40] According to Jordović, sycophants operated by bringing litigation against innocent aristocrats, to target them in a widespread "settling of scores" with the Four Hundred (presumably by falsely accusing those innocents of being part of the conspiracy). Jordović has some support in Lysias, one of whose clients (for Lysias's speeches were written for the use of others) suggests that after the fall of the Four Hundred, demagogues "persuaded [the people] to condemn some people to death without trial, to confiscate unjustly the property of many more, and to expel others and deprive them of citizen rights," and goes on to say that this "reduced the city to civil strife and very great disaster."[41] On Lysias's client's account, "oligarchy has twice been established because of those who were sycophants under the democracy."[42] If Jordović and Lysias's client are right, the zeal for retaliation after the first oligarchy helped bring about the second oligarchy, by undermining citizens' confidence in the legal system and winning public support for the first round of tyrannical executions.[43]

No surprise, then, that the strength *topos* began to get a grip in the public legal and political culture of Athens after the fall of the Thirty. Perhaps the success of the amnesty came about because the democrats learned from their prior mistakes.[44] Put differently, the Athenian citizens developed a preference for law over short-term political advantage.

D *The problems of commitment: disagreement and temptation*

But we must pause here and add something to the strength *topos* explanation. The mere recognition among those (elites) who were producing the oratorical corpus, history, poetry, and philosophy that the law was important to the strength of the democracy is not enough to fully explain the amnesty's success. For the citizens must also have *trusted* one another to share that recognition, and this must have been particularly difficult in the face of their dubious recent history of throwing aside the law in panicked lashing out at suspected oligarchs.

Particularly worryingly, there must have been a significant temptation to ignore the amnesty in the short run. And this temptation would be self-reinforcing: if the amnesty wasn't reliable because a citizen's fellows were subject to temptation, then the given citizen ought to give in to temptation himself and get rid of as many oligarchs as possible. Suppose an oligarch was facing trial for the crimes he committed. A citizen on the jury would have had good reason to worry: would the law be functioning tomorrow? If not, it would be better to eliminate the oligarch on the spot, in anticipation of future class conflict. Moreover, a citizen might worry that his fellow jurors were inadequately representative of the policy preferences of the public: suppose a majority happened to be political opponents of the amnesty?[45] Furthermore, who's to say that the jurors didn't see a given *particular* oligarch on trial at the given moment as sufficiently dangerous to justify ignoring the amnesty just once? How did the Athenians manage to, in the jargon of political science, *credibly commit* to the amnesty: to enforce it in support of their long-run interests even in the face of a short-run desire by aggrieved democrats to the contrary?[46]

Moreover, in order to successfully fight off future oligarchic threats, the democrats of Athens must have learned to trust one another. The elite, like all elites, were more powerful than members of the mass on a one-to-one basis; they had the capacity to do things like bribe or intimidate assemblies and juries. They also had greater capacity to coordinate their own actions to magnify their individual power, due to their smaller population and preexisting organizational capacity in the form of the *hetaireiai*.[47]

In order to counteract these advantages, the masses would have had to make full use of the only advantage they had: numbers. They would have to have been able to trust one another for support to resist future elite coups, even though elites would have had the power to do them harm on a one-to-one basis. And this need for support is reciprocal and extends across the political community. A depends on B's support, but B, in order to be able to support A, depends on A's reciprocal support, and both also depend on the support of citizens C and D:

each individual democratic, nonelite citizen, in order to be willing to stand up to a member of the oligarchic elite, must be able to rely on the support of each other individual democratic citizen. Otherwise, doing so is too dangerous. And it gets worse. Thucydides tells us that they were unable to so trust one another when the Four Hundred took over, suggesting that they must have had to build this trust out of nothing after the Thirty.

The democracy had a coordination problem: each nonelite citizen rationally should have done what each other nonelite citizen was doing. He would want to punish future elite transgressions if and only if each other citizen could be counted upon to do so – then he would get his most preferred outcome, a functioning democracy. However, he would want to refrain from attempting to punish elite transgressions if other citizens could not be counted upon to do so, because so refraining would allow him to avoid his least preferred outcome, being crushed by an overwhelmingly powerful member of the elite, although it would force him to accept his second least preferred outcome, living under an oligarchy.[48]

Political scientists have shown that law, understood as a common-knowledge mapping of conduct to evaluations ("legal" or "illegal"), with some mechanism for producing authoritative decisions about those mappings, can facilitate coordinated sanctioning systems.[49] However, in order to achieve coordinated punishment against some transgressor, the democratic masses must have had some settled way of determining when a transgression had occurred. And they must have been able to trust that one another would apply it faithfully. The upshot is that the Athenian democracy after the Thirty Tyrants critically depended on each citizen's ability to predict each other citizen's behavior; the law was the instrument for this prediction just to the extent that citizens knew one another could be depended on to uphold it.[50] But from where came this knowledge?

I contend that the mass jury served these functions. First, it provided the necessary authoritative resolution of disagreements about whether a given course of conduct was sanctionable under law, and thus made it possible for the democracy to coordinate itself by law in the first place. Second, it is this jury that would have heard charges against oligarchs, both amnesty-violating charges for crimes committed under the Thirty Tyrants, as well as charges for new oligarchic crimes committed after the Thirty; it is also the jury that would have heard charges against self-help amnesty violators, had any (other than the one we know of) happened. And – this is the key point – this gave the jurors reason to support the amnesty, because by doing so they could signal their willingness to one another to stand up for the law, and hence solve their coordination problem, and protect their democracy.

Because it was a *mass* institution, filled with hundreds of randomly selected citizens, and because trials were held in public, the jury could serve as an excellent informational proxy for the extent to which the citizen body was willing to enforce the laws, notwithstanding differences in policy preferences over the amnesty. A jury that ruled for a clearly legally correct outcome, especially when that outcome was contrary to the short-run self-interests or preferences of many of its members, and where that jury was drawn from a large and fairly representative sample of the population, demonstrated a widespread commitment to enforcing the laws and, consequently, the extent to which the laws were likely to be enforced in the future. Finally, because individual votes were secret, each individual citizen was not in danger of retaliation from voting to enforce the law, even if the vote was against the interests of powerful members of society. In short, the jury could build a record of lawful behavior without presupposing it: by safely allowing citizens to demonstrate their willingness to support one another and the law with their votes in the jury room, it allowed them to trust one another enough to be willing to take the risk to do so elsewhere, and hence allowed them to credibly threaten to resist future oligarchic coups in the streets as well as in the courts. The mass jury served the dual role of resolving legal disputes and demonstrating that the populace was committed to following the law.

This is a point similar to one that Ober has made about alignment in Athens in general.[51] As Ober suggested, because the jury was secret and nondeliberative, it could aggregate independent knowledge of individuals; in line with his account I'd emphasize that the knowledge it aggregated included not just facts about the world but also facts about individual preferences, particularly democratic legal preferences.

Moreover, the jury effectively eliminated the coordination problem in amnesty cases: a citizen voting (unlike, say, a citizen taking up arms) need not do what each other citizen does. If he votes, in violation of the amnesty, to convict an oligarch for prerestoration crimes, a majority of his fellow citizens can either also vote to convict, in which case at least the oligarch doesn't go free, or they can vote to acquit, in which case the amnesty is upheld. The same is true if he votes to acquit. In either case, the worst-case option, in which the rule of law fails and the citizen gets punished for trying, and failing, to kill an oligarch, is eliminated by operation of the secret ballot and aggregative mechanism.

This was at least sometimes a *costly* signal (unlike Teegarden's oath-taking), when democrats had to swallow what would otherwise very likely be their preferences for executing any given troublesome oligarch in order to uphold the law. Accordingly, their willingness to do so could serve as a credible signal of their conviction in the strength *topos*, and thus their willingness to uphold the law in general. For that reason, the amnesty was *self-reinforcing*: by obliging democrats to act against their short-run preferences, it enabled them to signal commitment to the law; this in turn established a record of consistent conduct upon which each citizen could rely in predicting the behavior of his fellow citizens; this in turn made it less risky for each democrat to use the legal system to resist any oligarchic threats that might arise. And this, in turn, suppressed those threats: in the jargon of game theory, attempting future oligarchic coups was off the equilibrium path, because the democrats could credibly threaten to collectively respond with overwhelming force against any such attempts.

On this analysis, the power of the demos and the power of law are fully reconciled through the strength *topos*. Prior scholars have sometimes thought that some of the references to what I call the strength *topos* in the oratorical corpus reflect a tension between the two. For example, Allen cites the following assertion from Aeschines as evidence against the Athenian rule of law: "The private man rules as king in a democratic city by virtue of the law and his vote." Allen suggests that this represents "some ambivalence over whether the laws or the jurors can ultimately be said to rule the city [because] [t]he citizen's vote must be given as much weight as the law."[52]

But there can be no choice between jurors and law, for the power of each was necessarily interdependent. Aeschines understood that the law ruled through citizens' votes, and citizens ruled through the existence of a well-functioning legal system. In fact, that passage is a near-perfect statement of the strength *topos* and the role of the law in constraining the powerful as well as – as I shall further discuss in Chapter 8 – the necessity of the rule of law to democracy. Aeschines goes on to argue that jurors make a grievous error in casting their votes for the interests of powerful politicians rather than the law: first, because the politicians cannot reward them (their votes being secret – and this is another way in which the jury was functional for encouraging people to signal legal preferences), but more importantly, because doing so encourages the *rhetors* in their hubris and threatens a recurrence of the Thirty. That is, Aeschines is telling the jurors to preserve their political power through fidelity to law. There is no ambivalence here: the law and the jurors must continue to rule the city together. And how could it be otherwise? As I discuss in the next chapter, no legal system can "rule" alone: in every society, there is a group of people who could overthrow it if they cease to be aligned to it; they are the rulers behind the rule of law; to observe that state power is reliably constrained is just to observe that there are strong institutional and political barriers to their alignment *except* through and under the terms of law. The Athenians were merely unusually perceptive in having seen this, and unusually honest in having said so.

E Athens as a case of transitional justice

"Transitional justice," in the sense used by contemporary human rights scholars, covers those legal and political mechanisms that promote community reconciliation in new or restored democracies after conflict, including accountability or amnesty for those who were responsible for atrocities in the previous regime. The Athenian reconstructions after the oligarchies of the Four Hundred and the Thirty were perhaps the first instances of transitional justice in recorded history, as many scholars have recognized.

Some have suggested that transitional justice arrangements should aim to publicly and collectively reaffirm the values of the society in question (e.g., to display and demonstrate disapproval of the crimes of the previous regime), in order, inter alia, to rebuild "civic trust" that those norms will be enforced in the future.[53] I have suggested that the Athenian jury was functional for this purpose, insofar as it allowed citizens to send signals of their willingness to enforce the law. However, ordinary citizen-initiated litigation was not the only Athenian legal practice to serve this function.

Athens also had something analogous to today's truth and reconciliation commissions, which seem to be a central feature of what we today label "transitional justice." The Thirty were required to subject themselves to formal *euthunai*, examination of former officeholders, in order to return to Athenian citizenship. And if collaborators wanted to take office under the restored democracy, they, like all candidates for office, were subject to *dokimasia*, formal examination of a prospective official's character, at which their crimes could be considered. Lanni argues that those institutions operated as a "safety valve for local resentments," allowing some measure of revenge to be exacted.[54] The analysis in this chapter suggests that her account is correct but incomplete: these measures also gave citizens an opportunity to choose the lawful method rather than some other method to seek accountability for past crimes, and hence to affirmatively and publicly show their commitment to the accountability mechanisms provided by law.

This similarity is striking. Understanding the function of the Athenian version of the truth and reconciliation commission in the context of the jury and the function of rebuilding trust and coordination may allow us to further understand the function of such institutions in the contemporary world. The functional isomorphism between Athenian institutions and contemporary ones suggests that such an approach may hold substantial promise.[55]

II FORMALIZING AND GENERALIZING ATHENS

The dynamics of the egalitarian rule of law in contemporary societies can be formalized by thinking about how Athens worked while abstracting from the particular institutional tools the democrats used in that one case (consistent with the general claim of this book that the rule of law is institution-independent – see Chapter 8 for more). I will begin with an intuition, and then a light game-theoretic model to flesh it out.

Athens is an example of how a state's regularity can be sustained by coordinated action from some subset of the subjects of its law. The size and distribution of that subset will vary depending on its distribution of political power, but in each state there is some critical mass of people such that if they can act in concert, they can threaten sufficiently large sanctions to force officials to obey the law. The type of sanctions to be threatened also vary across states; in stable democracies, the ordinary sanction will be voting disobedient officials out of office, while in others action might include coordinated labor strikes, rioting, revolution, and the like. In Athens, the sanctions available to the demos included both the prosecution of those seen to pose oligarchic threats to the rule of law, and active military action to restore the law when it had been overthrown.

For analytic purposes, we can abstract away from all these considerations and simply assume that there is some minimum coalition in each state such that, if it works together, it has the power to threaten costly enough sanctions, or, in the limit, forcibly remove disobedient officials from office. This assumption is essentially indisputable: at the limit, such a coalition could be every person except a single disobedient official.

However, attempting to exercise these sanctions is ordinarily costly. There are at least three types of costs attached to sanctioning officials. First are *direct costs* associated with some sanctions: if a subject joins the revolution, she must incur opportunity costs from the loss of alternative actions, must put herself in physical danger, must purchase arms, and so on. Second are *retaliation costs* inflicted by officials whom citizens resist. Third are *preference costs* associated with the sacrifice of a subject's personal preferences in defense of the law. Preference costs will be particularly significant for those subjects who are politically allied with the official, or who prefer the official's policies. Imagine, for example, the position of a white Southerner who cared about the law at the time of *Brown v. Board of Education*, but who held racist attitudes toward black people. Such a citizen would have incurred a preference cost to demand that her elected officials obey the law and desegregate the schools. Only if she valued the law more than she valued the subordination of black people would she help pressure officials to go along with the court's ruling.

Both direct and retaliation costs can be ameliorated by collective action: citizens acting in concert will both be able to take advantage of economies of scale in the costs of sanctioning officials (for example, a very large mass may only have to protest to bring a disobedient official to heel, where a smaller group may have to take more significant action) and be able to reduce the risk of retaliation. At the same time, citizens acting in concert increase their probability of success. However, preference costs are fixed as to each citizen. And the possibility of preference costs makes collective action more difficult: citizens might not know the extent of other citizens' alignment with officials.

We can thus imagine that for each citizen there is a number of other citizens (call this a citizen's "critical mass"), such that if that group is resisting the official, and she prefers the long-term advantages of staying in a rule of law equilibrium to the short-term achievement of the illegal policy implemented by the official (because she either dislikes the policy or likes the law more), she will be willing to resist the official.[56] Intuitively, each citizen's critical mass will depend primarily on her toleration of the risk of failure. If she attempts to sanction an official, but fails because not enough other citizens have gone along, she incurs direct and retaliation costs with no countervailing benefit. Assuming, for purposes of simplicity, that citizens' direct costs of resisting officials are constant, each citizen's critical mass will depend primarily on the extent to which she is willing to run the risk of being punished by an angry official if sanction efforts do not succeed (assuming, plausibly, that successful sanctioning also insulates sanctioning citizens from the risk of being punished).

The problem, of course, is that citizens don't know as to each individual incident of lawbreaking, or possibly even in general, the extent to which other citizens are willing to sacrifice the short-term achievements of their political preferences to preserve the rule of law. Consequently, coordination is difficult. Put differently, citizens lack knowledge of the preference costs incurred by their fellows. The core problem is captured by Timur Kuran: citizens who are unwilling to take the risk of punishing a regime may falsify their preferences about it, and pretend to support it insofar as they do not know they can rely on support from others.[57] Moreover, officials can increase some citizens' preference costs by side payments – sharing the benefits of an illegal policy to undermine opposition to it.

The best existing models explain how coordinated enforcement works despite direct and retaliation costs, and the role of consensus statements of the content of law in facilitating this coordination in a repeated game context.[58] The model by Hadfield and Weingast, which is particularly good, accounts for uncertainty about preference costs by suggesting that law enforcement can serve as a signal of preferences that are consistent with existing legal rules.[59] However, under the Hadfield/Weingast model, it is not clear how to account for the possibility of preference shifts, especially those induced by bad actors (e.g., by bribery or intimidation), but also those induced by broad-based shocks. For example, the situation of Euryptolemus in the trial of the Arginusae generals may have represented such a shock: due to a sudden hysteria, he found himself attempting to enforce the law in the face of a citizen body that just did not care.

Conditional retaliation costs also pose a threat to the Hadfield/Weingast model, which supposes that citizens may be tempted to not sanction misconduct because they pay fixed direct and retaliation costs, represented (abstractly) by a forgone trade, but does not take into account the possibility that the cost of sanctioning misconduct even in the present round may increase to the extent a citizen is uncertain about whether her fellows will also sanction that misconduct. Should both conditional retaliation costs and bribery/intimidation-induced shocks to preference costs be sufficiently low, the Hadfield/Weingast equilibrium still holds, but the prospect of those costs makes their equilibrium more brittle by making it more likely that, in any given round, the legal rules will fail to meet their sufficient convergence standard.[60]

The Hadfield/Weingast model relies on the abstract notion of an "authoritative steward" – such as a court – that makes determinations about the consistency of behavior with law. In the following, I construct a more robust variation on their model by supposing that the authoritative steward is the people themselves, or a representative sample thereof. Doing so allows that steward to serve not only a dispute resolution, but also a preference-signaling function; that is, this innovation reveals that it is possible for citizens considering the prospect of sanctioning the powerful to send a costless signal of their commitment to the legal order *before* confirming that signal with costly punishment. In doing so, they allow their fellow citizens to move on to the costly punishment stage while being able to account for the risk, omnipresent in an unstable legal system, that their prior commitment to the legal order, which has been signaled in earlier rounds, has been exogenously or endogenously undermined. The resulting equilibrium should be more robust both to preference alteration and to conditional retaliation costs. (However, it is somewhat more demanding with respect to the extent of the knowledge that citizens must have of the law.)

Ultimately, this model suggests that there are two paths for a state in which citizens actually are committed to the rule of law to stably achieve it. The two paths are the same path at the broadest level of generality, since both entail making it common knowledge that enough people are in fact committed to the rule of law.

First, such a state may have law and institutions that give people reason to believe that citizens in general do not incur preference costs, and thus will support the rule of law: a state that satisfies the principle of generality is likely (though not certain) to meet this condition, as the laws in such a state will be consistent with the interests of the population as a whole, and, by virtue of their justification by public reasons, it may be common knowledge that the law is in fact consistent with their interests. For similar reasons, a well-functioning democracy is also likely to meet this condition, since the laws in such a state will be the product of the consent of a substantial subsection of the population, and this, too, may be common knowledge.

Second, the state may build institutions that permit subjects to credibly signal their willingness to incur preference costs, and thus commitment to supporting the rule of law rather than pursuing short-term political preferences, and to do so in a particular fashion: by incurring preference costs *without* incurring direct or retaliation costs. This is the subject of the formal model in this chapter, demonstrating the possibility of an equilibrium such that people with preferences for the law can reveal themselves.

The most stable rule of law states can be expected to have all of these features. A democracy with general law, and that contains credible commitment signaling institutions, can be expected to have the most robust rule of law.

A *The model*

Start with a lawless political community. Assume, for simplicity, a one-dimensional policy space, which can be approximated as a scale from elite-preferring to mass-preferring policy. Such a policy space can be modeled as a division of a fixed surplus of goods, G (which can include things like political rights as well as economic resources), over a recipient class composed of N people, where the policy space indexes N (e.g., on one end is a pure extractive despotism [$N = 1$] or a regime like the Thirty Tyrants [$N = 3{,}000$], on the other is egalitarian utopia [N = population (P)], and in between are, e.g., aristocracies, societies like Athens that provide equal rights to citizen males but fewer to others, etc.).

The game is structured as follows. Each round, the ruler or ruling group (which models officialdom in general, acting in concert) chooses N, and then each citizen chooses whether or not to revolt. (Revolting can stand in for a wide variety of ways to resist and sanction rulers with no loss to the model.) If citizens do not revolt, the policy is implemented, and each citizen in N (including the ruler/ruling group) receives G/N, while each other citizen receives 0. If citizens do revolt, each citizen who revolts will pay a cost of C, and the revolt will succeed with probability KR, where K is a constant and R is the number of citizens revolting. Each citizen receives a payoff of G/P and the citizens impose an additional cost of F on the ruler if they succeed. If they fail, the policy is just implemented.[61] Note that in this sketch, C models both direct and retaliation costs, and the difference between G/N and G/P represents preference costs for those citizens in the preferred group.

Absent some kind of commitment mechanism of the sort to be outlined in a moment, citizens within N have no reason to revolt. Consequently, the upper limit of R is $P - N$. Under these assumptions, a citizen within the excluded group will prefer revolting to acquiescing in a ruler's policy when $KRG/P - C > 0$. Rearranging terms, this will be when $R > PC/KG$.

Suppose it is common knowledge that each excluded citizen will revolt when $P - N > PC/KG$ (in words, when enough citizens have been excluded to make it worthwhile to revolt). Call this the common knowledge condition. In such a case, $R = P - N$.

Under the common knowledge condition, the ruler has an incentive to set N at the smallest number (maximizing his own payoff) that makes excluded citizens indifferent between acquiescing and revolting (perhaps plus one), $P - N = PC/KG$, or, rearranging terms, $N = P - PC/KG$.[62]

The problem is that the common knowledge condition is likely to be false in most societies, because revolting is a public good. To see this, suppose the ruler sets $N = P - PC/KG - 1{,}000$. Rearranging, $P - N = PC/KG + 1{,}000$. Now suppose $P - N$ citizens revolt. The expected value of that revolt is positive relative to the situation in which no citizens revolt. But suppose one citizen declines to revolt. That citizen saves the cost C, and reduces the probability of success slightly: his payoff (the shirking payoff) is $K(R - 1)G/P$. The shirking payoff will be higher than the payoff for participating in the revolt when $K(R - 1)G/P > KRG/P - C$, which is true, after simplifying, whenever $C > KG/P$. Under those circumstances, our citizen prefers to shirk and free-ride on the provision of revolt by other excluded citizens. Each other excluded citizen, of course, can make a similar calculation. This reveals a classic public goods problem among the pool of excluded citizens. By induction, we would expect a maximum of PC/KG citizens to revolt.

This, in turn, poses serious problems related to selecting which group of PC/KG citizens, among the many possible subsets of the full group of P – N citizens available, will pay the cost of revolting. Consider the risk of strategic behavior: if exactly P – N citizens are poised to revolt, a citizen within that group has an incentive to threaten to shirk in order to force some other shirker to act. In sequential play, this problem goes away: it's trivial to predict that every citizen but the last PC/KG citizens shirks, and then the rest are left holding the bag. But in simultaneous play, the solution is much less clear; arranging the group of citizens who actually revolt is a difficult coordination problem.

Problems become much worse if we relax the implicit perfect information assumption of the discussion thus far. Suppose C is not uniform, but a private constant for each citizen representing, realistically, facts about that citizen such as his or her risk aversion, idiosyncratic preference costs, and the like. A citizen's C will determine the number of other participants for which it is worthwhile for her to revolt; without knowing C for each other citizen, it becomes impossible for any given citizen to predict the number of people who will revolt at any given N. Again, in sequential play, the problem might be resolved: Kuran's revolutionary cascades are one way, for appropriate distributions of C.[63] But matters are a mess in simultaneous decision contexts (that is, where citizens cannot observe one another's choices before themselves choosing, either because they actually act simultaneously, or because they simply lack the relevant information), or where C is not distributed such that the conditions are right for a revolutionary cascade (e.g., if there are no citizens with sufficiently low C that they might start a cascade).

To solve these problems, let us zoom out to multidimensional policy space. Suppose there is a common-knowledge set of criteria (aka "law") for acceptable policy along a number of dimensions, where each dimension represents an ordering of the population according to some different criterion (gender, race, socioeconomic status, land ownership, regional origin, religion, etc., as locally appropriate) and has some minimum lawful N along that dimension. Each person will find herself placed at a different location along each dimension, and will have a personal sense of whether the legal system as a whole – that is, the minimum N in each dimension – represents a compromise that she can live with (is more or less compatible with her interests, given the extent to which she recognizes the need for the system to be also compatible with the interests of others). This is equivalent to the setup of the Hadfield/Weingast model, which supposes each citizen has an "idiosyncratic logic" that may converge to a greater or lesser extent with the "common logic" represented by the law.

Model a repeated ruler–population interaction as follows. Each round of the game, the ruler/ruling group sets a new policy along some dimension, and each citizen simultaneously chooses to send a costless signal: accept or reject. Then the ruler chooses whether to insist on the new policy or reset it to the status quo, and if the ruler insists on the new policy, each citizen chooses whether to resist (revolt, etc.)

or not resist. If enough citizens resist, the resistance succeeds: the policy is reset to the status quo, and the ruler pays some positive cost. I submit that there is an equilibrium such that each citizen who thinks the legal system is generally in his interest sends the reject signal when the law is violated, and, for a sufficiently large number of citizens who think the law is in their interest, revolts if the ruler (off the equilibrium path) insists on the new policy.

First, some more intuition. Suppose the ruler violates the law along one dimension. Say, she enacts a law expropriating property from some disfavored religion and giving it to her allies in the majority religion. And suppose I am in the majority religion. Why might I want to nonetheless resist this enactment, even though it is in my interest? One reason is if I and the rest of the population are playing reciprocation strategies in which I can only rely on their support for resisting policies that hurt me if I support them in resisting policies that hurt them. If the legal system as a whole is more or less in my interest, such a reciprocation strategy may be sufficient to induce me to resist the illegal enactment. In other words, the reciprocal deal may lower my preference costs for any given policy by increasing the downside to me of the legal system's failure. And I can credibly signal that the law is more or less in my interest by announcing my objections to the law, so long as that announcement causes me no costs other than the surrender of the religious preference.

Formalize this more-or-less-in-my-interest idea by saying that, as to each citizen, she meets the *interests condition* if the discounted value of the minimum guaranteed her by the law, $g_{i,L}$ is greater than her discounted expected payoff in a situation in which the law fails and is replaced with lawless rule of the powerful in that society, $E(g_{i,A})$.

Now let us say that a group of people meets the *overwhelming power condition* if, should each member of that group who meets the interests condition resist the ruler, the probability of that group's succeeding is sufficiently high that it is common knowledge among that group that, given the levels of, for example, risk aversion, disparate power distribution, and so on in that society, no member of that group as to whom the interests condition is satisfied would view it to be too costly to resist the ruler. This is a condition that resists full formalization, but is easy to approximate. In a society in which power is roughly evenly distributed, a moderate supermajority is likely to meet this condition; in situations with more disparate power, it may require correspondingly larger majorities (or the participation of the powerful). I need not specify the size of the group necessary to meet the condition in every (or any) society; rather, it need only be intuitively plausible that a possible group that can meet the condition exists in every society – and I submit that it is. At the limit, in any real-world society, the group "everybody but the ruler" (president, members of parliament, etc.) clearly meets the overwhelming power condition.[64]

In slightly more formal terms, this condition rests on a model of rebellion such that each citizen controls a share Π of the overall distribution of power. These shares may vary (for example, military officers control more, small children control less), but I assume that the distribution is not so lopsided that a single official or small group of officials can hold off the rest – this merely excludes science-fictional societies in which a mad ruler controls a robot army by computer (and the undersigned dearly hopes that current drone technology does not progress to the point where this is possible in his lifetime, for it is difficult to see how the rule of law could survive in such a world). It is assumed that, if it can coordinate, the probability of a given side in a rebellion prevailing increases as the ratio of its aggregate power Πn_i to the aggregate power of the other side Πn_j increases, and is 1 at the limit; it is further assumed that as that ratio increases in favor of a rebellious party, the expected direct and retaliation cost $E(C_r)$ of rebelling to each member of that party approaches 0 (if everyone rises up at once, they win quickly, cheaply, and painlessly). Then the overwhelming power condition describes any group that controls a sufficiently large share of power such that for each member of the group who meets the interests condition the impact of the risk of loss and the cost of rebellion on his or her decisions is negligible, or, letting Φ designate the probability of the given group winning a conflict: for all i in the group, if $g_{i,L} > E(g_{i,A})$, then $\Phi(g_{i,L})+(1-\Phi)E(g_{i,A}) - E(C_r) > E(g_{i,A})$.

Finally, I specify one more condition, relating to the history of play: the *prior-consistency condition*. In every previous round in which the ruler announced an illegal policy, the number of people who signaled rejection met the overwhelming power condition; and in each such previous round in which in addition (a) the ruler did not withdraw the policy change, and (b) the number of people who signaled met the overwhelming power condition, the number of people who actually resisted met the overwhelming power condition.

With that in hand, I claim that the following strategy set is in subgame perfect equilibrium in indefinitely repeated games, for sufficiently low discounting, and if a sufficiently large number of people meet the interests condition: if the prior-consistency condition is true, the ruler specifies his or her most preferred policy that complies with the law, and if the prior-consistency condition is false, the ruler specifies his or her most preferred policy; in either condition, each nonruler citizen always signals acceptance of policies that comply with the law, and acceptance of all policies if the citizen does not satisfy the interests condition. Each nonruler citizen who satisfies the interests condition always signals rejection of policies that do not comply with the law. If the policy complies with the law, the round ends and the policy is implemented. Otherwise:

(A) the ruler withdraws the policy change and each citizen who signaled rejection resists if the ruler does not withdraw the policy change, if and only if:

  (A-1) the number of people who signaled rejection meets the overwhelming power condition, and
  (A-2) the prior-consistency condition is true; otherwise

(B) the ruler insists on the policy change and no citizen resists.

In all cases, the behavior of citizens who do not signal rejection and those who do not meet the interests condition is irrelevant; I shall assume they never resist or signal rejection, respectively.

1 Proof

The equilibrium is proved by the standard one-deviation principle for the folk theorem.[65] First, consider the ruler. If the prior-consistency condition is false, then the given strategy maximizes ruler payoff. If the prior-consistency condition is true, and if a large enough group of people meet the interests condition, thus making the overwhelming power condition true for equilibrium play by the citizens, then the ruler's choice is between getting the status quo policy this round and no change in future rounds (equilibrium play), or getting the status quo policy minus a penalty this round and no change in future rounds (deviation).

Now consider any individual citizen. If the prior-consistency condition is true, then a citizen's failure to resist an illegal policy to which she has signaled objection will risk (with positive probability) making it false in future rounds, insofar as that citizen's deviation leads to a failure of the overwhelming power condition; in turn, this risks permitting illegal policies not resisted by other citizens. So long as the citizen discounts the future sufficiently lightly, and so long as there's nonzero probability that the ruler's most preferred policy in future rounds will be illegal in a way that harms the interests of the citizen (for example, by expropriating that citizen's property), such a citizen has a long-term negative expected value from a deviation. Any citizen as to whom the interests condition is true must experience such a nonzero risk, for the interests condition captures just this long-term negative expected value relative to the law-preserving state of affairs. If the prior-consistency condition is false, then a citizen who resists will pay the cost of resisting without changing anything about present or future policy, and hence will simply suffer a one-round loss. If a citizen instead deviates by voting to accept an illegal policy, the risks are the same as those taken by a citizen who fails to resist. If she votes to reject a legal policy (perhaps because it fails to be the most advantageous to her of possible legal policies), or an illegal policy when the prior consistency condition is false, this vote will be ineffective with equilibrium play by everyone else, so she should be indifferent between those options. Q.E.D.

2 Analysis

Note the importance, in this equilibrium, of the interests condition. A citizen who does not meet the interests condition has no reason to signal opposition to an instance of official illegality – and this is consistent with the underlying intuition of the theory: if the legal system as a whole isn't in one's interest, relative to one's best estimate of the expected alternatives, one is, at best, indifferent between its continuation and its abolition; one might even prefer it to go away in the hope that something better will come along. Thus, if not enough citizens meet the interests condition, the overwhelming power condition will not be met, and the ruler cannot be controlled.[66]

This model is a close match to how the Athenian legal system worked: the mass jury stood up in defense of the laws; their votes signaled to elites that they couldn't get away with violating them, and they chose to vote that way – and to defend the legal system when it was overthrown, as with the quick elimination of the two oligarchies – in virtue of the fact that the legal system preserved their interests better than an oligarchy would have. Their continued votes in support of the law communicated to one another, and to the community at large, each individual Athenian juror's continued belief that the law was in his interest; since the jury was representative of the polis as a whole, the community at large could make inferences from jury votes about the likely consequences of ignoring the law.

Observe also the role of publicity in this model. Citizens must be able to know the law in order to coordinate to sanction violators. In Athens, this function was served by the settlement and communication functions of jury verdicts but also by the close connection between law and common-knowledge social norms. In the United States, a larger and more diverse society, and in the United Kingdom (somewhere in between, but closer to the United States), these functions are served by judicial rulings, which state (more or less) consensus interpretations of the law.[67] Moreover, where the law is difficult to apply, as in borderline cases, public adjudication in these modern states as in Athens also establishes a rough consensus determination and signal that the law has in fact been violated, establishing another precondition for effective coordination; the Athenian jury and the US Supreme Court are equally capable of serving that function.[68]

Note further that the basic idea of this model – that citizens can enforce the law themselves – is also directly built into the concept of publicity in the egalitarian conception of the rule of law. The egalitarian conception of the rule of law, unlike those in the previous literature, draws the normative concept in part from the strategic conditions under which it may exist, such that the definition of the rule of law restrains itself to institutional arrangements that are possible under realistic human political conditions.[69]

We now have a rough model for a sustainable rule of law. The rule of law is sustainable in a political community when (a) enough members of the community are committed to upholding the law, because they see it as being more or less in their own interest; (b) subjects have some common-knowledge method of determining when the law is obeyed or violated; and (c) the community either has a long-established record of mass commitment to the law or citizens have a two-stage method of communicating credible signals of commitment to the law to one another, relying on both retaliation-costless signals that allow citizens to signal legal preferences, plus the opportunity to send a costly signal by reinforcing their cheap talk with action when necessary.[70] This two-stage process solves the free rider problem by separating costless preference signaling from costly sanctioning: citizens have no incentive to shirk on the initial signal, but that signal commits them to (off-path) costly resistance should it be ignored, and the repeated play makes that threat credible. In addition, states in which the law is known to be in the interest (i.e., general, in a limited sense) of all may be stable without resort to such signals.

In this chapter, the normative model has become strategic; the role of the rule of law in establishing social equality has been revealed to be not just an ideal, but also a functional condition for the stability of rule of law practices. In the next chapter, we move from Athens to England, in order to increase the resolution of the abstract model we have been developing; in the one thereafter, lessons from Athens, England, and the United States are brought together to expand the abstract model still further.

Chapter 7

Parliament, Crown, and the rule of law in Britain

The North Atlantic rule of law tradition claims deep roots in the British common law as well as in the constraints on royal power expressed in the Magna Carta. At the same time, when we think of the concrete practices associated with rule of law in the modern world, we often think not of parliamentary supremacy and constitutional custom (indeed, as Chapter 5 showed us, the Athenian equivalents to both have been viewed as *threats* to the rule of law), but of something like American constitutional institutions: entrenched primary law, life-tenured judges with the power of judicial review, specific guarantees against bills of attainder, and the like. For that reason, a close look at the British rule of law is essential to a nonparochial understanding of the concept in general, particularly for scholarship produced in the United States. Accordingly, this chapter aims to shed light on two key questions. First, does the United Kingdom actually satisfy, to a reasonable degree, the demands of the rule of law? In the first section, I argue that the question cannot be conclusively answered absent empirical research, but offer an informal model demonstrating that – notwithstanding the doctrine of parliamentary sovereignty and the absence of binding judicial review – British officials could be sufficiently constrained to comport with the rule of law. Second, have egalitarian ideas similar to those I developed in Chapter 1 been available within the British rule of law tradition? In the second section, I argue in the affirmative.

Both sections are motivated by promissory notes issued in previous chapters. In Chapter 1, I argued that the concept of the rule of law should be treated separately from the practices of particular rule of law states. The institutional principles of the rule of law are functional generalizations from those observed practices, but they can be instantiated in different ways in different states.

In support of that *institutional independence claim*, I pointed out that we usually see Britain as a rule of law state, despite its absence of judicial review and its adherence to the doctrine of parliamentary supremacy, because constitutional customs, rather than the formal written constitutional constraints of the United States, sufficiently constrain British officials. Similarly, in Chapter 5, I argued that the supposedly absolute power of the Athenian assembly was not inconsistent with the rule of law in part by pointing to our standard evaluation of the United Kingdom as a rule of law state and its similarly de jure absolute legislative body.

But both of those arguments presuppose that the United Kingdom actually satisfies at least the weak rule of law – that is, that its officials are reliably constrained to comport with regularity and publicity. And it's not obvious that this is the case. Certainly, in the past, Parliament has itself acted like an unconstrained executive official, inter alia, by enacting acts of attainder and ordering people executed without trial. Perhaps written constitutions and judicial review and the like *are* necessary to reliably constrain officials to comport with the rule of law.

In the first section of this chapter, I will assuage these worries by developing an account of how Britain could have the rule of law despite its institutional structure. I will argue that we can evaluate the extent to which a state comports with the rule of law only through the empirical tools of positive political science, but I will offer an informal model of how the United Kingdom, even without formal legal restrictions on Parliament's behavior, might be so constrained.

The second section responds to the methodological criterion of normative robustness, showing that the legal material with which the early-seventeenth-century parliamentarians struggling for the rule of law worked (particularly the Magna Carta) carried latent egalitarian meaning for the parliamentarians to discover, and that they in fact discovered such meaning in their legal traditions and developed it into an argument with egalitarian overtones resembling the ideas presented in Chapter 1.

I THE BRITISH RULE OF LAW: ILLUSORY?

Many scholars have identified a tension between the rule of law and an absolutely sovereign British Parliament.[1] In the absence of binding judicial review or a written and entrenched constitution, Parliament arguably could retroactively abolish settled legal rights, order citizens imprisoned without trial, expropriate property, and so forth.[2]

Parliamentary supremacy has given way, moreover, to de facto supremacy of one house within Parliament. The House of Commons is effectively the unitary supreme legislative body: the House of Lords has very little formal power to constrain Commons; the judiciary, while independent (an independence that Parliament could revoke at will), has no power of judicial review; and the royal veto is de facto dead. Exacerbating these worries, in ordinary practice the cabinet controls the day-to-day legislative agenda; "backbenchers" have very little power in Commons; in practice, then, not only the legislature but also the executive might have unconstrained power.

It gets worse. The lack of anything like an entrenched codification of individual rights is (on some accounts) essential to the democratic self-conception of both the left and the right in Britain. As Prosser (1996, 481) puts it: "any entrenched system of rights has been seen in sharp opposition to democracy as limiting the sovereign power of the democratic will." Recall that we have already seen this problem in Athens, in the form of the question of whether radical popular sovereignty can be compatible with the rule of law. Prosser's summary of the ideology of British parliamentary supremacy sounds alarmingly like "It was a terrible thing if someone prevented the people from doing whatever they wished."

Nor can we simply say that the electorate constrains Parliament and the cabinet government, since Parliament controls the procedures of its own election and its term of office.[3] A truly runaway Parliament could, at least arguably, go so far as to abolish its susceptibility to election. Nor is this just an imaginary nightmare: in its history, Parliament has repeatedly changed the composition of the electorate, it has refused to dissolve (the Long Parliament), and it has executed people by attainder.

More recently, too, Parliament may have sent Britain beyond the bounds of the rule of law. Under current British law, the secretary of state is authorized to subject individuals to "terrorism prevention and investigation measures" for up to two years if the Secretary merely "reasonably believes" that the individual is "involved in terrorism-related activity," which can include as little as giving support to someone else who merely encourages terrorism.[4] These measures may include, inter alia, overnight curfews, travel restrictions, quarantines from specific places, restrictions on bank accounts, communications restrictions, employment restrictions, and electronic monitoring – all merely on "reasonable belief" of even indirectly facilitating terrorism-related offenses. This confers a quite extraordinary amount of discretion on executive officials to use the state's power of coercion based on only the thinnest of reasons.[5]

Such suspicion-based coercion violates the principle of publicity even when reviewed by an independent judiciary, since, at a minimum, a citizen about to be subjected to serious and long-term legal disabilities should have an opportunity to show that the conditions given by the law don't apply to her, rather than the much more difficult demonstration that executive officials didn't even have reason to suspect that those conditions applied. From the standpoint of regularity, this law also may confer open-ended threats on officials by virtue of the wide powers it grants and the broad set of citizens and circumstances subject to those powers.

One standard response to this cluster of worries is to claim that acts of attainder, statutes authorizing suspicion-based coercion, and so forth are aberrant measures imposed in times of political crisis, and it would be hasty to conclude from them that Parliament routinely exercises or authorizes executive officials to exercise unconstrained authority.[6] However, even if it's true (as it intuitively is) that British officials do not, in fact, make a habit of doing things like imprisoning people without trial, expropriating property, creating subordinate legal classes, or otherwise offending the rule of law in the sorts of egregious ways that would permit us to easily deny that Britain in fact comports with the three principles, a state does not count as having the rule of law if its officials merely comport with its principles out of the goodness of their hearts. As I argued in Chapter 1, officials must be reliably constrained, and to the extent we observe even episodic violations, we have reason to worry that no such constraints exist, or those that exist are unreliable.

A *Hobbesian sovereignty and the absolute-power coalition*

There is a formal sense in which we can say that all governments are unitary and absolute in the same way that Parliament is. Hobbes argued that sovereignty is ultimately indivisible and absolute. In chapter 19 of *Leviathan*, he explained that even in societies with ostensibly limited rulers, the actual absolute sovereign is the person or group who controls the terms of the nominal sovereign's limitation. And, in the abstract, Hobbes was, I submit, correct: in all states (assuming they are not dominated by foreign hegemons), there is always some possible coalition of citizens and officials that could exercise absolute power if all members had identical goals and were able to coordinate. In an extreme case, in any plausible state a coalition of all citizens but one could exercise absolute power over the outlier.

I will call this hypothetical group the "absolute-power coalition." Thus, in the United States, despite its formal separation of powers, any coalition of legislators amounting to two-thirds of both houses of Congress plus legislative majorities of three-fourths of the states could, in principle, exercise absolute power in virtue of its ability to amend the US Constitution; many other such coalitions are possible. If we assume that ordinary citizens in the United States are sufficiently attentive to their constitutional protections and able to coordinate, then the size of the de facto absolute-power coalition would increase to require the cooperation of a sufficiently large number of citizens to ensure ultimate (electoral, in extremis military) victory over the resistance of their recalcitrant fellows, but the absolute-power coalition still exists, at least in principle.

It just so happens that in the United Kingdom a majority of Commons is a de jure absolute-power coalition. For practical purposes, no de jure absolute-power coalition in the United States is likely to come together for any sustained length of time or large scope of issues, because the US institutional structure fills the offices that make up such coalitions with a large number of individuals with incentives that diverge from one another. The same cannot be said of the United Kingdom.

Those "practical purposes" are just the stuff out of which the rule of law is made. The extent to which official coercion is constrained by law, in any state, no matter its formal legal structure, depends on officials' ability and incentive to coordinate into a coalition sufficiently powerful to unshackle themselves from those constraints – that is, by retroactively revising or ignoring the legal prohibitions on whatever use they wish to make of the state's monopoly of violence. It also depends on the ability of those who would resist such official misbehavior to coordinate to put a stop to it.

This is not an original insight. Ignacio Sanchez-Cuenca has aptly argued that the rule of law does not require that no one have "the power to subvert the law," for such a situation would be impossible: someone, even if only "society as a whole," always has the power to subvert the law.[7] Rather, the relevant question is whether "given the laws and the incentives they create, men have no interest in subverting the institutional order." Admittedly, Sanchez-Cuenca took the claim rather too far: he concluded from it that the rule of law was "precarious" rather than dead altogether in Chile when Pinochet made it clear that he could and would discard legal constraints at whim. This is clearly wrong, and the reason it is wrong is that there is no "institutional order" at all when one person may wield the force of the state at whim without fear of sanction from others.

It follows that our evaluation of the extent to which a state comports with the rule of law is not going to depend, in the first instance, on the details of its formal legal structure, so long as that formal structure does not itself incorporate impermissible features (such as legal castes, rules providing for the retroactive effect of criminal statutes or requiring the law be secret, etc.). Instead, it's going to depend on the underlying distribution of power in that state, which is influenced by the state's formal legal structure, but also by many other properties of the sort that positive political scientists study. Among those properties are, intuitively, the following: (a) the diversity of interests among officials, (b) the size and coordination potential of any possible absolute-power coalitions under existing institutional structures, (c) the extent to which mass and elite actors have the institutional tools to facilitate coordinating to resist illegal official activity, (d) the extent to which subjects and competing officials have internalized the rule of law and are motivated to defend it against violation, and (e) the extent to which the legal rules then in existence are consistent with the interests of those citizens and officials whose cooperation is needed to sanction officials who violate the law.

I cannot consider all of these properties here; several would require extensive quantitative and/or ethnographic empirical research. However, in the British context, one is particularly interesting. It is not obvious to what extent the British people have the institutional tools to coordinate on a common-knowledge set of restrictions on their government, in light of the fact that the British have no written constitution.

B. Constraint, coordination, custom, and the constitution

Traditionally, British legal theorists claim that the British government is constrained by constitutional conventions, or constitutional customs. According to Dicey, the ministers who run the day-to-day executive business of British government are constrained by constitutional conventions because violating them will inevitably lead to punishable violations of written law.[8] He gives a example: ministers are obliged to follow the custom by which they step down or dissolve Parliament if they lose a no-confidence vote in Commons, even though no actual law requires it,[9] because if they fail to do so, sooner or later laws such as appropriations for the army will expire, and they'll be forced into crimes punishable by the judiciary (i.e., misappropriation of public funds) in order to run the government. But Dicey's argument only explains what might constrain a runaway cabinet; it cannot explain what constrains Parliament itself. Chrimes hazarded an attempt, suggesting that, in extremis, the royal prerogative could be revived to exercise the veto and then dissolve a runaway Parliament – but, in a vivid example of the absoluteness of parliamentary sovereignty, Parliament recently abolished the prerogative right to dissolve parliament, and could similarly eliminate the veto.[10]

Yet people still argue about whether an act passed by Parliament is "constitutional."[11] If such arguments are coherent, there must be some body of non-formally binding constitutional custom that nonetheless carries at least normative force in constraining Parliament's actions.

With that, we reach the crux of the matter. There need be no difference, in practical terms, between the constraint generated by written law and that generated by unwritten custom. If a sufficiently powerful group of citizens can credibly commit to sanctioning officials who violate a constitutional custom, the custom will be obeyed just as if it had been written into law, and regardless of whether the officials in question have the nominal power to legislate that custom away.

The chief difference between written and unwritten law for these strategic purposes then becomes that it's reasonably safe to assume reasonably widespread knowledge of the relevant written laws among those citizens potentially making up a coalition to sanction officials (or at least among the elites who coordinate citizen resistance) – an assumption of the Chapter 6 model. It's much less clear what sort of knowledge we can expect citizens to have of unwritten constitutional customs.[12] Something like this seems to have partly been behind the turmoil of the seventeenth century (about which much more later), which began with repeated and fundamental disagreements between Parliament and the Stuarts about the content of the customary constitution with respect to the legislative power of the church, ship money, the authority of the prerogative courts, and so on.[13]

I cannot make any conclusive claims about the effectiveness of unwritten constitutional constraint here. Instead, I suggest some intuitively plausible hypotheses to guide future research into the question of constitutional customs.

First, those customs that have been in continuous use for a longer period should, ceteris paribus, be more widely known among the population than more recent customs. Long-standing customs are more likely to have been published and taught to younger generations. Also, the longer a custom has been in operation without objection or alteration, the more reasonable it becomes for any given citizen to believe that fellow citizens endorse it.[14]

Second, the greater the extent of direct popular participation in a custom, the more likely, ceteris paribus, it should be known. Participation also gives citizens an opportunity to signal their acceptance or rejection of it.

Third, citizens might rely on authoritative third parties, such as de facto (if not firmly de jure) independent judges, to define the content of constitutional customs on an ongoing basis. Even if those judges lack the formal power of judicial review, as in the United Kingdom, citizens could coordinate on their signals. If a sufficiently influential group of citizens can credibly commit to resisting laws and executive actions that have been declared unconstitutional by the highest court, they should be able to coordinate to prevent such actions even in the absence of a common-knowledge body of constitutional law.

In the seventeenth century, the Stuarts tried to use judges to serve the inverse function: both James and Charles repeatedly sought, and obtained, rulings from the common-law and prerogative courts that their unusual revenue measures were legal, even while maintaining that their wills were superior to judicial rulings. We can interpret this as an attempt to convince the public that their acts were consistent with constitutional custom, and thus undercut any attempt by their opponents in Parliament to coordinate opposition. Unfortunately for the Stuarts, the credibility of the judges as consensus interpreters of the constitutional constraints on the Crown was impaired by their lack of independence, as both James and Charles had notoriously punished judges for disagreement. Instead, citizens seem to have coordinated on a signal from Parliament that the kings' actions were illegal; thus, parliamentary resistance to royal impositions led to public resistance.[15]

In the contemporary context, the House of Lords can also serve this third-party function in its legislative role. Formerly, the assent of Lords was necessary to enact a law. Now, its refusal to assent merely imposes a one-year delay on enactment.[16] In principle, however, such a refusal could signal to citizens that an act is unconstitutional, such that they could coordinate resistance.[17]

As noted, it is impossible to come to a reliable judgment about whether Britain comports to the rule of law without empirical work. For the purposes of hypothesis generation, however, the discussion thus far suggests an informal model of how its institutional structure plausibly could work to constrain Parliament, despite the doctrine of parliamentary supremacy and the absence of a written constitution.

Should Britain's constitutional traditions, and the rule of law, have sufficient support from the public, the institutional mechanisms discussed thus far have the potential to support coordination. The House of Lords and the judiciary are both insulated from direct electoral control and thus likely to have different interests from the elected officials that make up Commons, and both are deliberative, elite bodies in a good epistemic position to come to an independent judgment on the constitutionality of acts of Commons and the cabinet.[18]

Thus, in the event of unconstitutional action by Commons, the Lords may send a signal to the public at large by delaying the enactment of legislation,[19] and the judiciary may send a similar signal, not by overturning the legislation, but by very openly and clearly narrowly construing it to make it as consistent as possible with preexisting constitutional norms, or by openly criticizing it even while reluctantly applying it.[20] This hypothesis has observable implications: if these powers of Lords and the judiciary do constrain Commons, we ought to observe Lords refusing to assent to bills that authorize violations of the rule of law (e.g., imprisonment without trial, retroactive criminal punishment, etc.), and we ought to observe the judiciary stating objections to them if enacted over the objections of Lords. Moreover, we ought to observe a growth in public opposition to such enactments after Lords and/or the judiciary act. Ultimately, we ought to observe these laws failing in Commons after the Lords register their objections, or their repeal after the judiciary registers its objections.[21]

This model reflects the self-understanding of participants in the British legal system to some extent. At least one British jurist has suggested that the rule of law relies on political institutions getting information to the public to coordinate opposition:

> Parliamentary sovereignty means that Parliament can, if it chooses, legislate contrary to fundamental principles of human rights. The Human Rights Act 1998 will not detract from this power. The constraints upon its exercise by Parliament are ultimately political, not legal. But the principle of legality means that Parliament must squarely confront what it is doing and accept the political cost. Fundamental rights cannot be overridden by general or ambiguous words. This is because there is too great a risk that the full implications of their unqualified meaning may have passed unnoticed in the democratic process. In the absence of express language or necessary implication to the contrary, the courts therefore presume that even the most general words were intended to be subject to the basic rights of the individual. In this way the courts of the United Kingdom, though acknowledging the sovereignty of Parliament, apply principles of constitutionality little different from those which exist in countries where the power of the legislature is expressly limited by a constitutional document.[22]

Moreover, the Human Rights Act, 1998 c. 42, permits judges to issue a "declaration of incompatibility" between Acts of Parliament and the European Convention on Human Rights, which includes numerous rule of law provisions that roughly approximate the principles of regularity and publicity.[23] While such a declaration is formally toothless, it may have some political impact.[24]

There is reason for concern about the extent to which these signals actually coordinate public opposition, and thus lead to an effective constraint on officials: even though the Lords attempted to put a stop to it, the retroactive War Crimes Act 1991 was enacted (McMurtrie 1992), and while the judiciary managed to provoke the repeal of several troubling antiterrorist statutes providing for various sorts of executive coercion of suspected terrorists without an adequate opportunity to defend themselves (about which more in a moment), they were just replaced by almost equally troubling statutes. The most obvious explanation for this is that both were targeted against extremely unpopular groups – terrorists and war criminals. Still, each suggests that even if the British public take the rule of law as generating reasons for its support, those reasons may not be very strong – at least not strong enough to override considerations such as the fear of terrorists.

However, there is some evidence that Parliament is at least somewhat constrained by these mechanisms. The Anti-Terrorism, Crime and Security Act 2001 provided for indefinite detention for those whom the executive saw as a threat to national security. In 2004, the Law Lords ruled that the act was incompatible with the European Convention on Human Rights.[25] In response, Parliament replaced the ATCSA with the Prevention of Terrorism Act 2005, which replaced indefinite detention with control orders.[26] The courts declared this one incompatible with the European Convention on Human Rights, too.[27]

In response, Parliament again gave way, and enacted the Terrorism Prevention and Investigation Measures Act 2011, which I've already discussed. True, the TPIM Act is still objectionable from the perspective of the rule of law, but it's at least arguably better than the system of control orders it replaced, which was in turn arguably better than the detention rules that gave way to the control orders.

The foregoing example suggests that the British governmental structure can be consistent with the rule of law, just as long as the public in general remains willing to hold its representatives to it, with the help of such institutional signals as are available. It may fall far short of the rule of law in many cases, particularly relating to terrorism, but this is not a product of its unitary governmental structure or unwritten constitution. The United States, despite its extensive formal separation of powers and written constitution, has nonetheless recently claimed the right to hold alleged terrorists without charging them on a naval base in Cuba and assassinate US citizens with flying drones on the decision of the President alone. Ultimately, a state will have the rule of law only if its officials and citizens are willing to defend it, and recent history has shown us that this willingness may be difficult to find in the face of the fear of perceived existential threats, particularly when foreigners, racial and religious minorities, and the like are seen as the source of those threats.[28]

The parallel to Athens is striking. Athens, too, had institutions sufficient to maintain the rule of law under ordinary circumstances, yet succumbed to mass hysteria in wartime, both in the trial of the generals and in the affair of the Herms/Mysteries. In Athens, the United Kingdom, and the United States, we should draw a distinction between ordinary legal and political practice, which generally comports fairly well, more or less, with the rule of law, and moments of extraordinary political crisis, in which public support for the rule of law gives way to perceived exigency. This may be the best we can hope for from our political communities.

C *A historical precedent: customary manorial courts*

Parliament's absolute power, constrained only by constitutional custom today, bears an intriguing resemblance to the power of lords over their villeins in the thirteenth and fourteenth centuries. Before the Black Death of 1348–1350, legal protections for villeins steadily eroded.[29] However, the formal legal status of the lowest classes was significantly worse than the rules that were applied to them in practice. For example, if the treatise known as Bracton is to be believed, a lord had an absolute right to seize all property acquired by his villeins.[30] However, in practice, around the time of Bracton, lords respected villeins' customary property rights.[31] Perhaps more puzzlingly, lords appeared to respond inconsistently to economic incentives in managing their lands: before the time of the Black Death, faced with a labor surplus and a land shortage, they preferred to lease land to free tenants at the market rent rather than have the land worked by villeins at a submarket payment.[32] Nonetheless, they ordinarily did not simply expropriate land in the possession of villeins to convert it to more profitable leasehold land – an act within their legal rights as given by Bracton, yet contrary to custom – even though that would have been economically advantageous.[33]

Why did the lords, and their manorial courts, respect villeins' customary property rights, despite theoretically having absolute power over villeins' property and a financial incentive to exercise it? Local customs (which may have varied by region or by lord) would have been widely known, as they concerned the most fundamental aspects of peasants' lives – control over land, inheritance, the labor owed to the lord, and so forth. This licenses the assumption that villeins had common knowledge of the local informal legal rules, and suggests that they may have been able to coordinate to enforce them. Evidence that such coordination was possible on the local level is given by manorial court records showing a number of cases in which villeins stopped work en masse, and occasionally resorted to violence.[34] We can take this case as an application of the analytical framework of the previous chapter and this one. Once customary constraints on official power arise – due to either changing strategic circumstances or moral beliefs – those constraints can be enforced by their beneficiaries, even overriding formal rules to the contrary, if there is institutional support for common knowledge of those constraints and adequate incentives to enforce them. This is true whether the power at issue is baronial power over villeins in thirteenth-century manorial courts or parliamentary power today.

I now turn to the origins of the contemporary constraints on official power.

II THE RULE OF LAW AND EQUAL STATUS IN SEVENTEENTH-CENTURY ENGLAND

There is a strong English tradition of the rule of law, but that tradition seems to be inextricably associated with a conception of liberty. This association begins with the Magna Carta, which speaks of liberties and attaches its most important provisions to the "freeman," the *liber homo*. It continues into the conflict in the seventeenth century between Parliament and the Crown that led to the Petition of Right, the Long Parliament, the civil war, and, ultimately, the Glorious Revolution – a conflict that was influenced by religious division, to be sure, but which featured near-constant parliamentary appeals to the "liberty of the subject" against royal taxation and imprisonment unauthorized by law. This ideological heritage continued, of course, into the American Revolution.

Recently, Skinner has added some flesh to the seventeenth-century ideology of liberty.[35] On his account, the parliamentary party subscribed to a "neo-Roman" theory of liberty similar to that propounded, in the contemporary literature, by neorepublicans such as Philip Pettit. Skinner's analysis focuses on the political philosophers and parliamentarians writing after the execution of Charles I, and the influence they took from Roman ideas of freedom. But there was another intellectual stream within the parliamentary party, most prominent 20 years earlier in the debates leading up to the Petition of Right.[36] This stream comprised the common lawyers. Those in this line of thought, led by Coke and Selden, drew their inspiration from the legal traditions of England, particularly the Magna Carta, and were at best ambivalent to Roman civil law ideas – ideas from which the royalist party drew in support of absolutism.[37]

The content of and circumstances surrounding the Magna Carta and the parliamentary debates surrounding the Five Knights Case and the Petition of Right suggest that even if the common lawyers, too, may have accepted, or come to accept, something like Skinner's neo-Roman conception of liberty, that conception was closely associated with the equal status of the "freeman," that class of citizens, both commoners and nobility, who were hierarchically above serfdom. Rights to due process were the heritage of the *liber homo*, and in the king's attempt to undermine them the common lawyers saw the threat of a reduction of the ordinary Englishman's status to that of a villein – a drastic loss of political and social position.

The "free" of the *liber homo* and of Coke and his parliamentary confederates was a status term. "Free" status was the status of citizenship, of equal participation in political and economic institutions, and was contrasted with the status of villeinage or serfdom, a subcitizen status associated with a lesser entitlement to respect. Moreover, the parliamentarians held a relative of the hubris idea of Chapter 1: the threat was not that the king would hubristically raise his own status (he was, after all, *the king*: he already held higher status), but that he would lower that of the citizen body and render them subject to contempt. This was interwoven with a relative of the terror idea from Chapter 1: being subject to unconstrained royal power would render ordinary citizens fearful, and it was by virtue of that fear, and the cowardly behavior to which their fear would lead them, that they were subject to contempt.

I begin by offering an egalitarian interpretation of the Magna Carta. I then turn to the words of the seventeenth-century parliamentarians themselves.

A *Magna Carta as egalitarian text*

The Magna Carta, in the various versions in which it was issued and reissued, consistently refers to the "freeman" (*liber homo*) and his liberties.[38] From chapter 29:

> NO Freeman shall be taken or imprisoned, or be disseised of his Freehold, or Liberties, or free Customs, or be outlawed, or exiled, or any other wise destroyed; nor will We not pass upon him, nor condemn him, but by lawful judgment of his Peers, or by the Law of the Land. We will sell to no man, we will not deny or defer to any man either Justice or Right.

It's tempting to misunderstand this text as simply affirming something like the liberty thesis – that the protection against punishment or dispossession was intended to protect freedom or liberty. In fact, it also reflects an awareness that legal rights were attached to social and political status.

In order to make this argument clear, first, we should clarify some concepts. In modern speech, we refer to "liberty" as a unitary sort of thing with some presumptive normative value: liberty is, for example, the state of not being subject to interference with one's choices, or the state of being in control of one's own life. By contrast, there's another, older, use of the word in a plural sense, as "liberties." In that context, it refers to discrete property-like legal rights, which could also be called franchises or (if granted only to a particular class) privileges. "Liberties" in the second sense need not be contributions to "liberty" in the first sense, and need not have any particular normative value.[39] At the time the Magna Carta was granted, it was fairly routine to grant these liberties/franchises/privileges by royal charter, and, I shall argue, the Magna Carta did just that. Moreover, the most unusual fact about the Magna Carta, from the standpoint of its time, was that it granted these liberties on a relatively universal basis (to all those with the status of *liber homo*, about which more in a moment). The point is that while the Magna Carta greatly influenced the seventeenth-century parliamentarians, particularly Coke, we cannot take that fact as an indication that they were solely concerned with liberty in its indivisible, normative sense. The appeal to the Magna Carta must also be understood as an appeal to that document that established the nature of citizenship in the realm, and the "liberties" were what each citizen was entitled to just by virtue of his being a citizen.

"Free" itself referred to a social and economic status. Land could be held in freehold or in villeinage; the latter was both a social status and a tenancy in land.[40] The two could come apart: it was possible for a freeman to hold land under a villein tenancy.[41] Villeins were unfree in the unitary, normative sense in one important way – they did not have the choice to leave the employment of their lord – but the term "free" did not only, or primarily, refer to that lack of individual liberty, but to their status in the manorial system.[42]

Thus, in 1354, a statute of Edward III clarified the scope of chapter 29 of the Magna Carta:

> That no Man of what Estate or Condition that he be, shall be put out of Land or Tenement, nor taken, nor imprisoned, nor disinherited, nor put to Death, without being brought in Answer by due Process of the Law.[43]

To be noted here is that this text refers specifically to land tenure and social status. The passage (which followed an explicit confirmation of the Magna Carta) suggests that the live issue as to who would receive the protections of law was the social status of the citizen, and that the limitation to "freemen" in the Magna Carta was directed at specifying the social classes to which legal protection would apply.

Now, consider the term "liberties." Compare the text in chapter 29 to the text in one of the other chapters that is still law today, chapter 9:

> THE City of London shall have all the old Liberties and Customs [which it hath been used to have]. Moreover We will and grant, that all other Cities, Boroughs, Towns, and the Barons of the Five Ports, and all other Ports, shall have all their Liberties and free Customs.

The use of the word "liberties" here clearly refers to the political privileges of the various corporate entities, chief of which was London: at the time, purchasing such privileges, such as the right to hold courts or to appoint local sheriffs, was a common practice for boroughs.[44] Chapter 29 refers to the same sort of liberties: individuals, particularly in the nobility, also routinely purchased privileges from the Crown.[45]

As Holt has pointed out, there was nothing unusual about the specific "liberties" granted in the Magna Carta: they were of a type that had ordinarily been bought and sold and granted by earlier charters.[46] What was unusual was the Magna Carta's "universality, as a grant to all in the land." This is the innovation of the Magna Carta: to convert individual privilege, purchased or granted at the whim of those in power, to an equal right for all – or, at least, all of free status. In this respect, the Magna Carta is fundamentally an egalitarian document, concerned not only with the content of citizens' rights but with their distribution.

The Magna Carta is fundamentally egalitarian in another respect. Milsom has argued that the assize of novel disseisin was instituted as a mechanism to control lords' treatment of freehold tenants, to prevent lords from illegally dispossessing their tenants in the manorial courts by giving tenants a remedy in the royal courts.[47] This leads to another of Milsom's insights: that "when the Charter requires that the king should disseise only by judgment, it seeks to make him treat his own men as the law already makes them treat theirs."[48] In this way, the Magna Carta establishes the king and the barons on a footing of generality: it suggests that if a restriction is appropriate for the operation of manorial overlordship, it's appropriate for the royal overlordship; the difference in identity between king and baron is not a relevant distinction on which differential legal treatment ought to be based, at least when it comes to the legal power to take the property of one's feudal tenants.

Partial equality between the king and barons is similarly suggested by the provision requiring judgment by peers. It is not, as some modern readers have erroneously suggested, an enactment of anything like trial by jury.[49] In fact, however, the meaning of trial by peers is trial by one's social equals[50] – that is, for barons, by the standard royal court composed of the king's tenants in chief, rather than simply by the king himself; for lower classes of freemen, by the standard manorial courts, also composed of the local lord's free tenants. The best interpretation of this passage, then, represents a concern that justice not be given hierarchically – that the king not rule alone on the cases of his social inferiors, and likewise that lords not rule alone on the cases of their social inferiors.[51] This, in turn, contributes to the coordinated enforcement aspect of publicity: the class that benefited from the new legal rights was given a right to participate in their enforcement, and, consequently, access to information about the extent to which they were being obeyed.

Milsom's insight applies here as well: freemen, when they were being judged in the manorial courts of the barons, were entitled to be tried by their peers; the Magna Carta replicated that structure at the level of the royal courts with respect to the king's treatment of barons: again, the Magna Carta simply demanded that the king treat his vassals as other lords were required to treat theirs. Strikingly, this equality seems to go the other way as well: Henry III actively enforced the Magna Carta by requiring the barons to apply the rights granted therein to their free tenants, a policy that Maddicott interprets as evidence that "the higher nobility were not set apart by the legal privileges of a caste."[52]

Of course, I do not claim that the barons and other freemen (including both lower-level free tenants and churchmen) who imposed the Magna Carta on John did so out of egalitarian motives; the requirement of trial by peers, for example, was most plausibly motivated by strategic considerations, as an attempt to entrench the power of the baronial party against future royal expropriations.[53] But the motivation is not relevant here. What is relevant is the meaning that the Magna Carta could have had for later activists, particularly for Coke and the seventeenth-century parliamentarians. Similarly, I do not mean to claim that the rights granted by the Magna Carta can only be interpreted through an egalitarian lens. They may also be interpreted as grants of liberty in the unitary, normative sense – and such an interpretation does not hinge on whether it was so understood in the thirteenth century, but on the fact that a modern interpreter could easily argue that, for example, the right to not be imprisoned without trial protects one's liberty. I do not mean to exclude liberty-based interpretations of the Magna Carta, but simply to argue that it takes an equality-based interpretation just as well.

In this vein, Holt argues that the universal liberties granted by the Magna Carta "contributed to the emergence of the *communitas regni* both as a concept and [as] a political phenomenon."[54] This makes sense in the context of the egalitarian interpretation of the Magna Carta that I'm offering. If what matters about the Magna Carta is that it defined the entitlements of *all Englishmen*, or, at least, all Englishmen with the status of *liber homo* that was to develop into citizenship, as opposed to previous charters that had merely defined the entitlements of some Englishmen, then we can understand that the Magna Carta was defining just what it meant to *be* an Englishman. On this interpretation, the Magna Carta served the function that Waldron attributes to law in general: by converting privileges into rights, it makes universal the high status previously enjoyed only by the nobility, and, we can add to Waldron, defines membership in the political community (status as *liber homo*) as possession of those rights.[55]

Having offered an egalitarian interpretation of the Magna Carta, I now turn to the seventeenth century and its high point in British legal culture, to suggest that Coke and the parliamentarians could also have seen that what was special about the Magna Carta was that it gave rights to *all*[56] that had previously only been granted to *some*, and could have been influenced by the idea of equal citizenship as expressed in the Magna Carta. Their appeals to the "liberty of the subject" were appeals to the rights constituting the status of citizen, equal with all other citizens and a full member of the political community. Just as in Athens, the evidence is consistent with Coke and the parliamentarians seeing the royal threat to undermine the liberties of the Magna Carta as an attempt to undermine the political community itself, and its members' collective status as English citizens.

B *The parliamentary debates of* 1628

Starting in 1626, under increasing financial pressure from military needs, Charles I extracted forced loans from a variety of citizens.[57] In 1627, a number of citizens were committed to prison on royal orders for not giving the forced loans, and in the Five Knights Case, Lord Chief Justice Hyde refused the writ of habeas corpus. In response, Parliament, led by Coke, Selden, and others, began debating the alleged royal power to imprison citizens without trial, debates that ultimately led to the Petition of Right.[58] Often these debates appealed to the Magna Carta.[59] In this section, I review those debates to show how the parliamentary party appealed to egalitarian ideals underlying the rule of law to explain their resistance to the Crown's abuses.

In the debates following the Five Knights Case, I find three major themes that are relevant to the equality thesis.

The first is the claim that by imprisoning citizens and refusing to give the reasons or subject his actions to judicial control, the king reduces ordinary Englishmen to the status of villeins.

Second, and closely related, is an appeal to honor and dignity, both of the king and of ordinary citizens. Various parliamentarians suggest that to be subjected to imprisonment for no greater reason than the will of the king is a dishonor or indignity, and to actually bow to the royal demand for money under such threat is a worse dishonor still, and contemptible. This second claim appears with the claim that the king's unconstrained power reduces citizens to fearful, and hence dishonorable, behavior – a notion that tracks the idea of terror in Chapter 1, in which I argued that unconstrained officials force citizens to behave subserviently out of fear, and thereby lower their own status. Moreover, the parliamentarians suggest that the king's own dignity and honor are reduced along with the dignity and honor of his citizens, that it's a demotion for a king to rule over a nation of less than Englishmen.

These first two categories of claims add up to a variation on the hubris idea. By imprisoning citizens for no reason other than his own unconstrained will, the king did not quite express his own superiority (which was a given), but rather expressed the inferiority of ordinary citizens. Imprisonment at will deprives those subject to it of membership in the political community, membership in which entitles one to status and respect as an equal citizen.

Third, the parliamentarians often raise considerations of political liberty, rather than individual liberty in the contemporary liberal sense. This is consistent with Skinner's neo-Roman interpretation of the content of the parliamentary party's liberty motivation. Two things are important here for my purposes. First is the connection to *membership*: just as the legal entitlements granted by the Magna Carta were constitutive of the status of equal citizenship, so was parliamentary representation. To say that the king's abuse of power was a threat to Parliament itself was just to say that it was a threat to the status of those who could vote for Parliament and be elected to Parliament as full-fledged members of the political community. Second is the connection to *coordinated enforcement*: a threat to parliamentary representation and power, or the intimidation of Parliament by an unconstrained royal power to imprison, would also undermine the ability of the people to hold the Crown to the law in the future, just as, according to Andocides, Alcibiades' impunity undermined the power of the demos to use the jury to resist oligarchy.

Before moving into the details of the debates, note that all of this was transpiring during a period in which the common lawyers in general were beginning to follow Cicero in seeing the law as a countervailing force to traditional class distinctions. Brooks finds this trend in several legal treatises, and attributes it to the idea that "political society was founded to protect the weak from the strong."[60] Judson similarly suggests that the English of the period in general saw the law as "a binding, cohesive force in their polity" and "impartial – serving well both the king and the subject."[61] Even Bacon, royalist though he was, attested that the laws are "the equallest in the world between the Prince and People."[62] The debates in Parliament amply reflected this.

It is also important to note that the most salient event that provoked this controversy was, as the name suggests, a case about knights. A knight was within the top 5 or 10 percent of the population, in terms of social status, in the sixteenth century, although this number seems to have increased at some point in the seventeenth.[63] As the attack was against members of the gentry, the issue of the status consequences of arbitrary royal power over those attacked would have been particularly salient (recall that Coke himself was a knight). Moreover, as England at the time appears to have been experiencing what in modern times we would call "the disappearance of the middle class" (relative increase in the numbers of both the rich and high status and the poor and low status), we can expect status anxiety to have been high among the lower ranks of the elite, such as those who would hold seats in the House of Commons.[64] Furthermore, as wealth was required to maintain status, financial exactions could have been seen as a direct threat to status.[65]

1 Villeins and status

On April 3, 1628, Coke appealed directly to the hierarchical status relationship that the unconstrained royal power to imprison implies:

> [A]n imprisoned man upon will and pleasure, is 1. A bond-man. 2. Worse than bond-man. 3. Not so much as a man; for *mortuus homo non est homo*; a prisoner is a dead man. 1. No man can be imprisoned upon the will and pleasure of any, but he that is a bond-man and villain; for that imprisonment and bondage are *propria quarto modo* to villains: now *propria quarto modo*, and the Species, are convertible; whosoever is a bond-man may be imprisoned, upon will and pleasure; and whosoever may be imprisoned, upon will and pleasure, is a bond-man. 2. If Freemen of England might be imprisoned at the will and pleasure of the king, or his commandment, then were they in worse case than bond-men or villains; for the lord of a villain cannot command another to imprison his villain without cause, as of disobedience, or refusing, to serve, as it is agreed in the Year-Books.[66]

In that passage we see the direct relationship between at-will imprisonment and status: to allow a freeman to be imprisoned without cause is to render him even lower in status than a serf. In fact, Coke had made the comparison to villeinage even earlier, in discussing not the imprisonments, but the forced loans that led to them:

> Loans against the will of the subject are against reason and the franchises of the land, and they desire restitution. What a word is that "franchise." Villeins *in native habendo*, their lord may tax them high or low, but this is against the franchise of the land for freemen. "Franchise" is a French word, and in Latin it is liberty. In Magna Carta, *nullus imprisonetur* nor put out of his liberty or franchise ... The Magna Carta is called *carta libertates et franchisae* and to overthrow it makes slaves.[67]

Here we see a blending of liberty-talk and status-talk, according to which the right to be free from unauthorized taxes is a "franchise" attached to free status – a property right (one of the liberties in the plural sense) that Coke seems here to want to interpret as constitutive of liberty in the unitary sense.[68]

On March 27, Cresheld argued that even villeins were free from imprisonment at will, though not from expropriation of property, in the following terms: "the common law did favor the liberties not only of freemen but even of the persons of bondmen and villeins."[69] Here again, we see "liberties" in the plural sense – a bondman had the liberty of safety from physical imprisonment, but not the liberty of private property rights. Selden, by contrast, actually excluded villeins even from the protection against imprisonment at will:[70]

> The question is whether any subject and freeman that is committed to prison, and the cause not shown in the warrant, he ought not to be bailed and delivered. I think confidently it belongs to every subject that is not a villein, that he ought to be bailed or delivered.
>
> * * *
>
> All admit we are *liberi homines*, but do not consider the difference of villeins and freemen, and I know no difference in their persons, but only the one cannot be imprisoned as the other may: whosoever can say I can imprison him, I will say he is my villein. It is the body and sole distinction of freemen that they cannot be imprisoned at pleasure. In old time none but Jews and villeins could be imprisoned and confined. The Jews were as the demesne villeins of the King.[71]

Immunity from imprisonment appears here as a pure mark of status, the "sole distinction" of the *liber homo*. Here, the remark about the Jews is particularly telling, since there's no reason to believe that Jews were seen as unfree in the sense of not possessing or being entitled to liberty in the unitary normative sense, and not necessarily even in the sense of being unentitled to hold land in freehold tenancy, but they were certainly seen as of lower status, and were counted as nonmembers of the political community.[72]

Finally, the shortest but perhaps the most telling reference comes on March 22, when Wentworth described the king's actions as follows: "these illegal ways are punishments and marks of indignation." I take it that the claim here isn't that the king is indignant (why would he be?), but rather that the imprisonings, forced loans, and the like are indignities – status injuries – inflicted on the populace.[73]

2 Dishonor, fear, and contempt

On March 22, Seymour captures the essence of terror:

> Fear takes away freedom and the judgment that belongs to faithful counsel. We cannot speak our judgment while we retain our fears; nor know we how to give [money to the Crown] until we know whether we have to give or no, and no man can say that he hath to give if it may be taken away at pleasure. To prove this we may instance the billeting of soldiers and the imprisoning of those men that denied the loan; but if they had yielded through base fear, they had been as faulty as those that first broached these gauds.[74]

That passage begins with something resembling the chilling effects argument of Chapter 4, and then moves into a condemnation of those who would fear the king and pay the forced loans – an odd juxtaposition of claims: that fear of unconstrained royal power makes one unfree, but nonetheless that one ought to defy unconstrained royal power. One plausible reading of this passage that reconciles the two claims is that fear is the possession of the "base" – that is, of the dishonorable, of those having low status. Base citizens succumb to the fear of royal power and surrender their freedom; noble, honorable citizens resist it. To surrender to one's fear is to become base, dishonorable. But the king's terror tactics have the power to make citizens base by inflicting that fear on otherwise upstanding citizens. This is a close relative of the idea of terror presented in Chapter 1, in which the fear of unconstrained power gives citizens reason to behave in a subservient manner. Seymour just adds the gloss that such behavior is contemptible and blamable.

In the debates on March 22, Digges made repeated use of the claim that to be subject to forced loans and imprisonment without explicit legal authorization is to be reduced in status. First he remarks, "That king that is not tied to the laws is a king of slaves."[75]

Later that same day, Digges says the following: "I am afraid (and I have too great cause to fear) that our King is told he is no great king unless he be told so, but I believe his greatness lies in the observance of his laws. The king that is not limited rules slaves that cannot serve him." He goes so far as to suggest that the terror induced by unconstrained power makes worse soldiers out of people, echoing Seymour's suggestion that this fear makes those subject to it in some sense less virtuous than free Englishmen: "The Muscovites are so cowed with these arbitrary commands that I know the time when a few English and Scots have beaten I know not how many thousand of their best horsemen out of the field." He goes on to say, "The King cannot lose more than by degenerating us."[76] To impose forced loans and imprisonments without legal warrant or constraint is to reduce the status of ("degenerating") the ordinary citizens in part by reducing them to dishonorable cowards, like the Muscovites.

In a different version (from different notes) of the same debate, Digges reportedly says, "The monarch that doth not maintain the rights of the subjects is a monarch of none but slaves and vassals."[77] Here, the term "vassals" is telling. Vassalage, in a feudal sense, does not mean unfreedom; a lord could have free vassals, and, indeed, the highest nobles in the land were vassals of the king (even King John became a vassal to the Pope during the political troubles that led to the Magna Carta).[78] But vassalage did always imply lower rank in a hierarchy: a vassal was the subordinate of a lord. The usage "slaves and vassals" thus suggests that the feature of slavery that was being pointed to was not its unfreedom but its inequality.

On April 3, Coke follows his argument that royal at-will imprisonment would reduce ordinary Englishmen to the status of villeins by arguing that for the king to have such power would be "very dangerous for the king and kingdom" because "[i]t would be no honour to a king or kingdom, to be a king of bondmen or slaves; the end of this would be both *dedecus & damnum*, both to king and kingdom, that in former times hath been so renowned."[79] That is, by reducing the status of all his subjects to that of slaves, the king's status too is reduced, for it is lower to rule over a kingdom of slaves than over one of full citizens.[80]

3 Political liberty and coordination

Again, I begin with Coke:

> I shall produce therefore some reasons, first from the universality of the persons whom this concerns. *Commentaries*, 236, it is maxim that the common law hath so admeasured the King's prerogative that in no cause it can prejudice the inheritance of the subject, and how doth this absolute authority that is pretended concern not only the commonalty but the lords and all spiritual persons and all officers? For if he be committed and be called on for his office, his office is forfeited. It concerns all men and women, and therefore it deserves to be spoken of in Parliament. This may dissolve this House, for we may be all thus committed.
>
> 31 Hen.6. *rot.* 27, *rot. parl.*, no member of the Parliament can be arrested but for felony, treason, or the peace, and all here may be committed, and then where is the Parliament? Sure the Lords will be glad of this; it concerns them as well as us.[81]

This passage reveals two elements of Coke's thinking. First, he is concerned with the effect of the unconstrained power to imprison on the ability of Parliament to function: this power may be used to evade the restriction on interfering with the persons of members of Parliament. Second, the principle at stake is important enough to warrant parliamentary consideration in virtue of its universal effect – the king was threatening the rights of "all men and women." This fits nicely into my interpretation of the rights given by the Magna Carta, which Coke was endeavoring to defend, as universal among citizens and constitutive of their status *as* citizens. (This latter appears to also be a political argument: because it was universal, it affected the Lords, too, so they should join the fight.)

Eliot, on March 22, discussing the importance of the principle at stake, also referred to political liberty:

> But this reflects on all that we call ours, those rights that made our fathers free men, and they render our posterity less free. This gives leave to annihilate acts of Parliament, and Parliaments themselves.[82]

Here, Eliot seems to be suggesting that a free man is just someone who is entitled to parliamentary representation. Here, we see the conjunction between *liber homo* status and citizenship.[83] Note also, in the context of Chapter 6, that the abolition of Parliament meant the abolition of the power of the people to coordinate to resist the Crown: this reveals again the reciprocal relationship between the rule of law and nonofficial collective power that also appeared in the context of the Athenian strength *topos* (and, less directly, in the Fullerian conception of reciprocity discussed at the end of Chapter 4): compare it to Aeschines' warning that the scofflaw threatens to become "stronger than the courts."

4 Reviewing the evidence

The speeches in Parliament following the Five Knights Case and preceding the Petition of Right do not perfectly track the details of the egalitarian argument I offered in Chapter 1. For all the egalitarian innovations from the Magna Carta onward, the king was still of undoubtedly hierarchically superior status relative to everyone else in the realm; he could not be accused of hubris in the standard sense – that is, of illegitimately attempting to lay claim to that higher status. Nobody thought that the king ought to be fully equal to an ordinary citizen, although the Magna Carta did impose equality on him in a limited fashion.

However, the historical record reveals an approximation to the egalitarian argument of Chapter 1 in the worry, not that the king would aggrandize himself, but that he would degrade everyone else from their high status as *liberi homines*, members of the political community. Had the king the power to imprison at will, the parliamentarians claimed, the ordinary Englishman would be reduced to the status of, most often, a villein, but they also referred to slaves, vassals, Jews, and cowardly Muscovites – all markedly low-status groups. The mirror image of the hubris argument actually appeared in this context: were the king to become a ruler of citizens thus degraded, the king's high status too would be reduced. A version of the terror argument also appeared, in the claim that were the king to have the power to imprison at will, he would create cowardly, base, submissive citizens.

Moreover, in the same period that Parliament and the Crown were bickering over ship money and forced loans, the Puritans of the Massachusetts Bay Colony were building a thriving legal system. And the Puritans, too, had a *liber homo*: the "freeman" was a defined political status that carried with it voting rights and required membership in the church.[84] It was, essentially, *citizenship*, not mere nonslavery, and not exclusive possession of the liberal liberties.[85] "Freeman" in Massachusetts seems to have meant something much like "citizen" in Athens, and the term appeared as early as the 1629 charter of the Massachusetts Bay Colony, in which it referred to the members of the corporation.[86] The *liber homo* of the Magna Carta, Coke, and the Puritans, was, fundamentally, a full-fledged member, and this full-fledged membership is what the illegal exactions and imprisonments of the Stuarts threatened.

I conclude that the English case supports the robustness of the egalitarian account of the rule of law. I do not propose to dispute the claim of the traditional account that the British struggle for the rule of law was (also) rooted in a conception of liberty. Instead, I propose to add to it. I have offered evidence that considerations of terror and (a version of) hubris were on the minds of the parliamentarians in the seventeenth century. I have also offered evidence that the idea that protections against unconstrained royal power were the inheritance of equal members of the polis was within their political culture, and was immanent in the innovations of the Magna Carta. From this, we can see that the British case is consistent with the claim that the argument for the egalitarian conception of the rule of law is normatively robust: offering the argument in Chapter 1 would not have been objectionable to Coke and the other parliamentarians, and would have responded to concerns that they actually had.

III CIVIC TRUST AND THE BRITISH RULE OF LAW IN LATER YEARS

We can also see the strategic account of Chapter 6 making a critical appearance in the eighteenth century. In a groundbreaking paper, Margaret Somers argues that the working-class residents of "pastoral" regions of eighteenth-century England – rural regions with poor soil, and thus little interest from noble landlords, that developed an industrial textile industry – understood the ideal of the rule of law as grounding their claim to social, economic, and political equality on the basis of their identity as *liberi homines*, but the working-class residents of "arable" regions – good agricultural land dominated by the gentry – did not.[87]

Somers's explanation for this phenomenon is highly informative. Industrial production (i.e., the activity carried out in the pastoral regions) was regulated by ordinary local courts, which were themselves highly participatory, and whose officials were accountable to the public. Thus, I understand Somers to suggest, workers in pastoral areas both understood the law as a tool that could be put to use to protect their interests (rather than an instrument of top-down oppression) and had genuine access to institutions that could deploy the law to hold the powerful to account. Second, a combination of partible inheritance (primarily implemented in pastoral rather than arable regions) and apprenticeship concentrated economic and associational life into networks reinforced by kinship ties, promoting a higher degree of social capital. This, of course, implies a higher degree of trust among members of the working class, and thus a greater potential capacity to engage in coordinated action. In Somers's words: "[T]he greater solidarity and autonomy of villages in the pastoral areas were institutional preconditions for their greater capacity for association and participation and hence their ability to appropriate and convert regulatory laws into citizenship rights."[88] As a result, the claims of the working class in pastoral communities, on Somers's argument, became cast in the language of law, and particularly of rights associated with English citizenship.

Thus, interpreting Somers's argument in light of the points developed thus far, we can conclude that the residents of pastoral communities developed participatory institutions that allowed them to deploy collective sanctions against the powerful. Because they could do so, they could in fact (strategically) uphold the rule of law in support of their claims to equal status, and they began to understand (normatively) the law as expressing those claims. The strategic capacity to use the law to demand reasons from the powerful, that is, allowed the working class to see the normative power of the ideal of equal law.

From that further period in the development of the English rule of law, we can see that the strategic and the normative faces of the rule of law and its relationship to equality are interdependent and bidirectional. The strategic capacity to use law to call the powerful to account can develop the normative ideal of equality under law; as the next chapter will argue, the normative ideal of equality underlying the rule of law can also facilitate the strategic capacity to make use of it.

Chapter 8

The logic of commitment

It is now time to weave the themes of this book together into a unified account of the relationship between the rule of law and the ideal of equality. This chapter will not present new evidence (except insofar as the results from the computer simulation reported at the end count as such), but will focus on synthesis and extension. The goal is to generate relatively bold claims about how the rule of law works in the world – claims that, strictly speaking, go beyond what is fully substantiated by the evidence and analysis offered so far, but are suggested by them; that can be explored and tested by future researchers; and that, if true, can guide policy makers in making the world a more lawful and more equal place. (The next chapter draws out some preliminary empirical and policy implications of the account of this book.)

First, let us define an analytic ontology. This book thus far has made three kinds of claims about the rule of law: conceptual/normative, strategic, and empirical.

A conceptual/normative claim is about what the rule of law is – that is, about the necessary or sufficient criteria for it to be the case that a state satisfies (to some given degree) the rule of law. I combine conceptual and normative claims because, as the rule of law is supposed to be normatively valuable, to say that a state meets the classification criteria to satisfy the rule of law to some degree is also to say that the state is, ceteris paribus, more morally valuable than it otherwise would be to a similar degree. Claims about what follows from the rule of law can be redescribed as necessary conditions for the rule of law, and for that reason, fall into this category; for example, the claim that "the rule of law makes people more equal" (in the specified respects) entails that an improvement in equality is a necessary condition for the rule of law.

A strategic claim about the rule of law is about the behavioral incentives the rule of law tends to generate, and about the social facts that tend to generate incentives to behave in accordance with the normative prescriptions of the rule of law. For example, the claim that "the sorts of political and legal institutions that tend to enable states to establish the rule of law also tend to enable officials to credibly commit to punishing people for doing things they don't like" (Chapter 4) is a strategic claim. The strategic claims ought to be compatible with the normative claims: if we claim that the rule of law instantiates some normative value, then we would be embarrassed if it also gave people in rule of law states an incentive to undermine that value.

Finally, an empirical claim is what we would expect one to be: a claim about what we tend to observe or expect to observe about the rule of law in real states. Strategic claims obviously generate testable empirical claims, but so do normative/conceptual claims: as I have argued elsewhere, our account of what the rule of law is ought to respond to the cases of the rule of law we observe in the real world.[1] For the same reasons, empirical observations generate normative/conceptual claims, and also, of course, suggest strategic claims.

As a whole, this book has defended three key claims, which we may call "the equality claim," "the institutional independence claim," and "the coordination claim"; respectively, they are that the rule of law constitutes as well as promotes an important kind of equal status among the subjects of that law, and between ordinary subjects of law and those with official roles; that the rule of law is independent of particular kinds of formal institutions (which I have called "practices"), such as jury trials, written constitutions, nominally independent judiciaries, and the like; and that the rule of law both conceptually incorporates and practically requires widespread coordinated action to hold the powerful to account – requirements that are built into the concept of the rule of law and are both normatively valuable and practically useful for facilitating that coordination.

Thus, in Chapters 1 through 4, I argued for conceptual/normative reasons that the rule of law is about equality, commitment, and constraint of officials, and that it does not require any particular institutional form of achieving those ends. Chapters 5 through 7 drew out these claims empirically, by investigating Britain and Athens, both of which can be understood consistently with the egalitarian interpretation of the rule of law, and both of which lack many of the institutional structures with which, in contemporary discourse, we associate it.

Chapters 4 and 6 began the work of building strategic claims about the rule of law. In them, I argued that the rule of law is a general-purpose technology for coordinating to control the powerful, and that the rule of law can be established and maintained in a community if there is a widespread commitment to it among those of the population with enough (political, military, economic) power to uphold the law.[2] In this chapter, I will begin by drawing out that thesis about commitment to show that this suggests strategic defenses of the key claims. The rule of law should tend to be more sustainable over the long term when the law is more equal, which is to say (equivalently) that the weak version of the rule of law and less general versions of the strong version are less stable than strong instantiations of generality. Moreover, what matters is commitment, and that commitment is achievable when law is equal under a wide array of concrete political and legal institutions.

Next, this chapter examines the implications of those strategic claims for the relationship between the rule of law and democracy. Finally, it subjects them to the scrutiny of a complex computer simulation, to confirm that the strategic intuitions play out iteratively as expected.

I THE RULE OF LAW'S TELEOLOGY OF EQUALITY?

Commitment is a double-edged sword. Because citizens cannot abandon the legal system when the law they have proves inconvenient without undermining their ability to rely on one another for coordinated enforcement when the law serves their interests (Chapter 6), law that is against the interests of a given group of citizens can persist through their own collective enforcement, at least to the extent that the legal system as a whole is sufficiently congruent with their interests that they will be willing to enforce it.

This is not all bad. Under some plausible conditions, particularly, where preference intensities over particular laws vary between interest groups in the community, this dynamic supports political compromise: interest groups will be able to uphold the provisions that are most important to them and only slightly disliked by the rest of the citizen body, in exchange for similar concessions made by other groups. This, in turn, is how, as many scholars say, constitutionalism lowers the stakes of day-to-day politics:[3] by entrenching such provisions, and hence insulating them from the political process, constitutionalism only together with the rule of law (i.e., only when such provisions are actually obeyed) can effectively take the most important issues to some members of the community off the table, and hence support the commitment of those with intense preferences to the political community.

This same dynamic also contributes to the way that the rule of law may undermine citizens' liberty. This is an extension of the point about credible commitment in Chapter 4. An official who wants to externalize enforcement of her commands in order to credibly commit to having them obeyed has to find a source of power greater than those commands in order to insulate the enforcer from the costs of enforcement. Louis might create as many de jure independent judges as he likes, but if he retains the practical power to command the judges to refrain from expensively enforcing his orders, the judges will not be independent in fact. Accordingly, in order for the rule of law to support credible commitment of officials, there again must be a critical mass in the community of those who have the will and enough power to insist that the law be obeyed over the short-term wishes of officials. But if there is, citizens may be complicit in the undermining of their own liberty.

Of course, there's nothing surprising in this: even in Athens, we saw that the democrats necessarily restricted their liberty to ignore the amnesty in order to achieve their longer-term ends; one might debate whether this counts as a restriction on liberty as a whole.[4] However, in nondemocratic contexts, where the law is more or less in the interests of the citizen body as a whole (or those who hold power within it), this can genuinely restrict their liberty, to the extent citizens have the ability to coordinate to uphold the law as it is but do not have the ability to coordinate to impose substantive legal change on the ruler (i.e., because of conflicting interests), but prefer living under a less-than-optimal legal system to a state without the rule of law. This is essentially Hobbes's claim about the state of nature, but reframed in dynamic rather than static terms, and in terms of tyranny rather than anarchy: the members of a political community may offer continuing support to the institutions (like independent judges) that preserve their ruler's laws, including those laws they don't like, just in order to achieve the benefits of a legal order that is more or less compatible with their interests overall – and, in particular, to protect themselves from the hubris and terror that would come to them if the legal system collapsed without the collapse of the ruler, such that they could no longer collectively resist illegal force from that ruler. This is also the implicit bargain of the Magna Carta: by constraining the Crown's use of force to law, those who rebelled also built the groundwork for institutions facilitating royal attempts to regulate them by law.[5]

There is an internal limitation on this mode of restricting liberty, however: the rule of law has to be basically in the interests of those who are called upon to enforce it. Obviously, the nobility in 1215 would not have wanted to hold the Crown to the law if the law were radically against their interests: the law can be so bad that the relevant public prefers the unbounded but inefficient and ineffective depredations of a ruler, where those depredations are limited by the inability to credibly commit to costly enforcement, to the efficient and effective enforcement of a tyrannical law.

Note: "the nobility." Those who are called upon to enforce the rule of law need not be the masses – it might be that, for example, an elite, a bourgeoisie, or a nobility can call upon sufficient power to constrain top-level rulers and intermediate officials to respect the rule of law with respect to themselves, even as those below them in the hierarchy are ruthlessly oppressed. Before the abolition of slavery, continuing (albeit less so) through Jim Crow, and to some extent still today (as will be discussed in the Conclusion to this volume), the same can be said about race in the United States: the rule of law for whites only. Similarly, in Athens, in order for the rule of law to be sustained, the law had to be general with respect to citizen males, because citizen males had the power (ultimately, the wealth, arms, and coordination capacity) to force elites and magistrates to comply with the law. Women, slaves, and metics were not needed to enforce the law, and did not have the power to insist on legal rights for themselves. Thus, Athenian success in maintaining regularity and publicity went along with equal legal rights for the lowest socioeconomic citizen classes, but not women, metics, or slaves.

We can see this as a (limited) teleology of equality. Law that is not minimally consistent with the interests of those who are needed to enforce it against the powerful is unlikely to survive, because those people will have little incentive to enforce it. This suggests that we should expect to observe a greater incidence of law that treats them as equals at least to the limited extent of not disregarding their interests altogether, particularly in states whose legal systems have been stable for an extended period of time.

This is an empirically tractable functionalist account of the distribution of legal rights in states with constrained officials and elites, but one that does not depend on any kind of conscious pursuit of the rule of law. It so happened that Athens managed to maintain the rule of law, because the law was such that it was in the interests of the great mass of male citizens to uphold it. Had it not been in their interests, it would have been much less likely to have been successfully maintained. But that is not to say that equal law was enacted in order to recruit their support for the rule of law – it might be that equal law was enacted for any number of other reasons, including, inter alia, as a response to the need for expanded military participation, as a consequence of the increasing dispersal of wealth in a commercial society, or simply by revolutionary action. I do not propose to give an account of how societies achieve generality in this chapter, just how, if societies manage to do so, it helps them maintain regularity and publicity.

Because the scope of necessary generality depends on the distribution of power within a state, we should see more law that takes into consideration the interests of the most powerful (where how powerful one is tracks both one's ability to sanction officials and what one might expect to get from the resources one controls in the absence of a functioning rule of law, and hence how cheap it is to abandon support for the legal system); truly general legal systems will be advantageous only in societies in which the dispersion of power is general. But this shouldn't be surprising. The egalitarian advantage of the rule of law is not that it helps the powerless classes of society defy political reality, but that it allows classes with dispersed power to more easily coordinate to defend that power – it helps preserve preexisting mass power, but does not create it ex nihilo.

Moreover, the claim that nongeneral rule of law states are less stable does not come with a discrete time limit on it. A state might hobble on for centuries with radically nongeneral law if those who have the power to constrain rulers are never actually called upon to do so. This might happen if, for example, a state is ruled by an Olson-esque stationary bandit,[6] who is rational and does not heavily discount the future, and hence voluntarily sets out a system of prospective law and complies with it, and sees to it that subordinate officials comply with it, in order to maximize the ruler benefits from stable and prospective law, such as improved economic productivity, leading to more extractable rents. Ordinarily, a ruler who wants more rents must create alternate sources of power that can actually constrain her to resist the temptation to break her own rules. But suppose the temptation never arises. Then such laws might be on the whole disadvantageous to those with the power to constrain the ruler, such that if the ruler chooses to disregard the law, those people won't do anything to stop her, and the rule of law fails – but the ruler may never choose to disregard the law.

Looking at such a state one way, it lacks even the weak version of the rule of law: recall that the principle of regularity requires that officials be *constrained*, and here, the ruler is not constrained: she can abandon the rule of law any time she wants. However, we can also understand the state to satisfy the rule of law, at least partially, by virtue of the fact that subordinate officials are constrained; they're just constrained by other officials: namely, the top-level officials in the form of the ruler or ruling coalition. And these subordinate officials are constrained for exactly the same reason that all officials, including rulers, are constrained in more just rule of law states: namely, in view of the fact that the legal system as a whole is in the interest of the one(s) doing the constraining. It just so happens that the one doing the constraining here is the ruler.

This strategic intuition leads to others about when the rule of law can be expected to fail. Two kinds of exogenous shocks can undermine a system of collective enforcement. First, the group of people needed to enforce the rule of law might change (call this a *power-shifting shock*). For example, political, economic, and/or military power might shift from a hereditary aristocracy to a nouveau bourgeoisie. Officials who perceive this might ignore the law, in view of the fact that the aristocracy no longer has the power to enforce it, and the bourgeoisie have no interest in doing so. The end result of this kind of shock might be a dictatorship; a revolution by the bourgeoisie, who impose a new legal system that is more consistent with their interests; or a quiet preemptive updating of the legal system to accommodate the interests of the bourgeoisie – where selection between these results depends on other factors, like the extent to which the bourgeoisie have the power to act collectively.

Another power-shifting shock is a raw expansion in the set of people necessary to enforce the law. When rulers or other officials become more powerful – more able to inflict sanctions, and to resist sanctions inflicted on them – relative to the group of nonofficials that previously upheld the law, this may actually create pressure for greater generality (or dictatorship) in view of the fact that midlevel elites no longer have the power alone to resist them. This may happen, for example, where social, economic, or technological change facilitates the centralization of power, where rulers acquire new resources to make side payments (bribes) undermining coalitions within the population (as may be one of the causes of the infamous resource curse[7]), or when foreign hegemons prop up rulers for their own purposes (as happened all over the world during the Cold War).

Thus, imagine a feudal state that is more or less consistent with the rule of law with respect to midlevel nobility, in view of the fact that those nobles control the military force on which the king depends.[8] A bourgeois class exists, but because the landed nobles are powerful enough to enforce the monarch's compliance with the law on their own, and the bourgeois are not sufficiently powerful to generate a demand for law that takes their interests into account or to resist either crown or nobles, the law is general only with respect to the nobility. Now the monarch develops the administrative technology necessary to centralize military power; all of a sudden, the nobles do not have the power to resist her alone. The rule of law with respect to nobles only has become unstable. Should the monarch start violating it (and she might not), it might tip into a more general rule of law if the nobles are capable of recruiting the bourgeoisie to backstop their coordinated resistance to her (and if their combined forces are sufficiently powerful to do so), or it might tip into dictatorship if they are not.[9]

Still another kind of exogenous shock: the law might cease to be in the (perceived) interests of those who had previously coordinated to enforce it, whether because of changes in the law or changes in circumstances. A state facing an existential threat, for example, may throw out the rule of law because, based on the discount rate of those who are to enforce it, the net present value of the rule of law is less than that of taking lawless actions to, for example, squelch internal opposition. This is part of the story of Athens, in which the people, terrified by short-term oligarchic threats in the context of the war with Sparta, (mistakenly) saw the danger of conspiracies represented by the mutilation of the Herms and profanation of the Mysteries as greater than the danger of losing the legal system. This is also at least arguably part of the story of the contemporary American response to the acts of September 11, 2001, including the Patriot Act, no-fly lists, extrajudicial detentions and assassinations, and the like.

Because of all these potential sources of shocks, I claim that the rule of law's teleology of equality will have an expansive trend to it (albeit over time horizons that have the potential to be very long). All else being equal, where group A is a proper subset of group B, and assuming groups A and B are equally costly to coordinate, group B will have the capacity to resist those who would undermine its legal entitlements under a strictly broader set of strategic circumstances than group A. Ergo, in an environment characterized by shocks to legal system stability, we would expect law in the interest of broader groups of people to persist longer than law in the interest of narrower groups.

Of course, in ordinary coordination problems, groups A and B will not be equally costly to coordinate. However, law and collective trust are technologies of coordination that, by supplying a common set of norms and a common set of beliefs, are likely to reduce the coordination costs of larger groups once free-rider problems are eliminated, as in Chapter 6. We would still expect coordination to be less likely in large groups than in small groups, simply because at least some of the benefits of law are fixed-sum, such that the smaller groups would have more individual incentives based on capturing a larger share of the benefits.[10] Nonetheless, because some legal rules are essentially indivisible (I suffer no direct loss to my immunity from being arbitrarily beaten by the police if my neighbor gains the same), legal rules should trend in a more egalitarian direction than other kinds of goods that political states distribute. We ought to observe, for example, minimally egalitarian law more frequently than we observe egalitarian distribution of wealth.

There is also a potential trade-off with respect to preference intensity – that is, between the extent to which all in the community view the law as a little in their interests, as opposed to some viewing the law as greatly in their interests. Suppose a state may choose between a more or less egalitarian legal system that all, or almost all, subjects perceive as better than anarchy or dictatorship, and a hierarchical legal system in which the elites extract resources from the lower class, thus providing truly massive benefits to the elites. And suppose both possible legal systems are stable in the sense that the elites, as well as the citizen body as a whole, have the capacity to coordinate to defend the legal system. Against some shocks, the hierarchical legal system may be more robust: if a shock to the egalitarian system makes it just a little bit less in the perceived short-term interests of all, it might fall, because citizens don't care about it that much; a shock of similar magnitude to the hierarchical system might not damage the commitment of elites to defend it, because it provides them such great benefits that they will continue to see it as to their advantage even under slightly inferior conditions. However, this trade-off only goes so far: if a sufficiently strong shock arises such that the elites no longer have the power to defend their hierarchical legal system, all the preference intensity in the world will not save it.

What this all suggests is that the rule of law has a teleology of equality in a very limited, ceteris paribus kind of sense. However, a limited ceteris paribus kind of sense is still worth exploring, and can ground empirical predictions, like this one: legal systems that satisfy the strong version of the rule of law – in the limited sense of being minimally compatible with the interests of a larger share of the population – will be more robust against power-shifting shocks; for that reason, we should observe them more often than we observe legal systems that satisfy the weak but not the strong version of the rule of law, especially in states that have had stable legal orders for an extended period of time.

This provides all of the basics of an evolutionary account of the rule of law: a source of variation (the day-to-day struggles of politics and the diversity of social, economic, and military interests within and across states, leading to a wide variety of legal systems in the world); a source of replication (the year-to-year continuation of a legal system within a particular state); and a source of selection (the risk of exogenous shocks undermining less stable legal systems).[11] We can rephrase the claim and prediction of this section in evolutionary terms: the claim is that the compatibility of a legal system, as a whole, with the interests of more people is an advantageous trait, and the prediction is that we should see that trait grow within the population of legal systems over a sufficiently long time. Thus, the teleology of equality.[12]

But the point is not yet complete. This section has argued that the weak version of the rule of law, standing on its own, is unstable – that the rule of law will be more likely to persist in a state if the law in that state is general in the sense that it is compatible, as a whole, with the interests of more of the subject population. But that isn't the same generality that was elucidated in Chapters 2 and 3: generality in the sense that matters requires the law to be *publicly* in the interest of all in the community, in that it expresses their equality (or at least does not express their inferiority). This is a more demanding standard: ordinarily, a legal system that is worse for some members of the community than anarchy or tyranny will express disregard for those people as inferiors, since it totally disregards their interests, but not all legal systems that are better than anarchy or tyranny will be consistent with the equal status of all. The lower classes sometimes might be motivated to defend legal systems that treat them unjustly, just because the alternatives are so much worse. However, I now turn to a defense of the claim that it is real generality, not just Hobbesian better-than-anarchy for all, that is the teleology of the rule of law.

A *Commitment, full generality, and the internal point of view*

The most stable, commitment-worthy law is not merely coincidentally equal, or equal in the sense that it is more or less compatible with the interests of the class of people on whose commitment to the law the rule of law depends. Rather, the most stable law is *publicly* equal: it incorporates appeals to public reasons and thus is genuinely general.

In strategic terms, the reason for this turns on a problem of equilibrium selection. Chapter 6 showed that the rule of law can persist by collective enforcement in a society so long as enough of the people who are needed to enforce it think it's in their overall interests. But there are other equilibriums as well (technically, an infinite number), including equilibriums in which collective enforcement never gets off the ground. And getting into a collective enforcement equilibrium requires some up-front investment: subjects must create the signaling mechanism that allows them to enforce the law against officials (except when Louis has done so, per Chapter 4), and they must trust one another in the first round (or for a significant period of time in order to develop a reliable pattern of collective enforcement). This investment will be worth making only if subjects actually have good reason in advance to think that the law is compatible with the interests of others.

One way this might happen is if the state is a genuine democracy, in which those whose support is necessary to uphold the law are also those who are counted as citizens and the democratic institutions work properly (are not captured or corrupted, etc.). Thus, it may have been easier for the Athenians to initially build support for their legal system, and restore it after the oligarchies, just because the democratic laws were known to be in the interests of the masses.

Toward the end of this chapter, I will explore this connection between democracy and the rule of law in more detail. However, recall from Chapter 4 the argument that rulers have incentives to institute (the weak version of) the rule of law in nondemocratic states. In view of the claim (defended in Chapter 1) that the rule of law does not conceptually require democracy, as well as the claim that nondemocratic rulers have reason to institute it, we should not be surprised if we observe that not all (weak-version) rule of law states are democracies.[13] Also, of course, not all democracies function properly. Moreover, even in a well-functioning democracy, social choice theorists have shown that aggregative methods can fail to produce results preferred by the populace.[14] Citizens who know this may have good reason to suspect that not everyone sees even democratically enacted laws as consistent with their basic interests. Hence, in order to get into the rule of law equilibrium of Chapter 6 (other than by dumb luck), they need some way to come to an initial belief that the laws are in the interests of their fellows.

One way to achieve this, both in democracies and in nondemocracies, is for the law to be publicly justified or justifiable by reference to a legitimate conception of the collective good or the individual interests of all in society. If the legal system as a whole visibly takes the interests of all into account, that gives each in the community some substantial reason to think that it will be more or less compatible with the interests of her fellows; if it visibly disregards the interests or equal status of some people, that gives those in the community very strong reason to suppose that those whom it disregards will not be able to see it as in their interests. These evaluations will, in turn, influence whether it is rational for them to make the initial investments necessary to build trust in a legal system.

The foregoing discussion indicates the importance, at least at the beginning of a legal system, of laws that are truly general. But their importance does not end there. The extent to which subjects perceive the law to be in their interest is not a mere calculation of hedonistic self-interest. Someone who is insulted by the law, who is treated as a second-class citizen, can come to reject the legal system that allows such insults even if, as a whole, it nonetheless overall protects the person's basic interests and is better than the likely alternatives. Consider, for example, the way that the revolutionary wing of the civil rights movement, such as Malcolm X and the Black Panthers, stood in opposition to the legal system, rejecting its benefits and proposing radical resistance to it.[15] From a 1963 speech by Malcolm X:

> Jesus two thousand years ago looked down the wheel of time and saw your and my plight here today and he knew the tricky high court, Supreme Court, desegregation decisions would only lull you into a deeper sleep, and the tricky promises of the hypocritical politicians on civil rights legislation would only be designed to advance you and me from ancient slavery to modern slavery.[16]

Those are the words of an activist who has been driven by profoundly unequal treatment to abandon the law and reject even the progress and benefits offered by the legal system. And who could blame him? Yet it's unlikely that the revolutionary wing would have ever had a realistic chance to *win* the war some of their members hoped to spark, or would have prospered in the collapse of the legal system (if nothing else, white racists had the advantage of numbers). And it's implausible to think that the members of the revolutionary wing of the civil rights movement saw themselves as foils for the more peaceful side (even if some might have, and even if after the fact we can see that Malcolm was instrumental in the success of Martin). The revolutionary wing of the civil rights movement cannot be understood as rational without supposing that their members did not pursue self-interest in the narrow sense, but acted in accordance with their righteous rage against a legal (and social, and political) system that expressed their inferiority.

The same motivations can help us understand the 1992 Los Angeles riots, following the acquittal of the police who savagely beat Rodney King. The refusal of jurors to convict the police for beating a black man must have led at least some of the rioters to, however temporarily, cast aside their regard for the law, even though it's hard to understand a narrowly self-interested motivation for rioting under such circumstances, and there is no obvious reason to think that they were playing their role in a Chapter 6-style coordinated sanctioning equilibrium that ordinarily kept the police in line. Rather, we should understand the riots as a response to expressive, not pragmatic, motivations: at least some of the rioters felt that the legal system treated them with contempt, and so cast aside their allegiance to it.

As I finalize a draft of this chapter at the end of April 2015, the country seems to have been flung back into the 1960s. Last fall, the police killing of a black man sparked riots in Ferguson, Missouri, and just last week, the killing of a black man in Baltimore, Maryland, has sparked riots that are occurring today. Ta-Nehisi Coates, a prominent black journalist who has become a major establishment-located voice of the African-American left, just captured the heart of the matter:

> When nonviolence is preached as an attempt to evade the repercussions of political brutality, it betrays itself. When nonviolence begins halfway through the war with the aggressor calling time-out, it exposes itself as a ruse. When nonviolence is preached by the representatives of the state, while the state doles out heaps of violence to its citizens, it reveals itself to be a con. And none of this can mean that rioting or violence is "correct" or "wise" any more than a forest fire can be "correct" or "wise." Wisdom isn't the point, tonight. Disrespect is. In this case disrespect for the hollow law and failed order that so regularly disrespects the rioters themselves.[17]

Half a century apart, Coates and Malcolm X make the same point: when the law presents itself as "hollow" and "disrespects" those whom it is supposed to protect, the disrespected turn around and direct that disrespect right back at law. The physical manifestations of righteous anger in Ferguson and in Baltimore are poorly understood as some kind of calculating self-interest. Rather, they are evidence that people deeply value being publicly treated as equals by the legal system, and respond to that kind of equality – or to its absence – with action.

I will discuss the problems of racist policing in the United States at the close of this book. For now, let us imagine a more just society. Once we move beyond the narrow motivations of self-interest, we get into what H. L. A. Hart called the internal point of view.[18] Subjects can accept or reject the law in view of its expressive characteristics for its own sake rather than for reasons of brute instrumental rationality. Subjects who take the internal point of view on the law because they think that it as a whole expresses their equal status in the community, and instantiates values that they respect, need not engage in a calculus of self-interest each time they are called upon to support the law against disobedient officials; rather, they do so reflexively, based on the importance of the law to a political community they value, and that values them. Under those circumstances, the problem of Chapter 6 dissolves: a community has a legal culture in which subjects trust one another implicitly to support the law, in virtue of their long-run relationship of mutual regard with it.

Accordingly, we should expect genuinely general law to be more robust to the kinds of shocks described in the previous section than law that is merely compatible with the interests of all, given their alternatives (which might be lousy). "You should defend this legal system, which puts me in a hierarchically superior position to you and allows me to treat you badly, because I'm (however slightly) less likely to kill you or take your stuff in that system than in a Hobbesian anarchy" is convincing for only so long.

Moreover, the rule of law's teleology of equality may be more than a mere evolutionary claim. For it may be that the forms of law themselves create pressure to equality. Recall that in Chapter 3 I argued that the weak and the strong versions of the rule of law are rooted in the same abstract ideal, that of the demand that reasons be given for the use of power. As discussed in that chapter, others have seen this connection, prominently including the Levellers of the seventeenth century. Consequently, states that merely achieve the weak version of the rule of law may find their legal caste structure undermined by the persuasive power of the law to convince those within it – both those privileged participants in the system who take the internal point of view on it and those who are thrust into subordinate places in that system – that reasons must be given for the subordination of its lower-caste members. This is why Martin Luther King Jr. could decry Jim Crow, in the letter from the Birmingham jail, in terms of his respect for law.

E. P. Thompson (1975, 263), perhaps the scholar with the greatest insight into the function of the rule of law, explained all of this first. He noted, "In the case of an ancient historical formation like the law, a discipline which requires years of exacting study to master, there will always be some men who actively believe in their own procedures and in the logic of justice." In other words, carrying out the cognitive operation distinctively associated with (even unjust instantiations of) the weak version of the rule of law – the giving of reasons for the use of public power – has the potential to train participants to carry out that operation about the content of the laws themselves. This, in turn, has the potential to destabilize laws that are not justifiable by reasons that can be given to others.

II COMMITMENT AND INSTITUTIONS

Return, for a moment, to institutions. It's often supposed that particular kinds of "institutions" – by which those who do the supposing tend to mean concrete political arrangements, most commonly independent courts, but others are raised as well – are necessary for, or even constitutive of, the rule of law.[19] In Chapter 1, I disagreed, and offered that disagreement as a conceptual claim: the rule of law does not require, for example, judicial review, the separation of powers, or the jury trial. However, that claim might be subject to question on grounds of factual robustness: if, practically speaking, every stable rule of law state can be expected to have them for strategic reasons, then perhaps we ought to say that they're part of the concept of the rule of law as well.

To the contrary, I claim that there are institutional prerequisites for the long-term sustainability of the rule of law, but those prerequisites are malleable and contingent. As I have been arguing, the key difference between a successful rule of law state and one that does not succeed is the extent to which the people whose coordinated resistance is necessary to hold officials and powerful elites to the law are committed to doing so; the key determinant of that commitment ought to be the extent to which the law publicly takes their interests into account – that is, treats them as equals.

If this is true, it suggests that any institutional prerequisites will depend on what the people in a given state happen to need to support their coordination, which will depend on that state's history, distribution of power, existing level of trust, demographics, and other distinctive characteristics; moreover, multiple institutional arrangements may be sufficient to support coordination in a given state. In Athens, the mass jury was a powerful tool of coordination, because it allowed the citizen body to simultaneously signal their commitment to the rule of law (rebuilding the trust lost in the fifth century) and resolve legal disagreement. In the United States, with a longer tradition of reliable control of officials by law, such a signaling function is less urgent, and an elite judiciary does more or less fine in coordinating public opposition to illegal acts. In Britain, as described in Chapter 7, it has been supposed, plausibly, by scholars such as Dicey that the parliamentary system backstopped by constitutional custom is sufficient to leverage general acceptance of these constitutional norms into the constraint of the powerful.

Citizens who are committed to the rule of law will have a strong incentive to bring about the institutions that allow them to carry out their commitment. Thus, for example, we should expect that states whose citizens are committed to the law will create independent courts, juries, and the like, where none have previously existed.

Moreover, we should expect institutions like judicial independence and the jury trial to follow, not precede, a widespread commitment to law, for they presuppose such a commitment and something like a rudimentary version of regularity already existing in the community. To see this, consider the problem of *ineffectual courts*. A state might have judicial independence written in its constitution; it might be that judges are in fact independent from other officials, such that no official pressures judges to make any particular ruling. However, if that state does not satisfy the principle of regularity, there's no reason to believe that officials will obey the rulings of the independent judges. The same goes for juries or any of the other institutions that are supposed to support the rule of law. To the extent those institutions are themselves legal institutions – that is, institutions whose functions are specified by law – they can be effective only if there is a preexisting commitment to enforce their legal role, to make sure the court or the jury is obeyed, and if that preexisting commitment is cashed out in some baseline level of coordinated community action.[20]

In short, to say that "the rule of law will exist when there are independent judges" is a tautology. There cannot be genuinely independent judges (where the concept of "judges" includes an actual function in successfully adjudicating legal disputes and having their rulings obeyed) unless there is already the rule of law.

Consider for a moment how this argument applies to the American case. It looks like the US Supreme Court is enforcing its judgments directly against officials. However, I have argued elsewhere that such enforcement is effective only to the extent there is widespread knowledge that its rulings are backed by the prospect of political or other sanctions from ordinary citizens, who are committed to the rule of law.[21]

On such an account, the Court functions like a signaling device: within some constraints, when elected officials break the law, it says so; it having said so, the elected officials cease their illegal conduct because, if they do not do so, the people (to the extent they are part of the bargain) will be able to coordinate to punish them at the polls or elsewhere. What the Court provides is *information*: it resolves uncertainty about whether elected officials have broken the law – or, to be more accurate, it resolves each individual citizen's uncertainty about whether each other individual citizen will see the politicians as having broken the law, and thus allows them to depend on one another to punish the politicians in question, to the extent they trust one another to be committed to upholding the law. Because politicians know (or intuit) that the Court serves this function, they do not disobey it.

Suppose this account of how the US Supreme Court works is right. That explains why nobody had to visibly force politicians using sanctions to comply with *Roe v. Wade*: disobedience is off the equilibrium path. And with this conception of the role of a constitutional court in a stable rule of law state, we can see a number of features that are not required. First, such a court need not be composed of elite judges. A mass court such as the Athenian jury will do just fine. The court need not be independent of elections – many elected state judges in the United States also serve their signaling function just fine, and routinely strike down acts of other elected branches of government, or of the people themselves.[22] Nor need it have the formal power to strike down legislation: courts operating under the "new commonwealth model," which make nonbinding declarations of unconstitutionality, have been sometimes successful in motivating "voluntary" legislative action.[23] The previous chapter gave the British antiterrorism example.

More strikingly, on this model, the "court" need not be a court at all, and need not even be in government. Any independent sender whose signals the people come to trust can be used. For example, in a country with no independent judges, a particularly virtuous (or seen to be virtuous) newspaper editor could, hypothetically, serve this role, if a consensus builds such that if the editor condemns a government policy as unconstitutional, the people will punish the politicians if it isn't retracted. In principle, even decentralized information cascades – in which a few people signal that they see the government action as illegal, leading those who trust them to send such a signal themselves, and so forth – could do the trick, at least in a society in which the cost of sending such a signal is relatively low for the initial sender (i.e., not one in which dissidents are promptly shot).[24]

Nor need the court (or editorialist, or angry citizen) be enforcing a determinate written document. A consensus set of social norms will do; if those norms are accepted as a set of constraints on government and reliably enforced, there's nothing (at least for a legal positivist) preventing us from counting them as constitutional law, and, in countries like the United Kingdom, we already do so. In principle, we need not even have that much. Suppose our newspaper editor is believed to be *really* virtuous, such that the public at large trusts the editor's judgment about the appropriate constraints on official action; the public could just coordinate on that judgment without any preexisting law at all.

Of course, this can go only so far. Specific, preexisting, and public laws (written or otherwise) must exist to authorize direct official coercion over citizens, or the principles of regularity and publicity go out the window. But there's no particular reason that additional side constraints on official power, beyond those required by the weak version of the rule of law, can't be instantiated by the judgment of any old person. For example, our hypothetical virtuous newspaper editor might think that for particularly high taxes the legislature ought to have a supermajority; if the editor invalidates laws on that ground and the people successfully enforce it, nothing in the rule of law is offended. The point is that once we accept that independent judges work by sending a common knowledge signal of illegality that the public can coordinate around, we can see a variety of ways by which such signals can be sent. No particular method is necessary, and none will work absent public commitment.

That being said, institutions like judicial review will doubtless make it cheaper and easier to enforce the law against officials. Coordination is costly, and as the subgroups of the population of a state who must be coordinated become relatively mass rather than relatively elite (due to the rule of law's teleology of equality), we can expect these costs to become more meaningful. Signal senders – like courts – that have the credibility of a public office, formal protections against retaliation (which themselves can be enforced by coordinated judgments), and the focal point advantage of being picked out as the designated signal senders by law can be expected to facilitate mass coordination more cheaply than, say, newspaper editors.

For this reason, we would expect to see more helper institutions like independent formal judiciaries in states where the law is more general. The logic of this empirical prediction is as follows: where the distribution of power in a state requires mass coordination rather than merely midlevel elite coordination to enforce the law against top-level officials and elites, we would expect the law to be more general; only in such states will the masses have the *incentive* to coordinate (the teleology of equality). In such states, we would also expect to see helper institutions, for with such institutions the masses will be more likely to have the *ability* to coordinate. However, this empirical correlation, if it exists, will not imply that the rule of law can be created merely by installing independent judiciaries, for the means without the incentive will not be used (and, as the next chapter will discuss, the institutions installed must be locally legitimate). Similarly, we should see more helper institutions in more populous states, and more of such institutions in more politically, religiously, and culturally diverse states where citizens cannot so easily guess one another's views about the law.

All of this suggests that particular institutions, like independent judiciaries and judicial review, are good signs of the rule of law: they are more likely to exist in rule of law states, because in such states they may help preserve the rule of law, and the rule of law, in turn, is the precondition for their effective exercise of power. Hence, they can be used to proxy it in empirical measures. But they are imperfect proxies of the rule of law, and rule of law states can and have existed without them. In the next chapter, I discuss the implications of this idea for empirical measurement of the rule of law.

A *Democracy and the rule of law*

Mass coordination need not be the sole province of democracies. Consider the Ancien Régime *parlements*, which, in the buildup to the French Revolution, refused to enter a number of royal decrees, particularly relating to taxation, on the grounds that they were illegal; the royal response – exiling the *parlements* – led to copious public unrest that helped bring on the revolution.[25] And as I have argued, the rule of law can (conceptually) exist in the absence of democracy.

Still, the teleology of equality gives us some reason to expect an empirical association between the rule of law and democracy, for two reasons. First, as noted, a state may build collective trust in the commitment of each citizen to contribute to collectively upholding the law by structuring its lawmaking process in such a way that the laws are maximally likely to be compatible with the basic interests of all; a democratic process may serve this function to the extent it disperses influence over the substantive content of the law more broadly than other legislative processes.[26]

Second, and more basically, one of the ways in which law can be general is that it provides for more general influence over the legislative process. While nondemocratic legislative processes can comply with the principle of generality in appropriate social contexts (for example, a devout religious community may locate legislative power in the clergy without thereby expressing the subordination of anyone else), such processes are less likely to be so compatible in heterogeneous communities. For that reason, democracy may not be necessary for the weak version of the rule of law, but, in most real-world societies, we ought to expect it to be necessary for full instantiations of the strong version.[27]

The relationship between the rule of law and democracy along the conceptual, strategic, and empirical dimensions is proving to be complex. Before exploring further, we must get clearer on this notion of "democracy." It is probably an essentially contested concept, but any conception of democracy worthy of the name will be an evaluative standard for the relationship between the cognitions (wills, beliefs, desires, attitudes, intentions) of ordinary (nonelite) people and political outcomes. Most conventionally, democratic theorists suppose that there must be some intentional causal relationship between the latter and the former: for a state to be a democracy, people must be able to operate the levers of their political machinery to bring about political outcomes, and the political outcomes must be the products of those operations.

In other work (currently in progress), I am arguing against this view, and in its place I aim to construct a heterodox view about the relationship between democracy, popular sovereignty, and after-the-fact endorsement; I cannot defend it here. (Also, the view may turn out to be indefensible.) For present purposes, it will do to distinguish between two democratic ideas: a demanding *agency idea*, according to which the masses of ordinary people have to have substantial effective control (in one way or another) over political outcomes, and a less demanding *approval idea*, according to which the masses of ordinary people have to be able to approve of the sort of political outcomes that their system tends to generate. We can designate systems that comply with each conception as agency-democracies and approval-democracies, respectively. As I have not yet given an account of approval-democracies, and agency-democracies represent the conventional view, I will limit the discussion here to the latter only.[28]

The weak version of the rule of law is likely to be strongly correlated with agency-democracies (if not, strictly speaking, required for it). If the masses are to exercise genuine control over political outcomes, they are likely to need sophisticated coordination tools in order to overcome the natural monopolies of political states – hierarchical control over military force, concentrated wealth, and the like – and reliably hold on to authority. For the reasons described in Chapter 6, public law is just such a tool. Moreover, if they use law as a coordination tool, then that law must actually exercise effective control over officials in order for the state to be properly characterized as a democracy. Otherwise, the agency conception necessarily cannot be satisfied: the people are trying to direct their political outcomes by writing these things called "laws," but the political outcomes, given by the actions of officials using the tools of the state, are not tracking those efforts.

Moreover, not only is the rule of law likely to facilitate democratic control over political outcomes, but the institutions that facilitate democratic control over political outcomes are, for the reasons given in Chapter 6, more likely to facilitate the rule of law. Consistent with this hypothesis, Law and Versteeg have found, based on a worldwide data set, that democracy (proxied by polity scores) is a better predictor of states complying with constitutional rights than whether judicial review is included in a state's constitution.[29] This is to be expected, once we consider that more democratic states are open to more popular participation in all kinds of institutions for governing the powerful, and hence are more likely to be able to generate consistent signals of public support for the law.

However, in a very homogeneous democracy, the mass might rule without the aid of law. Recall that this characterizes many classicists' accounts of Athens, such as that of Adriaan Lanni: the people controlled political outcomes by coordinating to enforce customs and norms, not (prospective, reliably enforced, etc.) laws, through their political and legal institutions. In Chapter 5, I argued that we can understand as law those norms that Lanni identified, and in that way understand Athens as a rule of law state.

But suppose I am wrong. Maybe Athens was a "tyrannical democracy" that controlled the open threats represented by the wealthy by generating its own against them; those who complained of sycophants who abused the jury system in order to expropriate the wealthy alleged just such a tyranny. In essence, the accusation was that the masses collectively maintained the political authority of their democracy through terror. Suppose (contrary to what I argued in Chapter 5) that they were right: the possibility by empirical example of a democracy without the rule of law will have been established – but an example will have also been given of its instability, for it was the failure of democratic legal self-control that contributed, I argued in Chapter 6, to the fifth-century collapse and taught the demos to recommit to the rule of law in order to take fratricidal conflict between mass and elite off the political table.

As a whole, it seems as though we do best to understand democracy as most compatible with intermediate to advanced stages of the development of the rule of law: if it is possible in the absence of the weak version of the rule of law, the combination is strategically plausible only in relatively homogeneous societies in which the masses can act without sophisticated coordination tools; even in such societies it may not be stable. Once they exist in relatively rudimentary versions, democracy and the strong version of the rule of law can be expected to grow together, for they refer to the same fundamental idea of a state that is publicly compatible with the legitimate interests of all, and thereby expresses the equality of all.[30]

III DIVERSITY, GENERALITY, AND DEMOCRACY

Because of its relative homogeneity, Athens is in part a poor model for modern rule of law democracies. Modern mass democracies tend to be characterized by varying degrees of religious, ethnic, cultural, and other forms of diversity, leading to groups who may experience their interests as distinct. At the same time, these democracies may also be characterized by distinct social and economic elites (who may or may not be dispersed among demographically dissimilar groups) who may have disparate power. Athens, by contrast, is often understood as having been much more homogeneous, and though the standard one-dimensional division into mass and elite is distorting and reductive, it is close enough that it helps us understand quite a lot about what actually happened.

A population may be demographically diverse in at least three relevant respects, which may combine. First, it may have a higher degree of dissimilarity, in that there are more different kinds of people (for some meaningful conception of "kind-ness") in the population, independent of the quantity of people in each demographic classification. Second, the population may be dispersed more evenly among those different kinds of people (i.e., a population with half its members in one group and half in another group is more diverse, in this sense, than a population with 90 percent of its members in one group and 10 percent in the other). Third, relevant kinds of power (particularly, for present purposes, the power to sanction officials and others with concentrated power) may be dispersed more evenly among those different kinds of people.

These divisions are relevant for the maintenance of generality as well as democracy. Even modeling, as we have been, a modern state as a small group of very powerful elites and a large mass that must act in concert in order to keep the elites in place, diversity among that mass may impair its ability to coordinate. For example, the divide-and-conquer tools of elites may be deployed to ally with some portions of the nonelite, undermining the capacity of the latter to coordinate.[31]

The dynamics of legal stability in the face of the interaction of those three types of diversity has the potential to be highly complex, especially when population and power come apart; we might not observe the same macro-level consequences in states with, for example, few groups and dispersed power versus many groups and concentrated power, and it is hard to see how purely analytic predictions can be made. Accordingly, in order to extend the strategic ideas previously developed about homogeneous rule of law states (and rule of law democracies) in this chapter and in Chapter 6 to more complex diverse states, we can lay down both this chapter's strategic intuition development and Chapter 6's game theory and pick up computer modeling instead.

IV SIMULATING LEGAL STABILITY

I have programmed a computer simulation to further explore the strategic dynamics of rule of law states. The goal of the simulation is to iterate and flesh out the strategic intuitions given by the claims above: assuming that the micro-level intuitions are right, what follows on the macro scale?[32] Thus, this simulation makes rough mathematical representations of micro-level claims like "People are more likely to resist officials when they trust that others will do so as well" and "Elites and officials might attempt to bribe people to undermine their participation in collective coordination mechanisms to resist the law," and then iterates those representations over a large number of interactions, and for a very large number of randomly set starting conditions, such as (mathematical representations of) the extent of preexisting legal equality, the distribution of power and heterogeneity of social groups, and the initial level of trust present in a society.[33]

A computational model allows high levels of complexity to be analyzed, in order to generate insights that may be unattainable through purely analytic methods and unavailable to direct real-world observation, though at the cost of sensitivity to initial modeling choices. It also allows exogenous shocks to be introduced, in the form of round-by-round stochastic variance applied to model parameters. What follows is not, however, the same as what researchers in social science usually describe as an "agent-based model." An agent-based model typically involves networked agents who interact with one another, often with very simple decision rules (to aid interpretability) and with emergent complex systemic outcomes.[34] By contrast, the model described next features agents with fairly complex and often stochastic decision rules, reflecting the multitude of cross-cutting incentives facing actors at the inflection points of a legal system, but with relatively minimal interaction patterns. The model is written in the R statistical programming language, and the full code is available online.[35]

The population consists of 1,000 ordinary citizens and 100 elites, where an elite represents a powerful government official or a wealthy and high-status private citizen. There is also a distribution of 10,000 units of (legal) goods across mass and elite, where these distributions represent the benefits to be had from law that is consistent with one's interests (maximally general law is represented by an identical allocation of goods to each citizen). There is also a distribution of 10,000 units of power across mass and elite, where each unit represents the ability to influence the outcome of a conflict in the event the elite attempt to break free from the power of coordinated sanctions.

In each round, elites determine whether or not to (a) allocate all of the goods to themselves; (b) offer some bribe (as a portion of the legal goods) to some portion of the mass group (defined by subgroups, which are assigned randomly; the elite may bribe subgroups only in their entirety) and then allocate all of the rest of the goods to themselves; or (c) retain the status quo. The elite group makes this decision by searching over the space of choices (including the space of possible bribes) and then choosing the option that maximizes the individual elite expected utility function $EU_e = (1 - \pi\mu - \sigma\pi\Sigma(\rho_j/\gamma_j))\alpha_e$, where $\mu \in [0,1]$ represents the share of the power held by all mass subgroups that have not been bribed; α_e represents the total amount the elites allocate to themselves/100 (i.e., the amount of legal goods to be controlled by a single member of the elite under the given bribe); γ_j represents the amount the elites have spent to bribe group j, and ρ represents the total power of the members of group j, where j indexes all groups that have received a bribe. Much of this is meant to capture the notion that even bribed people may resist usurpation, depending on the degree of commitment and the amount they have been bribed, but at lower probability than unbribed people.[36] $\Pi \in [0,1]$ is the *trust* parameter, representing the degree of trust among the mass in the collective commitment to resist usurpation, which captures the baseline expectation about the proportion of the population who are likely to resist a power grab; π is an observation of Π with some error, such that $\pi = \Pi + \varepsilon$; $\varepsilon \sim N(0,\beta)$; $\beta \in (0.01,0.8)$. (values of π not in $[0,1]$ are constrained to the end points). Similarly, σ is an estimate of an unobserved *general commitment* parameter $Z \in [0,1]$, which represents the extent to which members of the public will resist even profitable bribes because of their long-term commitment to the system; the estimate σ is constructed in an identical fashion as is π. Where the elite choose to retain the status quo, π is constrained to be 0. Accordingly, the expression $(\pi\mu + \sigma\pi\Sigma\rho_j/\gamma_j)$ represents the subjective probability a member of the elite has in being overthrown.

If the elites decide to attempt to take all the goods for themselves or bribe some subgroup and take the rest, each member of the masses decides whether to reject any bribe and revolt or to acquiesce and take any offered bribe, by choosing the larger of the expected utility functions (ties go to resistance) $EU_{i,revolt} = \alpha_i - (1 - \theta_i\mu - \sigma_i\theta_i\Sigma (\rho_j/\gamma_j))\psi$, $EU_{i,acquiesce} = (1 - Z_i)(\delta_j/\gamma_j)$ where α is the initial distribution of goods to that individual; δ_j represents the amount of the bribe, if any, to that individual's subgroup; γ_j represents the number of members of this subgroup, $\psi = U_e\tau\alpha_m$; that is, it represents the penalty for attempting to resist and losing, which is the product of the mean amount of legal goods allocated to members of the mass α_m, the proportion of power held by the elite U_e, and a random penalty parameter $\tau \in [0.5,5]$. Z_i is the individual's personal commitment parameter, which tracks the extent to which the person is willing to sacrifice individual short-term self-interest to preserve the legal system; θ_i represents that individual's estimate of the trust parameter Π, calculated in the same way as π, but on an individual-by-individual basis (i.e., with individual error), likewise σ_i. All other variables represent the same as they represented in the elite expected utility function. The individual commitment parameter is determined by the extent to which the citizen is treated fairly relative to other members of the mass by the distribution of legal goods, the citizen's perception of the extent of trust in the community, and the overall level of commitment in the community, such that $Z_i = (Z + \theta_i(\alpha_i - \lambda))/2$, $Z_i \leq 1$. Here, λ represents the average share of the goods allocated to the mass under the status quo distribution, that is, the total mass share divided by 1,000, and the expression $\alpha i - \lambda$ is constrained to be nonnegative. The expression $1 - \theta_i\mu - \sigma_i\theta_i\Sigma(\rho_j/\gamma_j)$, $\in [0,1]$ represents citizen i's subjective probability of losing a revolt.

The starting parameters of the model are an initial distribution of goods,[37] a distribution of power,[38] a number of subgroups within the masses ($n \in [2,5]$), a distribution of those subgroup identifiers among the mass,[39] an initial trust parameter value $\Pi \in [0.1, 0.9]$, a general commitment parameter Z, a value for the trust and commitment estimation error variance β, the penalty parameter τ, a distrust decay term Δ of either 0 or. 01, and a shock variance parameter $\kappa \in [0.05, 0.9]$ to be described later. One simulation run consists of a random assignment of each initial parameter from a uniform distribution over their possible ranges, and repeats for 1,000 rounds or until the elites successfully change the distribution of legal goods in their favor (i.e., they overcome the potential of coordinated resistance); the output of each simulation is a description of the original parameters plus the number of rounds it took for the elite group to steal some or all of the goods.

Each round after the first experiences a shock to the distribution of power: from the set of subgroups of the mass plus the elite, two groups are randomly chosen from a uniform distribution, and then a proportion φ of the power from the first is transferred to the second (taken equally from each member of the former and distributed equally to each member of the latter), where $\varphi \sim N(0, \kappa)$. In each round in which the elites attempt to loot, the masses successfully resist them with probability $\Sigma_{i=1...k}\, \mu_i$, where $(1 \ldots k)$ are the members of the mass who resist – that is, with probability equal to their aggregate share of the total power. If the elites win, the run immediately ends. If they lose, Π changes to equal the proportion of the mass who resisted the takeover attempt, and the run continues with a new round.[40] If they do not attempt to loot, Π increases by $\Delta\Pi$ (up to a limit of 1) and the run continues with a new round.

One final concern motivates the addition of some additional complexity to the model. The power of a group is to some extent endogenous to the legal rights of that group, for groups that are deprived of legal rights may become deprived of power as a result. We see a contemporary example of this in the condition of African-Americans in the United States: racially disparate policing (which in the model is captured by a relative lack of legal goods) leads to mass incarceration, and thus both to reduced economic power in the African-American community and to reduced political power (especially through felony disenfranchisement laws). It may be that this dynamic makes unequal legal systems more stable than they otherwise would be, because groups that are the subject of severe inequality over time become less important for the preservation of the legal order. In order to model this effect, a power decay parameter $\chi \in [0,0.5]$ is randomly assigned at the start of each run. Each round, before shocks are applied, each member of any group whose mean goods endowment is more than 1.5 standard deviations below the mean groupwise goods endowment among the mass suffers a decay equal to χ multiplied by the individual's power. This will allow us to test the effect of any such disempowerment tendency.

Even this complicated model simplifies important calculations. Most serious is that players consider only current-round payoffs. Based on the parameters in play, it is impossible to generate a convincing account of how players will estimate future-round payoffs. In principle, we could do so for modeling purposes by calculating, for each round, discounted expected payoffs for every future round based on given assumptions about, for example, the prospects for a successful countercoup if the elites take over. However, doing so would not only drastically complicate even the programming of the computer simulation for this model, but would also impose unrealistic assumptions about the extent to which human beings can or ever would form meaningful expectations about such things. I suggest that the existing simulation actually better models the likely real-world human decision-making process in a situation of dire political conflict, constitutional crisis, or even civil war, when short-term outcomes are likely to be extremely salient and discounting is likely to be very high (not least because in many such situations death is a realistic prospect).

Other parameters are constrained for the purpose of simplification. The ratio of elite to mass is fixed; however, this is unimportant, because the strategically important information that ratio might provide is the difference in the distribution of power and goods between mass and elite; rather than vary the populations, those underlying distributions themselves are allowed to vary. More important, it is assumed that elites act in unison; this simplifies away an entire body of literature about intra-elite competition (although some of this is indirectly captured by the round-by-round shocks to the distribution of power, where one of the real-world events that can cause such a shock is intra-elite competition reducing the elites' ability to coordinate). Similarly, the model allows for only one level of elite, as opposed to the hierarchical ordering of them found in many societies and often considered quite relevant to the development and maintenance of the rule of law to the extent that midlevel elites can facilitate or impede the initiatives of high-level elites.[41] Finally, the utility calculations have been constrained in the interest of simplifying the ultimate maximization problem: the elite optimize only over a limited (but well-dispersed) subset of possible bribes, and both mass and elite take account of the magnitude of bribes in calculating the expected behavior of others in a somewhat ad hoc way rather than directly representing the expected utility functions of others. These simplifications should not change the direction or the effect of any of the parameters,[42] although they may shift the cut points, for example, at which a given bribe expenditure is large enough to stave off a result, and thus, for example, the point in distributional inequality for given values of the other parameters at which N members of the mass will revolt.

Results of the simulation (run 201,000 times) generally confirm the strategic intuitions laid out earlier, albeit with some reservations and surprises. Table 8.1 represents the coefficients of several slightly different linear regression models, where the dependent variable was the number of rounds – that is, the extent to which initial parameters were stable (88.5 percent of the runs lasted the full 1,000 rounds). Changes between the various models, as can be seen from the table, relate primarily to the inclusion of interaction terms for the shock magnitude parameter κ, the inclusion and removal of terms capturing individual and groupwise inequality in the distribution of goods and power (both of which are derived from the same underlying distribution), and the removal of power parameters. All predictors were centered and scaled for comparability. As almost all predictors are highly significant (the original model output was just filled with triple-star coefficients), for readability

TABLE 8.1: Results of rule of law stability simulation

	Rounds (Stability)				
	(1)	(2)	(3)	(4)	(5)
Shock Variance (κ)	0.108	0.123	0.162	−0.280	−3.139
Mean Mass Legal Goods (MMLG)	−10.686	−10.294	−13.343	−12.685	−4.339
Gini Coef. Mass Legal Goods (GMLG)	24.973	21.694	−28.310	—	67.057
Mean Mass Power (MMP)	−12.409	−12.721	−22.257	−13.107	—
Gini Coef. Mass Power (GMP)	−81.565	−69.345	−205.794	—	—
Number of Subgroups (Num)	4.662	4.619	3.353	—	−24.506
Groupwise Legal Goods Gini (GLGG)	−56.425	−52.314	—	−28.168	−102.458
Groupwise Power Gini (GPG)	−133.357	−144.496	—	−212.935	—
Trust (Π)	0.008	−0.622	−0.054	−0.474	0.663
Commitment (Z)	14.380	14.878	14.843	14.850	11.017
Resistance Penalty (τ)	8.266	7.781	7.136	7.895	11.270
Observation Error (β)	−21.200	−21.127	−21.141	−20.972	−21.589
Trust Growth (Δ)	−1.631	−1.274	−0.862*	−1.713	−5.024
Disenfranchised Power Decay (X)	5.357	5.143	4.484	5.387	—
κ * MMLG	—	−4.449	−2.781	−2.399	−6.290
κ * GMLG	—	−15.894	4.228	—	5.384
κ * MMP	—	41.720	39.435	45.289	—
κ * GMP	—	−22.495	−42.149	—	—
κ * Num	—	−4.475	−4.388	—	−22.032
κ * GLGG	—	22.456	—	5.370	0.656
κ * GPG	—	−22.500	—	−48.037	—
κ * Π	—	−3.789	−3.350	−4.338	−2.635
κ * Z	—	−2.657	−2.282	−2.775	−5.795
κ * τ	—	−0.186	−0.026	−0.022	7.199
κ * β	—	14.942	14.938	14.996	14.138
κ * Δ	—	−1.784	−0.695	−2.488	1.547**
κ * X	—	−0.558	−0.548	−0.236	—
R^2	0.520	0.534	0.527	0.532	0.040

I have bolded those that were not significant at a .05 level, and then removed the triple stars from those (majority) that are significant at the .01 level.[43] However, it should be noted that the only unambiguously meaningful features of these results are the signs on the coefficients. All else could be artifacts of the specification of the underlying utility functions. (For example, had the coefficients on θ and π been larger, or Π been on a larger scale in the utility functions underlying the simulation, the magnitude of the effect of trust in the results would have been larger.)

These results indicate that the distributions of power and goods (the latter of which equates to legal rights) dominate the stability results. More unequal power, particularly on the level of groups, most reliably predicts the failure of a simulated legal order, the most obvious reason for this being that such inequality facilitates elite bribery: if one group has much more power than the rest, it may be bribed by elites at lower cost, consistent with the strategic intuitions laid out in this chapter. Likewise, more unequal distribution of goods on the level of groups (although not individuals independent of groups) also strongly predicts the failure of the legal order. Commitment behaves as expected, which again is to be expected if the dynamics of the model are dominated by attempts at bribery of disproportionately powerful groups. Most of the interactions with the shock variance magnitude also behave in predictable ways: as the distribution of power becomes noisier, inequalities in power among mass groups increasingly undermine stability. Several mysteries appear. The ambiguous effect of inequality in goods distributions on an individual level is most plausibly explained as a representation of preference intensity: those who receive more than their fellows have the highest individual commitment, and hence are most likely to resist. However, I cannot fully explain the weak and ambiguous effect of trust. More complex nonlinear analytic strategies might make such anomalies disappear (and would also increase the low overall R^2), but only with a severe cost to interpretability; for present purposes the existing analysis is sufficient, and provides moderate support to the overall argument of this chapter.

This chapter has given a case for a truly full-blooded egalitarian theory of the rule of law. I have argued that the weak version of the rule of law carries with it a strategic pressure to equality – that is, toward the strong version. Even though the full strategic dynamics of any legal system are complex and not amenable to reduction to simple aphorisms like "More equal legal systems will be more stable," an attempt to capture some of this complexity with a computer simulation is at least consistent with such less granular claims. Most important, I have argued that the most stable rule of law systems will be those that can partly break free of purely strategic considerations – that can induce a commitment to support the law on behalf of their people, notwithstanding their short-term self-interested preferences, and can induce public knowledge of that commitment. In the next chapter, I will draw out the implications of that claim for the development and measurement of the rule of law.

Chapter 9

The role of development professionals: measurement and promotion

Let us suppose that the rest of this book is to be believed. The rule of law is about equality, in the dual sense that its moral value is derived from its contribution to the equal standing of those subject to the law, and it will be maintainable for the long term only in states that actually have legal systems that treat their citizens as equals. This contrasts sharply with the conventional views of the rule of law according to which it is primarily about liberty (philosophers) or economic development (social scientists), and will be maintainable through Western-style constitutional and judicial institutions. The egalitarian theory of the rule of law represents an opportunity to open a new conversation about how policy makers and development specialists should understand the rule of law.

That conversation, however, should be focused on empirical potential, not policy prescription. I am not an experienced development practitioner, nor do I have the local expertise necessary to propose concrete rule of law development initiatives in actual states. What I, with the aid of the egalitarian theory of the rule of law, can offer, however, is (a) a set of potential policy approaches that may be adapted to real-world contexts, but that should be implemented on a large scale only with the aid of local expertise and after being empirically validated – as well as a new kind of argument in support of those who have already advanced similar approaches, and (b) an approach to measuring the rule of law that can help in the task of empirical validation by giving us some way to test how policy interventions work on a state-by-state level, as well as test the theoretical claims often made about the side benefits of the rule of law, such as its usefulness for economic development.

I RULE OF LAW DEVELOPMENT

The previous chapters suggest three general principles for rule of law promotion, which may be tested and empirically evaluated. I will call them persuasive commitment-building, generality development, and radical localism. The key idea underlying each is from the previous chapter: rule of law promotion will be more likely to succeed if the people in the communities in which policy makers are attempting to promote it can come to endorse and be committed to preserving their state's legal systems. This, in turn, suggests that those systems must serve their interests, must be implemented in a way compatible with their local ideals and cultures, and must be advocated for with respect for the role of the actual citizens of the communities in which the law is to be promoted.

While my aims in this section are modest, they still represent a radical contrast to the "Washington consensus" school of rule of law promotion, which aims to promote the rule of law in order to promote so-called market reforms – that is, to make the world safe for capitalism, where the capital owners often are from the promoting countries rather than from the countries in which the rule of law is being promoted. Something of the priorities of this school can be seen in the following quintessential development community passage, from a market-oriented review essay on the development of the rule of law in Latin America:

> While the swift and decisive decision-making needed to implement first-generation market reforms often requires a pliant judiciary, second-generation economic reforms aimed at anchoring the institutional foundations of the market economy require precisely the opposite. Market-oriented economic reforms are not sustainable without restoring and strengthening the credibility of the rule of law. As the reliability of the legal and judicial process increases, so does the credibility of the public policymaking process. More fundamentally, government by executive decree, while an asset in the initial phase of economic reform, progressively becomes a liability in the second phase of reform.[1]

That author evidently views the rule of law in purely instrumental terms, not for its inherent moral value, or even for its direct effects on the well-being of the people in whose communities it is to be promoted. To the contrary, "government by executive decree" is to be *supported* in the first stage of "economic reforms." The author never says what this first stage is, but the undersigned cannot help but fear that he's talking about Pinochet-style market authoritarianism: precisely the opposite of the rule of law. I submit that this attitude is bound to lead to failure, as those in the communities in question have zero reason to support a legal system that is not viewed even by its promoters as independently valuable or even worth keeping if it turns out to impede their preferred form of economic organization. In addition, this method of promoting the rule of law fails to attend to the underlying normative value of the ideal; unsurprisingly, without a clear normative concept of the rule of law in the heads of its promoters, they find themselves simply attempting to transpose bits and pieces of their own institutions into other countries – a practice that Martin Krygier has aptly diagnosed as "abuse of the rule of law."[2]

As the wave of global activism beginning in the globalization protests of the late 1990s and continuing with the recent Occupy movement has shown, many do not believe that market reforms and legal institutions meant to support capitalism are in the interests of the masses in the countries in which they are promoted. The truth of that question is open to debate, and many economists and policy makers would argue that they genuinely are in the long-term interests of all in the communities in question, but attempting to promote the rule of law on the basis of such controversial economic as well as normative claims is a recipe for failure, and represents a lack of respect for the legitimate views and concerns of those in the societies with whose legal institutions the development community is involved. Little wonder, then, that rule of law promotion has had decidedly mixed international results: to me it seems most likely that this is a consequence, at least in part, of inadequately inclusive processes as well as outcomes, ones that, in the terms of this book, fail to be general.

In discussing the rule of law's potential to serve the cause of justice, E. P. Thompson also inadvertently explained why instrumentalist rule of law promotion in the interests of global capital is a doomed enterprise:

> [P]eople are not as stupid as some structuralist philosophers suppose them to be. They will not be mystified by the first man who puts on a wig. . . . Most men have a strong sense of justice, at least with regard to their own interests. If the law is evidently partial and unjust, then it will mask nothing, legitimate nothing, contribute nothing to any class's hegemony. The essential precondition for the effectiveness of law, in its function as ideology, is that it shall display an independence from gross manipulation and shall seem to be just. It cannot seem to be so without upholding its own logic and criteria of equity; indeed, on occasion, by actually *being* just.[3]

This argument seems quite right to me: even from the standpoint of the self-interested desires of the Western economic powers, law that is blatantly aimed at promoting their economic interests will not be effective, as Thompson puts it, "in its function as ideology." Accordingly, it will not be effective at promoting those interests. Evidently unjust law, or law imported by outsiders that fails to pay due regard to the interests of the actual stakeholders in a society, cannot expect to win the support of those stakeholders. It is far more likely to encounter their active resistance.

Sadly, some elements of the rule of law development industry are in dire need of reform. The worst example I have ever discovered is from one of the international experts who was brought in to help build the rule of law in Afghanistan, but whose published writings display an open contempt for the country, its traditions, and its people. A professor at the University of Copenhagen, he, according to his online faculty profile,[4] "set up the ongoing legal training programmes of the Max Planck Institute in Afghanistan." He also has written a book chapter, in which he said the following about the Afghan resistance to the Soviet invasion: "Self-serving descriptions by its protagonists notwithstanding, the Afghan conflict was only marginally a national defence against a foreign aggressor. Primarily, it was a civil war fought between those who favoured accelerated modernisation and those who resisted this change with reference to an atavistic understanding of religion."[5] Speaking of the "atavistic" religion of the Afghan people: "However aggressive, intolerant, and backward widely prevailing notions of Islam in this country have been, it is the lack of effective governance, not religious parochialism, that brings about chaos and poverty."[6] On the very same page, he tellingly asserts that "the general quality of legal expertise going into the [constitutional drafting] process must be described as poor" because (the causal implication is unstated but unavoidable) "[o]utside technical assistance was available in principle but was utilised only very haphazardly and incoherently; by and large outside legal expertise was seen at best as an irritant to inter-factual horse-trading and at worst an attempt at cultural domination."[7] One might dare to think that the writer, qua member of the "outside legal expertise," was indeed engaged in an attempt at cultural domination over the "backward" and "atavistic" version of Islam endorsed in the community. Nor does the state itself escape his scorn. In his two-sentence summary of the entire history of Afghan statehood he describes it as "depend[ing] on foreign largesse" and "extract[ing] significant rents" from the world powers.[8]

Of course, the sins of a few cannot be visited on the rule of law development enterprise as a whole. However, it is hard not to suspect that the Washington consensus approach to rule of law development might encourage this kind of attitude. And there is something about this lack of respect for existing traditions that seems to be more widespread than the extreme example I have just quoted. Such externally imposed rule of law development patterns have been described by Ugo Mattei as "imperial."[9] As Mattei points out, the US/Western legal system denies that legal systems unlike its own actually count as legal systems – what Mattei calls "de-legalization."[10]

Accordingly, I offer this book in part as a theoretical grounding for those who endorse alternative approaches to rule of law development, particularly what might be called the "bottom-up" rule of law development movement (associated, inter alia, with Carothers, Kleinfeld, and others associated with the Carnegie Endowment for International Peace), and offer the following as a catalog of ways in which the theoretical material of this book may connect with the kinds of efforts they support.[11]

A *Persuasive commitment-building*

One of the themes of this book is that the rule of law in the first instance requires a general commitment to the law. That commitment is the precondition for, not a consequence of, functional formal institutions like courts. Thus, the egalitarian account of the rule of law suggests that the task of rule of law development is partially to persuade people that it is in their interests to act collectively to enforce the rule of law.

Of course, to persuade citizens to support a rule of law that is not, actually, in their interests is to subject them to oppression; to dishonestly persuade citizens that they can safely act in concert to defend the law is not only to subject them to potentially brutal retaliation, but also to undermine the extent to which they will believe in the viability of collective enforcement of the law later. For that reason, persuasion is necessarily subordinate to substantive reforms to make the legal system worth supporting.

B *Generality development*

As Chapter 8 argued, members of a political community will have reason to support the rule of law only if the law is compatible with their interests, and more so if it is publicly fair – that is, if the law is general. Accordingly, the egalitarian theory of the rule of law suggests that rule of law development efforts focus on making the law general, by, inter alia,

(a) Controlling violence under color of the state, particularly against the most vulnerable, and ensuring that all have access to legal remedies against violence.
(b) Eliminating legalized discrimination by gender, race, religion, class, caste, sexual orientation, and other group identities.
(c) Actively promoting social equality through the law by implementing legal protections against private discrimination.
(d) Actively promoting political equality by giving members of all groups access to the legislative process, thereby allowing all groups to see that their interests are taken into account in the making of the laws that they're being asked to support.
(e) Dispersing access to nonlegislative sources of political power, such as property, the press, the professions, civil society, and military participation.
(f) Implementing a program of economic egalitarianism and a social safety net, to increase the pool of stakeholders in the stability of society in general.

C *Radical localism*

Even though no particular institutions are necessary to establish the rule of law in a state, the account in Chapters 6 and 8 suggests that some institutions will be helpful in bringing it about, particularly those institutions that permit citizens – having been convinced of the value of a secure legal system to protect their interests, and in an environment where the legal system actually does treat them as equals – to credibly signal their commitment to that system. However, what those institutions are will vary from society to society. Many societies will have preexisting institutional resources that can be adapted to this signaling function, rather than attempting to transpose institutions wholesale from the North Atlantic liberal democracies.[12]

For example, many communities in India feature local councils, the *panchayats*.[13] A rule of law development in such a community could feature efforts to expand access to the *panchayat*, and encourage the government to recognize decisions of a *panchayat* as binding on state officials. To the extent a community's *panchayat* is already generally accepted as a legitimate source of rulings, this may be more effective at producing widespread participation in legal adjudication and enforcement – and hence widespread signaling of legal commitment – than reforms to courts.[14]

Religious authorities may also be recruited in communities with a tradition of religious involvement in civil dispute resolution.[15] So may civil society organizations, the press, and other unofficial methods of communicating public sentiment about the law. We might imagine a state, for example, in which the government is held to comply with law not through courts, but through local and informal methods of imposing social sanctions on disobedient officials – shunning, perhaps, or gossip, or the refusal to trade with misbehaving officials. To the extent that sanctions deployed by such institutions can be seen to represent the will of a critical mass of the community, and to the extent they can be brought to use those sanctions against officials who disobey the law, these – the theory of Chapters 6 and 8 suggests – can provide institutional support for the rule of law.[16]

Such institutions may do better than Western-style elite judicial institutions at supporting the rule of law in communities where there is no widespread common knowledge of public endorsement of the state and legal system, on the basis of the model given in Chapter 6. Participatory mass, or representative, rather than elite, adjudications can be used not only to rule on the question of whether officials obeyed the law, but also to cheaply signal commitment to the law, and to the particular outcome of a case. Imagine a small town and a police beating, and suppose that the victim of the beating can turn for justice either to an out-of-touch and widely distrusted court operated by the central government (and built by the United States on the model of its own judicial system) or to a local religious leader, where the latter will call upon a community forum to judge the dispute and settle upon a remedy. The latter is, all else being equal, more likely to be effective, not only at finding a remedy for the misconduct, but also in deterring this misconduct in the first place, for police officers in a community with active mass adjudication will know that their fellows are committed to carrying out the result of decisions made in common, and will know that there are consequences to abuses that turn the community against them.

Moreover, such institutions are likely to draw additional public support not only from their direct recruitment of public participation but from the fact that the norms upon which they draw to constrain the use of power – be they customary law, statute law, religious norms, or the like – necessarily must be compatible with that popular participation. Accordingly, they are likely to enforce norms that are widely accepted within the community (or at a minimum accepted by the powerful, which is better than accepted by nobody).[17]

Moreover, Katharina Pistor has pointed out that legal institutions that are locally derived are the products of learning and institutional evolution over time, and are more likely to be adapted to local conditions than imports, however certified by external expertise.[18] Her argument applies not just to substantive law, but also to procedural law, such as the details of the legal mechanisms at work in a community. If a community has, for example, eschewed centralized Western-style courts for hundreds of years, it behooves external rule of law promoters to consider the possibility that perhaps the absence of such tools is embedded in a coevolved local ecosystem in which cultural and moral norms, dominant social (and religious, etc.) beliefs, adjudicative forums, and substantive legal rules are mutually interdependent, such that transplanting external institutions will be ineffective.[19]

Of course, not all evolved systems are maximally beneficial to the organism, whether that organism is a person or a state. Evolution finds local optima, not global optima; an institution that is too costly to abandon might nonetheless be harmful overall for the society in which it is embedded, as a trait to a person (witness the human appendix and the American electoral college). But observing that a given legal institution ("customary," "informal," or otherwise) has survived in its social context gives us some reason to believe that there may be hidden costs to abandoning it and supplanting it with institutions that have succeeded in other states.

"Local" in this subsection has been used to contrast with "foreign," to refer to the institutions that are native to the country and culture in which the rule of law is being promoted, rather than to the promoter countries and cultures; in that first sense, "local" is a rough synonym for "traditional." However, "local" also carries the meaning of "decentralized," and there, too, the theory of this book can connect with concrete policy potential for rule of law promoters.

There is empirical evidence suggesting that radically local development can successfully serve a violence-reducing dispute-resolution function. Blattman, Hartman, and Blair recently implemented an experiment in which community members in Liberia were trained in problem solving and alternative dispute resolution within their local cultural contexts (including the effective use of traditional forms of dispute resolution, such as "adjudication by community leaders").[20] The result was a persistent decline in violent dispute resolution among treated groups, even though the central state had largely failed to provide them with legal resources. Importantly, this produced positive change even though, before the experimental treatment, local residents had reported a multiplicity of conflicting central ("formal") as well as traditional ("informal") authorities, leading to "forum-shopping" and clashing unenforced judgments.[21] Training in the effective use of traditional forums seems to have ameliorated the downside of local and pluralistic adjudication. Moreover, some of the positive effect seems to have resulted from making adjudication even more decentralized than it already was: subjects reported resolving disputes within the community, rather than taking them to a mishmash of central and traditional authorities (who were all corrupt, albeit in different ways).[22]

Better yet, subjects reported that these methods led to dispute resolutions that were actually in the interests of the parties, and thus "self-enforcing," and led "traditionally low-powered groups" to demand improvements in their social position; that is, it tapped into the rule of law's pressure toward generality (Chapter 8).[23] This was only one experiment, and the experimenters did see some negative effects (particularly an increase in unjust extralegal punishment, such as witch-hunting[24]), but, on the whole, it is a promising result.

Additional promising evidence on radical localism comes from Afghanistan.[25] Kleinfeld and Bader report on a program that identified those likely to be recruited as leaders by insurgent groups and jumped the gun on them, recruiting the nascent leaders instead for community infrastructure-building projects based on local materials and knowledge, such as soil conservation.[26] This effort successfully kept those leaders out of insurgent groups, and their communities began to see them "as leaders who could be counted on for advice and wisdom" and "agents of reconciliation."[27]

Strikingly, over time the leaders recruited for things like soil conservation actually found themselves mediating civil disputes over, for example, land rights, and, as Kleinfeld and Bader point out, this "prevented insurgents from exploiting such community conflicts by providing shadow governance services themselves."[28] Even when the outside development agencies were only trying to create leaders to work on physical infrastructure projects, they ended up accidentally creating leaders in local justice, which successfully competed with the Taliban and other violent groups. The results of that project offer substantial reason to hope that more intentional local justice projects have a strong chance of succeeding.

The Special Inspector General for Afghan Reconstruction reports that such "informal" justice programs as exist have succeeded in both bringing people to justice and advancing women's rights:[29] they got no fewer than 5,192 elders to agree to stop using *baad* – a traditional practice in which women are traded as compensation in civil disputes[30] – as a dispute-resolution method, and found that citizens who turned to elders who had participated in the program "showed improved perceptions of procedural fairness and overall justice."[31]

1 Locally driven project design

Just as one way to bring it about that the law is substantively general is to enact it pursuant to a (deliberative) democratic process that generates enactments based on reasons that citizens understand to apply to them, one way to bring it about that the legal system is procedurally legitimate, such that it is likely to win the commitment of the public, is to involve the public in its design. Rule of law development projects in which the leaders are drawn from the local population, rather than from international organizations or distant central governments, may benefit from greater knowledge of local conditions, a greater ability to recruit widespread community support, and superior access to preexisting local institutions.[32]

This is not to deny a role for external expertise: economists, political scientists, lawyers, sociologists, and others have valuable knowledge that can be put to work in implementing or reforming rule of law institutions even in unfamiliar countries. However, there are more and less locally driven ways to deploy this expertise.

In the engineering and product design fields, a minor revolution has taken place in recent years surrounding a concept known as "design thinking," which is more user-oriented than traditional methods. For example, it begins with a process of "needfinding," consisting essentially of open-ended conversations with potential users where the designer aims to produce a product that actually meets needs, rather than produce a product that looks exciting to the designer and then find the needs that it meets after the fact. Similar close-in empathetic interactions with the user are carried out throughout the development process.[33]

Lately, design thinking has gone beyond the product world to the field of social design, applying empathetic and interactive processes to social organization and institutions.[34] Design-thinking principles might also be applicable in the international design of legal systems (i.e., the use of international expertise primarily to support the express rather than implicit legal needs of those in the local community).

"Design," here, includes both procedural and substantive elements. Procedurally, it can mean building the institutions that the local citizens say they need, rather than those that external experts think they need. Substantively, it can mean focusing on problems that are a priority to the local people rather than to external stakeholders such as international commercial interests. If the people say they need immediate protection from police violence, for example, building courts to assist them in resolving private land disputes, while worthy, may not be as effective at winning their endorsement or participation as addressing police misconduct would be.[35]

II STUDYING THE RULE OF LAW: NEW EMPIRICAL DIRECTIONS

Accurate cross-national measures of the rule of law would be useful to evaluate policy interventions to promote it as well as claims about the benefits associated with it. Unfortunately, no existing measure of the rule of law is adequate. The problems with existing rule of law measures are widely recognized. Preexisting rule of law measures have been criticized for, among other things, paying little or no attention to conceptualization;[36] inappropriately including nonlegal factors, such as crime rates;[37] adopting proxy variables that are riddled with measurement error, are miscoded, and make unwarranted assumptions about the relationship between the proxy and the rule of law;[38] being unduly focused on legal rules relevant to business and property rights;[39] including copious redundancies as well as irrelevant ideas;[40] focusing (in some cases) on meaningless de jure claims written into a country's laws without regard for whether they are enforced;[41] and being unclear or inconsistent about how different alleged dimensions of the rule of law are to be aggregated and weighted.[42]

Unfortunately, these criticisms are, on the whole, warranted. A brief review of some of the most prominent or recent measures will shed some more light on the problem.[43] By far the best of the existing rule of law measures is that given by the World Justice Project (WJP), on whose data set my own measure is based. The WJP's rule of law index is based on carefully designed original survey instruments, and surveys a large number of both experts and members of the general population across the world. It has also been subject to careful and independent statistical scrutiny.[44] However, the WJP's interpretation of its data is marred by a lack of conceptual ambition: it divides its understanding of the rule of law into eight factors – "limited government powers," "absence of corruption," "order and security," "fundamental rights," "open government," "regulatory enforcement," "civil justice," and "criminal justice" – and does not attempt to unify these factors into a single scale. As discussed in the next section, this raises significant interpretive problems in, for example, figuring out how to classify a state that scores highly on one factor but poorly on another. Moreover, the WJP's factors include a number of irrelevancies: for example, its survey measures how often bribes have to be paid to obtain medical treatment, the effectiveness of national environmental enforcement, and the effectiveness of local arbitration, which may shed some light on the effectiveness of a state's legal system in general, but do not shed any particular light on *the rule of law* as such.

Other measures are significantly worse. The World Bank produces what it calls "Worldwide Governance Indicators," which simply concatenate a variety of other organizations' measures, and are heavily biased toward both the views of business interests and data reflecting those interests, such as the "business cost of crime and violence" and "intellectual property rights protection."[45] Moreover, the World Bank indicators do not permit cross-country comparison, as the variable coverage is different across countries and regions.[46] While the Bank's researchers have attempted to answer these criticisms, the chief answer they offer is that their measures are highly correlated – commercial evaluators are highly correlated with noncommercial evaluators, and the various kinds of measures for a different concept, such as corruption, are highly correlated with each other in the countries in which they do overlap.[47] However, while that reduces the impact of these criticisms, it does not eliminate them completely. Consider the example the Bank's researchers offer: suppose country A has only a score on a judicial corruption scale, while country B has only a score on an administrative corruption scale.[48] It may be that those two sorts of corruption are sufficiently correlated that we can sensibly suppose that both are measuring a latent variable of corruption in general, as the Bank's researchers claim. But we evaluate our measurement tools with reference to the available alternatives, and those alternatives include measures consciously aimed at tracking the same kind of corruption, such as the WJP's, which necessarily feature less room for the error introduced by using different measures to capture a latent variable idea of corruption. And this is before we even get to generalizing from "corruption" to the rule of law – a point on which this example sheds particular light, since, as a conceptual matter, judicial corruption is far more relevant for the rule of law than administrative corruption, since administrative corruption might include corruption in domains that do not relate to the control of state coercive power (such as in the provision of public services), while judicial corruption raises serious doubts about the ability of the courts to control state violence.[49]

The design of the proposed United Nations Rule of Law Indicators instrument is somewhat better than the World Bank's. However, it also includes a number of irrelevant items, such as access to health care in prison, effectiveness of the police at controlling crime, "budgetary transparency," and the like.[50] More signficantly, it doesn't come attached to any data: the UN merely provides a standardized instrument that it advises stakeholders to use to measure the rule of law in their states. Standardized is a step in the right direction: at least this can avoid the methodological difficulties inherent in the World Bank's approach, and should this instrument be used on a worldwide scale, it could produce data comparable to, or even better than, the WJP's. However, the instrument would also be very difficult and expensive to use, as it suggests drawing not only from survey data but also from field research and review of national documents.

Finally, the most interesting recent entrants in the rule of law measurement races are Nardulli, Peyton, and Bajjalieh, who use a novel method based on interpreting a cross-national data set of the content of constitutions.[51] Their measure is characterized by a careful attention to conceptualization issues, an attempt to base the measurement on "objective" data, and a data set that spans across time as well as across many countries. It also has the distinct advantage of treating the rule of law as a unidimensional concept rather than a noncomparable set of factors. However, the Nardulli et al. measurement suffers from one fatal flaw: one of its variables, the "objective" one, is purely de jure, consisting entirely of claims written into nations' constitutions, and need bear no relationship to the actual constraints on official coercive power in a state. The other measure is simply the extent to which a nation has a robust field of legal periodicals ("legal infrastructure"). To see the problems with this measure, we need only note that the 1936 Soviet constitution provided for judicial independence and the supremacy of law, equal rights, free speech, free press, and a whole host of other liberal-democratic ideals that Josef Stalin obviously had no intention of fulfilling.[52] Moreover, as far as I can tell from the literature available in this country, the Soviets had at least a fair amount of legal scholarship.[53] The Soviet Union was quite possibly the most efficient system for wielding arbitrary power against a population that the world has heretofore seen, but the Nardulli, Peyton, and Bajjalieh measure would categorize it as having achieved a high degree of the rule of law.

Accordingly, I have created a novel measure of the rule of law. This is only a proof of concept, for I do not have access to data sufficient to make a measure that can be repeated over multiple years, or over as large a set of countries as may be desired. Instead, thanks to the kindness of the World Justice Project, I have received one year of their data, and have extracted a unidimensional measure from that data. As will be seen, this measure behaves much like we would expect a rule of law measure to behave, and accordingly reflects a credible technique for proxying an observation of the property in real-world states. Researchers with access to more data may use similar methods to achieve wider-scale and multiyear measures that may be of practical use in social science as well as in program management.

A *The new measure: methods*

The alternative rule of law measure here is based on its theoretical conceptualization as a undimensional property of states, suitable to be approximated on a unidimensional scale.

1 Structure and scaling

As we've seen, the conventional approach to measuring the rule of law, and the one taken by the best of the existing measures, is to conceive of it as a multidimensional construct – an odd composite idea comprising a series of factors tracking, loosely, a mishmash of ideas that have more or less traditionally been associated with the rule of law. This method carries with it a number of problems, however. First, on an empirical level, it's not clear how to interpret the notion of a state having the rule of law to a greater or lesser extent, if the rule of law is a multidimensional concept. Suppose a state has a really good informal justice system, but its formal justice system is corrupt. Does that state count as having more or less of the rule of law than a state with no institutions of informal justice, but with a pristine and uncorrupted legal system? In the statistical literature, this is the problem of weighting factors.[54] It is widely recognized as a critical problem in the existing attempts to measure the rule of law, one that has led some scholars to propose abandoning the attempt to measure the rule of law as a whole altogether and just measure each factor individually.[55] By contrast, a unidimensional concept imagines that each measurement item (such as a survey question) is an observation of the same thing. The only reason one needs to include multiple items in a measurement of a unidimensional latent variable is that each item measures the variable with some error.

Second, on a practical level, the point of measuring a multidimensional construct is not at all clear. We presumably attempt to measure the rule of law because we want to know where and how it obtains, and its effect on the world. If we wanted to measure "open government" and "effective criminal justice," we could measure those things on their own; if we wanted to measure the effects of having both of those things together, or any linear combination of the various factors in these multidimensional constructs, then we can use interaction terms in ordinary multivariate regressions to do so. We don't add any insight or explanatory traction to the world by imagining that there's some odd multidimensional thing lying behind these factors.

Compare the rule of law to another notoriously difficult-to-measure concept, democracy. We might say that democracy is a multidimensional concept comprising, say, "political equality" and "popular sovereignty." But the person who wants to do so owes us an explanation about why, if that's the case, we ought, morally, to care about "democracy" at all, distinct from the independent reasons we have to care about "popular sovereignty" and "political equality." If we're consequentialists, we might think that having both popular sovereignty and political equality produces more good things than having just one, but that still doesn't warrant saying that their combination is one good thing, rather than two good things that just happen to be better together. Put differently, salt is different from the mere combination of sodium and chloride. We enjoy consuming salt qua thing; we wouldn't enjoy consuming a bunch of sodium and a bunch of chloride mushed together. The rule of law is an object worthy of study only if it's one thing rather than just the mushing together of some other things. A multidimensional account of a social scientific phenomenon just begs the thoughtful researcher to reduce the concept to its dimensions.

By contrast, conceiving of the rule of law as a unidimensional concept also clears away some of the confusion about what particular items go into a measure of the rule of law. We can distinguish what the rule of law is from social phenomena that are either tools to achieve the rule of law or arguable consequences of it. Some of those things may still be worth including in a measure of the rule of law. For example, judicial independence is merely a tool to achieve the rule of law (it's conceptually possible to have the rule of law without it), but it's a very common and important tool, and given that we cannot observe the rule of law directly, it may be worthwhile to include judicial independence in a measure of the rule of law as a proxy. But we can do so consciously, without succumbing to the illusion that judicial independence is a component of the rule of law or a dimension of it.

In the foregoing chapters, I have given a conceptual and normative analysis of the rule of law as a unidimensional concept. There are three principles of the rule of law, but those principles are largely hierarchical: one must have regular legal rules constraining those in power for those legal rules to be public; one must have public legal rules for them to be general. The rule of law measure in this chapter takes advantage of the unidimensional properties of the underlying concept by taking existing data for the rule of law and composing them into a scale using the tools of item response theory (IRT). IRT is a method borrowed primarily from psychological research, which measures a unidimensional construct (a latent variable; in psychology, things like the big five personality traits, IQ, etc.) by measuring individual *items* (e.g., answers to a test), with the model that those who have greater degrees of the latent variable will also answer more of the items in the predicted way.

Some IRT models, like the Guttman scaling methods from which they were derived, suppose that the individual items exist in a hierarchy of difficulty that track greater or lesser degrees of that concept, such that we would ordinarily expect to see the more difficult items only in the presence of the less difficult items. (I will call these "hierarchical models.") For example, if such a scale is measuring racial tolerance, we would expect everyone who answers "I would be willing to allow my children to marry people of other races" to also say "I would be willing to live in the same town as people of other races." Likewise, on a test measuring mathematical knowledge, we would ordinarily expect correct answers to the calculus questions only on the tests that have correct answers to the arithmetic questions. IRT models improve on Guttman scales by being more accommodating of random measurement error, such that the results of an IRT model might deviate from a perfect Guttman scale.[56]

Such hierarchical models track the hierarchical properties of the rule of law, in that individual variables on the scale reflecting generality will be more difficult, in this sense, than items reflecting publicity, which in turn will be more difficult than items reflecting regularity. However, hierarchical models tend to depend on strong assumptions about item-by-item ordering. For example, the Mokken model of double monotonicity requires items that have a consistent difficulty ordering across all subjects.[57] This is an implausible standard to meet in a rule of law index with multiple items tracking different parts of each of the three principles. For example, generality may be captured by variables measuring both the racial equality in a state's laws and its gender equality; it may be that some legal systems are nongeneral with respect to race but not gender, and others are nongeneral with respect to gender but not race, even though all legal systems that are general with respect to either also satisfy regularity and publicity to a substantial degree. Accordingly, I make use of the Mokken model of monotone homogeneity, which benefits from substantially weaker assumptions. Monotone homogeneity requires only three assumptions: first, that there is an underlying unidimensional latent trait (this is the assumption on which the whole enterprise is based); second, that each item is more likely to be true (for polytomous items, to a higher degree) if the latent trait is found to a stronger degree (a fairly straightforward scale requirement); and third, that there are no omitted variables influencing scores on multiple items ("local stochastic independence").[58]

2 Item selection and scale-fitting

Data from the World Justice Project's 2012 expert and general population surveys were used.[59] First, I personally reviewed the survey questions for their correspondence to the elements of the rule of law described in Chapters 1 and 2. Selected questions (items) were generally in the following categories: political influence and financial

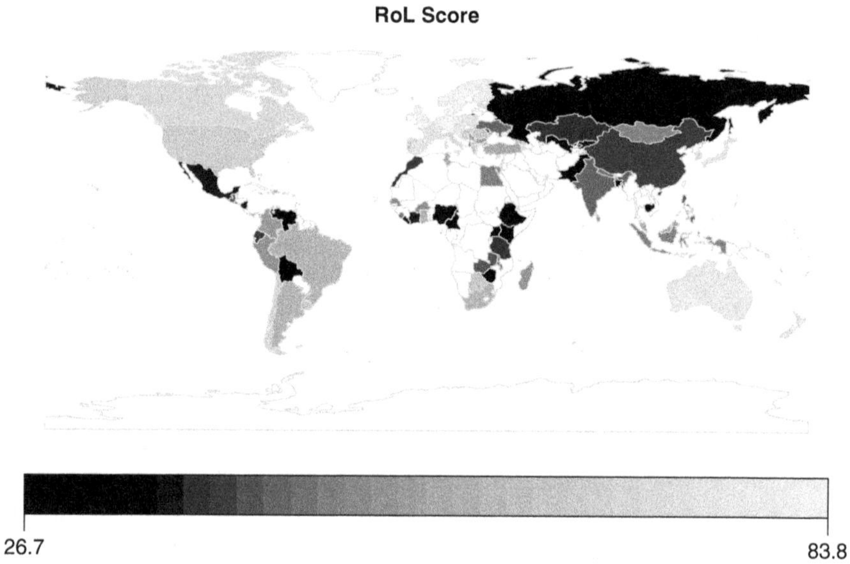

FIGURE 9A Rule of law scores across the globe

corruption in the judicial process, executive obedience to the law, opportunity for citizens to resist government power (included to capture the notion of coordinated defense by beneficiaries of law), discrimination in the criminal process, information about legal rights, and police misconduct. Unfortunately, the WJP data set contains little data on the substantive generality of the law, so data about discrimination in the criminal process will have to stand in for this principle as a whole. After this initial review, all items with missing data were removed, except where that missing data was clustered in one or a few states; on examination, four states were found to have an excessive amount of missing data and were removed from the data set. The resulting initial set of items contained 92 items across the 93 remaining countries.

Next, the data were fit to a Mokken monotone homogeneity scale (with minimum scalability coefficient H set to default at .3) using the genetic algorithm described by Straat, van der Ark, and Sijtsma, using the Mokken package for the R statistical programming language.[60] All 92 items were found to fit the scale, with Cronbach's alpha at .987. Finally, scores along each included item were summed across each country, yielding an ultimate rule of law score for each state, suitable at least for interpretation as an ordinal ranking. (These rule of law scores should not be interpreted as cardinal values.)

Each state's rule of law score is included in an appendix to this chapter. Overall, total scores quite well match intuitive evaluations of the rule of law conditions of the most salient states in the world (see Figure 9A). On the whole, the North Atlantic liberal democracies and the most economically developed Asian nations rank the highest. For example, Sweden ranks first, the United Kingdom 11th, Japan 14th, the United States 26th, Iran 69th, Russia 79th, Venezuela 92nd, and Zimbabwe last.

B Limitations

The World Justice Project's data set contains several inherent limitations for this task. First, it does not cover every country. Second, it does not contain extensive data capturing the generality principle; data considering, for example, the extent to which women and members of religious, linguistic, national, and/or racial minorities are subject to de jure or de facto legal discrimination would greatly improve the content validity of the scale given in this chapter. Third, the survey questions were not designed to fit a unidimensional model, and would be more useful had they been written with an intuitive scale of difficulty suitable for more hierarchical models. Fourth, the data do not measure public attitudes toward the legal system; direct data on public commitment to the rule of law would be highly useful. Fifth, the data were based on surveys connected between 2009 and 2012, depending on country, and political change between those years may make comparisons between countries surveyed in different years less reliable.[61] The methods used here are also limited. The equal weighting of each scale item and the disparate number of items for the various principles of the rule of law may introduce distortions into the ultimate scoring.

C Behavior of the measure

Validating the proof of concept scale, we may note that it behaves in roughly the way expected by theory. In order to confirm its match to the rough theoretical consensus about the functions of the rule of law, I examined a series of bivariate regressions with indicators of economic development, individual freedom, and democracy. All are in the expected direction and are highly significant. Of course, this should not be taken as evidence that the rule of law itself is associated with these properties, as a proper inferential investigation would, among other things, include things like control variables. These regressions are merely reliability checks for the underlying scale: we would have reason to distrust a rule of law scale that was negatively associated with something like democracy or economic development.

Accordingly, per capita gross domestic product (GDP) (from World Bank 2012 data) is a significant predictor of rule of law scores in a bivariate linear regression with p essentially indistinguishable from zero (values are listed in Table 9.1).[62] The same is true of personal autonomy scores from Freedom House, Freedom House's scores for states' electoral processes and political pluralism and participation, and the Heritage Foundation's scoring for the protection of private property rights.

TABLE 9.1: Bivariate regressions – rule of law scores

RoL ~	Coefficient	p
GDP Per Capita	$6.65\ 10^{-4}$	$< 2\ 10^{-16}$
GDP P.C. (log-transformed)	0.17	$< 2\ 10^{-16}$
Personal Autonomy	4.22	$< 2\ 10^{-16}$
Electoral Process	2.58	$7.19\ 10^{-10}$
Political Pluralism	2.52	$3.37\ 10^{-13}$
Property Rights	4.22	$< 2\ 10^{-16}$

Since the dominant theories in the social sciences suggest that the rule of law is more likely to be found in wealthy liberal democracies that protect property rights, the strong associations of the rule of law measure developed in this chapter with all of these indicators is good reason to think that it measures the variable of interest to political scientists, economists, and development professionals. Moreover, since that variable was constructed on the basis of survey questions that closely reflect the concept of the rule of law as developed by philosophers and lawyers, these results strongly suggest that the rift in the two rule of law conversations can be healed: social scientists can measure what normative and conceptual theory suggests the rule of law is, and it can give us some empirical traction on the questions of concern to real-world practitioners. A *unified approach to the rule of law is possible.*

III APPENDIX: SCORES AND STATES

This appendix contains several figures representing the results of the proof-of-concept rule of law measure. First, Table 9.2 is a complete listing of states, rule of law scores, and ordinal ranks. The graphs are scatterplots with fitted regression lines capturing bivariate relationships between the rule of law scores and various observable features often thought, in the theoretical domain, to relate positively to the rule of law. Figure 9B relates the rule of law to economic development, expressed as per capita gross domestic product (GDP); Figure 9C is the same as Figure 9B, but log-transformed to more clearly show the relationship given the scale differences between the variables and the clustering of GDP on the low end. Figure 9D relates the rule of law to a popular measure of individual liberty. Figures 9E and 9F relate the rule of law to two popular measures of democracy, expressed as the quality of a state's electoral process (9E) and the extent of its political pluralism and participation (9F). Finally, Figure 9G relates the rule of law to a popular measure of a state's level of property rights protection. Full color, interactive, and additional graphs are available online at rulelaw.net.

TABLE 9.2: Rule of law scores by state

State	Score	Rank	State	Score	Rank	State	Score	Rank	State	Score	Rank
Sweden	83.85	1	Uruguay	64.81	25	Colombia	47.03	49	Morocco	38.60	73
Norway	83.61	2	United States	63.08	26	Madagascar	46.96	50	Kazakhstan	37.81	74
Finland	82.27	3	Portugal	62.96	27	Jamaica	46.95	51	Mexico	37.47	75
Netherlands	80.57	4	Georgia	61.44	28	Peru	46.72	52	Côte d'Ivoire	36.55	76
Denmark	80.48	5	Romania	60.79	29	Mongolia	46.01	53	Kyrgyzstan	36.22	77
Germany	76.93	6	Botswana	60.56	30	Senegal	46.01	54	Kenya	35.76	78
New Zealand	76.33	7	Greece	58.21	31	Panama	45.41	55	Russia	35.53	79
Belgium	73.57	8	Hungary	58.06	32	Indonesia	44.41	56	El Salvador	34.75	80
Australia	73.28	9	Croatia	57.44	33	Egypt	44.13	57	Liberia	34.10	81
Austria	73.15	10	Bosnia and Herzegovina	55.77	34	Burkina Faso	44.12	58	Pakistan	33.68	82
United Kingdom	73.13	11	UAE	55.30	35	Nepal	43.46	59	Uganda	33.57	83
Estonia	72.98	12	Macedonia	54.11	36	Albania	42.60	60	Bolivia	33.51	84
Poland	72.95	13	Lebanon	52.07	37	Sierra Leone	42.30	61	Ethiopia	33.43	85
Japan	72.04	14	Argentina	51.94	38	Malawi	41.33	62	Nicaragua	32.62	86
Singapore	71.95	15	Brazil	51.83	39	Ukraine	40.80	63	Bangladesh	31.57	87
Hong Kong	71.74	16	South Africa	51.68	40	India	40.72	64	Uzbekistan	30.43	88
Spain	71.26	17	Ghana	51.20	41	Philippines	39.96	65	Nigeria	30.17	89
France	71.23	18	Malaysia	50.72	42	Guatemala	39.67	66	Cameroon	29.65	90
South Korea	70.74	19	Sri Lanka	50.55	43	Zambia	39.62	67	Cambodia	28.69	91
Canada	70.03	20	Tunisia	50.42	44	China	39.33	68	Venezuela	27.84	92
Czech Republic	69.03	21	Serbia	49.58	45	Iran	39.23	69	Zimbabwe	26.66	93
Slovenia	66.52	22	Turkey	49.22	46	Moldova	39.21	70			
Chile	65.99	23	Dominican Republic	49.17	47	Ecuador	39.11	71			
Italy	65.06	24	Bulgaria	47.26	48	Tanzania	39.07	72			

B The rule of law and other measures of political well-being

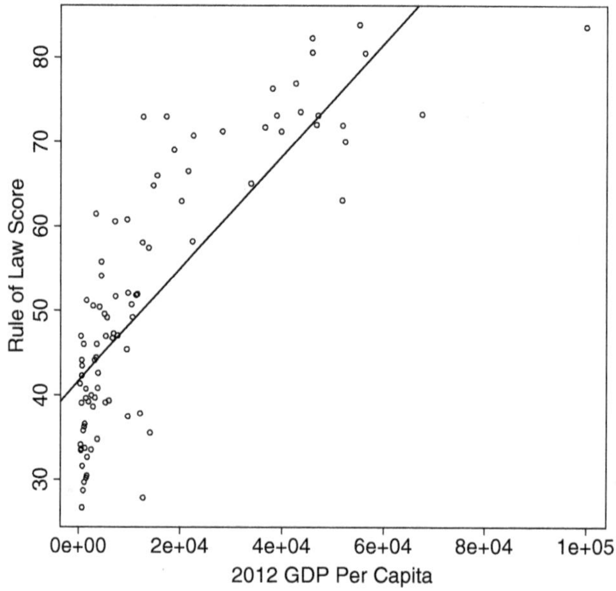

FIGURE 9B Rule of law scores and per capita GDP

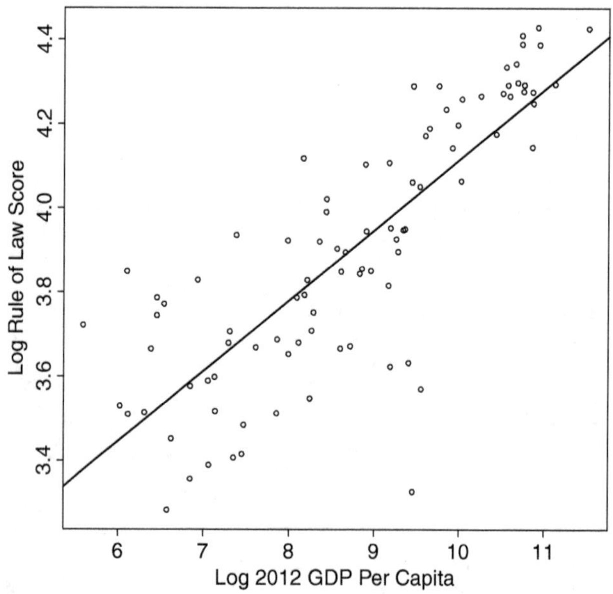

FIGURE 9C Log-transformed rule of law scores and per capita GDP

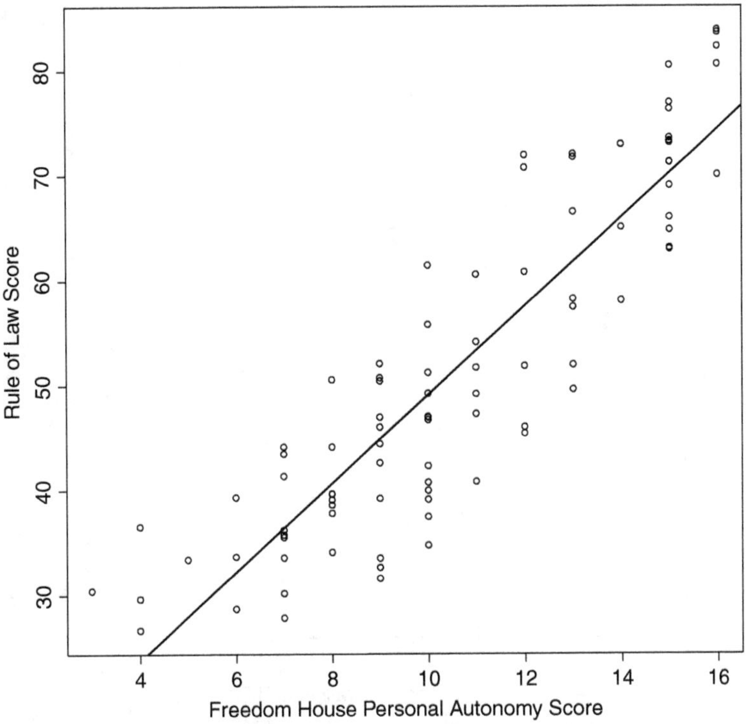

FIGURE 9D Rule of law and individual autonomy scores

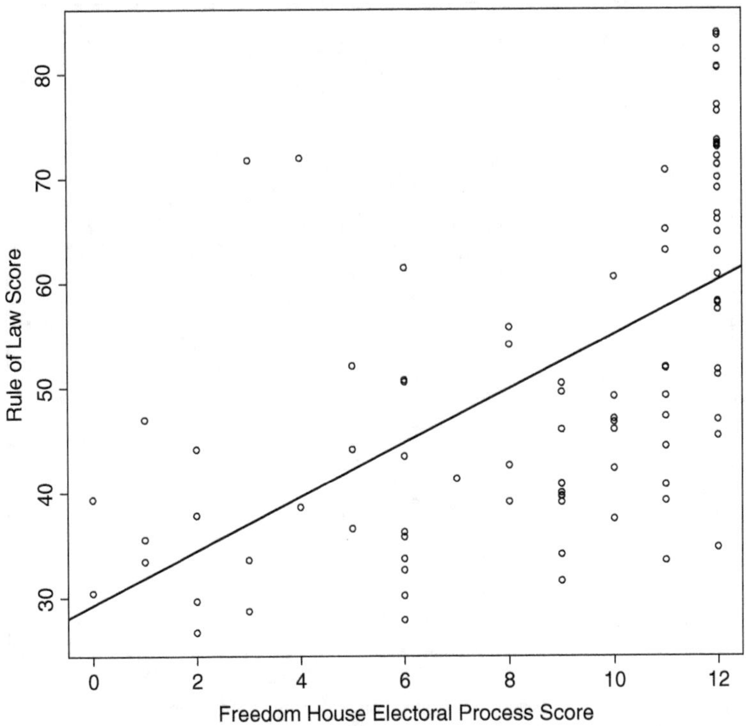

FIGURE 9E Rule of law and electoral process scores

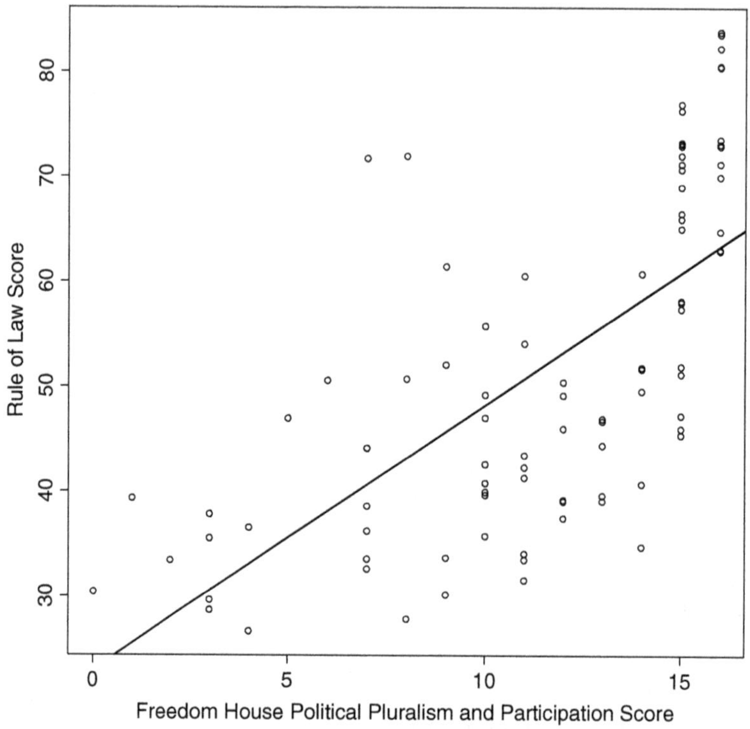

FIGURE 9F Rule of law and political pluralism scores

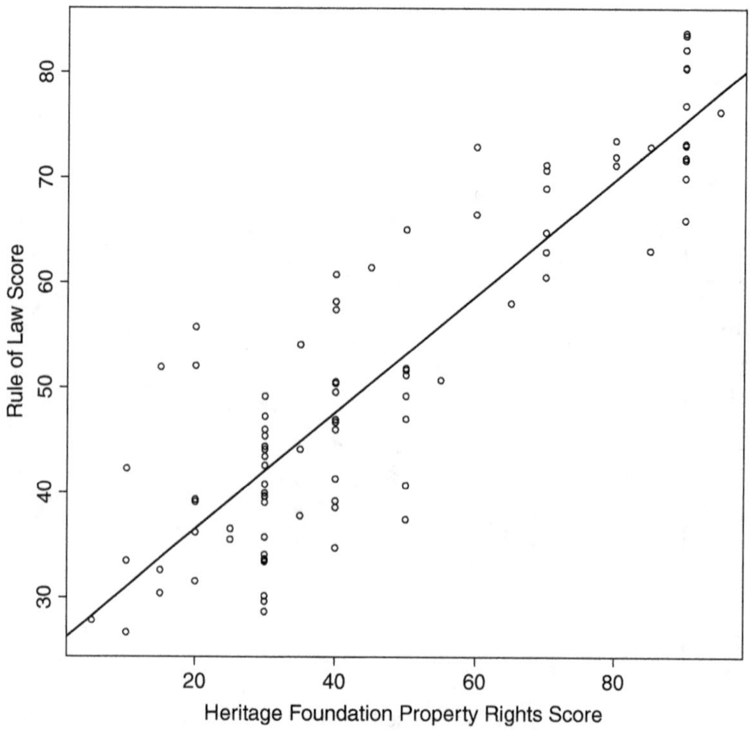

FIGURE 9G Rule of law and property rights scores

Conclusion

A commitment to equality begins at home

To build a legal system that is regular, public, and general is to set the state on a course in which its overwhelming power is to be used against the people in the community only when those who wield it can explain, to the satisfaction of a watchful public, how its use is consistent with the equal standing of those against whom it is to be used. To establish such a system is to declare a commitment to equality; to maintain it is to rely on that commitment across the political community. That, in two sentences, has been the argument of this book.

The promotion and maintenance of the rule of law is an urgent human rights problem. There are countless people living and dying in terror at the hands of thugs in uniforms, and more who are doomed to social, economic, and political inferiority and misery by unjust and hierarchical legal systems. I do not expect that this small book can contribute much to resolve these problems. If it helps at all, it may only be by offering a language in which we can discuss the rule of law without focusing on the self-absorbed economic and political interests of the wealthy and powerful. The rule of law is a way of respecting the equal moral worth of all humans; we ought to say so, and work to build this equality across the world.

Contemporary rule of law talk often sounds like those who seek to promote the law in the developing world placidly assume that it's being exported from countries in the developed world that have successfully held on to the value. But critics within the developed world have called this into question. For example, many have argued that the war on terror has undermined the commitment of the United States and other Western democracies to rule of law values in favor of regimes of so-called enhanced interrogation, secret and procedurally bare military trials, extrajudicial assassinations, torture, and the like.[1]

Nor may we be complacent about maintaining the rule of law in the Western democracies to the extent it does exist. One important implication of the strategic analysis in Chapter 6 is that the rule of law is sensitive to shifts in political, economic, and military power. If power shifts away from the lowest socioeconomic classes, there is a long-term risk to the generality of the legal system: if the lowest classes are no longer needed to hold officials to complying with the law, then the law need not take their interests into account. Similarly, if power shifts away from nonofficials as a whole, even the weak version of the rule of law is put at risk, to the extent nonofficials no longer have the resources to effectively sanction officials for ignoring the law. Several developments in the Western democracies – particularly the United States – over the past few years appear to pose these dangers. The most obvious developments include increasing economic inequality[2] and the capture of political institutions by powerful and narrow interests.[3]

Equally worrying is the advent of private military contractors, and the potential for increased use of professional and elite military units, automated drones, and other developments that shift military force away from mass publics and toward centralized control. To the extent that top-level officials have greater centralized control over military force, this deprives ordinary citizens of the power to resist officials by, for example, refusing to fire on their fellow citizens to enforce illegal policies (as we saw during the Arab Spring in Egypt[4]), and midlevel officials of the administrative power to resist higher-level officials by depriving them of military force or by turning it against them.[5] Even the "big data" revolution poses risks: a government that has copious information about its citizens thereby increases its discretion over them: imagine if traffic police could monitor all our driving activity, and choose to punish any of us for the numerous minor traffic violations we may commit each day. Open threats can appear in the aggregate as well as the discrete.

As alarming as the way the Western democracies are treating those who are perceived as an external threat is the way minorities are being treated in our own communities. In the United States, African-Americans in particular (but also other racial minorities, particularly Latinos in the border states) are subject to extraordinary police paranoia and misconduct. In Europe, the targets du jour are Muslims (who are, of course, not free from official discrimination in the United States, either).[6] Some basic data are incredibly damning: according to the National Association for the Advancement of Colored People (NAACP), blacks and Latinos together make up only about a quarter of the population, but (as of 2008) 58 percent of the prison population; the incarceration rate for blacks is six times that of whites; and "[i]f current trends continue, one in three black males born today can expect to spend time in prison during his lifetime."[7] The racial composition of juries has an alarming effect on conviction rates by race: with no black people in the jury, conviction rates go significantly up for black people and down for white people.[8] White crime victims receive significantly faster and more effective responses from the police than do black victims.[9] Blacks receive significantly harsher sentences.[10]

The consequences of this system have been amply documented by Michelle Alexander: the United States effectively operates a racialized system of segregation via the criminal justice system in which blacks are grossly disproportionately stopped, arrested, convicted, and punished, and then subjected to lifelong disabilities, including exclusion from employment, housing, juries, the franchise, and public benefits, all of which lead to reincarceration, poverty, and broken families.[11]

Defenders of racial profiling allege that there are statistical correlations between race and crime, which, if true, might conceivably constitute a public reason for the practice. However, that argument falls prey to three fatal problems. First is the easy one: even when whites unambiguously commit crimes as often or more often than blacks, it's blacks who are disproportionately subjected to every stage of the criminal justice system.[12] Second is a simple confusion about generality: as the argument in Chapters 2 and 3 establishes, to the extent the state is substantially responsible for the poverty and inequality of subordinated minorities, as it doubtless is, it cannot use the consequences of that poverty as an excuse to impose unequal policing on those groups consistent with public reason.[13] Third, such practices become a self-fulfilling prophecy: investigating more crimes among racially subordinated groups means that more crimes will be discovered among those groups, even relative to their rates of criminal behavior; the consequence will be further apparent justification in crime statistics for profiling in a vicious cycle that leads to the creation of presumptively criminal classes; additional investigation and disparate punishing will exacerbate also the cycle of poverty in a community, and thereby increase actual as well as perceived crime rates.

Communicating to racial, ethnic, and religious minorities that they are seen as subordinate legal classes predisposed to criminality will make it more difficult for the subordinated minorities to take the internal point of view on the law. Substantially more blacks than whites think that the US criminal justice system does not give fair trials or treat people equally.[14] A substantially higher proportion of blacks than whites in the United States view the criminal justice system as unfair to blacks.[15] This disparity extends to juveniles: black and Latino teenagers hold less positive views of the police than white teenagers hold.[16] The obvious surmise is that this suspicion and contempt are caused by police misconduct toward blacks; this surmise is supported by the data.[17] Not only does this plausibly feed individual crime, but it also feeds collective violence: racial disparities in policing and racial police brutality have contributed to numerous riots in the United States.[18] And it feeds organized opposition to criminal justice institutions: police violence was a major factor in the formation, for example, of the Black Panther Party and its revolutionary ideology.[19]

To the extent we in the Western democracies are unwilling to defend the legal rights of those in our societies whom we perceive as threatening, either because of statistical and stereotypical association with criminality or because of religious and ethnic similarity with some of the members of one particular subgroup of terrorists, we undermine our ability to defend the rule of law for other, less unpopular, groups in the future. This is a straightforward implication of the coordination account in Chapter 6. To the extent the courts disregard the rights of blacks or Muslims, they undermine their power to signal violations of the rule of law in the future; to the extent the white/non-Muslim public does not resist lawless official action against blacks and Muslims, they undermine the collective trust and faith in the system necessary to deter lawless official action against themselves tomorrow. Of course, that's not the only reason to defend the rights of the victims of racism in contemporary democracies. There's a moral obligation to do so. But sometimes powerful majorities need more self-interested reasons: here's one that advocates of the rule of law can offer.[20]

The case of the black community in the United States can stand as the final, abbreviated case study with which to conclude this book. The risk of imprisonment by age 30 for African-American men born in the late 1970s has been calculated at more than 25 percent – a figure that does not even include interactions with the criminal justice system short of imprisonment such as constant police harassment, serving time in local jails, and taking plea bargains leading to suspended sentences (and all the lifelong collateral consequences of a criminal record).[21] As Alexander details, much of the racial disparity in mass incarceration is driven by a legal system that permits unbounded discretion in the war on drugs, both to police (to carry out pretextual stops and notional "consent" searches based on conscious and unconscious racial bias, and to focus their enforcement efforts on blacks even when whites commit crimes at the same or higher rates) and to prosecutors (to grossly overcharge blacks, channel blacks to the harsher federal system, and leave blacks languishing in prison with steep bonds in order to extract plea bargains even from the innocent) and in doing so impose a life of stigma and civil disability on a huge proportion of the black community, and reestablish the racial caste system supposedly destroyed by the civil rights movement.

As I write these words in the summer of 2015, the United States has just suffered through a heartbreaking year of astonishing police-initiated bloodshed of African-Americans. Ezell Ford, John Crawford, 12-year-old Tamir Rice, Eric Garner, Akai Gurley, Michael Brown, Walter Scott, and Freddie Gray have died, among others. Protests have shaken dozens of American cities. Riots have broken out in Ferguson, Missouri, and in Baltimore, Maryland. Worse, this year has simply made salient the fears of black families across the nation. America's police departments seem to have learned nothing from the long history of shock and horror at their treatment of blacks, like Oscar Grant, Rodney King, Amadou Diallo, Abner Louima, and many others. And there is precious little evidence of accountability. Officers are often not charged; if charged, they are often not convicted, and are sometimes given preferential treatment; in one notorious example in the Baltimore case, a killer cop was given a lighter bail than one of the rioters who rose up in response, even though the cop was charged with murder and the rioter had merely vandalized a police car.[22]

Freddie Gray is believed by many to have died after a "rough ride" – an informal custom of illegal police violence in which a victim is put in a police vehicle without a seatbelt and then thrown around by its motion. In Los Angeles, a similar technique is apparently called a "screen test," the twisted witticism referring both to the native movie industry and to the screen that separates arrestee from officer in a police car, and into which the arrestee is thrown by deliberately erratic driving.[23] One longtime Baltimore city journalist explained the customs that, in the days prior to the war on drugs, used to govern the illegal police use of arbitrary arrests and arbitrary violence.[24] According to this journalist, there used to be an informal "code" indicating which kinds of behavior would generate an arbitrary arrest (what he called "a humble" – "a cheap, inconsequential arrest that nonetheless gives the guy a night or two in jail before he sees a court commissioner"). The code also regulated the conditions under which the police would inflict arbitrary violence on a citizen, to an astonishingly fine-grained level: calling an officer a "motherfucker" was okay, but calling one an "asshole" meant "you're going hard into the wagon in Baltimore."

However, astonishingly, that world – in which police brutality was apparently governed by an informal and unenforced code specifying the degree of disrespect one was allowed to show before being subjected to arbitrary extreme violence – was the "good old days," when there were rules (albeit illegal and corrupt ones) governing the violent abuse of the authority of the police and the weapons with which they are entrusted, before the pressure of the war on drugs undermined even those rules. Today, if this journalist is to be believed, all bets would appear to be off. Even the mayor of New York has felt the need to warn his son about the dangers of having dark skin and dealing with the New York Police Department.[25] In retaliation for Mayor de Blasio's expression of concern for his child, and apparently horrified at the notion that anyone in authority would acknowledge their out-of-control racial aggression in public, the police turned their backs on him at an officer's funeral and staged a work slowdown.[26] According to one anonymously sourced press report, the public housing authority in New York has told its workers to wear bright orange vests in order to not be mistaken for residents and shot by the police.[27]

In famously liberal San Francisco, a number of police officers were fired for sending text messages among themselves that included repeated use of the term "nigger," references to cross burning, "white power," and this lovely sequence of messages: (1) "I hate to tell you this but my wife friend is over with their kids and her husband is black! If is an Attorney but should I be worried?" (2) "Get ur pocket gun. Keep it available in case the monkey returns to his roots. Its not against the law to put an animal down." (3) "Well said!"[28] Does "pocket gun" mean a gun to be planted on the officer's dead victim? Does it just mean a secondary gun to be used to kill the victim based on the concession that one ought not to commit a murder with one's actual service revolver? Who can tell?

Arbitrary violence against African-Americans is not the only gross misconduct to which the modern American police department seems to be susceptible. The unrest in Ferguson was also driven by an egregious record of petty authoritarianism in St. Louis County, in which poor African-Americans were aggressively taxed by an endless parade of penny-ante regulations and citations, leading to endless cycles of fines, penalties, arrest warrants for not paying the fines and penalties, further fines and penalties, and so forth, and an astonishing statistic:

in 2013, Ferguson issued 1.5 arrest warrants per resident.[29] This state of affairs can only be described as a conspiracy between the police, local elected officials, and local courts against poor blacks – and if it took a killing and a riot to bring the conditions in St. Louis County to the attention of the rest of the country, how many more have not been revealed?

Moreover, while blacks get the brunt of the abuse, there have also been astonishing stories of nonracial (or less obviously racial) abuse. Most astonishingly in the past year, *The Guardian* broke the story of the "black site" maintained by the Chicago police department, where off-the-books interrogations were conducted.[30]

All of these stories came out in the past twelve months, as of this writing. Broader trends are equally alarming. The police have come up with a name for their own (apparently routine) perjury: "testilying."[31] Police departments regularly seize the assets of citizens who are not convicted of any crime, and keep the money.[32] And they do it with a growing arsenal of totally unnecessary military-level equipment and tactics, going so far as to serve minor warrants with heavily armed SWAT teams.[33] The deaths of young black men are also not new: the killings of black men by police have outstripped those of white men consistently since 1960.[34]

It is extremely difficult to avoid the impression that police departments in the United States have gone completely out of control, and in some communities act more like an occupying military force than the police of a stable liberal democracy under the rule of law. And the rest of the population has not responded to these infamies in the way one would expect from a stable rule of law state (i.e., demanding that politicians bring the police to heel, and removing them from office if they fail to do so). African-Americans seem to have been excluded from the rule of law collective commitment and enforcement bargain. And the fact that police abuse is showing signs of expansion to citizens of other races (black sites, asset forfeitures, etc.) is just what the theory of this book would predict in such a situation: the police are learning that the rest of the community does not always credibly threaten to hold them to account for their use of power; the rest of the American public is becoming habituated to allowing police misconduct to pass by unsanctioned.

This cannot be tolerated. As police slip further out of control without public intervention, it becomes harder to believe that the American people are genuinely committed to the rule of law, and harder for us to trust one another to enforce it more generally. We doubtless have a long way to go before the rule of law melts down altogether – but American whites should pray that the day never comes when the defense of their rights requires coordinated political action from long-neglected and abused blacks and other racial minorities, for it is hard to see why the latter should see themselves as having a stake in the system. And it is a great moral stain: the United States reinforces the social subordination of people of color by subjecting them to daily hubris and terror from law enforcement.

The time may have come to seriously contemplate truly radical reforms to American policing. I am no criminal justice expert; however, several policy options seem worthy of consideration. For example, we might abolish civil asset forfeiture altogether. We might remove SWAT teams from the operational control of ordinary police, and place them under the operational control of locally elected civilian leaders, to be deployed only when both police and civilians agree that they are necessary. We might institute mandatory grand jury inquiries in the case of every civilian killed in police custody or by a police weapon. We might consider restricting ordinary patrol officers to carry nonlethal weapons only.

We may even borrow some of the ideas about radical localism developed in the previous chapter and apply them at home. Existing methods of incorporating citizens into the legal system are not fully optimized for recruiting public support for their judgments: grand jury proceedings are entirely secret and totally controlled by prosecutors, while petit juries deliberate in secret and are hampered by the sanitized information that makes it through the rules of evidence and a limited decisional scope ("questions of fact").

We could involve the public more deeply. Trials of police officers whose actions have led to citizen deaths could, for example, be conducted by wholly public (and large) deliberative assemblies, selected genuinely randomly from the whole population (rather than from the subset with driver's licenses and voter registrations and subject to challenge from lawyers), with the authority to come to an all-things-considered judgment on the propriety of the officer's act, subject only to deferential appellate review by professional judges.

Whatever we do, we must stop the racial disparities that exist at every level of the criminal justice system. Police officers need to be punished for using unnecessary violence against African-Americans. Police departments need to be punished, or even disbanded, for maintaining policies and training programs that encourage this behavior. The private citizens who facilitate racist policing by summoning the state whenever they come across a neighbor who seems suspicious only because of the color of his or her skin should be fined for filing frivolous police reports. Municipalities that fund their operations via the systematic juridical expropriation of racial minorities and the poor should lose their charters and be annexed into larger urban areas that are more resistant to capture. Policy options need to be investigated to ameliorate the truly difficult root problem underlying these disasters – the persistent de facto residential segregation that allows the United States to be divided into poor minority neighborhoods with oppressive local governments and richer and whiter neighborhoods with solicitous ones.[35] Criminal sentences need to be overturned or reduced on appeal to the extent that the variation among them can be attributed, statistically, to broader patterns of racial disparity in charging and sentencing; arrests and charges need to be dismissed on the same grounds.[36] Felon disenfranchisement must end. Only then will we be able to hold out American institutions as the model of the rule of law to be followed across the world. Rule of law reform begins at home.

Notes

INTRODUCTION

1. Dworkin (1986). The best overall review of the rule of law literature is in Tamanaha (2004). An excellent more recent overview is in Goldston (2014).
2. Waldron (2002, 137–64).
3. Index specification online at http://info.worldbank.org/governance/wgi/pdf/rl.pdf.
4. Index specification online at http://worldjusticeproject.org/?q=rule-of-law-index/dimensions.
5. Fukuyama (2010, 33–34).
6. Pinochet's Chile combined capitalism and the protection of property rights with a system of state terror against dissidents (Letelier 1976; Silva 1993). Barros (2003, 214) claims that Chile achieved a form of the rule of law because legislative power was subject to some constitutional controls; however, in view of the fact that Pinochet possessed what Barros delicately describes as "discretionary authority to restrict individual freedoms without legal justification," including "a number of extrajudicial executions," the notion that Chile satisfied the rule of law to any degree whatsoever is highly implausible.
7. On "the conventional wisdom," "the rule of law appeals as a remedy for every major political, economic, and social challenge facing transitional countries," and is "considered indispensable for democracy, economic success, and social stability" (Carothers 1999, 164).
8. See the discussion in Haggard, MacIntyre, and Tiede (2008, 205–34).
9. For the most extreme case, Walker (1988, 24–41) gives twelve requirements described over seventeen pages of text.
10. For example, Allan (2001).
11. Williamson (1990); Santiso (2001, 1–22). For an example of this kind of talk, see Fukuyama (2004, 29–30), who runs together "institutions," "state capacity," "state strength," "smoothly functioning legal institutions," and "formal, enforceable property rights" into a general notion of a state that, while it doesn't interfere in the economy, nonetheless provides solid and reliable rules of the game in which it can operate. For an apt critique of the abuse of

the concept of the rule of law by the participants in the Washington consensus, see Tamanaha (2008, 537–41).

CHAPTER 1 THE RULE OF LAW: A BASIC ACCOUNT

1. Gowder (2013, 2014c, 2014d).
2. Gowder (2013). Other obvious objections are addressed in Gowder (2014c).
3. This is the part that has been elaborated in much more detail elsewhere (Gowder 2014d, "Institutional Values"). The first few sentences of this paragraph are a close paraphrase, bordering on quotation, from the first page of that paper.
4. *Ibid.*
5. I use "coercion," "power," and "violence" interchangeably throughout; the state's coercive power is always backed up by the use or threat of violence.
6. See Raz's (1979, 30) argument that the law necessarily claims that its authority is legitimate and Weber's (1946, 83) argument that the state monopolizes legitimate force.
7. This last idea is drawn from Nagel (2005, 113–47).
8. Here, I draw inspiration from Sally Haslanger's (2012, 303) conceptual analysis of gender and race. As Haslanger argues, our concepts can be underdetermined by descriptive facts, and it is appropriate under such circumstances to build our concepts in part based on "what we want them to be," that is, on the real-world uses for our concepts. Haslanger thus defends race and gender concepts that are appropriate to pursue social justice; likewise, we should build our concept of the rule of law in such a way that it allows us to pursue legal justice.
9. It makes no difference whether we say that officials ought to be bound by "rules" or by "legal rules." I count those social rules that constrain state power or authorize its use as legal rules (for rule of law purposes) regardless of the form in which they appear. Also, I will use "laws," "rules," and "legal rules" interchangeably.
10. This idea goes back to Aristotle (Pol. 3.1287a), who asserts that equality demands that those who govern be mere "guardians" of the law. It makes a contemporary appearance in North, Wallis, and Weingast (2009), who argue that the rule of law is one facet of an impersonal social order in which institutional roles are separate from personal identities.
11. The title has also been given as "Pamcayata" and "Pamca-Paramesvara," and is usually translated roughly as "The Panchayat Is the Voice of God." I have relied on the translation by Nopany and Lal (1980).
12. Of course, not all rule of law societies have all of these features, and certainly do not instantiate them in the same way. The three principles are functional generalizations from the practices of a variety of rule of law societies.
13. Traditionally, these practices have been captured under the notion of "predictability." I have argued against the predictability conception of the rule of law elsewhere (Gowder 2013, 576–78).

14. Macedo (1994) cogently argues that this is a necessary property of general rules.
15. Burton (1992) argues that to judge in good faith in the face of legal indeterminacy or discretion is to weigh the legal reasons – the considerations given by legal sources, rather than by personal interests and beliefs independent of legal sources – in coming to a decision. This is similar to Hart's (2013) notion that discretion is not a matter of unfettered choice, but an act of sound judgment – an exercise of judicial virtues. The principle of regularity requires judges as well as other officials to engage in such a weighing process whenever they are faced with a discretionary decision. We may also understand the considerations of policy or value that can be reasonably seen as underlying a grant of discretion as legal reasons. If officials are constrained to act in good faith in this sense, they do not have open threats – they might be able to reach more than one decision, but they will not be able to reach decisions that are explainable only as exercises of unfettered will.
16. Dworkin (1967).
17. In order to satisfy the principle of publicity, subjects must be able to know and make use of these other sources of constraint: they must, for example, be able to offer unwritten extensions to de jure rules as arguments in court, or deploy social and political institutions to sanction judges for abusing their discretion.
18. The law can be public with respect to some subjects but not others (e.g., if women must rely on male guardians to appear for them in court).
19. Waldron (2011b) offers an extensive list of judicial procedures that contribute to satisfying his version of the publicity principle.
20. This argument owes much to Diver (1983), who argued that the notion of "precision" in legal rules refers to "transparency," the extent to which their words are meaningful among those who are to obey and enforce them; "accessibility," or how easy to apply they are; and "congruence," or tracking of the intentions of the lawmaker.
21. Note that a law written in Officialish has another name in the real world: a secret law.
22. To the extent her interpretation is available for use in future cases, either as authoritative or persuasive precedent, this translation process is more effective, for it confers on subjects in those cases additional epistemic and argumentative resources for use in them.
23. Cohen (2010). In the words of Judge Kozinski, dissenting from the refusal to punish a judge who issued a ruling "just because I said it": "No one knew why the district judge had done what he did – the order gave no reasons, cited no authority, made no reference to a motion or other petition, imposed no bond, balanced no equities. The two orders were a raw exercise of judicial power." *In re: Complaint of Judicial Misconduct*, 9th Circuit No. 03–89037, unpublished opinion of September 29, 2005, available online at http://caselaw.findlaw.com/9th-circuit-judicial-council/1023783.html.
24. Schauer (1995, 633–59) points out that reason-giving behavior can be an expression of relative status in this way. See also Schwartzman (2008, 1004),

who argues that giving reasons is necessary to "respect the rational capacities of those subject to their authority," and works cited therein.

25. Kramer (2007, 65–66) aptly argues that an official who makes rulings solely on the basis of her own interests shows "contempt" for the interests of those who have come before her. My position is more ambitious, since it does not depend on the official's rulings being self-interested.
26. When I say that a legal act *expresses respect* (or disrespect), I mean to invoke the conception of expressing value with actions given by Anderson and Pildes (2000, 1510), broadly speaking, to act in a way appropriate for someone who has respect for the other. For much more about how legal acts express values, see the next chapter.
27. For this reason, officials must actually be constrained, just as in the principle of regularity, to offer reasons for their uses of coercive power. If an official explains herself to a subject out of the goodness of her heart, that explanation is not a product of the official's being accountable to the subject, and cannot express that accountability. This is part of why publicity depends on regularity.
28. Compare Allan (2001, 79), who suggests that legal systems in which subjects of law are entitled to offer arguments to the decision maker and receive reasons for their treatment express respect by recruiting their acceptance of the outcome, either as fully justified or at least as "fairly adopted by [democratic] procedures enabling all citizens to exert an influence." My claim is weaker: an official act of coercion carried out pursuant to the principles of regularity and publicity might be carried out without any claim that the law applied is justifiable to the subject, but nonetheless is minimally respectful insofar as the official carrying out the coercion at least acknowledges some source of authority other than her own will that grounds her use of power over the subject, and acknowledges the subject as someone who is capable of responding to reasons.
29. Even in a state where the monarch is the final judge, the monarch cannot make every decision; most day-to-day interactions between citizens and the state will involve officials applying someone else's general judgments.
30. For more on role separation, see Gowder (2014e).
31. Shklar (1998) interprets Montesquieu's account of the rule of law as essentially concerned with protecting the populace from fear.
32. Pettit (1996, 584) has aptly caught the gist of this form of inequality in the form of the concept of "domination":

    > The powerless are not going to be able to look the powerful in the eye ... the asymmetry between the two sides will be a communicative as well as an objective reality. Conscious of this problem, John Milton deplored "the perpetual bowings and cringings of an abject people" that he thought were inevitable in monarchies. And a little later in the seventeenth century, Algernon Sydney could observe that "slavery doth naturally produce meanness of spirit, with its worst effect, flattery."

    (Internal citations, footnotes omitted.)

33. See Dershowitz (2003, 275–94) on this possibility. I thank David Dyzenhaus for raising this point.
34. Here, I disagree with Allan (2001, 63), who implies that it is only "in the context of a liberal democracy" that "departures from [the weak version of] the rule of law are properly occasions of moral censure." Brettschneider (2011, 60) seems to have the right of it when he points out that "nonarbitrariness" (about which, see Chapter 3) is an "entitlement[ ] that individuals enjoy distinct from their participatory rights."
35. Gowder (2013) defends the factual robustness idea further.
36. Those in the "status egalitarian" school of thought associated with, inter alia, Anderson (1999, 287–337) and Scheffler (2003, 5–39) are particularly likely to endorse the notion that hubris and terror are forms of status or dignitary inequality. Hegel (1991, sec. 132, 215, 228, 258) offers an autonomy-centered version of the same idea, suggesting that the "right of self-consciousness," a "right to recognize nothing that I do not perceive as rational," grounded on the individual's "intellectual and ... ethical worth and dignity" entitles individuals to know the law, and also shields individuals from exploitation by those who do know the law, who would otherwise be reduced to an underclass in "serfdom." Waldron (2012) has similarly argued that the law contributes to individual dignity in virtue of the fact that it is "self-applying" – that individuals are expected to apply its commands to themselves.
37. Those who subscribe to Christiano's (2008) conception of egalitarian democracy should agree that publicity is required for what Christiano calls "public equality," a principle requiring that citizens not only be treated as equals but be able to observe their equal treatment.
38. For example, the approach in Sen (1980/2011, 195–220) would be compatible with such an argument.
39. Pseudo-Xenophon (1968).
40. Pseudo-Xenophon (1968, 479–81).
41. The term used here is ισηγοριαν, which usually means political equality. Obviously, slaves and citizens did not have political equality in Athens. Marr and Rhodes (2008, 79) suggest that a literal translation of the word as "equality of free speech" is appropriate, in which case it appears to amount to the claim, consistent with my account, that slaves were permitted to talk back or mouth off to citizens; that is, they did not need to behave deferentially.
42. "Commands backed up by the threat of violence" includes not only the traditional sort of command on which the pre-Hart positivists focused ("pay your taxes or go to jail"), but also power-conferring rules and the like that can authorize the eventual application of state violence. For example, the laws permitting citizens to make contracts are backed up with violence insofar as one consequence of breaching a contract is a civil judgment for money damages, and civil judgments are backed up by force (armed police seizing one's property, etc.).
43. Ordinary language users routinely criticize individual officials' behavior on rule of law grounds. We should understand such criticisms in one of two ways.

Sometimes they amount to the claim that *if the behavior became routine* it would threaten the rule of law. Thus, if we say to a police officer, "The rule of law gives you reason not to have beaten that citizen just because you were in a bad mood," what we mean is that his behavior is not generalizable consistent with the rule of law. Other times, they refer to the effects of an individual action on the state as a whole. For example, when we criticize a judicial opinion for offending the rule of law, we often are concerned with its precedential effect and the behavior it will authorize for other officials.

44. As Levi (1990, 403) points out, the term "institution" often goes invoked but undefined.
45. Summers (1999, 1695) calls these "devices" to achieve the more abstract goals of the rule of law. His distinction between devices and principles is essentially the same as mine between practices and institutional principles.
46. Dworkin (1986).
47. The rule of law does require that officials respect such property rights as exist.
48. For a defense of the formality of the rule of law, see Summers (1993); for a defense of the proposition that the rule of law does not require extensive property rights, see Waldron (2011a).
49. Allan (2001, 38) denies this, apparently on the misapprehension that to say that a value can be satisfied to a greater or lesser extent, or is "only a matter of degree," is to deny that it is obligatory. Characterizing Raz's view: "since [the rule of law] may be possessed to a greater or lesser degree, it should not be permitted to impede the pursuit of important governmental purposes" (*ibid.*). But a value can be a continuum rather than a binary and still be obligatory; utilitarians, for the most obvious example, can coherently say that we are absolutely obliged to maximize aggregate utility, even though aggregate utility is a continuous variable. Moreover, most political values on most accounts (saving those of value monists), be they binary or continuous and whether they generate an absolute normative "must" or not, may conflict and must sometimes be subject to trade-offs.
50. For some of the landscape, see Waldron (2008), Sevel (2009), and Raz (1979). The view that the rule of law and law itself are different tends to be associated with positivists, and I tend to accept positivism; I also tend to accept the separation between law and the rule of law. However, since nothing is at stake in that separation, this account of the rule of law ought to also be compatible with nonpositivist views.
51. Simmonds (2007, 46–54).
52. Fuller (1969).
53. Lovett (2002, 41–78); Marmor (2007); Rijpkema (2013, 806).
54. To be clear, it's not in virtue of the moral properties of regularity and publicity that law must be minimally regular and public; it's merely a pragmatic necessity of command-giving behavior. In Kantian terms, we expect moral principles to issue categorical imperatives, but the claim at issue is merely a hypothetical imperative: "If you want to effectively boss people around, then you should make sure they know your commands and can anticipate their

enforcement." Nonetheless, the state of affairs generated by officials who act in accordance with this hypothetical imperative may itself be morally valuable.

55. This is a point that Marmor (2007) seems to miss – in defending Fuller's claim that those elements of the rule of law necessary for the law to effectively function confer moral value on the state, he ignores the fact that officials can operate a "dual state" (Fraenkel 1941), in which it runs government under law for ordinary business, while still preserving a prerogative power allowing it to totally vitiate the moral value of the rule of law by disregarding legal rules when those in power so desire.

CHAPTER 2 THE STRONG VERSION OF THE RULE OF LAW

1. Just about every scholar who thinks that generality is part of the correct conception of the rule of law credits it with egalitarian moral value. This goes at least as far back as Dicey (1982, 114–15). The most interesting version of the idea is Waldron's (2012) suggestion that the general distribution of the protections of modern law represents a concept of "human dignity" that makes universal the high status previously enjoyed only by the nobility. Habermas (1996, 473) interprets Kant and Rousseau as claiming that legal generality is an egalitarian principle. Hayek (1960, 85, 209) claims that it's the *only* permissible sort of legal equality. Ignatieff (2004, 30) deploys the egalitarian view of generality to criticize the detention of Arabs and Muslims in the contemporary United States.
2. Hayek (1960, 150–55).
3. Rawls (1999b, 237).
4. Hart (1958, 623–24).
5. Raz (1979).
6. Rousseau (2003, 2.6). Moore (1985, 316) offers another minimal conception, suggesting that the "treat like cases alike" principle only requires courts to respect stare decisis.
7. As Schauer (1995) points out, the practice of giving reasons amounts to an appeal to general propositions: to say "I did X for Y" is to assert that in other cases in which Y applies, one will do X. This suggests that there can be no purely formal conception of generality with any normative appeal, because any reason for a decision, even a terrible one like "I convicted the defendant because I don't like him," is formally general.
8. This idea has made an appearance in US law, in *Royster Guano Co. v. Virginia*, 253 U.S. 412, 415 (1920) ("the classification must be reasonable, not arbitrary, and must rest upon some ground of difference having a fair and substantial relation to the object of the legislation, so that all persons similarly circumstanced shall be treated alike").
9. For example, Fuller (1969, 47, 51–52 n. 10) describes the version of the principle of generality that forbids law with proper names, and describes the motivation for the bill of attainder clause in US Constitution as a commitment to the principle of generality.

10. Hayek (1960, 153, 209).
11. Examples include Hayek (1960, 150–55), Rawls (1999b, 237); Hart (1958, 623–24).
12. One might argue, in favor of the minimal conception, that it forbids legislatures from targeting people (e.g., out of malice). However, the minimal conception is insufficient to do this: even were it coherent, it might prohibit some official from enacting a malicious law against one person, but might not prohibit someone from enacting a malicious law against a whole disfavored class (such as anti-Semitic laws).
13. This is a well-known philosophical problem. Quine (1969, 119) describes it as one of defining similarity over an infinite set of possible kinds (like "red things" or "round things").
14. West (2003, 121–24) describes a similar critique of the similarity conception from the critical legal studies movement.
15. Hayek (1960, 155) points out that under the formal conception of generality officials have to be subject to the same law as everyone else. This seems intuitively important, and might make up a defense of the formal conception, except that it's impossible. Officials cannot be subject to the same law as everyone else, because they have official powers, given by law, that others lack. Since they must be subject to some different legal rules from the rest of us, we must have some criterion by which we can pick out which differences are acceptable and which are not.
16. Contrary to the position of Schauer's (2003, 205) "skeptic," this is not to claim that the principle of equality is "empty." Rather, it is to claim that the relevant conception of equality is not one that demands that people be treated identically, but instead that people be treated as equals. For more, see Gowder (2014c).
17. Cf. Amar (1996, 209–17, 226), who seems to move back and forth between an epistemic formal conception of generality and a substantive egalitarian one.
18. Cohen (2009) argues that democracy requires the giving of public reasons in order to express the equality of all citizens. His point applies equally well to the rule of law, once we accept that the rule of law too serves equality.
19. Waldron (2001, 777–81) has a similar (though more demanding) idea. He too recognizes that the principle of treating like cases alike (what he calls "the consistency value of formal justice") requires legal actors to give reasons to one another, and argues that the reasons offered must be ones that treat individuals as ends in themselves, that eschew "aggregate justifications."
20. Along these lines, Solum (1993, 738) suggests that "when the requirements of the rule of law are observed, laws and regulations are addressed to the public at large." This leads him to the idea that public reason is appropriate for "public discussion about the coercive use of state power." This notion – that state power is addressed to the public at large – also helps us understand why the rule of law requirement of generality, as the principle governing state discrimination, might be different from (and more stringent than) the moral principles governing private discrimination. In particular, purely arbitrary

kinds of distinction, such as dispreferring those whose last names begin with "A" (discussed in Segev 2014, 58), may or may not be morally objectionable as grounds for private decision, but they are surely objectionable as grounds for public decisions, just because the state is obliged to offer public reasons when it coerces people with its laws.

21. West (2003, 149); Cohen (2009).
22. Anderson and Pildes (2000).
23. Rawls (1999a, 136–37).
24. This is equivalent to Schauer's (2003, 219) worry about the "treat like cases alike" principle, even interpreted consistently with the idea that it commands us to track relevant distinctions between people. Schauer argues that the principle is "either superfluous or irrelevant," because those who wish to viciously discriminate will (falsely) suppose that there are relevant differences (e.g., between blacks and whites in the Jim Crow era). The aim of the public reason conception of generality is to provide a ground for excluding some of those supposedly relevant differences, particularly those that require the attribution of inferiority to some citizens. To the extent it succeeds in doing so, it answers Schauer's worry.
25. Rawls's own elaboration of the requirement tends in this direction. For example, he suggests that relying on controversial economic theories is forbidden by public reason (Rawls 2005, 225).
26. I borrow the phrase from Nagel (1986).
27. Anderson (1993, 17–18).
28. The possibility of making such a determination is the key point in favor of understanding public reason as expressive: it gives one some social facts on which to hang one's evaluative hat in determining the extent to which a given reason is public.
29. At any rate, the legislature need not state its reasons for enacting a law, and different members of a legislature may support a law for different reasons. (Or legislators may utter sham reasons to disguise wicked or politically divisive intentions.) Under such circumstances, the attribution of reasons for some enactment will unavoidably be constructive: we actually attribute reasons to the legislature; we do not try to guess the beliefs and values held by individual legislators.

    However, public reasons must be able to justify the actual law enacted; in order to do so, it must be possible to plausibly say that the reasons under consideration are the actual reasons for the law (sham reasons or insincere reasons are not justifying). This need not require that any actual legislators hold the reasons in question, just that it must be possible to say with a straight face that they did.
30. This point was first noticed by Baker (2001, 593), who also makes similar points about what I call the conventional nature of legal meanings.
31. Here, I follow, and basically accept, Raz's (1979, 29–30) account of law's claim to authority.

32. On the notion of laws being enacted in citizens' names, see Nagel (2005, 128–29). Nagel's argument, on its terms, is not limited to democracies, and it has long been suggested that even nondemocracies act in the name of their citizens (e.g., by Hobbes, about monarchies).
33. It is worth noting that the assertion that the laws are enacted in the name of the people in the territory is most naturally associated with the Weberian property described in Chapter 1, that is, the state's claim that its monopoly over force is legitimate. The most obvious reason to think that state force is in fact legitimate (and the one relied on by political philosophers from Hobbes and Rousseau to Nozick) is that it is in some sense attributable to those over whom it is used; the Weberian claim and the "in citizens' names" claim go together.
34. This truth, of course, is embedded deeply into our constitutional ideas. Thus, the Supreme Court applies rational basis review to every legislative act, even those not impinging on a fundamental right or protected class (e.g., *Cleburne v. Cleburne Living Center*, 473 U.S. 432 [1985]). But the idea goes deeper: positive law is purpose-driven activity (the legislature is trying to bring something about by its enactments), and purpose-driven activity is under a rational requirement to take the means necessary to achieve its ends (Kant 2002, 31–34).
35. Davidson (2001a, chs. 9–10); Lewis (1974).
36. The final quote, and the principles of coherence and charity, come from Davidson (2001b).
37. Ordinarily, these attitudes will be beliefs; however, the expressive meaning of a law could comprise some other propositional attitude. Nothing in the argument turns on this. Beliefs might be about social, physical, or normative truths, or some combination of them – a law may require attributions of beliefs about, for example, economic theories, moral claims, or the character traits of particular persons or groups. Multiple sets of attitudes may supply the expressive meaning of a law – for example, we may attribute to the legislature that enacts a regressive tax the inclusive disjunction of hatred of the poor and/or a belief in supply-side economic theory. In such a case, both would count in the candidate reasons by which the law might be justified; if either is public, the law is general.
38. Street (2010, 363).
39. However, members of the community must be able to give the laws the interpretation claimed for them – the interpretation shouldn't be routinely met with a blank stare of confusion.
40. Such meanings are established by convention, similar to Lewis's (1975, 3–35) account of the relationship between meaning and convention. In the case of symbolic meanings embedded into law, the conventions that give meaning to the symbol will also give meaning to the law: if the state commands an utterance that symbolically means X (for example, commanding redheads to wear dunce caps, and thus to symbolically send the message "redheads are stupid"), that law will mean X just because people

in the community ordinary take the utterance the law commands to have that meaning.

41. This point isn't limited to utilitarianism, but applies to all forms of moral reasoning in which evaluations of institutions depend on facts about the world. For example, one might think that the laws creating a military draft are permissible only because one's state has institutions ensuring that it fights only just wars; if those institutions go away, the draft will become impermissible.

42. I thank Enrique Guerra for pressing me to clarify why public reasons are necessary from all three standpoints. Intuitively, those reasons also must be at least basically consistent with one another, in that, for example, a reason from the third-person standpoint that entails the negation of the only possible public reason from the first-person standpoint will not suffice. However, as I do not presently have any argument for that constraint beyond the intuition, this issue must be reserved for future work. (The intuition is driven by the notion of a principle of rational consistency that spans the three standpoints, but I am not certain that such a demand is required.)

43. Conceivably, a legislator might also have enacted the law to accommodate the racist attitudes of white private citizens. However, this amounts to the same idea of inferiority as that given in the text, since it requires the supposition that it is right that the members of the subordinate caste give way to accommodate the distaste held toward them by the dominant caste.

44. Here, I disagree with Hayek (1960, 154), one of whose formulations of the ideal of general law is that a law that carves out different classes of application is acceptable to the extent it is equally acceptable to those inside and outside of the relevant group. Hayek fails to attend to the possibility of false consciousness, leading some to endorse their own social inferiority.

45. Fiss (1976) gives an anticaste principle that has been dominant in the equal protection clause literature, but, oddly, has not made an impression in the rule of law literature on generality. Jeffries (1985, 213–14) has also aptly identified this as a goal of the rule of law.

46. Gowder (2015a) gives the history of state-invented and state-warped racial ascriptions in the United States, and references to the history in Rwanda.

47. I thank Kristen Bell for drawing my attention to this line of reasoning. It was also inspired by an argument for a reciprocity-based obligation to obey the law discussed in a workshop paper by Liam Murphy, as well as Sangiovanni's (2007) argument that claims to reciprocity from fellow citizens who have contributed to the institutional framework of a productive economy give rise to obligations of distributive justice. Michelman (2002, 974–77) considers a similar idea in a very abstract way, suggesting that public reason is a "reciprocity-tending" value that might guide judges.

Note that this conception of reciprocity is not the same as Fuller's. Fuller suggested that the rule of law establishes a relationship of reciprocity between ordinary people, who obey the law, and officials, who restrict their conduct to that consistent with the rule of law. (Fuller's explication of this point is somewhat obscure; Murphy's (2005, 242) explanation is helpful, though her interpretation of Raz's contrary position seems seriously mistaken.) By contrast, I have argued that the rule of law does not require nonofficials to obey the law, and am instead arguing that generality establishes a relationship of reciprocity among subjects of law, who do not receive special legal privileges against one another. In other words, what matters is not that subjects *actually obey* the law, but that they are subject to the same law, and subject to sanction on the same terms if they do not obey it. However, at the end of Chapter 4, I consider an interpretation of Fuller's version of reciprocity (Rundle 2012) that is quite congenial to mine.

48. Nozick (1974, 90–95) has an influential objection to this sort of fairness argument: in the course of rejecting the argument that citizens have obligations of distributive justice in virtue of their having received the benefits of an overall system of cooperation, he suggests that it's unreasonable to demand that our fellow citizens accept their share of the costs of a public good that we've imposed on them without their consent. However, Nozick's objection does not apply here, because this argument isn't directed at those who do not consent to the public good. Those who defend unequal legal systems typically want to have those whom they oppress regulated by state power, while accepting a lighter (or no) burden of state regulation for themselves: they demand the public good, but refuse to share it. I do not propose to offer an answer to the anarchist who flat-out rejects law's demands; many philosophers have done so elsewhere.

CHAPTER 3 GENERALITY AND HIERARCHY

1. Thus Justice Harlan, dissenting in a case involving public accommodations, worried that unless full civil rights were extended to freed slaves "the recent amendments [would] be splendid baubles thrown out to delude those who deserved fair and generous treatment at the hands of the nation." *Civil Rights Cases*, 109 U.S. 3, 48 (1888).
2. Brennan (2011). Brennan disclaims the further step of claiming that those who have a moral duty not to vote ought to be disenfranchised. Still, that step is arguably available to the supporter of a literacy test.
3. Mill (1977).
4. *Ibid.*
5. Sticht (2002) recounts Southern laws against educating slaves.
6. In Kantian terms, to demand that someone who suffers from a socially imposed disability sacrifice important interests in order to spare that same society from the consequences of that disability is to disrespectfully use that person's capacity to respond to reasons as a mere means for the ends of others. It's a form of moral exploitation.
7. France (1914).
8. E.g., Mitchell (1997, 303).
9. Waldron (1991) gives an apt analysis of this problem.

10. Ripstein (2009, 278) attributes a similar position to Fichte: property rights are unenforceable against the poor who have been neglected by the political community.
11. Thus, Locke (2002, IX.123–27) argues that the state's primary end is the protection of property rights.
12. Rawls (2001, 114, 138) describes the normative space for "liberal socialism," which preserves private property rights in personal property in order to facilitate individual autonomy, but does not permit private property in the means of production.
13. Consider Hobbes's argument in chapter 15 of *Leviathan*.
14. Ripstein (2009, 280).
15. Cf. Sepielli (2013, 698), who points out that wealth and poverty can be understood as state-imposed distributions of the burdens of complying with the property laws.
16. Allan (2001) makes this suggestion first.
17. I thank Patricia Broussard for suggesting this interpretation.
18. Note that we can't be sure that a decision is nongeneral just because it fails the test of decision-maker independence – two decision makers may come out to different results because they interpret facts or exercise discretion differently, within a range of reasonable variation; by contrast, a single decision maker may vary in obviously nongeneral fashions (as by flipping a coin). For this reason, this doesn't work as a (formal) conception of generality. However, a decision that isn't decision-maker independent is at least suspicious.
19. Curtis (1991) provides a good discussion. I thank Elizabeth Anderson for suggesting I consider the Levellers.
20. Brettschneider (2011) aptly suggests that the substantive face of the rule of law is an ideal of "nonarbitrariness," which means offering citizens reasons for the state's coercion that are consistent with their equal status.
21. E.g., Fallon (1997, 8).
22. Postema (2015). In response to such examples, Postema argues that law must offer people general guidance in structuring their relationships with one another. I take this to be roughly equivalent to the claim that people must ordinarily obey the law, or at least take it as reason-giving, even in wholly private interactions that do not carry with them the taint of state power.
23. The standard account is Simmons (1979). See also Raz (1979) and Edmundson (1999).
24. What about a duty to refrain from more serious lawbreaking like violence against other citizens? It's hard to see why we might need the rule of law to impose such duties on people, or even what the law itself might add to those duties. We may need the law to *enforce* those duties, but laws such as "no murdering" are probably the least convincing cases for the application of the notion that one has a moral duty to obey the law *as such*: one is not obliged to refrain from killing people because there's a law against it, one is obliged to refraining from killing people because murder is wrong. Perhaps the prohibition of theft is a special case, since the law at least serves the settlement/

coordination function of defining the details of property rights. Still, it's hard to see why we ought to locate any such duties the property laws impose under the head of "the rule of law," understood as a condition to be achieved through states; there is plenty of social scientific evidence that often people manage to handle such matters without availing themselves of states and formal law (Ostrom 1990; Ellickson 1991).

25. This objection may be avoided by supposing that the rule of law requires states to generate obedience without requiring states to obey. However, that position seems fairly implausible: do we really want to think that the state is *obliged* to prevent people from smoking marijuana, merely in virtue of the fact that it has forbidden the behavior?

26. One railroad went so far as to challenge a Mississippi law requiring it to enforce segregated cars within the state, and took the case all the way to the Supreme Court. It lost. *Louisville, New Orleans, & Texas Railway Co. v. Mississippi*, 133 U.S. 587 (1890).

27. It may be urged against this point that even if the rule of law does not require ordinary citizens to collaborate in the enforcement of profoundly unjust law, it still, on my argument, requires officials to do so. But this isn't right: officials are not required to actively enforce unjust law, but simply to refrain from using their power illegally and, like ordinary citizens, to work to resist the illegal uses of power of others This is a position perfectly consistent with the officials of evil regimes *declining to use their power at all*, as a form of passive resistance. They may also, of course, just resign their positions. The rule of law did not give the Nazi camp guards, or the South African officials under apartheid, or any of the other standard examples routinely trotted out in this situation a reason to obey their evil orders, even though those orders came cloaked in the forms of law. I have previously suggested something approaching the opposite position (Gowder 2013), but I now think this was a mistake.

28. Many times, blacks were outright forced to flee lynch-heavy communities (Tolnay and Beck 1992, 103–16).

29. Holden-Smith (1996, 36).

30. Howard's story is reported by King (2013, 101–04). A substantially more detailed version is given in chapter 4 of Hobbs (2004). That same year, a police constable in the same county forced yet another black man to jump to his death in the same river; he got a year in jail and a thousand-dollar fine (King 2013, 104).

31. Dunn (2007).

32. King (2013, 91–93, 98–99) gives the vivid example of the case of Sheriff Willis McCall, who not only recognized and protected the ringleaders of a mob (which itself included law enforcement officers) attempting to lynch four black men accused of rape, but also allowed them to burn the houses of some black citizens unmolested, and enforced only against blacks, not against whites, an order to disarm citizens seen roaming around with guns. In general, "fewer than 1 per cent of the lynchings before 1940 were ever followed by a

conviction of those responsible" (Clarke 1998, 281). Carr (2015) collects several studies on official complicity in lynching, which universally suggest deep official involvement; the most striking statistic is that in one 50-year period, victims were kidnapped out of police custody in 80 percent of the lynchings in Georgia and 94 percent of the lynchings in Virginia.

33. Holden-Smith (1996, 41–42).
34. *Ibid.*, 58.
35. I use the phrase "were accused" advisedly, since another common practice was the use of torture to extract false confessions from blacks accused of crimes against whites. Examples and details are given by Klarman (2000, 48–97).
36. Nor was this an unusual strategy: rogue states have often deliberately blurred the boundaries between private and public violence and used private violence to reinforce their political ends. Heaslet (1972, 1032–47) discusses one of the more prominent recent examples.
37. Carr (2015).
38. *Palmer v. Thompson*, 403 U.S. 217 (1971).
39. Gordy (1997) gives the history.
40. Cohen (2011, chs. 7–8).
41. The extent to which property rights generate open-ended threats depends on overall market conditions, as I discussed in Gowder (2014f).
42. Alexander (2012).

CHAPTER 4 EGALITARIAN LIBERTY AND RECIPROCITY IN STRATEGIC CONTEXT

1. Huth (1999).
2. Machiavelli (1997, 1.52, 3.19).
3. Suppose Louis gets some positive payoff (L) from punishing a citizen (e.g., he gets to loot that citizen's goods) and L > M. Under those circumstances, he still cannot enforce his commands: punishment of those with enough lootable goods is a strictly dominant strategy, such that the only subgame perfect equilibrium is citizen always disobeys, Louis always punishes. (Intuitively, a citizen has no reason to obey if he prefers to disobey and he'll be punished no matter what he does.) This predicts a kleptocracy similar to the Thirty Tyrants – discussed at length in the next two chapters – who executed and confiscated the goods of the wealthy without regard to whether their victims had obeyed the laws (Xen. Hel. 2.3.21, 2.4.1, Lys. 12.6–20).
4. Cf. Fearon (1997) on costly signals of willingness to use violence.
5. Of course, as in real states, we may see disobedience and punishment due to lack of information and erroneous calculation about the costs of punishment, the likelihood of discovery, and the like.
6. On audience costs, see Lohmann (2003). On audience costs in nondemocracies in general, see Weeks (2008).
7. The rules may also help Louis control Richelieu. Cf. Turner (1992, 32–33, 40–41), who finds evidence that rule of law principles with respect to clear laws

and defined punishments were pursued in Imperial China, motivated by the attempt to keep corrupt or incompetent magistrates from wasting "human and material resources for [the state's] use."

8. Even if the rule of law is established in response to the demands of nonrulers rather than by the initiative of rulers or other high officials, its establishment is still likely to give rulers the tools to precommit to carrying out threats. For, as I will show in Chapters 5 and 6, in order for the masses to establish and uphold the rule of law, they must themselves be able to credibly commit to enforcing the law as written, regardless of their substantive preferences about the content of that law. If officials who are not accountable to the masses are choosing the substance of what is to be enacted into that law, then a successfully mass-established rule of law will entail that the masses are committed to enforcing those official preferences, at least to some extent.

9. What about democratic societies? Well, they might have more or less liberty-preserving law, depending on things like the extent to which they have permanent cultural minorities, and so on. The rule of law (as discussed in Chapters 5, 6, and 8) may help them preserve their democratic character.

10. BBC World News, "Why Does Singapore Top So Many Tables?," October 23, 2013, available online at www.bbc.co.uk/news/world-asia-24428567, notes that Singapore is routinely rated extremely low crime, extremely low corruption, extremely friendly to business, extremely wealthy, and extremely low freedom, by the enterprises that study such things. For anyone who accepts both conventional conceptions of the rule of law, in which the rule of law supports both economic development (social scientists) and freedom (philosophers), and in which the rule of law is often measured with variables including property rights, crime control, and corruption (see Chapter 9), this must count as a serious anomaly. Another example is Turkey, at least circa 2013, which has been accused of having effective constitutionalism in the absence of liberal democratic rights (Isiksel 2013). For that reason, we would expect Turkey to have at least a substantial degree of the weak version of the rule of law, since the constitution too is law that might be reliably obeyed or not obeyed by the state. (However, I do have one reservation about the notion that Turkey as Isiksel describes it is a rule of law state, because the constitution in question permits its own violation through extensive "emergency" provisions.)

11. Accordingly, Singapore does have a rule of law score, from my analysis in Chapter 9, more than one standard deviation above the mean, even as Freedom House rates it below the mean on scores of political liberty, free expression, and free association. By contrast, Turkey's rule of law score ranks it just below the mean, and its Freedom House ratings all cluster around the mean.

12. Hayek (1960, 155). Assaf Sharon (2012) traces this argument back to Locke. *Federalist* No. 57 offers the point as a defense of the claim that the House of Representatives will not be able to make "oppressive measures" because "they can make no law which will not have its full operation on themselves and their friends, as well as on the great mass of the society."

13. The conception of the rule of law articulated in Chapters 1 and 2 also requires officials to apply the laws to themselves, except in those rare cases where public reasons can be offered for their exclusion.
14. See, e.g., Brian Murphy, "Saudi Arabia Partying: Elite, Boozy, and Secret," Associated Press/*Huffington Post*, December 8, 2010, www.huffingtonpost.com/2010/12/08/saudi-arabia-partying-eli_n_793997.html, reporting on leaked diplomatic memoranda describing a secret alcohol/prostitute party thrown by a Saudi prince.
15. It is far from obvious that enforcing alcohol and cross-gender fraternization laws against the Saudi elite would lead to the liberalization of those laws in the face of the strong elite as well as mass religious identity in Saudi Arabia. It might just force the rulers to limit their own hedonism – a nice result from the perspective of eliminating hypocrisy, but cold comfort to liberals.
16. Consider, for example, the rights of gays and lesbians: in heterosexual-dominated societies, officials are unlikely to be particularly concerned about preserving their own liberty to engage in same-sex intercourse.
17. *Railway Express Agency, Inc. v. New York*, 336 U.S. 106, 112 (1949) (Jackson, J. concurring).
18. Rawls (1999b, 207–10).
19. Kramer (1999, 54–55) makes two other apt points against the relationship between legal certainty and freedom. First, uncertainty about the enforcement of too constraining legal rules can effectively expand citizens' choice sets by allowing them to gamble on the nonenforcement of some law. Second, some of citizens' choices may involve interfering with other citizens' choices; legal uncertainty that chills those choices may provide an overall benefit from the standpoint of liberal liberty.
20. This also assumes that the identities of rulers are stable. This may be less plausible for individual autocracies – citizens of Rome might be justly afraid that Claudius could die tomorrow and be replaced by Nero – but more plausible for ruling parties and coalitions, military governments, and so on.
21. Kramer (1999, 69) points out that irrational rulers who impose punishment when citizens have not violated their rules thereby reduce the incentive citizens have to obey; this may actually make them more free, in practical terms.
22. Linz 2000, 159.
23. See Herndon and Baylen (1975, 493–97) on the military and political cost of Stalin's purge of the Red Army, and Birt (1993) on Stalin's paranoia in general.
24. North and Weingast (1989).
25. It might be objected that this holds for top-level rulers but not for their subordinates, who may also be vested with unconstrained power over ordinary citizens but whose preferences may be harder to know (if only because there are more of them). But that objection is unconvincing, because the same incentives apply to lower-level officials. If the neighborhood centurion hates birdbaths, he can get rid of them at a lower cost if he puts up a flyer

announcing that those who display birdbaths will be punished rather than simply punishing everyone who has a birdbath and relying on them to guess the reasons.

26. For example, Mao Zedong facilitated the Cultural Revolution by creating copious propaganda announcing to citizens what they were expected to do and guiding the Red Guards in their use of violence.
27. Obvious examples include Napoleon and Catherine the Great (1768).
28. Replacing precise legal rules with less precise principles that are to be filled out on a case-by-case basis in common-law fashion by judges does not help matters: those principles rigidify into increasingly complex rules once the precedential cases are decided.
29. North, Wallis, and Weingast (2009, ch. 5).
30. Raz (1979, 220); Wall (2001, 221–22). Hayek has a version of the argument in which he suggests that citizens who are aware of the conduct that will bring about official punishment are thereby *not coerced*, because they can plan their lives to avoid force by the state. That is obviously wrong (and quite bizarre): the threat of force is just as coercive as its actual application. Otherwise the mugger who says "Your money or your life" is not coercing you unless you're foolish enough to say "No."
31. Gowder (2013).
32. E.g., Christman (1991).
33. For a lucid presentation of this sort of autonomy ideal, see Benn (1976).
34. Moreover, as Waldron (2011a) points out, markets can price such risks (e.g., by insuring them). That offers another way those risks can be incorporated into citizens' plans.
35. I have argued elsewhere (Gowder 2014f) that the economic choices of others constitute meaningful infringements on one's freedom, in virtue of their use of force-backed property rights, to the extent they leave one without a domain of independent choice sufficient for a life that goes tolerably well.
36. This may be true of some legal rules as well. For example, Rantanen (2015) argues that US patent rights are indeterminate and malleable.
37. It is inspired by Elster (2000).
38. Like Olson's (1993) "stationary bandit" (e.g., a tyrant, as opposed to a roving bandit).
39. This corresponds to Fraenkel's (1941) account of the "dual state" in Nazi Germany. Fraenkel argued that Germany simultaneously had a functioning administrative apparatus under a (conditional) rule of law that enforced contracts, protected (some) property rights in the means of production, and so on, in order to permit the predictable and orderly working of a quasi-capitalist economic system, while simultaneously operating a "prerogative state" completely unbounded by the rule of law in all noneconomic and some economic (especially labor regulation) domains.
40. To be sure, as discussed in Chapter 6, the rule of law both requires and facilitates citizens' coordination to collectively defend themselves against official power. But this public law kind of coordination can exist without the

freedom-facilitating private law sorts of coordination the law of property and contract makes possible.

41. Hayek (1978, v. 1, ch. 5). I thank Bill Simon for pressing this point on me.
42. A similar argument could be made about systems of statutory law in democratic states, to the extent the democratic process ensures that legislation tracks community norms. Such an argument would be subject to the same objections raised here.
43. Hayek (1978, 106–10).
44. Pettit (1997, 173–77).
45. Pettit (1996, 584).
46. Pettit (2003, 394).
47. Gowder (2012b).
48. Simmonds (2007, 104).
49. At one point, Simmonds (2007, 143) seems to shift from the proposition that the rule of law is *sufficient* to secure a freedom from private domination to the proposition that it is *necessary* for "enjoying some domain of entitlement that is secure from the power of others." If by "others" Simmonds means to include state officials, then this is in part a tautology, because (the weak version of) the rule of law is constituted by the control of state power. If "others" means only private citizens, then the necessity claim is false: the example of Pinochet, who established private capitalist rights in conjunction with arbitrary state power, as well as the general claims given as far back as Hobbes, are sufficient to refute it. (From the other direction, we might also consider the arguments of contemporary anarchists or libertarians such as Nozick and Hasnas, who have imagined that freedom from private violence – and hence presumably from domination – can exist without a state at all. I am not quite sure whether those are to be believed, however.)
50. Dworkin (1995).
51. Rousseau (2003, 2.6). Brudner (2004, 127–42) gets a conception of generality much like my own out of a theory of democracy as collective autonomous self-rule. He claims that the state has an obligation to only regulate subjects by general law based on "a duty on authority to submit for validation to the rational assent of the subject such that the subject is as much ruler as subject and the ruler as much subject as ruler" (*ibid.*, 130). My conception of generality can be read as a rational assent requirement, but I deny that such a requirement applies only in states in which subjects are also rulers. Even in relationships of one-way supervision and authority, the one with authority treats the one given orders with respect only if the orders given are justifiable by reasons that count as reasons for the one given orders. A good boss, for example, gives orders to a subordinate that are justifiable in terms of the collective goals of the firm; a good parent gives orders to a child that are justifiable in terms of the child's well-being; in both cases, such orders are susceptible to interpretation in terms of compatibility with the rational assent of the one being ordered around, and that interpretation has moral value as

consistent with due respect for that individual independent of any notion of self-rule.

52. Hayek (1960, 155).
53. Raz (1979, 220–22). Marmor (2007) similarly claims that retroactive law shows disrespect for citizens' autonomy.
54. Darwall (1977, 48–49) offers a compelling account of what it might mean to respect someone's autonomy. Gerald Dworkin (1988, 4) characterizes Ronald Dworkin's notion of equal concern as a requirement of "equal respect for the autonomy of citizens." See also Hill (1973, 93–94), who argues that the servile person "does not, strictly speaking, violate his own rights," but "fails to acknowledge fully his own moral status," and thus displays a failure of self-respect in virtue of the fact that he "denies his moral equality" with others. I have further discussed the notion of what it might mean to offer an "insult" in the rule of law context in Gowder (2014c).
55. Fuller (1969, 162).
56. I thank Arash Abizadeh for suggesting this phrasing.
57. Habermas (1996).
58. Rundle (2012, 97–101, 139).
59. Rundle (2012, 130).

CHAPTER 5 ισονομια: THE DAWN OF LEGAL EQUALITY

1. In this chapter and the next, I draw from copious sources in translation from Attic Greek. With the exceptions noted, the translations in this book are those given by the Perseus Digital Library, at www.perseus.tufts.edu/. Exceptions, which appear separately in the general list of references for this book, include Aristotle (1996), Herodotus (2009), Lysias (2000), Plato (1997), Thucydides (1996), Xenophon (2009), and Pseudo-Xenophon (1968). Where particular words are significant for the argument, I have endeavored to verify the translations with my own (fairly rudimentary) Greek. Citations are typically given to original Greek texts in the style used by classicists. Also, in this chapter, "citizens" takes the narrower meaning of full members of the political community, in contrast to metics, slaves, and the like. It does not take the broader meaning (the same as "subjects") used in the rest of the book.
2. Ober (1989, 128).
3. Here, I disagree with Ostwald (1986) and Lanni (2009). Recently, Edward Harris (2013) has also taken up this question in book-length form, and also argues that Athens did have the rule of law to a substantial extent.
4. Except where otherwise noted, the details in this section are drawn from Hansen (1999) and MacDowell (1978, 214–17).
5. *Graphe* is not the only type of action that classicists typically call a "public suit," but the details of the distinction are unimportant for present purposes.
6. For discussion of this, see Schwartzberg (2013, 1049–62).
7. Fisher (1992).
8. Ober (1989, 53–103).

9. Cohen (1995, 56–57). The prohibition against double jeopardy can be found across several of Demosthenes' speeches; see Loening (1987, 133) for references.
10. Andoc. 1.87.
11. I focus in this section on control of elites, and of private citizens occupying roles in the jury and assembly. These are the sites for which the claim that Athens had the rule of law is most controversial. There seems to be very little disagreement about the proposition that day-to-day magistrates were constrained by law; for a discussion, see Harris (2013, 26–28).
12. Pseudo-Xenophon (1968).
13. Hansen (1999, 230).
14. The account in this paragraph is drawn from Lanni (2010).
15. Fisher (1992, 1); Ober (2005, 113–16).
16. Fisher (1992, 38–43).
17. Carawan (2007, 43–46).
18. Lanni (2009, 693, and sources cited therein) suggests that the legal system as a whole was good at restraining private violence, getting elites to pay their taxes, and so on. However, as Lanni notes, there is some debate about the extent to which private violence was actually restrained. Karayiannis and Hatzis (2012, 621) allege that Athens's legal system was also effective in serving functions such as protecting property rights and enforcing contracts. Taylor (2002, 100) points out that the assassination of Androcles and other killings leading up to the oligarchy of the 400 were "the first known political murders in Athens since the assassination of Ephialtes" (that is, in about a 50-year period – a record comparable to those of modern rule of law states; compare, for example, the four US presidents assassinated in a 98-year period: Lincoln in 1865, Garfield in 1881, McKinley in 1901, and Kennedy in 1963). Although the relative absence of political assassinations is not a direct indication of the Athenian rule of law, the relative absence of cases where people felt the need to resort to such extra-legal means of achieving political ends certainly is indirect evidence that core functions of the state were ordinarily handled in orderly fashion.
19. On the jurors' oath, Harris (2007) argues that jurors did not consider nonlegal evidence except in fixing penalties. Maio (1983) argues that the juries followed the law when it existed, and exercised something like policy-making power in the gaps. Cohen (1995) is often cited for the suggestion that the law courts simply ruled on political disputes or feuds, and that the precise legal charges brought were not material to jury decisions (e.g., Lanni 2006, 41), though I have some difficulty discerning such an extreme position in his argument. Lanni (*ibid.*, *passim*) argues that Athens had a broad notion of relevance that included extralegal evidence when consistent with justice. Carey (1996, 36) suggests that there was a strong Hellenic norm limiting the extent to which law could just be disregarded. Also see Carey (1994), Cronin (1939), and Blanshard (2004).

20. Lanni (2009, 692–94). Harris (2013, ch. 6) argues, by contrast, that juries generally rejected aggressive interpretations of the law.
21. Lanni (2009, 701–07).
22. Moreover, rule of law skeptics such as Lanni have offered no evidence that litigants asked juries to ignore the law in favor of social norms; it's striking that the extant forensic speeches pair appeals to social norms with appeals to law, and accuse their opponents of violating both. Norms seem to function as a complement rather than a substitute for laws. Allen (2000, 176–77) suggests that jurors were asked to ignore the law, but the evidence for that proposition comes from various orators who say that their opponents' demands that the jury ignore the law should be disregarded – which seems to me more likely to be tendentious characterization on the part of the orators ("My opponent wants you to cast aside the laws!") than fair summary of the opposing argument. Also, the oratorical claim that jurors should "act as legislators" (*ibid.*, 177) may be little different from the contemporary acknowledgment that common-law judges may make new legal rules, or that the Supreme Court may change constitutional doctrine. In fact, Lysias (14.4) asks the jurors to act as legislators in explicit recognition of the fact that the case will set a precedent for cases in the future – that is, that legal norms the jurors set will be at least potentially binding.
23. Lanni (2012).
24. Consistent with this approach, Thomas (1995, 64–66) suggests that the distinction between written laws and unwritten laws or binding customs developed only toward the end of the fifth century, and became politically significant primarily because the Thirty manipulated the unwritten laws for their own advantage. Ober (2008, 190–91) argues that Athenian jurors had a "shared repertoire of common knowledge, along with a common commitment to democratic values," such that they "would often align in more or less predictable ways" even in the face of formal legal ambiguity.
25. Thuc. 2.37. I thank Dan-El Padilla Peralta for drawing this to my attention. For Aristotle, see *Politics* 6.5, 1319b.40–41 and 3.17, 1287b6–7. Demosthenes also refers to the unwritten law in "Against Aristocrates" (Dem. 23.70). See also Lys. 6.10.
26. Hayek (1978) argues that the common law is superior, from the standpoint of the rule of law, to legislative enactments in virtue of the fact that the common law is discovered and evolved from community norms rather than decreed by someone's will. Like so many twentieth-century arguments, this was anticipated by the Athenians: Aristotle declared that "a man may be a safer ruler than the written law, but not safer than the customary law" (*Politics* 3.17, 1287b6–7). That passage could also be read to say that the customary law is more authoritative and less changeable.
27. Carugati (2014, 144). However, Allen (2000, 173) suggests that consistency between cases was "a core goal of Athenian judicial decisions."
28. Thus, in contemporary America, Paul Butler (1995) suggests that black jurors do and should engage in jury nullification to resist racially biased law

enforcement – or, in other words, to police the legal system's compliance with the (social as well as legal) norm of racial equality. While Butler suggests that such jury nullification is permissible because the rule of law is a "myth" (*ibid.*, 706–77), I would say that it is an *example* of the rule of law, in its chief function of controlling powerful officials.

Fissell (2013) points out that a jury's morality and a community's morality (or positive justice) can diverge, such that juries might run amok and exercise power contrary to the rule of law. This is true, and the solution is to impose constraints on juries run amok – in Athens, these constraints were probably the need for the general community to actually enforce judgments; in the United States, the appellate process makes jury nullificatory discretion appropriately asymmetric: they can free a criminal against the law, but cannot, for example, impose large verdicts or convict the innocent without being subject to at least some judicial scrutiny. I say much more about collective enforcement and a little more about informal norms in the following chapters.

29. Todd (1993, 100).
30. *Ibid.*, 113.
31. Todd (1993, 113–15); Hansen (1975).
32. Lanni (2012).
33. Harris (2013, 114–28) gives an extensive argument and evidence for the claim that the scope of litigation was limited to the complaint filed by the prosecutor. This, by facilitating a defense, further supports the principle of publicity.
34. MacDowell (1978, 64). Harris (2013, 74–75) suggests that there was a penalty for losing private suits (*dike*) as well as public suits (*graphe* – although there were other kinds of public suits as well), however, most other sources only mention a penalty for public suits (e.g., MacDowell 1978, 64–65; Hansen 1999, 192; Christ 1998, 26). Moreover, Harris's claim contradicts Demosthenes 22.27.
35. Hansen (1999, 162–63).
36. MacDowell (1978, 48).
37. *Ibid.*, 45–46. This worry is ameliorated somewhat if Lanni (2009) is right that the Athenian courts enforced a great deal of unwritten social norms, since those norms, to be norms at all (let alone to be willingly enforced by mass randomly selected juries) must have been widely known (and accepted).
38. Nightingale (1999, 107–12) argues that ordinary Athenians did not in fact have substantial legal knowledge. If true, that nonetheless does not directly threaten the conclusion that Athens comported with the principle of publicity, so long as knowledge of the laws was available (fairly cheaply) to those citizens who cared; compare Athens here, again, to modern societies – the US Code does not offend against the rule of law because citizens don't have it memorized, so long as it is relatively easy for citizens to learn their obligations and rights when they need to do so. See further the discussion by Harris (2013,

7–8), who cites evidence of efforts to make the law consistent and available to the public, and *ibid.* (11) for an argument that litigants typically agreed about the content of the law in actual cases. In view of the problems with legal complexity discussed in Chapter 4, Athens probably did better than modern societies at bringing legal knowledge to the masses.

39. Exceptions to this were in assignment to branches of the military service and mandatory "liturgies" (contributions to the military and to festivals) for the rich. For liturgies, see Ostwald (1995, 370). On military assignments, see *ibid.* (377–78).
40. For the details and a discussion of a passage where Demosthenes explains this idea, see Osborne (1985, 40).
41. Vickers (1995, 348).
42. Recall Pseudo-Xenophon's explanation of this phenomenon, discussed in Chapter 1.
43. To be clear here, the idea of democracy in Athens did not simply mean popular legislation (democracy in a minimal modern sense); rather, political equality was partnered with, and in many ways a tool of, social and economic equality; to preserve the former was to preserve the latter. Aristotle (Ath. Const. 2.1–3, 9.1) makes this clear: popular institutions were a solution to widespread oppression of the poor by the rich, culminating in slavery for debt and civil disorder.
44. Vlastos (1953, 337).
45. *Ibid.*, 350–52.
46. Ober (1989, 75).
47. Ostwald (1969, 153–54). Elsewhere, Ostwald (1986, 27) suggests that *isonomia* meant "political equality between the ruling magistrates, who formulate political decisions, and the Council and Assembly, which approve or disapprove them."
48. Ostwald (1969, 159).
49. Hansen (1999, 84). *Isegoria* is a particular term for political equality as a democratic citizen (i.e., having an equal voice in the decisions of the city). There can also be found *isokratia*, equal power, used by, for example, Herod. 5.92 in contrast to tyranny. Raaflaub (1996, 140) and Cartledge (1996, 178) both collect other terms for various sorts of equality.
50. Hansen (1999, 81–82). Rosivach (1988, 47–51) has a similar view, but argues that *isonomia* just meant political equality among those entitled to participate, which could include, for example, just oligarchs. Hayek (1960, 164–65) seems to have held the opposite view – that *isonomia* just meant the rule of law, not political equality – but he was no philologist. Raaflaub (1996, 144–45; 2004, 94–96) argues that *isonomia* shifted in meaning, first expressing the equality of aristocrats as against tyrants and only later mass democracy.
51. Rosivach (1988).
52. Rosivach (1988, 43, 56–57).
53. Lewis (2004).
54. Lanni (2009, 701).

55. Isoc. 20.
56. Dem. 19.296–97.
57. Dem. 19.313–14.
58. Andoc. 4.13. For "equality," Andocides uses *koinotes*, usually translated as "community" or "in common." It is important to note that many classicists think this speech is a forgery, although there is some debate on the question (Gribble 1997). Nonetheless, it has evidentiary value, for, as Gribble discusses, it has sometimes been thought to be a speech delivered by someone else, but may also have been a rhetorical exercise of the late fourth century. Either possibility is consistent with it reflecting genuine knowledge about and concern for the social dynamics in Athens during the democratic period. For convenience, I will continue to refer to it as Andocides 4, but the reader is advised to discount it accordingly.
59. Isoc. 20.
60. Demosthenes (Dem. 51.11) makes a similar claim: "[I]f a poor man through stress of need commits a fault, is he to be liable to the severest penalties, while, if a rich man does the same thing through shameful love of gain, is he to win pardon? Where, then, is equality for all [πάντας ἔχειν ἴσον] and popular government [δημοκρατεῖσθαι], if you decide matters in this way?"
61. Dem. 21.219–25.
62. Cohen (2005, 218–19) reads Demosthenes to argue that the jury's enforcement of the laws "regardless of the wealth or status of the defendant" is what prevents ordinary citizens from having to live in fear. In Cohen's words: "All of this reflects an understanding of criminal law and the rule of law as the bulwark of society by which impunity for any person because of their status undermines the law which is the protection of everyone. Only punishment of those who act with impunity can preserve that order." Gowder (2015d) offers an interpretation of Plato's *Crito* along similar lines.
63. Andoc. 4.17.
64. Andoc. 4.18.
65. Andoc. 4.21.
66. If Andocides 4 was genuinely a forgery composed in the late fourth century, this supports the claim of the next chapter that the Athenians learned, between the third and fourth centuries, about the importance of the rule of law for the stability of their democratic equality.
67. Aes. 3.6.
68. Aes. 3.7.
69. Aes. 3.234–35. A *rhetor* was a professional orator, seen with suspicion for his manipulative powers (Arthurs 1994). On Aeschines' pejorative use of the term in "Against Ctesiphon," see *ibid.* (6).
70. Again, Plato is in accord, pointing out that the tyrant is surrounded by enemies whom he must continually fight (*Rep.* IX.579).
71. Aes. 1.4–5. See the discussion in Hansen (1999, 74).

72. Hyp. 6.25. (Though Hyperides was a forensic orator, the speech in question was not given before a court. Also, "ruler's" in the given translation is ανδρος, which might be better translated as "man's.")
73. Raaflaub (2004, 233–35) argues based on evidence from Herodotus, Thucydides, and Euripides that "[r]espect for *nomos* made it possible to defend the community's freedom from," inter alia, "attacks by authoritarian opponents."
74. Ari. *Politics* 2.12, 1273b.35–1274a.5, as translated by Ostwald (1986, 5).
75. *Ibid.*, 5–15.
76. Ari. *Politics* 3.16, 1287a.9–24.
77. Thuc. 2.37, translated in Hansen (1999, 73). Thucydides (3.37) also gives us a version of a speech of Cleon including the claim that a city is stronger in international competition when its politicians subordinate their own cleverness to stable laws.
78. Thuc. 6.15.4.
79. Eur. Supp. 429–43. In the last line, Euripides uses the comparative adjective form of *isos*, the general term for equality, which does not have any particular political or legal connotation, in contrast to *isegoria*, generally used to refer to political equality, and *isonomia*, as discussed earlier. "Equal justice" is δίκην ἴσην, which could also be translated as "equal rights." N.b., no inferences should be drawn from the use of "reviled" in the given translation, which is rather too strong (the Greek is κακως): I would have preferred "mistreated."
80. Aeschylus, *Eum.* 680–710. See also Rottleuthner's (2005, 38) description of that passage, which he sees as a creation myth for the law, and particularly for the law captured in the notion of the impartial judge: on his account, it "lays the foundations for the precedence of the *polis* over the *genos*. On the world's stage there has now appeared a court that is formed by persons not related to the parties and that is vested with the competence to pass a binding judgment."
81. Plato, *Crito* 53b–c. I discuss *Crito* and the strength *topos* at length in Gowder (2015d).
82. Herod. 3.80.
83. Herod. 3.80.5–6.
84. Dicey (1982, 292–304).
85. Ostwald (1986, 497).
86. Carugati (2014) has criticized my prior work for conflating the notions of the rule of law and the sovereignty of law. On her account, the "sovereignty of law" means something like the supremacy of formal law as adjudicated by the judicial organs. As she aptly points out, Athens is perhaps more accurately compared to a dual sovereignty system featuring both formal and informal norms as well as centralized and decentralized institutions of enforcement. I wholeheartedly take Carugati's point. The rule of law is essentially about power being constrained by rules, and it is not, strictly speaking, necessary to take on commitments about whether any particular (or even single) entity has "sovereignty" or what kind of enforcement mechanisms are dominant in

order to judge whether a state has the rule of law. If Ostwald also maintains a rule of law/sovereignty of law distinction (and I am not sure whether he does), then he may have no objection at all to the proposition that Athens had the rule of law, wherever "sovereignty" might have been located. For present purposes, I shall assume that Ostwald, or others, meant "rule" by "sovereignty." (As an aside: it is also not clear that "sovereignty of law" in Carugati's sense of the term would be possible without the rule of law, about which see Chapter 8 of this volume.)

87. Hardin (2008); Eskridge (2005, 1279).
88. On the identification of the law code of 403 with the ancestral laws, see Finley (1975, 39–40).
89. Some contemporaneous recognition of this function of entrenched law can be found in Plato (*Laws* 715), who cautions against competition for office on the grounds that in such societies "the winners take over the affairs of state so completely that they totally deny the losers and the losers' descendants any share of power," leading to a cycle of retribution that can be resolved by selecting officials who are "best at obeying the established laws."
90. On the reforms that arguably did promote the rule of law, Ostwald (1999, 523) notes that the reformers forbade both magistrates enforcing unwritten law (the scope of this provision is unclear) and the enactment of laws targeting particular individuals. The codification and publication of the written laws was also an improvement from the rule of law standpoint.
91. Cohen (1995, 40–41) nicely expresses this tension through a discussion of Aristotle's worries, on rule of law grounds, about radical democracy. Lewis (2011, 25) argues that before the post-Thirty reforms, the assembly increasingly disregarded legal restrictions on its own behavior.
92. Xen. Hel. 1.7.12.
93. Colson (1985, 133) denies, contra what appears to be a prior consensus to the contrary (see sources cited therein), that the trial of the generals was illegal. The debate is immaterial for present purposes. Either the trial was illegal or the *ekklesia* had and exercised the power to execute people en masse as a kangaroo court. Both are extremely worrisome from the rule of law standpoint. On the much clearer prohibition of assembly executions after the Thirty, see Carawan's (1984, 111–21) discussion.
94. Roberts (1977, 107). Asmonti (2006, 2) gives other references for the standard account of the trial as an exceptional incident, though Asmonti argues, somewhat in opposition, that the trial actually reflected broader political worries about the distribution of power in Athenian society.
95. Xen. Hel. 1.7.35. Plato *Apology* 32b has Socrates claiming that everyone later recognized that the trial of the generals was illegal.
96. Hansen (1974, 55–61).
97. Hansen's account of the relationship between the *ekklesia* and the *dikasterion* is controversial. He cites the relevant sources (and defends himself) elsewhere (Hansen 2010). By way of caveat, as Hansen notes (*ibid.*, 525–26), the priority of *dikasterion* over *ekklesia* that he identifies may be a particularly

fourth-century (that is, post-Thirty and post–legislative reform) phenomenon.

98. Demosthenes explicitly said the two were compatible, and that the assembly could and did restrain itself: "[T]he civic body of Athens, although it has supreme authority over all things in the state, and it is in its power to do whatsoever it pleases, yet regarded the gift of Athenian citizenship as so honorable and so sacred a thing that it enacted in its own restraint laws to which it must conform" (Dem. 59.88).
99. There are good accounts by McGlew (1999) and in Rhodes (2010, 166–67); Furley's (1996) is the most comprehensive account of which I'm aware.
100. Herod. 9.5.
101. I thank Danielle Allen for suggesting this point to me.
102. Allen (2000, 178–79).
103. All dates are drawn from Rhodes (2010).

CHAPTER 6 THE LOGIC OF COORDINATION

1. Thus, the Athens case is used as an "analytic narrative" as practiced by scholars in the new institutional school of economics: an application of formal analytics to rich historical facts, as in Bates, Greif, Levi, and Rosenthal (1998).
2. The account in this paragraph and the next two is drawn, unless otherwise noted, from a combination of Ostwald (1986, 339–95) and Lang (1967, 176).
3. Thuc. 8.65.
4. Thuc. 8.66.
5. Thuc. 8.70.
6. Ostwald (1986, 387).
7. Thuc. 8.71.
8. Ostwald (1986, 401–04).
9. On the overlapping personnel, see *ibid.* (460–61, 466).
10. The account of the rise of the Thirty is taken from Ostwald (*ibid.*, 460–96) and Krentz (1982) except as otherwise noted.
11. There's some dispute about the extent of the property they stole. Krentz (1982, 81–87) suggests that the property expropriations of the Thirty were overstated, and that they may not have engaged in expropriations on a larger scale than the democracy did. However, Krentz's argument is unconvincing. Elsewhere (105) he suggests that the expropriations of the Thirty were on a large enough scale to raise serious problems of accounting in the reconciliation settlement. And certainly the Thirty's *throwing everyone but the 3,000 out of the city* suggests that they must have done something with the in-town property of those evicted – an expropriation of stunning scale all on its own, at least if we help ourselves to the modest assumption that a significant proportion of the 90 percent of citizens thus excluded had some property in the city.
12. Confirmed by both Aristotle (*Ath. Const.* 35.4) and Aeschines (Aes. 3.235).
13. Lanni (2010, 566).

14. Krentz (1982, 120) notes that "no prosecutors are known to have violated the amnesty successfully." There is, however, some dispute (*ibid.*, 120–22) about whether the oligarchs or the democrats started the conflict, shortly after the peace agreement, that led to the reconquest of Eleusis and the killing of the generals who were there. Moreover, Lanni (2010, 568) suggests that there is at least one known case where a prosecutor managed to use novel legal tactics to get around the amnesty, though she agrees that in general it was respected.
15. Kagan (1991, 163) suggests that "there is no reason to think that the exiles and imprisonments were widespread" either. However, Gallia (2004, 451) claims that Thucydides understated the crimes of the Four Hundred. On the opposite extreme, Lewis (2011, 25, 35) claims the Four Hundred "governed non-violently." If nothing else, we can confidently say that the regime of the Four Hundred was less blood-soaked than that of the Thirty (not a terribly impressive achievement, all things considered).
16. Taylor (2002). On her account, the Athenian masses mostly quietly accepted the Four Hundred at first. Rex Stem (2003, 18, 32) suggests that fraud – the false promise that they would hand over power to a broader oligarchy of 5,000 – had more to do with their accession than force. (The false promise of Persian support can't have hurt.)
17. I infer the relative mildness of the Four Hundred also from the charges against them at their subsequent trials. Ostwald (1986, 401–04) lists a number of trials, all of which appear to be for treason or subverting the democracy, but not for murder. This would be surprising, were the Four Hundred guilty of a significant number of murders. The Athenians attached religious importance to the pollution incurred by murders (Visser 1984, 193; Blickman 1986, 193). This suggests that they wouldn't have just ignored murders committed by the Four Hundred. By way of contrast, in the post-Thirty amnesty we know that the democrats explicitly reserved the right to try murderers as such.
18. On the Corinthian War, and the Athenian politics surrounding it, Roberts (1980) has a good account.
19. Lanni (2010, 573) agrees.
20. Carawan (2006, 68–69) describes what little is known of the details of the reconquest. Strauss (1987, 114) suggests that the democrats might have taken revenge on the oligarchs had the *thetes* (lower-class citizens who served in the navy) not been seriously weakened by losses in the Peloponnesian War. However, the weakness of the *thetes* cannot explain the demos's restraint. Both the victory over the oligarchic enclave at Eleusis and the successful resistance of the men of the Piraeus against the Thirty, even supported by a Spartan garrison, suggest that it would have been common knowledge that the democrats had enough military force to impose their will on the oligarchs. Moreover, the Thirty had just murdered a number of people equal to about 5 percent of the citizens; in doing so, they must have made enemies across the social spectrum.

    Elster (2004) claims that the democrats respected the amnesty in order to reintegrate the elites into the community and again have use of their services. But this, standing alone, is not a sufficient explanation for the difference between their behavior after the Thirty and after the Four Hundred, for the elites would also have been useful in prosecuting the Peloponnesian War.

21. Teegarden (2012, 433).
22. Siegel and Young (2009, 765) helpfully explain why cheap talk often does not facilitate credible commitment.
23. Ostwald (1986, 500–01).
24. Wolpert (2001, 46); Loening (1987, 116–19).
25. Lanni (2010).
26. Cohen (2001, 349).
27. Plato captures this sentiment nicely in the *Laws* (715d), suggesting that where the government is not subordinate to the laws, "the collapse of the state, in my [the Athenian stranger's] view, is not far off."
28. The number of votes for each side was public in addition to the outcome (Ober 2008, 193), facilitating the public use of jury verdicts as a signal of the level of social commitment.
29. This argument depends on the fact that the amnesty was imposed on the legal system by Sparta. If we accept the argument, from Carawan (2006, 57–76), that the provision giving the Thirty themselves amnesty if they passed their *euthynai* was enacted by a decree of the assembly after the original reconciliation agreement, my argument rests on the assumption that this was done for transient military or political reasons (e.g., to head off a short-term counter-revolutionary threat). This assumption, however, seems fairly plausible: right after the restoration, the Athenians must have been particularly afraid of a Spartan return, and would have had some reason to try to quickly reconcile Sparta's oligarchic allies to the community. This is also consistent with the general Athenian pattern after the war of superficial obsequiousness to their victorious enemies, and divergence at first only in secret (Rhodes 2010, 261–62). (In Gowder 2014b, I misstated the implications of Carawan's hypothesis for my argument.)
30. Lanni (2010, 589).
31. Bolt (1990).
32. Thuc. 3.84.
33. Teegarden (2012) thus has the wrong answer, but the right question, viz., how could the Athenians have credibly signaled to one another their willingness to enforce the law?
34. Thuc. 8.66, from the translation given in Taylor (2002).
35. Rhodes 2010, 169–70.
36. Buggle (2013).
37. Also see Harris (2013, ch. 9), who argues that a growing practice of using the courts to attack political opponents contributed to the fall of the democracy.
38. Christ (1998).
39. Xen. 2.3.12. The actual prevalence of sycophants in Athens is a subject of some dispute (Christ 1998).

40. Jordović (2008, 36).
41. Lys. 25.25–26.
42. Lys. 25.27.
43. Asmonti (2006) argues that the execution of the generals too was a move by the democrats against elites who were seen as a potential oligarchic threat.
44. In further support of the tentative hypothesis that the failures of the rule of law contributed to the two oligarchic coups, note that the Athenian polis suffered similar disasters in 430–427 (a major plague), 353 (defeat in the Social War), and 338 (after the crushing defeat by Macedon at the battle of Chaeronea), yet these disasters didn't go hand in hand with major failures of the law, and, after them, Athenian democracy did not collapse. I thank Josiah Ober for bringing this point to my attention. Note also that the democrats began attempting to reform their legal code after the first oligarchy fell (Rhodes 2010, 296–97), suggesting a recognition that the laws had something to do with the oligarchic threats even before that was fully driven home by the Thirty.
45. I know of no direct evidence that the amnesty was controversial, but indirect evidence can be gleaned from the fact that the council felt it necessary to summarily execute the first violator to indicate their intention to vigorously enforce it. This would not have been necessary were the amnesty met with universal approval. Moreover, again, the Thirty killed a number of people equal to a solid 5 percent of the citizen population; for comparison, this would be like killing off fifteen million Americans, or three million British. It beggars imagination to suppose that the amnesty was universally popular.
46. On the idea of credible commitment, see North (1993).
47. On the advantage of small groups, see Olson (1965).
48. This is a simplification: it may require the cooperation of fewer than all democrats to effectively resist threats. Nothing turns on this.
49. Law (2009); Hadfield and Weingast (2012, 2014).
50. In effect, the demos faced a problem of equilibrium selection: it could have ended up in a non-rule of law oligarchic equilibrium in which the rich and the powerful did what they pleased and the others suffered, or a rule of law democratic equilibrium in which the weaker masses successfully used the law to coordinate their resistance to the power of the elite.
51. Ober (2008, ch. 5).
52. Allen (2000, 181). She also (*ibid.*, 179–83) gives further oratorical references for the strength *topos*. For example, she cites a claim of Demosthenes that "laws that are masters make the jury masters," which I would read much like I read Aeschines. I would go so far as to say that all of the oratorical references she cites for the proposition that the power of the law rested on (or was even epiphenomenal on) the power of juries is evidence for, not against, the rule of law in Athens, although space only permits me to discuss this one example.

    Two other elements of Allen's account of Athenian law fit nicely into the model presented in this chapter. First is her argument (*ibid.*, 192–95) that law is a form of social memory: I would say that what the jurors do is remembered by the community as a whole, and shapes expectations about what will be done in the future; this is how knowledge about mass commitment to the law is propagated. Second is her analysis of the characterization, in the tragic corpus, of the law as a collective possession of the people rather than of tyrannical individuals (*ibid.*, 89–93). I disagree with Allen, however, about the concept of possession in play. It seems odd to assimilate the personal *possession* of the laws, associated with tyrants, to individual authorship or legislation – after all, the democratic laws of Athens were strongly associated with the legislation of Solon, Cleisthenes, and Pericles. Rather, it seems better to associate possession with the *control* of the laws by individuals as opposed to the demos acting through assembly and jury.

53. "Civic trust" comes from de Greiff (2012, 44–48). Similarly, Dyzenhaus (2012), drawing from Hobbes, has suggested that a function of transitional justice is to provide a civic education in the rule of law. I agree, but submit that what is being taught is not the importance of the rule of law in the abstract, but that citizens may rely on one another to support it: the education is collective and interdependent rather than individual. Murphy (2010) contains a stellar discussion of the way in which rebuilding broken networks of "political trust" ought to be a goal of transitional justice. However, I do not mean to suggest that trust has some independent normative value (though it might), but rather to use it, in Levi's (2003, 78) well-known terms, as "a holding word for a variety of phenomena that enable individuals to take risks in dealing with others, solve collective action problems, or act in ways that seem contrary to standard definitions of self-interest" (or at least the first two of those).

54. Lanni (2010).

55. Blanton and Fargher (2008) attempt a more ambitious version of this, arguing that rational choice approaches to understanding collective control of the powerful (like that developed in this chapter) can help explain numerous premodern states in similar terms as have been applied to modern ones, and this social form appears quite broadly, rather than being tied to particular continents, cultures, or religions – not something that demarcates the difference between Western and non-Western societies. Obviously, this result (which I lack the global historical expertise to evaluate) is highly congenial to the theory developed in these pages.

56. This is a slight simplification, since other citizens may not have equal power to sanction the ruler; I discuss how relaxing this assumption affects the dynamics of the rule of law in Chapter 9. A second simplification, which I cannot here lift, is that I assume that citizens' preference intensities and cost tolerances are independent; in reality, a citizen who very strongly prefers the existing legal system will be willing to risk higher direct and retaliation costs to preserve it.

57. Kuran (1991, 121–25). In other work (Gowder 2015d), I discuss the application of Kuran's preference falsification idea to Athens in greater depth through a reading of Plato's *Crito*. While the preference falsification idea is most relevant to understanding the barriers to trust among a mass public seeking to hold rulers, officials, or elites to the rule of law, there is a substantial related literature, which Lohmann (1994, 2000) helpfully reviews and extends.

Johnston (1996) describes, from a sociological perspective, stages of resistance in a number of repressive states, which we may interpret as the gradual and partial revelation of antiregime preferences. One important point (suggested to me by Gary Fine) is that information among a mass public is likely to be heterogeneous; the extent to which subjects are aware of one another's preferences or views about officials will depend on social network composition. On this, see Ikegami (2000). (It may be that the claims that "civil society builds trust" and "dense networks distribute information about preferences" are essentially identical.)

58. Weingast (1997, 247–51); Hadfield and Weingast (2012); Law (2009, 759–65).
59. Hadfield and Weingast (2013, 10–11).
60. In the Hadfield and Weingast (2012) model, a preference alteration, by shock or bribery, is equivalent to reducing their inequality 8 by changing buyers' idiosyncratic logics in order to count fewer deviations as harmful to them. Conditional retaliation costs are equivalent to adding some $\pi\mu$ to the right side of their inequality 7, where μ represents the retaliation suffered by a citizen who sanctions ruler illegality and π represents a citizen's subjective probability that not enough fellow citizens will join in the sanction to preclude that retaliation.

    Note also that preference alteration by bribery must be backed up by a ruler credible commitment to be a threat to either the Hadfield/Weingast equilibrium or mine. Otherwise, those who are bribed in round *n* know that in the future, after the officials doing the bribing eliminate some of their opponents or otherwise increase their power (including by undermining community trust in one another's commitments to upholding the law against officials), they can turn on their former allies. Accordingly, so long as citizens discount the future sufficiently lightly, if they value the legal system as a whole, they should be able to resist the temptation to take a short-term bribe.
61. This model contains a number of simplifying assumptions: in the real world, C probably varies with R, and F may as well. However, for present purposes, this simplification doesn't change anything: the important idea, that revolts are more likely to be worth it the more citizens participate, can be captured in the probability term alone.
62. I assume here that a sufficiently large group of citizens can sanction the ruler enough to make her prefer avoiding a revolt (i.e., that F entails losing one's head or other very costly punishment).
63. Kuran (1989, 41–74).
64. In real-world societies, a sample of the population that is known to be representative, such as a jury or a parliament, can reliably signal the intentions of the community; accordingly, we can safely suppose for modeling purposes that such a sample can meet the overwhelming power condition in a signaling model like the one under discussion.
65. Osborne and Rubinstein (1994, 122–23, 153, 316).
66. Incidentally, signaling opposition to a law violation when one is being bribed to support it, or otherwise prefers the policy, is a costly signal. However, it is

free from retaliation and all-but-nominal direct costs; this is the point of the model; moreover, because preferences are private, one's fellow citizens need not know that such a signal incurs preference costs (i.e., for all relevant purposes this is a cheap talk model). Incidentally, cheap talk works here, though not in Teegarden's (2012) oath-giving explanation, because (a) in repeated play citizens can condition on the honesty of one another's repeated signals, and (b) in Teegarden's model actually not signaling (i.e., refusing to give the oath) would have been costly, which further reduces the credibility of the signal he proposes.

Also, in many real-world situations described by something like the model of this chapter, citizens can act as if their fellows' signals are costly when they resist a policy, to the extent they can observe a substantial amount of political support in the community for that policy. Without knowing the preferences of their fellows, they may infer that their fellows are incurring preference costs by the mismatch between the proportion of people known to politically support a policy and the proportion of the population observed to resist it either at the signaling (jury) stage or the active resistance/rebellion stage.

67. See Gowder (2014a) for more.
68. Compare to the law merchant model of Milgrom, North, and Weingast (1990). In addition to serving as a repository of otherwise-uncertain knowledge about who violated generally accepted rules (as in the law merchant), the jury can serve as a repository of knowledge about the otherwise-uncertain appropriate application of rules to generally known acts. Also, see Gowder (2014a) for an account of the similar signaling role of constitutional courts.
69. Compare Rousseau (2003, 13) ("men as they are and laws as they might be"), and Rawls (2001, 4) on stability and "realistic utopia."
70. This suggests that more participatory legal institutions will make more of a contribution to the maintenance of the rule of law in states that have had less stable legal systems in the recent past. It is striking in this context to observe the apparent greater currency of ideas like jury nullification and popular constitutionalism in the United States shortly after the American Revolution, relative to today. However, I cannot explore this issue here.

CHAPTER 7 PARLIAMENT, CROWN, AND THE RULE OF LAW IN BRITAIN

1. E.g., the "intuitive" objection noted by MacCormick (1999, 68–69). For more, see Frohnen (2012) and Harden and Lewis (1988, chs. 2–3).
2. For simplicity, I ignore the possibility that the European Union exercises an authority that permits it to constrain Parliament. For an answer to this, see MacCormick (1999, ch. 6).
3. See, e.g., Fixed-Term Parliaments Act 2011 c. 14.
4. Terrorism Prevention and Investigation Measures Act 2011 c. 23.
5. Also, several successive Parliaments renewed an antiterrorism law permitting detention without charge for seven days, even after an adverse ruling by the European Court of Human Rights (Marks 1995). The pretrial detention

period fluctuated over the years; from 2006 to 2010 it reached a height of 28 days. Terrorism Act 2006 c. 11, sec. 23.

6. Jennings (1959, 52, 56–58) gives a litany of parliamentary violations of the rule of law, but nonetheless declares that "it is the general tendency which matters most," and that truly illegitimate laws would lead to mass opposition.
7. Sanchez-Cuenca (2003, 62).
8. Dicey (1982, 292–304).
9. As of 2011, Dicey's example was obsolete: the Fixed-Term Parliaments Act requires the cabinet to step down on a no-confidence vote.
10. Chrimes (1965, 11), and Fixed-Term Parliaments Act 2011 c. 14(3)(3), forbidding the dissolution of Parliament, and the explanatory notes thereto (online at www.legislation.gov.uk/ukpga/2011/14/notes/division/6/3), which specifically note that the statute abrogates the royal prerogative. The Parliament Act 1911 also abolished the veto of Lords.
11. See, e.g., McMurtrie (1992), taking seriously the possibility that the War Crimes Act 1991 might be unconstitutional, in virtue of its (alleged) retroactive criminal effect. Tellingly, she closes with the lament that "it is discouraging to realize that there exists no effective domestic constitutional check against the enactment of such legislation" (*Ibid.*, 149).
12. Customs can change gradually over time, including by the deliberate action of officials. Intuitively, customs that have grown up out of the practices of chronologically and geographically diverse officials and citizens are also more likely to conflict with one another than are the provisions of a written law code created with the aim of consistency and containing explicit priority rules to reconcile apparent conflicts (like the standard interpretive rule that later enactments implicitly repeal earlier ones).

    A similar problem can arise in common-law systems with conflicting precedents. Moreover, even if citizens know the constitutional customs that are currently practiced, they may not know the extent of their fellow citizens' commitment to them; indeed, there may be disagreement about the appropriateness of the customs, but this, of course, is true in states with a written constitution as well.
13. For an account of the facts, see Hart (2003, chs. 1–4).
14. Moreover, as McHarg (2008) aptly argues, a constitutional convention cannot be said to exist until it has persisted over time; otherwise there would be no way to distinguish the conventions that attach to a given official role from the individual preferences of the occupants of that role. McHarg infers from this, plausibly, that even deliberate, legislated constitutional changes (including, it seems to follow, the recent parliamentary innovations on the fundamentals of British government, such as the Fixed-Term Parliaments Act, 2011) cannot be seen as binding constitutional provisions until they are consistently implemented.
15. The details are in Hart (2003).

16. Parliament Act 1911 c. 13; Parliament Act 1949 c. 103. Anything written in this chapter about the Lords may become obsolete by the time of printing, as the powers of the Lords have been in flux for some time.
17. McMurtrie (1992) accordingly attributes the Lords' rejection of the War Crimes Act to constitutional worries. Of course, this rejection did not in fact lead to popular resistance to the law, perhaps because the public supported it, or perhaps because they were nonetheless unable to coordinate.
18. For what it's worth, the independence of the judiciary is provided for, to some extent, by statute. See Constitutional Reform Act 2005 c. 4(2)(3).
19. The House of Lords may also simply criticize the bill. It has a constitution committee that publishes reports on the constitutional implications of proposed bills and actively scrutinizes parliamentary business.
20. At least one former Law Lord has suggested that judges are obliged to narrowly construe acts of Parliament to the extent possible to make them compatible with the constitution (Bingham 2007).
21. This optimistic picture of what empirical political science might observe is complicated by the possibility that leaders in Commons might look down the game tree and not proffer bills likely to generate objections from the Lords and the judiciary, thus eliminating the evidence for their own constraint. However, we may still observe such objections in situations where the Commons fails to correctly apprehend the extent to which proposed laws are objectionable; recent events in the context of antiterrorism legislation, discussed later in this chapter, offer at least one example of such a circumstance.
22. *Regina v. Secretary of State for the Home Department, Ex parte Simms* [1999] UKHL 33 [2000] 2 AC 115, per Hoffman.
23. The Human Rights Act creates other devices by which political pressure might be brought on Parliament to comply with the rule of law. Most interestingly, it requires a minister proposing a bill to either declare the bill's compatibility with the act or "make a statement to the effect that although he is unable to make a statement of compatibility the government nevertheless wishes the House to proceed with the Bill" (sec. 19). (Of course, the minister might just lie.) The act also requires judges to interpret legislation to be compatible with the Convention to the extent possible.
24. Gardbaum (2013) gives the most complete account of the functioning of nonbinding judicial review.
25. *A v. Secretary of State for the Home Department* [2004] UKHL 56; [2005] 2 AC 68.
26. The details are given by Bogdanor (2009, 72–73).
27. *Re M.B.* [2006] EWHC (Admin) 1000; *Secretary of State for the Home Department v. MB* [2006] EWCA Civ 1140. For more details of the reception of these matters in the British courts, see Pether (2008, 2283–91).
28. Nor is this a new trend: Justice Brennan (1988) traces it throughout US history. In Britain, there have been several low points of the rule of law since the Glorious Revolution; possibly the most dramatic was the Black Act, enacted in

1723, which permitted summary execution of proclaimed offenders for such grave crimes as poaching and cutting down trees (Thompson 1975, 22).

29. Hilton (1965).
30. Henry Bracton, *De Legibus et Consuetudinibus Angliæ*, Samuel E. Thorne translation (1968), v. 2, 87 (online at http://hlsl5.law.harvard.edu/cgi-bin/brac-hilite.cgi?Unframed+English+2+87). (Legal historians these days do not tend to think that Bracton actually wrote the treatise that bears his name.)
31. Hatcher (1981, 9).
32. Hatcher (1981, 15–18).
33. Importantly, the lords controlled the courts in which villeins would have had to dispute the extent of permissible noble exactions – the unfree brought suit in manorial courts, not royal courts (Ault 1923, 7–8, 127); see also the sources cited by Clarkson and Warren (1940, 483–84). Note, however, that the restriction to manorial courts may have applied only to *land* held in villeinage, not personal litigation brought by villeins – see Briggs (2008) for the distinction. Moreover, unlike the ordinary manorial court, comprised of the baron and his free tenants, the court to which villeins must appeal was, at least on some accounts, judged only by the lord's steward (Maitland 1908, 49). Maitland expresses some skepticism about this conventional view, for reasons not explicitly given but that seem to revolve around the worry that, if this were true, villein interests would be totally unprotected; this subsection suggests that Maitland's skepticism on those grounds can be relieved, since, even if the barons did in fact totally control the courts to which villeins must appeal, the villeins could have coordinated to defend their customary rights.
34. Hilton (1949, 127–29); Ault (1954, 386–89).
35. Skinner (1998).
36. There can be no doubt that the earlier phase influenced the latter; to note just one detail, the Long Parliament ordered Coke's *Second Institute* published in 1641 (Holt 1993, 74).
37. Christianson (1993, 119–27).
38. I draw the language from the 1297 version, the most important part of which is chapter 29, as enrolled on the British statute books, with the "traditional" translation given by the British government online at www.legislation.gov.uk/aep/Edw1cc1929/25/9.
39. The classic defense of the claim that medieval Englishmen were concerned more with "liberties" qua specific legal privileges than with the unitary, normative notion of liberty is Pollard (1926/1972); see especially p. 153. Harding (1980) gives much more detail on the topic. The term "liberties" was used in this way at least into the eighteenth century. Thus, in the Pennsylvania Charter of Privileges (1701), describing the constitutional structure of the Pennsylvania colonies, we find a references to the "divers Liberties, Franchises and Properties" granted by William Penn to the residents of the territory, as previously described in the Frame of Government of the Province of Pennsylvania (1682); for its part, the Frame describes the form of government of Pennsylvania and its electoral rules, not anything like the standard

liberal liberties, and does not refer to individual liberty in the unitary, normative sense, though that document also contains a preamble that appears to make use of a unitary conception of liberty.

40. Pollock and Maitland (2010, 379).
41. Hyams (1980, 320).
42. Harding (1980, 424) cites a passage of the treatise known as Bracton in which the author notes that villeins are free under a Roman definition of having "the natural power of every man to do what he pleases, unless forbidden by law or force."
43. 28 Edward III, cap. 3; *Statutes of the Realm* I, 345. Holt (1993, 63) suggests that the universal language in the quoted statute of Edward III was not meant to extend due process rights to villeins. Rather, it was a reaction to the narrowing sense of "freeman." In 1215, it was understood that the *liberi homines* comprised all citizens above the status of villein. In 1354, however, the term took a narrower meaning, so the language was revised in the statute of Edward III to make clear that it referred to all citizens.
44. On the purchase of such privileges, see Holt (1992, ch. 3). Particularly, see a charter, reproduced *ibid.* (67–68), describing as "liberties" concessions like the number of horsemen the local royal official was allowed to keep, and the courts to which local residents were allowed to be summoned. Maddicott (1984) gives an in-depth overview of the municipal liberties.
45. Further support for this interpretation can be gleaned from the verb "disseised" in chapter 29 – to disseise a freeholder was to take his land ("freehold"), and, particularly, refers to the taking of land by the feudal lord who had granted it (hence the assize of novel disseisin, targeted against lords who seize tenants' land; see Milsom 2003, 104–06), suggesting by implication from the phrase "disseised of his Freehold, or Liberties, or free Customs" that liberties can be disseised just as can land, and were thus also property interests granted by the king.
46. Holt (1993, 47).
47. Milsom (1976, 36).
48. *ibid.*, 25. Milsom's view of novel disseisin is controversial (the debate is described by Brand 1992, 212–25), but the controversy (over the extent to which lords had untrammeled power beforehand) is not material to the point here. (I thank Tom Gallanis for drawing my attention to the controversy.)
49. On the myth that the Magna Carta is the source of the jury trial right, a myth that apparently took in, among others, Blackstone, see Darbyshire (1991, 742–43).
50. Holt (1992, 328).
51. Thus, Selden, 400 years later, points out that "if I bring an appeal of murder against a nobleman, which is my suit, he shall not be tried by his peers; but if he be indicted for that murder which is the King's suit he shall" (Johnson et al. 1977 [hereafter JKCB], 151). That is, the Magna Carta protected specifically against being both accused and tried by the king, qua legal superior.

Darbyshire (1991, 742) suggests that the demand is "for a tribunal in which they would not be judged by their inferiors," but this is an implausible interpretation in the context of increasing royal jurisdiction in which the barons were at continual threat of being judged by the king and summarily deprived of their property; moreover, if this was the danger against which the Magna Carta guarded, it was notably ineffective: there's evidence that lords were put to judgment by their free tenants in their own manor courts shortly thereafter (Ault 1954, 389).

52. Maddicott (1984, 52).
53. On this, it nicely fits the administrative power model of Greif (2008) and De Lara et al. (2008); the barons attempted to increase their own administrative power in order to protect the substantive legal concessions given them in the rest of the charter.
54. Holt (1993, 49).
55. Waldron (2012).
56. Again, I say "all" only in the same sense that they might have said "all" in Athens – all full-fledged citizens, or *liberi homines* – a putatively universalistic class that in fact excluded, inter alia, villeins, slaves, sometimes various sorts of religious dissenters, and other nonmembers or subordinate members of the political community.
57. The details of the Five Knights Case are drawn from Hart (2003, ch. 4).
58. Arbitrary imprisonment (for refusing arbitrary expropriation) was not the only rule of law issue in the Five Knights Case: there was also some suspicion that the King's advisors had tampered with the court records (recounted in Willms 2006, 97–99).
59. E.g., JKCB 1997, 45, 122–23.
60. Brooks 1993, 87. Brooks (*Ibid.*, 88) also quotes an anonymous common lawyer: "If we would perfectly execute justice wee must make no difference betweene men for their frends[hi]p, parentage, riches, pov[er]tye, or dignitye."
61. Judson (1964, 4–6).
62. Quoted *ibid.* (44–46).
63. Stone (1966).
64. On the disappearance of the middle class, see *ibid.* (28–29).
65. On the correlation of status with wealth, and the threat to status from loss thereof, see *ibid.* (39–40) and also Heal and Holmes (1994, 13–15, 97–99).
66. From a report to Lords, in Coke (2003, 1244).
67. JKCB (64), on March 22 (internal citations omitted). Harding (1980, 429–31) discusses the "franchise" at some length and concludes that the term referred to discrete jurisdictional privileges of the sort noted earlier (i.e., to run one's own courts, etc.). See also Maitland (1889, xxxii–xxxv), who describes numerous additional examples of these liberties/franchises.
68. On March 25, there appear two interesting turns of phrase. From Eliot, referring to imprisonment and to sending citizens overseas: "How do these concur with the liberty of free men?" And from Phelips: "I suppose it will appear evidently that liberty is the stamp of a free man." (Both on JKCB 99.)

Here, both seem to be using "liberty" in its indivisible liberal or republican sense, but to be declaring that it is a marker of status. That is, neither Eliot nor Phelips simply refers to liberty, but also refers to a particular category of person who is to hold it, denoted by "free man" used as a status term. (Phelips's statement would read particularly bizarrely if "free man" were understood as the possessor of liberty, rather than *liber homo* status: "liberty is the stamp of one who has liberty"?)

Later, Selden specifically suggests replacing the phrase "subject of England" with "free man" in the text of a proposed Parliamentary resolution against exactions, forced loans, and the like (JKCB 289), which again seems to suggest the equivalence of the *liber homo* with an equal citizen in the political community.

69. JKCB 148.
70. Later, he adds, "The law is for every man, the process only for freemen" (JKCB 158). This may be a reference to the fact that villeins were, at least in theory, given justice as an act of their lords' grace (i.e., in manorial courts controlled by their lords, as discussed at the end of section I) rather than being entitled to claims of right in the royal courts. If so, then the comparison between citizens subject to royal at-will imprisonments and villeins makes more sense, for such citizens would likewise have no authority to enforce their legal entitlements, but would receive them only at the grace of the king. Littleton suggests something similar: that due process of law applies only to those above villein status (JKCB 335). Sherfield argues that the law protects villeins from imprisonment (JKCB 189), but it is not clear whether he thinks villeins have the right to judicial process to enforce that protection. Compare these ideas to those of the Levellers (discussed in Chapter 3), who directly recognized the relationship between access to process and social status.
71. JKCB 150–51.
72. At least until 1271, Jews could own land in freehold; after then, they appeared to have property rights strong enough to make loans. See Herman (1993, 53–55) for the statute barring Jews from holding freehold land, and Jewish property rights up until that point. Note in particular that when a Jewish lender foreclosed on land, the sheriff "required the villeins [of that estate] to do fealty to him" (*ibid.*, 53). It seems most reasonable to understand the Jews as free citizens of higher status than villeins but of lower status than Christians. I have been able to find at least one royal charter (which also refers to an earlier charter) granting Jews (some or all Jews – it is unclear) the right to "reside in our land freely and honorably," serve as witnesses, pass property to heirs, and have trial by peers (Charter of Richard I, reprinted and translated in Jacobs 1893, 134–38). See also Pollock and Maitland (2010, 494–500), who argue that the Jews were freemen with respect to all except the king.

Of course, the expulsion was still in effect when Selden was speaking, so the "old time" to which he referred must just have been that period up to 1290, when the Jews were expelled. On the other hand, Hyams (1974, 287–88) notes that the status of Jews was often compared to that of serfs in the relevant period – but this comparison is implausible unless we're to believe that serfs had sufficiently strong property rights to get in the business of moneylending. Also, Selden later says that "the Jews are in the same degree with slaves" and the insane in being subject to confinement by proclamation (JKCB 259), but this is in the present tense, and appears to refer to the state of affairs after the expulsion.

73. This is a nonstandard usage, but not a wholly unfamiliar one: cf. Charles James Fox's 1800 parliamentary speech, "On the Refusal to Negotiate with France" (online at www.bartleby.com/268/4/7.html; accessed March 3, 2014): "The right honorable gentleman who opened this debate may remember in what terms of disdain, or virulence, even of contempt, General Washington was spoken of by gentlemen on that side of the House. Does he not recollect with what marks of indignation any member was stigmatized as an enemy to this country who mentioned with common respect the name of General Washington?"
74. JKCB, 71–72.
75. JKCB, 66.
76. JKCB, 71.
77. JKCB, 75.
78. Green (1879, 154).
79. Again from a report to the Lords, in Coke (2003, 1246–47).
80. There's also a claim that the king sullies his hands by personally imprisoning people, which Coke credits to Fortescue (JKCB, 192).
81. JKCB, 191.
82. JKCB, 57.
83. This may have been the case under law. The records of the parliamentary debate of March 21 reveal an open question as to whether two MPs returned by Coventry were eligible to sit in Parliament despite their "being no freemen"; that is (as I read it), they were of subcitizen status, and thus not eligible for political office (JKCB, 44).
84. Brown (1954, 865–83) gives the legal structure of Massachusetts freemanship in some detail.
85. Cf. *Ibid.* (873), recounting a case in which a court gave a servant "liberty to dispose of himself," and then freeman status four years later, and another in which a nonfreeman "inhabitant" owned real estate.
86. The Charter of Massachusetts Bay: 1629, available at avalon.law.yale.edu/17th_century/mass03.asp.
87. Somers (1993, 593–94).
88. *Ibid.*, 603.

CHAPTER 8 THE LOGIC OF COMMITMENT

1. Gowder (2014d). Of course, our classification of cases of the rule of law in the real world also depends on our account of what the rule of law is. That should be unsurprising: observation is theory-laden. Ultimately, we end up with a

holistic relationship between the concept of the rule of law and our empirical observations.

2. Hadfield and Weingast (2014) agree that the rule of law is independent of political institutions, and that it is fundamentally about achieving coordination, though they flesh out the details differently from the way I do.
3. Eskridge (2005). Reenock, Staton, and Radean (2013) offer and empirically support an account of legal institutions according to which they support political compromise by allowing citizens to coordinate to sanction rulers for violating that compromise.
4. This is an instance of the general problem of self-binding discussed by Elster (1979).
5. This is also how Olson's (1993) stationary bandit manages to collect rents. She creates the rule of law in order to guarantee the power of those who control her authority (independent judges, decentralized military forces in the hands of nobles, rebellious masses, or whoever), so she can credibly commit to allowing economically productive activity. In doing so, and in recruiting the support of these actors (judges, nobles, masses, etc.) to hold her to those constraints, however, she also recruits their support for the legal system that permits those exactions that she still allows herself.
6. We might imagine a stationary bandit who binds herself as well as subordinate officials, or we might imagine a stationary bandit who binds only her subordinates, not herself.
7. Robinson, Torvik, and Verdier (2006, 447–68) suggest that patronage is one of the causes of the resource curse.
8. Greif (2008).
9. This may be how customary legal norms that provide broader rights than formal rules, such as those discussed in the previous chapter, come about: those who are protected by formal rules suddenly need the help of others to enforce them.
10. Cf. Olson (1965).
11. See Boyd and Richerson (2008, 314) for these classic assumptions of natural selection. This kind of evolutionary account requires the supposition that these exogenous shocks actually happen, but of course they do, being generated by, inter alia, external political competition, technological development, migration, and economic, religious, and social change.
12. These strategic intuitions run on the top of far more complexity. Consider the hypothetical case of a state with a powerful elite group from which most officials are drawn, and two groups of ordinary citizens of roughly equal power, but with unequal legal rights, which have the capacity to resist elite depredations only when working together. If the elite were unable to use bribery to undermine that cooperation, it would make sense to predict that the status quo distribution of legal rights granted to each of the two ordinary-citizen groups would persist, absent exogenous shocks to the balance of power in the community, in view of the likelihood that the only options accessible to the worst-off group would be to

defend the existing state of affairs against elite threats or fail to cooperate and watch their situation get worse after the elites take over altogether. In a world in which they may be bribed, however, they have a third option: accept a slight improvement in their existing situation as a bribe in exchange for defecting from the cooperative arrangement with the other group, allowing the other group to be wholly exploited. Of course, such a strategy would be unhelpfully myopic in the context of long-term interaction, as the elite could make a similar offer later to the other (now more oppressed) group; these dynamics quickly become intractable when we consider issues like the impact of social prejudice on inequality (and vice versa). On the whole, however, the overarching evolutionary claim remains plausible; moreover, progress toward testing some (though not all) refinements in this category is made in the simulation given at the end of this chapter. The simpler claim will do for now.

13. Arguable historical examples could include the late Prussian monarchy (Ledford 2004); the Chinese imperial system, particularly as evidenced and influenced by Legalist thought (Turner 1992); the reforms attempted by Catherine the Great in Russia (Griffiths 1973, 325–27, 332–33); and the law of the Islamic Caliphate from the Prophet through the Ottoman Empire (Baderin 2003, 89; Hallaq 2005, 182–92; Jennings 1979, 152).
14. Riker (1988).
15. Courtright (1974, 249–67).
16. Karim (1971, 61–80).
17. Ta-Nehisi Coates, "Nonviolence as Compliance," in *The Atlantic*, April 27, 2015, available online at www.theatlantic.com/politics/archive/2015/04/nonviolence-as-compliance/391640/.
18. Hart (1997).
19. For example, Steyn (2006) suggests the necessity of independent judges for the rule of law, as does Ferejohn (1999, 366–68). For a similar view from someone with rather significant experience in the matter, see Archibald Cox's (1996, 565–84) discussion.
20. Lohmann (2003, 97) similarly argues that what she calls a "fiat institution" will be effective only "when the political commitment to the institution is backed up by an audience that can and will execute state-contingent punishment strategies."
21. Gowder (2014a). A more elaborate account of how this mechanism works is given by David Law (2009, 723–801).
22. As we saw recently in the wave of state-constitution legalizations of gay marriage in the United States.
23. Gardbaum (2013).
24. For a general discussion of the role of information cascades in mass resistance to their governments, see Ellis and Fender (2011) and Lohmann (1994, 2000).
25. Doyle (2002, 76–77).

26. Relatedly, democratic institutions may help people develop political knowledge and skill in coordinating that, in turn, may make it less costly for them to coordinate to defend the rule of law.
27. A genuine democracy may not only be necessary for the strong version, but may also be sufficient for it, depending on the demandingness of one's conception of democracy. Those deliberative democrats who hold a conception of democracy according to which the interests of all must be taken into account just read the strong version into their accounts of what democracy is.
28. The strong version of the rule of law may be required for approval-democracies, for on the account that I am giving elsewhere of them (or, more carefully, for an approval-conception of popular sovereignty), they require a general acceptance of the core practices of the state; if there is such a general acceptance, it would seem to follow (absent extreme cases of false consciousness) that those core practices are understood to treat all as equals.
29. Law and Versteeg (2013, 926–29).
30. I have said more about the relationship between the rule of law and democracy in Gowder (2015b).
31. A real-world example of such a strategy can be found in one important account of the rise of racialized slavery in Colonial America. In Allen's (2012) account, the racial categories that were attached to enslavement were essentially invented by the planter elite and the governments they controlled, particularly in Virginia in the late seventeenth century, in order to split a nascent alliance between workers of European descent and workers of African descent (see the discussion in Gowder 2015a).
32. This is consistent with the general method proposed by Epstein (1999, 48).
33. This is what Epstein (1999, 52) refers to as "sweep[ing] the parameter space," although it would be more accurate to say that I sample, not sweep, the parameter space: not every possible parameter setting is tested. (The reason for this is a matter of brute combinatorics: the number of possible settings of even one parameter, such as the distribution of 10,000 goods over 1,100 people, is mind-bogglingly large.) As he notes, it is much harder to sweep "the space of possible individual rules" for agents' decisions, although I have attempted to ameliorate this problem by making as much of agents' decisions as possible depend on randomized parameters.
34. Axelrod (1997, 18).
35. All supplemental material for this book is available at rulelaw.net.
36. In order to reduce the search space for this maximization problem (which is otherwise subject to combinatorial explosion), bribes may only be given to groups in increments of budget (.1), where the budget is the total number of goods available, less the amount assigned to the elite in the status quo ante. As paying out the whole budget has a maximum payoff equal to the payoff achieved with certainty by not attempting to overthrow, elite utility for that strategy is not calculated. An alternative approach would use an optimization algorithm more sophisticated than the simple grid search I have implemented, but this simulation is already a gross approximation of a complex dynamic

pattern; deploying fancier algorithms to allow a more granular optimization would not make a meaningful improvement.

37. Goods are set as follows: first, the elites are randomly assigned a proportion of the goods between .1 and .4, which are divided equally among them; then the remaining goods are assigned randomly one at a time to each member of the mass with equal probability.
38. Power is assigned the same way as are goods, except that the elites share ranges from .2 to .49, and the distribution is constrained such that no member of the mass has as much power as a member of the elite. In order to ensure adequate variance in the resulting data, in 25 percent of the runs, both goods and power are allowed to dramatically vary from these initial assignments, concentrated in the first mass subgroup.
39. Each member of the mass is assigned to a subgroup from a uniform distribution over the available groups.
40. In order to motivate this behavior, we may imagine that the elites are punished by a one-round loss of goods, but experience no further consequences, or that they are removed and replaced; it makes no difference, for we may safely assume that a sufficiently powerful group of resisters may choose a punishment sufficiently severe to deter elites.
41. E.g., Greif (2008). However, the existence of bribable subgroups in the mass can, when one such subgroup is particularly powerful, roughly model the idea of an intermediate level of elite who may be induced to enter coalitions either upward or downward.
42. This is because they vary with others in the expected ways. For example, the subjective probability the elites have in a group participating in a revolt ought to decrease with the bribe paid to that group; the model conforms to that.
43. Full data, plus R code to run the simulation and subsequent analysis, are available at rulelaw.net.

CHAPTER 9 THE ROLE OF DEVELOPMENT PROFESSIONALS: MEASUREMENT AND PROMOTION

1. Santiso (2003, 119).
2. Krygier (2006, 129–61). Krygier argues that before we try to promote the rule of law, we should figure out the ends that it's meant to serve – a claim that I obviously endorse.
3. Thompson (1975, 262–63).
4. Faculty biography of Ebrahim Afsah, available at http://jura.ku.dk/english/staff/research/?id=422468&vis=medarbejder (visited May 4, 2014).
5. Afsah (2012, 128).
6. *Ibid.*, 137.
7. *Ibid.*, 137.
8. *Ibid.*, 145.
9. Mattei (2003, 383–448).

10. *Ibid.* (445–46). This disdain for non-Western legal systems has been described elsewhere as "legal Orientalism" (Ruskola 2002).
11. E.g., Carothers (1999, 2003); Kleinfeld (2012); Kleinfeld and Bader (2014). Most recently, the contributors to Marshall (2014) have offered various versions of the strong case for bottom-up development; this volume gives an excellent overview of the territory. For an important critical discussion of bottom-up rule of law development, see van Rooij (2012).
12. This point holds true not just for outsiders attempting to create the rule of law in other nations, but also for central governments attempting to do so in their own. For more on the problems of centralized, top-down institutional imposition, see Scott (1999). For an analysis that uses the case study of Kosovo to make points similar to those of this chapter, including a focus on the importance of norms rather than formal institutions, and on actually attending to local cultures and traditions, see Brooks (2003, 2275–340). See also the discussion by Upham (2002), who points out that a "legal system is too complicated to be planned from the top down," such that supplanting local institutions with foreign legal institutions may do more harm than good once those new institutions fail. For a history of the rule of law development industry's attempts to deal with "legal pluralism," and the prior attempts of some in that industry to supplant traditional legal systems with centralized state-run systems like those in the North Atlantic liberal democracies, see chapter 2 of Grenfell (2013); for a general discussion of the potential and perils of relying on local institutions, see Tamanaha (2011).
13. For an overview of the *panchayats*, see Klock (2001, 275–95).
14. This is meant to be an example rather than a specific institutional prescription for India, a country in which I have no expertise. Those with expertise in India have, in fact, criticized attempts to work through the *panchayats* (e.g., Galanter 1972, 53–70). The point is that this is the type of strategy that should be considered and empirically tested, and policy makers should work with those who actually do possess local expertise.
15. This tradition extends beyond today's developing world. In medieval Ireland, for example, the Catholic Church had a role in enforcing some economic regulations, for example, by punishing contract breakers (Watt 1998, 168, 175).
16. Buscaglia and Stephan (2005) aptly discuss other factors favoring local methods of dispute resolution.
17. Fiseha (2013, 118–19) also attributes this property to traditional adjudication, although this argument is mated to a confused equation of traditional adjudication with the rejection of positive law, which misses that customary law is consistent with legal positivism.
18. Pistor (2002, 97–130).
19. For an account of such phenomena at an even higher level of generality that includes individual psychologies, see Boyd and Richerson (2008, 305–23).
20. Blattman, Hartman, and Blair (2014).
21. *Ibid.*, 107.
22. *Ibid.*, 118–19.

23. *Ibid.*, 120.
24. *Ibid.*, 113, 119. Fiseha (2013, 114–15) argues that "community dispute resolution mechanisms" have the dual role of resolving disputes between individuals and generally quelling violence by "restoring broken relations and putting order in the community," in contrast to centralized state mechanisms that fail at "dealing with the psychological and cultural traumas that often trigger retribution."
25. Bassiouni and Rothenberg (2007) point out that the "formal" justice sector in Afghanistan is widely seen as corrupt and lacking legitimacy, while the "informal" justice sector, including local institutions known as the *shura* and *jirga*, is generally seen as legitimate, as is Islamic law. The *shura* and *jirga* mainly operate by deploying community disapproval of those who they condemn (Checchi and Company 2005), and thus are particularly promising sites, based on the theory given in Chapters 6 and 8 of this book, for promoting the kind of civic trust, on a local level, necessary to develop the rule of law: they call upon ordinary people to signal their support for their judgments and willingness to impose sanctions on those who violate them. Souaiaia (2013, 11) notes that there is substantial historical precedent for local Islamic mosques taking on a governance role in the failure of central governments.
26. Kleinfeld and Bader (2014).
27. *Ibid.*, 15.
28. *Ibid.*, 17.
29. One key problem with the use of local and traditional institutions to implement the rule of law is that, in many contexts, they have traditionally excluded or actively carried out the subordination of women. However, efforts to actively encourage women's participation in local institutions have shown some success. US/World Bank support of the National Solidarity Program, a locally oriented public works program in rural Afghanistan, has placed a number of women in nontraditional leadership roles in local councils (Coleman 2010, 188–92). Drumbl (2004, 349–90) suggests that the international community could encourage traditional institutions to include women.
30. Stromseth, Wippman, and Brooks (2006, 337).
31. Special Inspector General for Afghan Reconstruction, report to Congress of April 30, 2014.
32. Cf. Carothers (1999, 257–70), who describes the lack of "local ownership" in development projects. External actors may lack "input legitimacy," in Krasner and Risse's (2014) terms.
33. The "design thinking" process is described by Stanford's Hasso Plattner Institute of Design at http://dschool.stanford.edu/use-our-methods/ (accessed March 3, 2014).
34. For example, the Parsons Design for Social Innovation and Sustainability (DESIS) lab at the New School (www.newschool.edu/desis/) has sponsored projects relating to New York City public housing and other social services. Also see Soule (2013).

35. In particular, commercial legal reforms may make matters worse. The object of rule of law development is to build widespread support for the rule of law, and institutions that allow the subjects of law to coordinate in its defense. The citizens of developing states are not stupid, and can tell if external rule of law development efforts are intended to benefit the country's social and economic elite and foreign corporations associated with the states that are sending the development agencies, rather than the immediate legal needs of ordinary people. Such efforts can be expected to induce cynicism and opposition from the neglected populace.
36. Ginsburg (2011, 271–74); Skaaning (2010, 449–60); Ringer (2007, 178–208); Nardulli, Peyton, and Bajjalieh (2013); Merkel (2012).
37. E.g., Davis (2004, 141–61).
38. Ginsburg (2011, 275–77).
39. Krever (2013, 131–50).
40. Skaaning (2010).
41. See the sources cited by Haggard and Tiede (2011, 676), as well as the discussion by Rios-Figueroa and Staton (2008).
42. Skaaning (2010) and Haggard and Tiede (2011, 677–78).
43. More extensive literature reviews can be found in Skaaning (2010), Haggard and Tiede (2011), Rios-Figueroa and Staton (2008), Davis (2004), and Haggard, MacIntyre, and Tiede (2008).
44. See Saisana and Saltelli (2012).
45. Variable specification available online at http://info.worldbank.org/governance/wgi/index.aspx. For an apt critique of the conceptualization problems, in the (roughly equivalent) language of construct validity, see Thomas (2009, 38–41).
46. "Note that not all of the data sources cover all countries, and so the aggregate governance scores are based on different sets of underlying data for different countries." *Ibid.* The Bank insists that its data are suitable for cross-country comparisons (Kaufmann, Kraay, and Mastruzzi, 2011), on the grounds that "all of our sources use reasonably comparable methodologies over time" (*ibid.*, 15), but this is nothing more than a blunt (and imprecise) assertion.
47. Kaufmann, Kraay, and Mastruzzi (2007). Alarmingly, this paper also scornfully dismisses the poor conceptualization objection as "definitional nitpicking" (*Ibid.*, 23–24).
48. *Ibid.*, 7–8.
49. Haggard, MacIntyre, and Tiede (2008, 221–27) note that some of the correlations we would expect between Bank governance indicators and some of the other measures used for the rule of law are surprisingly weak. See Gowder (2014e) for more on the relationship between corruption and the rule of law.
50. United Nations, *Rule of Law Indicators: Implementation Guide and Project Tools* (2011).
51. Nardulli, Peyton, and Bajjalieh (2013, 139–92).
52. Starr (1936, 1143–52). On "sham constitutions" in general, see Law and Versteeg (2013). It might be possible to get something useful out of the

Nardulli et al. measure by weighting it with the Law and Versteeg constitutional performance scores.

53. E.g., works cited by Lissitzyn (1952, 257–73), Hazard (1947, 223–43), and Schlesinger (1955, 164–82). There is also a rather odd one-page bibliographic entry (Sharlet 1974, 156), which at least hints at the existence of a 144-page bibliography of them, and claims that the aforesaid bibliography is incomplete.
54. Organisation for Economic Co-operation and Development (2008, 31–33).
55. Rios-Figueroa and Staton (March 26–27, 2008).
56. Van Schuur (2003, 141).
57. *Ibid.*, 150. Other models, such as the Rasch model, are even stricter.
58. *Ibid.*, 145. Local stochastic independence may be dubious, also, reliability statistics will be inflated because of the large number of items; very little should be inferred from this scaling exercise.
59. I thank Alejandro Ponce of the World Justice Project for permitting me to use the WJP data. Unfortunately, due to confidentiality concerns relating to the expert respondents, the WJP has requested that the item-by-item raw data not be further shared. The text of selected items is available online at rulelaw.net.
60. Straat, van der Ark, and Sijtsma (2013, 75–99).
61. However, the impact of this limitation should not be substantial. Three years is ordinarily not a period in which we would expect to see radical changes to a country's legal system. Exceptions include those countries that were involved in the Arab Spring, and countries that had coups. States that are potentially problematic on these grounds include Lebanon, Morocco, Thailand, Turkey, and the United Arab Emirates.
62. This (unlike the other relationships) is not linear. As the plots suggest, there appears to be substantially more rule of law variation in the lower income levels than in the higher income levels. However, after log-transforming the variables, the strong relationship between the two can be seen (see the charts in the appendix to this chapter).

CONCLUSION A COMMITMENT TO EQUALITY BEGINS AT HOME

1. Just a handful among many: Scarry (2010), Steyn (2004), Satterthwaite (2007), Drumbl (2005).
2. Keister and Moller (2000).
3. Lessig (2011).
4. See David Kirkpatrick, "Mubarak's Grip on Power Is Shaken," *New York Times*, January 31, 2011, www.nytimes.com/2011/02/01/world/middleeast/01egypt.html; Katherine Marsh, "Syrian Soldiers Shot for Refusing to Fire on Protesters," *The Guardian*, April 12, 2011, www.theguardian.com/world/2011/apr/12/syrian-soldiers-shot-protest. Similar refusals were noted in Tunisia and Libya (Silverman 2012).
5. See the discussion of administrative power in Greif (2008) and De Lara et al. (2008). For a nuanced discussion of the implications of military privatization for the control of state-level violence, see Avant (2005).

6. For a general account of the European discrimination against Muslims (which is not focused on the criminal justice system), see Modood (2003).
7. NAACP "Criminal Justice Fact Sheet," available online at www.naacp.org/pages/criminal-justice-fact-sheet (visited December 19, 2013).
8. Anwar, Bayer, and Hjalmarsson (2012).
9. Hurwitz and Peffley (2010, 460).
10. Franklin (2013).
11. Alexander (2012).
12. For example, Alexander (2012, 7) cites statistics showing similar rates of drug offenses for whites and blacks, even though blacks are by far the disproportionate targets of the drug war.
13. For an argument that the state is in fact responsible to a substantial degree for this poverty and inequality, see Gowder (2015a). On the relationship between poverty and crime, see Hsieh and Pugh (1993); Pridemore (2011).
14. Hurwitz and Peffley (2010, 464).
15. Chaney and Robertson (2013, 483).
16. Wu, Lake, and Cao (2013).
17. Tuch and Weitzer (1997, 643) found "a precipitous decline in approval ratings," particularly among black citizens, following a series of widely publicized police beatings of black citizens, and black and Latino citizens held more disapproving attitudes toward the police longer after these incidents than did whites. Obviously.
18. Perez, Berg, and Myers (2003).
19. Harris (2001, 412–13).
20. Critical race theorists call this the "interest convergence" thesis: advances in the standing of minority groups tend to come about only when they happen to be in the interests of the majority (Bell 1980).
21. Western and Pettit (2010, 11). By contrast, whites in the same age cohort have an imprisonment risk by age 30 of barely 5 percent (*ibid.*).
22. Danny Vinik, "An 18-Year-Old Baltimore Rioter Faces a Higher Bail Than the Cop Accused of Murdering Freddie Gray," *New Republic*, May 2, 2015, www.newrepublic.com/article/121702/baltimore-rioter-gets-bail-above-freddie-grays-alleged-cop-murderer.
23. Frank Stoltze, "'Rough Rides' in Baltimore Police Cars Are 'Screen Tests' in LA," KPCC radio, May 2, 2015, www.scpr.org/news/2015/05/02/51400/rough-rides-in-baltimore-police-cars-are-screen-te/.
24. Bill Keller, "David Simon on Baltimore's Anguish," The Marshall Project, April 29, 2015, https://www.themarshallproject.org/2015/04/29/david-simon-on-baltimore-s-anguish.
25. Leonard Levitt, "NYPD v. Bill de Blasio: Why New York's Mayor, Police Are at Odds," *Reuters*, December 31, 2014, http://blogs.reuters.com/great-debate/2014/12/31/nypd-v-bill-de-blasio-why-new-yorks-mayor-police-are-at-odds/.
26. *Ibid.* Keldy Ortiz, Steven Trader, and Barry Paddock, "Police Union Silent Day after Commissioner Bratton Acknowledged NYPD Slowdown," *New York*

Daily News, January 10, 2015, www.nydailynews.com/new-york/nyc-crime/police-union-quiet-bratton-acknowledged-nypd-slowdown-article-1.2073467.

27. Larry Celona and Bob Fredericks, "City Housing Puts Workers in Bright Vests in Fear of NYPD Shootings," *New York Post*, May 25, 2015, http://nypost.com/2015/05/25/city-housing-puts-workers-in-bright-vests-in-fear-of-nypd-shootings/.

28. Firings: Timothy Williams, "San Francisco Police Officers to Be Dismissed over Racist Texts," *New York Times*, April 3, 2015, www.nytimes.com/2015/04/04/us/san-francisco-police-officers-to-be-dismissed-over-racist-texts.html. Content of texts: Aleksander Chan, "The Horrible, Bigoted Texts Traded among San Francisco Police Officers," *Gawker*, March 3, 2015, http://gawker.com/the-horrible-bigoted-texts-traded-between-san-francisc-1692183203.

29. Extortionate practices: Radley Balko, "How Municipalities in St. Louis County, Mo., Profit from Poverty," *Washington Post*, September 3, 2014, www.washingtonpost.com/news/the-watch/wp/2014/09/03/how-st-louis-county-missouri-profits-from-poverty/. Arrest warrants: Monica Davey, "Ferguson One of 2 Missouri Suburbs Sued over Gantlet of Traffic Fines and Jail," *New York Times*, February 8, 2015, www.nytimes.com/2015/02/09/us/ferguson-one-of-2-missouri-suburbs-sued-over-gantlet-of-traffic-fines-and-jail.html. Original court record of arrest warrant numbers: https://www.courts.mo.gov/file.jsp?id=68845. According to Balko, even higher ratios of arrest warrants to residents can be found in Grandview, Independence, and, astonishingly, Kansas City, Missouri. Unsurprisingly, Balko also reports a number of racial disparities in these practices.

I find the occupancy permit notion most astonishing. In order to move to a new residence in Ferguson, one apparently needs to show up in person with a stack of documents and $80. From an FAQ section of the Ferguson city website, as of my visit to it on May 5, 2015:

> 1. Do I need an occupancy permit?
> Yes. Occupancy permits are required for both residential and commercial properties. All permits must be paid in person; cash, checks, money orders, debit or credit cards are accepted.
> 2. What is required to get a residential occupancy permit?
> To get a residential occupancy permit, you will need proof of ownership or authorization to occupy residential property form, a photo ID, birth certificates for children to show proof of relationship, a complete application, and the $40 fee.
> *An inspection is required when there is a change in occupancy and/or ownership. The inspection must be requested by the property owner and a fee of $40 must be paid separate from the occupancy permit fee. The fee must be paid in person; cash, checks, money orders, debit or credit cards are accepted.

www.fergusoncity.com/Faq.aspx?QID=71. This kind of obscure, bureaucratic, and expensive regulation is a ready-made tool to give police open threats in the brute pursuit of municipal banditry. The poor, unable to pay the $80; the working poor, unable to find the time to show up in person, dig up things like their children's birth certificates, and arrange for an inspection; and the uninformed, unaware of the regulation's very existence, become susceptible to official coercive power at will. It's also striking just how far from the assumed norm of American culture this is. Who would imagine that you have to dig up a bunch of documents and get a special license from the government after an inspection to move to a new apartment, or show up for a second round when, for example, a romantic partner moves in with you? This kind of regulation smacks of the sort of tale American schoolchildren in the 1980s were told about the Soviet Union, all internal passports and officious bureaucrats covering the ordinaries of day-to-day life with a miasma of long lines and forms to be filled out in triplicate. Nor does the oppressive potential of such regulations go unused. The most egregious abuse shows up on page 81 of a March 4, 2015, report of the US Department of Justice, available at www.justice.gov/sites/default/files/opa/press-releases/attachments/2015/03/04/ferguson_police_department_report_1.pdf, where we learn of at least two cases in which calling the police to report a "domestic disturbance" (which I read as meaning "domestic violence") got the complaining witness (i.e., *victim*) either summonsed or arrested for an occupancy permit violation; in one horrifying case the victim was arrested because the boyfriend, who (as I read it) was the alleged *perpetrator* of the domestic violence, was not listed on the occupancy permit. The capacity for that kind of outrageous arbitrary abuse of power is what an open threat looks like in a country that makes a show of the rule of law.

30. Spencer Ackerman, "The Disappeared: Chicago Police Detain Americans at Abuse-Laden 'Black Site,'" *The Guardian*, February 24, 2015, www.theguardian.com/us-news/2015/feb/24/chicago-police-detain-americans-black-site.
31. Slobogin (1996, 1040) gives the name and (*ibid.*, 1041–44) describes its prevalence.
32. Worrall (2001).
33. For example, Balko (2013, xii–xiii) recounts a 2010 nighttime SWAT raid in Columbia, Missouri, to serve a warrant for marijuana possession, which involved the shooting of several pet dogs, in a house with a 7-year-old child. The ultimate charge: possession of a marijuana pipe.
34. Krieger, Kiang, Chen, and Waterman (2015). American police have also been criticized for neglecting violence against blacks (Kennedy 1997, 29 et seq., especially 69 et seq.).
35. Gowder (2015a, 373–85).
36. In principle it is possible for courts (or pardon boards) to collect data on the extent of criminal behavior (facilitated, for example, by special verdict forms) in a given time period as well as sentences by race, and then retroactively lower the sentences for racial minorities until race no longer predicts sentence length after controlling for criminality.

References

Aeschines. "Against Ctesiphon." In *The Speeches of Aeschines*, translated by Charles Darwin Adams, 305–511. London: William Heinemann, 1919.

Afsah, Ebrahim. "Constitutionalism without Governance: International Standards in the Afghan Legal System." In *International Law in Domestic Courts: Rule of Law Reform in Post-Conflict States*, edited by Edda Kristjansdottir, Andre Nollkaemper, and Cedric Ryngaert, 125–52. Series on Transitional Justice. Cambridge: Intersentia, 2012.

Alexander, Michelle. *The New Jim Crow: Mass Incarceration in the Age of Colorblindness*. New York: New Press, 2012.

Allan, T. R. S. *Constitutional Justice: A Liberal Theory of the Rule of Law*. New York: Oxford University Press, 2001.

Allen, Danielle. *The World of Prometheus: The Politics of Punishing in Democratic Athens*. Princeton: Princeton University Press, 2000.

Allen, Theodore. *The Invention of the White Race, Volume II: The Origin of Racial Oppression in Anglo-America*. 2nd ed. New York: Verso Press, 2012.

Amar, Akhil Reed. "Attainder and Amendment 2: Romer's Rightness." *Michigan Law Review* 95 (1996): 203–35.

Anderson, Elizabeth S. *Value in Ethics and Economics*. Cambridge, MA: Harvard University Press, 1993.

"What Is the Point of Equality?" *Ethics* 109, no. 2 (1999): 287–337.

Anderson, Elizabeth S., and Richard H. Pildes. "Expressive Theories of Law: A General Restatement." *University of Pennsylvania Law Review* 148, no. 5 (2000): 1503–75.

Andocides. "Andocides: *On the Mysteries*." In *Minor Attic Orators in Two Volumes*, translated by K. J. Maidment, §1.87. Cambridge, MA: Harvard University Press, 1968.

Anwar, Shamena, Patrick Bayer, and Randi Hjalmarsson. "The Impact of Jury Race in Criminal Trials." *Quarterly Journal of Economics* 127, no. 2 (2012): 1017–55.

Aristotle. *The Politics and the Constitution of Athens*. Edited by Stephen Everson. New York: Cambridge University Press, 1996.

Arthurs, Jeffrey. "The Term Rhetor in Fifth- and Fourth-Century B.C.E. Greek Texts." *Rhetoric Society Quarterly* 23, no. 3–4 (1994): 1–10.

Asmonti, Luca A. "The Arginusae Trial, the Changing Role of *Strategoi* and the Relationship between *Demos* and Military Leadership in Late-Fifth Century Athens." *Bulletin of the Institute of Classical Studies* 49, no. 1 (2006): 1–21.

Ault, Warren. *Private Jurisdiction in England*. New Haven: Yale University Press, 1923.

"Village By-Laws by Common Consent." *Speculum* 29, no. 2 (1954): 378–94.

Avant, Deborah D. *The Market for Force: The Consequences of Privatizing Security*. New York: Cambridge University Press, 2005.

Axelrod, Robert. "Advancing the Art of Simulation in the Social Sciences: Obtaining, Analyzing, and Sharing Results of Computer Models." *Complexity* 3, no. 2 (1997): 16–22.

Baderin, Mashood A. *International Human Rights and Islamic Law*. Oxford: Oxford University Press, 2003.

Baker, C. Edwin. "Injustice and the Normative Nature of Meaning." *Maryland Law Review* 60, no. 3 (2001): 578–606.

Balko, Radley. *Rise of the Warrior Cop: The Militarization of America's Police Forces*. New York: PublicAffairs, 2013.

Barros, Robert. "Dictatorship and the Rule of Law: Rules and Military Power in Pinochet's Chile." In *Democracy and the Rule of Law*, edited by José María Maravall and Adam Przeworski, 19–61. New York: Cambridge University Press, 2003.

Bassiouni, M. Cherif, and Daniel Rothenberg. "An Assessment of Justice Sector and Rule of Law Reform in Afghanistan and the Need for a Comprehensive Plan." Presented at the Conference on the Rule of Law in Afghanistan, Rome, Italy, July 2, 2007.

Bates, Robert H., Avner Greif, Margaret Levi, and Jean-Laurent Rosenthal. *Analytic Narratives*. Princeton: Princeton University Press, 1998.

Bell, Derrick A., Jr. "*Brown v. Board of Education* and the Interest-Convergence Dilemma." *Harvard Law Review* 93, no. 3 (1980): 518–33.

Benn, S. I. "Freedom, *Autonomy and the Concept of a Person*." Proceedings of the Aristotelian Society 76 (1976): 109–30.

Bingham, Lord. "The Rule of Law." *Cambridge Law Journal* 66, no. 1 (2007): 67–85.

Birt, Raymond. "Personality and Foreign Policy: The Case of Stalin." *Political Psychology* 14, no. 4 (1993): 607–25.

Blanshard, Alastair J. L. "What Counts as the Demos? Some Notes on the Relationship between the Jury and 'The People' in Classical Athens." *Phoenix* 58, no. 1 (2004): 28–48.

Blanton, Richard, and Lane Fargher. *Collective Action in the Formation of Pre-Modern States*. New York: Springer, 2008.

Blattman, Christopher, Alexandra C. Hartman, and Robert A. Blair. "How to Promote Order and Property Rights under Weak Rule of Law? An Experiment in Changing Dispute Resolution Behavior through Community Education." *American Political Science Review* 108, no. 1 (2014): 100–20.

Blickman, Daniel. "The Myth of Ixion and Pollution for Homicide in Archaic Greece." *Classical Journal* 81 (1986): 193–208.

Bogdanor, Vernon. *The New British Constitution*. Portland: Hart Publishing, 2009.

Bolt, Robert. *A Man for All Seasons*. New York: Vintage Books, 1990.

Boyd, Robert, and Peter J. Richerson. "Gene-Culture Coevolution and the Evolution of Social Institutions." In *Better Than Conscious? Decision Making, the Human Mind, and Implications for Institutions*, edited by Cristoph Engel and Wolf Singer, 305–23. Cambridge, MA: MIT Press, 2008.

Bracton, Henry. *De Legibus et Consuetudinibus Angliæ*. Translated by Samuel E. Thorne. Cambridge, MA: Belknap Press of Harvard University Press, in association with the Selden Society, 1968.

Brand, Paul. *The Making of the Common Law*. London: Hambledon Press, 1992.

Brennan, Jason. *The Ethics of Voting*. Princeton: Princeton University Press, 2011.

Brennan, William J., Jr. "The Quest to Develop a Jurisprudence of Civil Liberties in Times of Security Crises." *Israel Yearbook on Human Rights* 18 (1988): 11–21.

Brettschneider, Corey. "A Substantive Conception of the Rule of Law: Non-Arbitrary Treatment and the Limits of Procedure." In *Nomos L: Getting to the Rule of Law*, edited by James E. Fleming, 52–63. New York: New York University Press, 2011.

Briggs, Chris. "Seigniorial Control of Villagers' Litigation beyond the Manor in Later Medieval England." *Historical Research* 81, no. 213 (2008): 399–422.

Brooks, Christopher. "The Place of Magna Carta and the Ancient Constitution in Sixteenth-Century English Legal Thought." In *The Roots of Liberty: Magna Carta, Ancient Constitution, and the Anglo-American Tradition of Rule of Law*, edited by Ellis Sandoz, 34–56. Indianapolis: Liberty Fund, 1993.

Brooks, Rosa Ehrenreich. "The New Imperialism: Violence, Norms, and the 'Rule of Law.'" *Michigan Law Review* 101, no. 7 (2003): 2275–340.

Brown, B. Katherine. "Freemanship in Puritan Massachusetts." *American Historical Review* 59, no. 4 (1954): 865–83.

Brudner, Alan. *Constitutional Goods*. New York: Oxford University Press, 2004.

Buggle, Johannes. "Law and Social Capital: Evidence from the Code Napoleon in Germany." In progress, 2013.

Burton, Steven J. *Judging in Good Faith*. New York: Cambridge University Press, 1992.

Buscaglia, Edgardo, and Paul B. Stephan. "An Empirical Assessment of the Impact of Formal versus Informal Dispute Resolution on Poverty: A Governance-Based Approach." *International Review of Law and Economics* 25, no. 1 (2005): 89–106.

Butler, Paul. "Racially Based Jury Nullification: Black Power in the Criminal Justice System." *Yale Law Journal* 105, no. 3 (1995): 677–725.

Carawan, Edwin. "Akriton Apokteinai, Execution without Trial in Fourth-Century Athens." *Greek, Roman, and Byzantine Studies* 25, no. 2 (1984): 111–21.

"Amnesty and Accountings for the Thirty." *Classical Quarterly* 56, no. 1 (2006): 57–76.

"The Trial of the Arginousai Generals and the Dawn of Judicial Review." *Dike* 10 (2007): 19–56.

Carey, Christopher. "Legal Space in Classical Athens." *Greece & Rome (Second Series)* 41, no. 2 (1994): 172–86.

"Nomos in Attic Rhetoric and Oratory." *Journal of Hellenic Studies* 116 (1996): 33–46.

Carothers, Thomas. *Aiding Democracy Abroad: The Learning Curve*. Washington, DC: Carnegie Endowment for International Peace, 1999.

Carothers, Thomas. *Promoting the Rule of Law Abroad: The Problem of Knowledge*. Washington, DC: Carnegie Endowment for International Peace, 2003. http://carnegieendowment.org/files/wp34.pdf.

Carr, Jesse. "The Lawlessness of Law: Lynching and Anti-Lynching in the Contemporary USA." *Settler Colonial Studies*, forthcoming (2015).

Cartledge, Paul. "Comparatively Equal." In *Demokratia: A Conversation on Democracies, Ancient and Modern*, edited by Josiah Ober and Charles Hedrick, 175–85. Princeton: Princeton University Press, 1996.

Carugati, Federica. "What Is the Rule of Law *Good For*? Democracy, Development and the Rule of Law in Classical Athens." *Buffalo Law Review* 62, no. 1 (2014): 119–56.

Catherine II. *The Grand Instructions to the Commissioners Appointed to Frame a New Code of Laws for the Russian Empire*. Translated by Michael Tatischeff. London: T. Jefferys, 1768.

Chaney, Cassandra, and Ray V. Robertson. "Racism and Police Brutality in America." *Journal of African American Studies* 17, no. 4 (2013): 480–505.

Checchi and Company Consulting, Inc., for the USAID Afghanistan Rule of Law Project. "Field Study of Informal and Customary Justice in Afghanistan and Recommendations on Improving Access to Justice and Relations between Formal Courts and Informal Bodies" (2005), 29–30.

Chrimes, S. B. *English Constitutional History*. London: Oxford University Press, 1965.

Christ, Matthew Robert. *The Litigious Athenian*. Baltimore: Johns Hopkins University Press, 1998.

Christiano, Thomas. *The Constitution of Equality: Democratic Authority and Its Limits*. New York: Oxford University Press, 2008.

Christianson, Paul. "Ancient Constitutions in the Age of Sir Edward Coke and John Selden." In *The Roots of Liberty: Magna Carta, Ancient Constitution, and the Anglo-American Tradition of Rule of Law*, edited by Ellis Sandoz, 115–84. Indianapolis: Liberty Fund, 1993.

Christman, John. "Liberalism and Individual Positive Freedom." *Ethics* 101, no. 2 (1991): 343–59.

Clarke, James W. "Without Fear or Shame: Lynching, Capital Punishment, and the Subculture of Violence in the American South." *British Journal of Political Science* 28, no. 2 (1998): 269–89.

Clarkson, Paul S., and Clyde T. Warren. "Copyhold Tenure and Macbeth, III, ii, 38." *Modern Language Notes* 55, no. 7 (1940): 483–93.

Cohen, David. *Law, Violence, and Community in Classical Athens*. New York: Cambridge University Press, 1995.

"The Rhetoric of Justice: Strategies of Reconciliation and Revenge in the Restoration of Athenian Democracy in 403 BC." *European Journal of Sociology* 42, no. 2 (2001): 335–56.

"Crime, Punishment, and the Rule of Law in Classical Athens." In *The Cambridge Companion to Ancient Greek Law*, edited by Michael Gagarin and David Cohen, 211–35. New York: Cambridge University Press, 2005.

Cohen, G. A. *On the Currency of Egalitarian Justice, and Other Essays in Political Philosophy*, edited by Michael Otsuka. Princeton: Princeton University Press, 2011.

Cohen, Joshua. "Procedure and Substance in Deliberative Democracy." In *Philosophy, Politics, Democracy: Selected Essays*, 154–80. Cambridge, MA: Harvard University Press, 2009.

Cohen, Mathilde. "The Rule of Law as the Rule of Reasons." *Archiv fuer Rechts- und Sozialphilosphie* 96, no. 1 (2010): 1–16.

Coke, Edward. *The Selected Writings and Speeches of Sir Edward Coke*, edited by Steve Sheppard. Indianapolis: Liberty Fund, 2003.

Coleman, Isobel. *Paradise between Her Feet: How Women Are Transforming the Middle East*. New York: Random House, 2010.

Colson, Darrel D. "On Appealing to Athenian Law to Justify Socrates' Disobedience." *Apeiron: A Journal for Ancient Philosophy and Science* 19, no. 2 (1985): 133–51.

Courtright, John A. "Rhetoric of the Gun: An Analysis of the Rhetorical Modifications of the Black Panther Party." *Journal of Black Studies* 4, no. 3 (1974): 249–67.

Cox, Archibald. "The Independence of the Judiciary: History and Purposes." *University of Dayton Law Review* 21, no. 3 (1996): 565–84.

Cronin, James F. "The Athenian Juror and Emotional Pleas." *Classical Journal* 34, no. 8 (1939): 471–79.

Curtis, Michael Kent. "In Pursuit of Liberty: The Levellers and the American Bill of Rights." 8 *Constitutional Commentary*, 359–93, 1991.

Darbyshire, Penny. "The Lamp That Shows That Freedom Lives – Is It Worth the Candle?" *Criminal Law Review* (1991): 740–52.

Darwall, Stephen L. "Two Kinds of Respect." *Ethics* 88, no. 1 (1977): 36–49.

Davidson, Donald. *Inquiries into Truth and Interpretation*. New York: Oxford University Press, 2001a.

"Three Varieties of Knowledge." In *Subjective, Intersubjective, Objective*, by Donald Davidson, 205–20. New York: Oxford University Press, 2001b.

Davis, Kevin E. "What Can the Rule of Law Variable Tell Us about Rule of Law Reforms?" *Michigan Journal of International Law* 26 (2004): 141–61.

de Greiff, Pablo. "Theorizing Transitional Justice." In *Nomos LI: Transitional Justice*, edited by Melissa Williams, Rosemary Nagy, and Jon Elster, 31–77. New York: New York University Press, 2012.

De Lara, Yadira González, Avner Greig, and Saumitra Jha. "The Administrative Foundations of Self-Enforcing Constitutions." *American Economic Review* 98, no. 2 (2008): 105–09.

Dershowitz, Alan. "The Torture Warrant: A Response to Professor Strauss." *New York Law School Law Review*, 48 (2003): 275–94.

Dicey, Albert Venn. *Introduction to the Study of the Law of the Constitution*, edited by Roger E. Michener. Indianapolis: Liberty Fund, 1982.

Diver, Colin. "The Optimal Precision of Administrative Rules." *Yale Law Journal* 93, no. 1 (1983): 65–109.

Doyle, William. *The Oxford History of the French Revolution*. New York: Oxford University Press, 2002.

Drumbl, Mark A. "Rights, Culture, and Crime: The Role of Rule of Law for the Women of Afghanistan." *Columbia Journal of Transnational Law* 42, no. 2 (2004): 349–90.

"Guantanamo, *Rasul*, and the Twilight of Law." *Drake Law Review* 53 (2005): 897–922.

Dunn, Marvin. "Justice for Willie James." *Tampa Tribune*, November 18, 2007. http://tbo.com/list/news-opinion-commentary/justice-for-willie-james-190797.

Dworkin, Gerald. *The Theory and Practice of Autonomy*. New York: Cambridge University Press, 1988.

Dworkin, Ronald. "The Model of Rules." *University of Chicago Law Review* 35, no. 1 (1967): 14–46.

"Political Judges and the Rule of Law." In *A Matter of Principle*, by Ronald Dworkin, 9–32. Cambridge, MA: Harvard University Press, 1986.

"Constitutionalism and Democracy." *European Journal of Philosophy* 3, no. 1 (1995): 2–11.

Dyzenhaus, David. "Leviathan as a Theory of Transitional Justice." In *Nomos LI: Transitional Justice*, edited by Melissa Williams, Rosemary Nagy, and Jon Elster, 180–217. New York: New York University Press, 2012.

Edmundson, William A., ed. *The Duty to Obey the Law: Selected Philosophical Readings*. Lanham: Rowman & Littlefield, 1999.

Ellickson, Robert C. *Order Without Law: How Neighbors Settle Disputes*. Cambridge, MA: Harvard University Press, 1991.

Ellis, Christopher, and John Fender. "Information Cascades and Revolutionary Regime Transitions." *Economic Journal* 121, no. 553 (2011): 763–92.

Elster, Jon. *Ulysses and the Sirens: Studies in Rationality and Irrationality*. New York: Cambridge University Press, 1979.

Ulysses Unbound: Studies in Rationality, Precommitment, and Constraints. New York: Cambridge University Press, 2000.

Closing the Books: Transitional Justice in Historical Perspective. New York: Cambridge University Press, 2004.

Epstein, Joshua M. "Agent-Based Computational Models and Generative Social Science," *Complexity* 4, no. 5 (1999): 41–60.

Eskridge, William N., Jr. "Pluralism and Distrust: How Courts Can Support Democracy by Lowering the Stakes of Politics." *Yale Law Journal* 114, no. 6 (2005): 1279–1328.

Euripides et al. *The Complete Greek Drama: All the Extant Tragedies of Aeschylus, Sophocles and Euripides, and the Comedies of Aristophanes and Menander, in a Variety of Translations*. Edited by Whitney J. Oates and Eugene O'Neill Jr. New York: Random House, 1938.

Fallon, Richard H., Jr. "'The Rule of Law' as a Concept in Constitutional Discourse." *Columbia Law Review* 97, no. 1 (1997): 1–56.

Fearon, James D. "Signaling Foreign Policy Interests: Tying Hands versus Sinking Costs." *Journal of Conflict Resolution* 41, no. 1 (1997): 68–90.
Ferejohn, John. "Independent Judges, Dependent Judiciary: Explaining Judicial Independence." *Southern California Law Review* 72 (1999): 353–84.
Finley, M. I. *The Use and Abuse of History*. New York: Viking Press, 1975.
Fiseha, Assefa. "Customary Dispute Resolution Mechanisms and the Rule of Law: Areas of Convergence, Divergence, and Implications." In *Law and Development, and Legal Pluralism in Ethiopia*, edited by Elias N. Stebek and Murado Abdo, 111–40. Addis Ababa: Justice and Legal Systems Research Institute, 2013.
Fisher, N. R. E. *Hybris: A Study in the Values of Honour and Shame in Ancient Greece*. Oxford: Aris & Phillips, 1992.
Fiss, Owen M. "Groups and the Equal Protection Clause." *Philosophy and Public Affairs* 5, no. 2 (1976): 107–77.
Fissell, Brenner M. "Jury Nullification and the Rule of Law." *Legal Theory* 19, no. 3 (2013): 217–41.
Fox, Charles James. "On the Refusal to Negotiate with France." In *The World's Famous Orations, Volume IV: Great Britain – II*, edited by William Jennings Bryan and Francis W. Halsey, 37–59. Accessed March 3, 2014. www.bartleby.com/268/4/7.html.
Fraenkel, Ernst. *The Dual State: A Contribution to the Theory of Dictatorship*. Translated by E. A. Shils. New York: Oxford University Press, 1941.
France, Anatole. *The Red Lily*. Translated by Frederic Chapman. London: John Lane, 1914.
Franklin, Travis W. "Race and Ethnicity Effects in Federal Sentencing: A Propensity Score Analysis." *Justice Quarterly* (2013): 1–27.
Frohnen, Bruce P. "A Problem of Power: The Impact of Modern Sovereignty on the Rule of Law in Comparative and Historical Perspective." *Transnational Law & Contemporary Problems* 20 (2012): 599–632.
Fukuyama, Francis. "The Imperative of State-Building." *Journal of Democracy* 15, no. 2 (2004): 17–31.
"Transitions to the Rule of Law." *Journal of Democracy* 21, no. 1 (2010): 33–44.
Fuller, Lon L. *The Morality of Law*. New Haven and London: Yale University Press, 1969.
Furley, William. *Andokides and the Herms: A Study of Crisis in Fifth-Century Athenian Religion*. Supplement 65. London: University of London Institute of Classical Studies, 1996.
Galanter, Marc. "The Aborted Restoration of 'Indigenous' Law in India." *Comparative Studies in Society and History* 14, no. 1 (1972): 53–70.
Gallia, Andrew B. "The Republication of Draco's Law on Homicide." *Classical Quarterly* 54, no. 2 (2004): 451–60.
Gardbaum, Stephen. *The New Commonwealth Model of Constitutionalism: Theory and Practice*. New York: Cambridge University Press, 2013.
Ginsburg, Tom. "Pitfalls of Measuring the Rule of Law." *Hague Journal on the Rule of Law* 3 (2011): 269–80.

Goldston, James A. "New Rules for the Rule of Law." In *The International Rule of Law Movement: A Crisis of Legitmacy and the Way Forward*, edited by David Marshall. Cambridge, MA: Harvard University Press, 2014.

Gordy, Sondra. "Empty Classrooms, Empty Hearts: Little Rock Secondary Teachers, 1958–1959." *Arkansas Historical Quarterly* 56, no. 4 (1997): 427–42.

Gowder, Paul. "An Egalitarian Theory of the Rule of Law." *PhD diss.*, Stanford University, 2012a.

"The Liberal Critique of Domination," Presented at the 2012 Western Political Science Association conference, Portland, Oregon, March 22–24, 2012b.

"The Rule of Law and Equality." *Law and Philosophy* 32, no. 5 (2013): 565–618.

"The Countermajoritarian Complaint." *Transnational Law and Contemporary Problems* 23 (2014a): 7–33.

"Democracy, Solidarity, and the Rule of Law: Lessons from Athens." *Buffalo Law Review* 62, no. 1 (2014b): 1–67.

"Equal Law in an Unequal World." *Iowa Law Review*, 99, no. 3 (2014c): 1021–81.

"Institutional Values, or How to Say What Democracy Is." *Southwest Philosophy Review* 30 (2014d): 235–42.

"Institutional Corruption and the Rule of Law." *Les Ateliers de l'ethique/The Ethics Forum*, 9, no. 1 (2014e): 84–102.

"Market Unfreedom." *Critical Review* 26, no. 3–4 (2014f): 306–47.

"Racial Classification and Ascriptive Injury." *Washington University Law Review* 92, no. 2 (2015a): 325–96.

"The Rule of Law against Sovereign Immunity in a Democratic State." *Texas Law Review See also* 93 (2015b): 247–262.

"Trust and Commitment: How Athens Rebuilt the Rule of Law." In *Theorizing Transitional Justice*, edited by Claudio Corradetti, Nir Eisikovits, and Jack Volpe Rotondi, 225–36. Farnham, UK: Ashgate, 2015c.

"What the Laws Demand of Socrates – and of Us." *The Monist*, 98, no. 4 (2015d): 360-374.

Green, John Richard. *A Short History of the English People*. New York: Harper & Brothers, 1879.

Greif, Avner. "The Impact of Administrative Power on Political and Economic Developments: Toward a Political Economy of Implementation." In *Institutions and Economic Performance*, edited by Elhanan Helpman, 17–63. Cambridge, MA: Harvard University Press, 2008.

Grenfell, Laura. *Promoting the Rule of Law in Post-Conflict States*. New York: Cambridge University Press, 2013.

Gribble, David. "Rhetoric and History in [Andocides] 4, Against Alcibiades." *The Classical Quarterly* 47, no. 2 (1997): 367–91.

Griffiths, David M. "Catherine II: The Republican Empress." *Jahrbücher für Geschichte Osteuropas* 21, no. 3 (1973): 323–44.

Habermas, Jürgen. *Between Facts and Norms: Contributions to a Discourse Theory of Law and Democracy*. Translated by William Rehg. Cambridge, MA: MIT Press, 1996.

Hadfield, Gillian, and Barry Weingast. "What Is Law? A Coordination Account of the Characteristics of Legal Order." *Journal of Legal Analysis* 4, no. 2 (2012): 471–514.

"Law without the State: Legal Attributes and the Coordination of Decentralized Collective Punishment." *Journal of Law and Courts* 1, no. 1 (2013): 3–34.

"Microfoundations of the Rule of Law." *Annual Review of Political Science* 17 (2014): 21–42.

Haggard, Stephan, Andrew MacIntyre, and Lydia Tiede. "The Rule of Law and Economic Development." *Annual Review of Political Science* 11 (2008): 205–34.

Haggard, Stephan, and Lydia Tiede. "The Rule of Law and Economic Growth: Where Are We?" *World Development* 39, no. 5 (2011): 673–85.

Hallaq, Wael B. *The Origins and Evolution of Islamic Law*. New York: Cambridge University Press, 2005.

Hansen, Mogens. *The Sovereignty of the People's Court in Athens in the Fourth Century B.C. and the Public Action against Unconstitutional Proposals*. Translated by Jorgen Raphaelsen and Sonja Hoboll. Odense: Odense University Press, 1974.

Eisangelia: The Sovereignty of the People's Court in Athens in the Fourth Century B.C. and the Impeachment of Generals and Politicians. Odense: Odense University Press, 1975.

The Athenian Democracy in the Age of Demosthenes: Structure, Principles, and Ideology. Translated by J. A. Crook. Norman: University of Oklahoma Press, 1999.

"The Concepts of *Demos, Ekklesia*, and *Dikasterion* in Classical Athens." *Greek, Roman and Byzantine Studies* 50 (2010): 499–536.

Harden, Ian, and Norman Lewis. *The Noble Lie: The British Constitution and the Rule of Law*. London: Hutchinson, 1988.

Hardin, Russell. "Constitutionalism." In *The Oxford Handbook of Political Economy*, edited by Barry R Weingast and Donald Wittman, 289–311. New York: Oxford University Press, 2008.

Harding, Alan. "Political Liberty in the Middle Ages." *Speculum* 55, no. 3 (1980): 423–43.

Harris, Edward. "The Rule of Law in Athenian Democracy: Reflections on the Judicial Oath." *Ethics & Politics* 9, no. 1 (2007): 55–74.

The Rule of Law in Action in Democratic Athens. Oxford: Oxford University Press, 2013.

Harris, Jessica C. "Revolutionary Black Nationalism: The Black Panther Party." *Journal of Negro History* 86, no. 3 (2001): 409–21.

Hart, H. L. A. "Positivism and the Separation of Law and Morals." *Harvard Law Review* 71, no. 4 (1958): 593–629.

The Concept of Law. New York: Oxford University Press, 1997.

"Discretion." *Harvard Law Review* 127, no. 2 (2013): 652–65.

Hart, James S., Jr. *The Rule of Law: 1603–1660: Crowns, Courts and Judges*. Harlow: Pearson Education, 2003.

Haslanger, Sally. *Resisting Reality: Social Construction and Social Critique*. Oxford: Oxford University Press, 2012.

Hatcher, John. "English Serfdom and Villeinage: Towards a Reassessment." *Past & Present*, no. 90 (1981): 3–39.

Hayek, Friedrich A. *The Constitution of Liberty*. Chicago: University of Chicago Press, 1960.

Law, Legislation and Liberty, Volume 1: Rules and Order. Chicago: University of Chicago Press, 1978.

Hazard, John. "The Trend of Law in the U.S.S.R." *Wisconsin Law Review* (1947): 223–43.

Heal, Felicity, and Clive Holmes. *The Gentry in England and Wales, 1500–1700*. Stanford: Stanford University Press, 1994.

Heaslet, Julia Pennington. "The Red Guards: Instruments of Destruction in the Cultural Revolution." *Asian Survey* 12, no. 12 (1972): 1032–47.

Hegel, Georg Wilhelm Friedrich. *Hegel: Elements of the Philosophy of Right*. Edited by Allen W. Wood. Translated by H. B. Nisbet. New York: Cambridge University Press, 1991.

Herman, Shael. *Medieval Usury and the Commercialization of Feudal Bonds*. Berlin: Duncker & Humblot, 1993.

Herndon, James S., and Joseph O. Baylen. "Col. Philip R. Faymonville and the Red Army, 1934–43." *Slavic Review* 34, no. 3 (1975): 483–505.

Herodotus. *The Landmark Herodotus: The Histories*. Edited by Robert B. Strassler. Translated by Andrea Purvis. New York: Anchor Books, 2009.

Hill, Thomas E., Jr. "Servility and Self-Respect." *Monist* 57, no. 1 (1973): 87–104.

Hilton, R. H. "Peasant Movements in England before 1381." *Economic History Review* 2, no. 2 (1949): 117–36.

"Freedom and Villeinage in England." *Past & Present*, 31, no. 1 (1965): 3–19.

Hobbes, Thomas. *Leviathan*. Edited by Richard Tucker. New York: Cambridge University Press, 1996.

Hobbs, Bradley. "Hitler Is Here: Lynching in Florida during the Era of World War II." *PhD diss.*, Florida State University, 2004.

Holden-Smith, Barbara. "Lynching, Federalism, and the Intersection of Race and Gender in the Progressive Era." *Yale Journal of Law and Feminism* 8 (1996): 31–78.

Holt, J. C. *Magna Carta*. Cambridge and New York: Cambridge University Press, 1992.

"The Ancient Constitution in Medieval England." In *The Roots of Liberty: Magna Carta, Ancient Constitution, and the Anglo-American Tradition of Rule of Law*, edited by Ellis Sandoz, 32–74. Indianapolis: Liberty Fund, 1993.

Hsieh, Ching-Chi, and M. D. Pugh. "Poverty, Income Inequality, and Violent Crime: A Meta-Analysis of Recent Aggregate Data Studies." *Criminal Justice Review* 18, no. 2 (1993): 182–202.

Hurwitz, Jon, and Mark Peffley. "And Justice for Some: Race, Crime, and Punishment in the US Criminal Justice System." *Canadian Journal of Political Science* 43, no. 2 (2010): 457–79.

Huth, Paul K. "Deterrence and International Conflict: Empirical Findings and Theoretical Debates." *Annual Review of Political Science* 2 (1999): 25–48.

Hyams, Paul R. "The Jewish Minority in Mediaeval England, 1066–1290." *Journal of Jewish Studies* 25, no. 2 (1974): 270–93.

King, Lords, and Peasants in Medieval England: The Common Law of Villeinage in the Twelfth and Thirteenth Centuries. New York: Oxford University Press, 1980.

Ignatieff, Michael. *The Lesser Evil: Political Ethics in an Age of Terror*. Princeton: Princeton University Press, 2004.

Ikegami, Eiko. "A Sociological Theory of Publics: Identity and Culture as Emergent Properties in Networks." *Social Research* 67, no. 4 (2000): 989–1029.

Isiksel, Turkuler. "Between Text and Context: Turkey's Tradition of Authoritarian Constitutionalism." *International Journal of Constitutional Law* 11, no. 3 (2013): 702–26.

Isocrates. "Against Lochites." In *Isocrates in Three Volumes*. Translated by George Norlin. Cambridge, MA: Harvard University Press, 1980.

Jacobs, Joseph. *The Jews of Angevin England: Documents and Records from Latin and Hebrew Sources, Printed and Manuscript*. London: David Nutt, 1893.

Jeffries, John. "Legality, Vagueness, and the Construction of Penal Statutes." *Virginia Law Review* 71, no. 2 (1985): 189–245.

Jennings, Ivor. *The Law and the Constitution*. London: University of London Press, 1959.

Jennings, Ronald C. "Limitations of the Judicial Powers of the Kadi in 17th C. Ottoman Kayseri." *Studia Islamica*, no. 50 (1979): 151–84.

Johnson, Robert C., Mary Frear Keeler, Maija Jansson Cole, and William B. Bidwell, eds. *Commons Debates*, 1628. New Haven: Yale University Press, 1977.

Johnston, Hank. "'Let's Get Small': The Dynamics of (Small) Contention in Repressive States." *Mobilization* 11, no. 2 (1996): 195–212.

Jordović, Ivan. "Critias and Democracy." *Balcanica* 39 (2008): 33–46.

Judson, Margaret Atwood. *The Crisis of the Constitution: An Essay in Constitutional and Political Thought in England, 1603–1645*. New York: Octagon, 1964.

Kagan, Donald. *The Fall of the Athenian Empire*. Ithaca, NY: Cornell University Press, 1991.

Kant, Immanuel. *Groundwork for the Metaphysics of Morals*. Translated by Allen Wood. New Haven: Yale University Press, 2002.

Karayiannis, Anastassios, and Aristides N. Hatzis. "Morality, Social Norms and the Rule of Law as Transaction Cost-Saving Devices: The Case of Ancient Athens." *European Journal of Law and Economics* 33, no. 3 (2012): 621–43.

Karim, Imam Benjamin, ed. *The End of White World Supremacy: Four Speeches by Malcolm X*. New York: Seaver, 1971.

Kaufmann, Daniel, Aart Kraay, and Massimo Mastruzzi. "The Worldwide Governance Indicators Project: Answering the Critics." *World Bank Policy Research*, Working Paper no. 4149 (2007).

"The Worldwide Governance Indicators: Methodology and Analytical Issues." *Hague Journal on the Rule of Law* 3, no. 2 (2011): 220–46.

Keister, Lisa A., and Stephanie Moller. "Wealth Inequality in the United States." *Annual Review of Sociology* 26 (2000): 63–81.

Kennedy, Randall. *Race, Crime, and the Law*. New York: Pantheon, 1997.
King, Gilbert. *Devil in the Grove: Thurgood Marshall, the Groveland Boys, and the Dawn of a New America*. New York: Harper Perennial, 2013.
Klarman, Michael J. "The Racial Origins of Modern Criminal Procedure." *Michigan Law Review* 99, no. 1 (2000): 48–97.
Kleinfeld, Rachel. *Advancing the Rule of Law Abroad: Next Generation Reform*. Washington, DC: Carnegie Endowment for International Peace, 2012.
Kleinfeld, Rachel, and Harry Bader. *Extreme Violence and the Rule of Law: Lessons from Eastern Afghanistan*. Carnegie Endowment for International Peace white paper, April 2014.
Klock, Kimberly. "Resolution of Domestic Disputes through Extra-Judicial Mechanisms in the United States and Asia: Neighborhood Justice Centers, the Panchayat, and the Mahalla." *Temple International and Comparative Law Journal* 15 (2001): 275–95.
Kramer, Matthew H. *In Defense of Legal Positivism: Law without Trimmings*. New York: Oxford University Press, 1999.
Objectivity and the Rule of Law. New York: Cambridge University Press, 2007.
Krasner, Stephen D., and Thomas Risse. "External Actors, State-Building, and Service Provision in Areas of Limited Statehood: Introduction." *Governance* (2014). doi:10.1111/gove.12065.
Krentz, Peter. *The Thirty at Athens*. Ithaca, NY: Cornell University Press, 1982.
Krever, Tor. "Quantifying Law: Legal Indicator Projects and the Reproduction of Neoliberal Common Sense." *Third World Quarterly* 34, no. 1 (2013): 131–50.
Krieger, Nancy, Matthew V. Kiang, Jarvis T. Chen, and Pamela D. Waterman. "Trends in U.S. Deaths Due to Legal Intervention among Black and White Men, Age 15–34 Years, by County Income Level: 1960–2010." *Harvard Public Health Review* 3 (2015), online publication, available at http://harvardpublichealthreview.org/190/.
Krygier, Martin. "The Rule of Law: An Abuser's Guide." In *Abuse: The Dark Side of Fundamental Rights*, edited by András Sajó, 129–61. Utrecht: Eleven International Publishing, 2006.
Kuran, Timur. "Sparks and Prairie Fires: A Theory of Unanticipated Political Revolution." *Public Choice* 61, no. 1 (1989): 41–74.
"The East European Revolution of 1989: Is It Surprising That We Were Surprised?" *American Economic Review* 81, no. 2 (1991): 121–25.
Lang, Mabel. "Revolution of the 400: Chronology and Constitutions." *American Journal of Philology* 88, no. 2 (1967): 176–87.
Lanni, Adriaan. *Law and Justice in the Courts of Classical Athens*. New York: Cambridge University Press, 2006.
"Social Norms in the Courts of Ancient Athens." *Journal of Legal Analysis* 1, no. 2 (2009): 691–736.
"Transitional Justice in Ancient Athens: A Case Study." *University of Pennsylvania Journal of International Law* 32, no. 2 (2010): 551–94.
"Publicity and the Courts of Classical Athens." *Yale Journal of Law and Humanities* 24, no. 1 (2012): 119–35.

Law, David. "A Theory of Judicial Power and Judicial Review." *Georgetown Law Journal* 97, no. 3 (2009): 723–801.

Law, David, and Mila Versteeg. "Sham Constitutions." *California Law Review* 101, no. 4 (2013): 863–952.

Ledford, Kenneth F. "Formalizing the Rule of Law in Prussia: The Supreme Administrative Law Court, 1876–1914." *Central European History* 37, no. 2 (2004): 203–24.

Lessig, Lawrence. *Republic, Lost: How Money Corrupts Congress – and a Plan to Stop It*. New York: Twelve/Hachette Book Group, 2011.

Letelier, Orlando. "The Chicago Boys in Chile: Economic Freedom's Awful Toll." *The Nation*. Last modified August 28, 1976. www.tni.org/article/chicago-boys-chile-economic-freedoms-awful-toll.

Levi, Margaret. "A Logic of Institutional Change." In *The Limits of Rationality*, edited by Karen Schweers Cook and Margaret Levi. Chicago: University of Chicago Press, 1990.

"A State of Trust." In *Trust and Governance*, edited by Valerie Braithwaite and Margaret Levi, 77–101. New York: Russell Sage Foundation, 2003.

Lewis, David. "Radical Interpretation." *Synthese* 27, no. 3–4, (1974): 331–44.

"Languages and Language." In *Minnesota Studies in the Philosophy of Science*, edited by Keith Gunderson, 3–35. Minneapolis: University of Minnesota Press, 1975.

Lewis, John David. "Slavery and Lawlessness in Solonian Athens." *Dike* 7 (2004): 19–40.

"Constitution and Fundamental Law: The Lesson of Classical Athens." *Social Philosophy and Policy* 28, no. 01 (2011): 25–49.

Linz, Juan J. *Totalitarian and Authoritarian Regimes*. Boulder: Lynne Rienner Publishers, 2000.

Lissitzyn, O. J. "Recent Soviet Literature on International Law." *American Slavic and East European Review* 11, no. 4 (1952): 257–73.

Locke, John. *The Second Treatise of Government; and, A Letter Concerning Toleration*. Mineola: Dover, 2002.

Loening, Thomas Clark. *The Reconciliation Agreement of 403/402 B.C. in Athens: Its Content and Application. Hermes: Einzelschriften, Volume* 53. Stuttgart: Franz Steiner Verlag Wiesbaden, 1987.

Lohmann, Susanne. "The Dynamics of Informational Cascades: The Monday Demonstrations in Leipzig, East Germany, 1989–91." *World Politics* 47, no. 1 (1994): 42–101.

"Collective Action Cascades: An Informational Rationale for the Power in Numbers." *Journal of Economic Surveys* 14, no. 5 (2000): 655–84.

"Why Do Institutions Matter? An Audience-Cost Theory of Institutional Commitment." *Governance* 16, no. 1 (2003): 95–110.

Lovett, Frank. "A Positivist Account of the Rule of Law." *Law & Social Inquiry* 27, no. 1 (2002): 41–78.

Lysias. *The Speeches of Lysias*. Translated by S. C. Todd. Austin: University of Texas Press, 2000.

MacCormick, Neil. *Questioning Sovereignty: Law, State, and Nation in the European Commonwealth*. New York: Oxford University Press, 1999.

MacDowell, Douglas M. *The Law in Classical Athens*. Ithaca, NY: Cornell University Press, 1978.

Macedo, Stephen. "The Rule of Law, Justice, and the Politics of Moderation." In *Nomos XXXVI: The Rule of Law*, edited by Ian Shapiro, 148–77. New York: New York University Press, 1994.

Machiavelli, Niccolò. *Discourses on Livy*. Translated by Harvey C. Mansfield and Nathan Tarcov. Chicago: University of Chicago Press, 1995.

Maddicott, J. R. "Magna Carta and the Local Community 1215–1259." *Past & Present*, no. 102 (1984): 25–65.

Maio, Dennis Peter. "*Politeia* and Adjudication in Fourth-Century B.C. Athens." *American Journal of Jurisprudence* 28, no. 1 (1983): 16–45.

Maitland, F. W., ed. *Select Pleas in Manorial and Other Seignorial Courts, Volume 1: Reigns of Henry III and Edward I*. London: Bernard Quaritch, 1889.

The Constitutional History of England – A Course of Lectures Delivered. New York: Cambridge University Press, 1908.

Marks, Susan. "Civil Liberties at the Margin: The UK Derogation and the European Court of Human Rights." *Oxford Journal of Legal Studies* 15, no. 1 (1995): 69–95.

Marmor, Andrei. "The Rule of Law and Its Limits." In *Law in the Age of Pluralism*, by Andrei Marmor, 3–38. New York: Oxford University Press, 2007.

Marr, J. L., and P. J. Rhodes, trans. *The "Old Oligarch": The Constitution of the Athenians Attributed to Xenophon*. Oxford: Aris & Phillips Classical Texts, 2008.

Marshall, David, ed. *The International Rule of Law Movement: A Crisis of Legitimacy and the Way Forward*, Cambridge, MA: Harvard University Press, 2014.

Mattei, Ugo. "A Theory of Imperial Law: A Study on U.S. Hegemony and the Latin Resistance." *Indiana Journal of Global Legal Studies* 10, no. 1 (2003): 383–448.

McGlew, James F. "Politics on the Margins: The Athenian *Hetaireiai* in 415 B.C." *Historia: Zeitschrift für Alte Geschichte* 48, no. 1 (1999): 1–22.

McHarg, Aileen. "Reforming the United Kingdom Constitution: Law, Convention, Soft Law." *Modern Law Review* 71, no. 6 (2008): 853–77.

McMurtrie, Sheena N. "The Constitutionality of the War Crimes Act 1991." *Statute Law Review* 13, no. 2 (1992): 128–49.

Merkel, Wolfgang. "Measuring the Quality of Rule of Law: Virtues, Perils, Results." In *Rule of Law Dynamics in an Era of International and Transnational Governance*, edited by Michael Zurn, Andre Nollkaemper, and Randy Peerenboom 21: 47. Cambridge: Cambridge University Press, 2012.

Michelman, Frank. "Relative Constraint and Public Reason: What Is 'the Work We Expect of Law'?" *Brooklyn Law Review*, 67 (2002): 963–85.

Milgrom, Paul R., Douglass C. North, and Barry R. Weingast. "The Role of Institutions in the Revival of Trade: The Law Merchant, Private Judges, and the Champagne Fairs." *Economics & Politics* 2, no. 1 (1990): 1–23.

Mill, John Stuart. "Thoughts on Parliamentary Reform." In *The Collected Works of John Stuart Mill, Volume XVIII*, edited by John M. Robson, 311–39. London: Routledge and Kegan Paul, 1977.

Milsom, S. F. C. *The Legal Framework of English Feudalism: The Maitland Lectures given in 1972*. New York: Cambridge University Press, 1976.

A Natural History of the Common Law. New York: Columbia University Press, 2003.

Mitchell, Don. "The Annihilation of Space by Law: The Roots and Implications of Anti-Homeless Laws in the United States." *Antipodes* 29, no. 3 (1997): 303–35.

Modood, Tariq. "Muslims and the Politics of Difference." *Political Quarterly* 74, no. s1 (2003): 100–15.

Moore, Michael S. "A Natural Law Theory of Interpretation." *Southern California Law Review* 58 (1985): 277–398.

Murphy, Colleen. "Lon Fuller and the Moral Value of the Rule of Law." *Law and Philosophy* 24, no. 3 (2005): 239–62.

A Moral Theory of Political Reconciliation. Cambridge: Cambridge University Press, 2010.

Nagel, Thomas. *The View from Nowhere*. New York: Oxford University Press, 1986.

"The Problem of Global Justice." *Philosophy & Public Affairs* 33, no. 2 (2005): 113–47.

Nardulli, Peter F., Buddy Peyton, and Joseph Bajjalieh. "Conceptualizing and Measuring Rule of Law Constructs, 1850–2010." *Journal of Law and Courts* 1, no. 1 (2013): 139–92.

Nightingale, Andrea Wilson. "Plato's Lawcode in Context: Rule by Written Law in Athens and Magnesia." *Classical Quarterly* 49, no. 1 (1999): 100–22.

North, Douglass C. "Institutions and Credible Commitment." *Journal of Institutional and Theoretical Economics* 149, no. 1 (1993): 11–23.

North, Douglass C., John Joseph Wallis, and Barry R Weingast. *Violence and Social Orders: A Conceptual Framework for Interpreting Recorded Human History*. New York: Cambridge University Press, 2009.

North, Douglass C., and Barry R. Weingast. "Constitutions and Commitment: The Evolution of Institutions Governing Public Choice in Seventeenth-Century England." *Journal of Economic History* 49, no. 4 (1989): 803–32.

Nozick, Robert. *Anarchy, State, and Utopia*. New York: Basic Books, 1974.

Ober, Josiah. *Mass and Elite in Democratic Athens: Rhetoric, Ideology, and the Power of the People*. Princeton: Princeton University Press, 1989.

Athenian Legacies: Essays on the Politics of Going on Together. Princeton: Princeton University Press, 2005.

Democracy and Knowledge: Innovation and Learning in Classical Athens. Princeton: Princeton University Press, 2008.

Olson, Mancur, Jr. *The Logic of Collective Action: Public Goods and the Theory of Groups*. Cambridge, MA: Harvard University Press, 1965.

"Dictatorship, Democracy, and Development." *American Political Science Review* 87, no. 3 (1993): 567–76.

Organisation for Economic Co-operation and Development. *Handbook on Constructing Composite Indicators: Methodology and User Guide* (2008). www.oecd.org/std/42495745.pdf.

Osborne, Martin J., and Ariel Rubinstein. *A Course in Game Theory*. Cambridge, MA: MIT Press, 1994.

Osborne, Robin. "Law in Action in Classical Athens." *Journal of Hellenic Studies* 105 (1985): 40–58.

Ostrom, Elinor. *Governing the Commons: The Evolution of Institutions for Collective Action*. Cambridge/New York: Cambridge University Press, 1990.

Ostwald, Martin. *Nomos and the Beginnings of the Athenian Democracy*. Oxford: Clarendon Press, 1969.

From Popular Sovereignty to the Sovereignty of Law: Law, Society, and Politics in Fifth Century Athens. Berkeley and Los Angeles: University of California Press, 1986.

"Public Expense: Whose Obligation? Athens 600–454 B.C.E." *Proceedings of the American Philosophical Society* 139, no. 4 (1995): 368–79.

Perez, Anthony Daniel, Kimberly M. Berg, and Daniel J. Myers. "Police and Riots, 1967–1969." *Journal of Black Studies* 34, no. 2 (2003): 153–82.

Pether, Penelope. "Militant Judgment? Judicial Ontology, Constitutional Poetics, and 'The Long War.'" *Cardozo Law Review* 29, no. 5 (2008): 2279–317.

Pettit, Philip. "Freedom as Antipower." *Ethics* 106, no. 3 (1996): 576–604.

Republicanism: A Theory of Freedom and Government. New York: Oxford University Press, 1997.

"Agency-Freedom and Option-Freedom." *Journal of Theoretical Politics* 15, no. 4 (2003): 387–403.

Pistor, Katharina. "The Standardization of Law and Its Effect on Developing Economies." *American Journal of Comparative Law* 50, no. 1 (2002): 97–130.

Plato. *The Laws of Plato*. Translated by Thomas L. Pangle. New York: Basic Books, 1980.

Plato: Complete Works. Edited by John M. Cooper and D. S. Hutchinson. Indianapolis: Hackett, 1997.

Pollard, A. F. "Parliament and Liberty." 1926. Reprinted in *Magna Carta and the Idea of Liberty*, edited by J. C. Holt. New York: John Wiley & Sons, 1972.

Pollock, Frederick, and F. W. Maitland. *The History of English Law before the Time of Edward I*. Reprint of 2nd ed. Indianapolis: Liberty Fund, 2010.

Postema, Gerald. "Fidelity in Law's Commonwealth." In *Private Law and the Rule of Law*, edited by Lisa M. Austin and Dennis Klimchuk. Oxford: Oxford University Press, 2015.

Premchand, Munshi. *Twenty Four Stories*. Translated by Nandini Nopany and Purushottama Lal. New Delhi: Vikas, 1980.

Pridemore, William Alex. "Poverty Matters: A Reassessment of the Inequality-Homicide Relationship in Cross-National Studies." *British Journal of Criminology* 51, no. 5 (2011): 739–72.

Pseudo-Xenophon. *Xenophon Scripta Minora*. Translated by E. C. Marchant. Cambridge, MA: Harvard University Press, 1968.

Quine, W. V. *Ontological Relativity & Other Essays*. New York: Columbia University Press, 1969.

Raaflaub, Kurt. "Athens: Equalities, Inequalities." In *Demokratia: A Conversation on Democracies, Ancient and Modern*, edited by Josiah Ober and Charles Hedrick, 139–74. Princeton: Princeton University Press, 1996.

The Discovery of Freedom in Ancient Greece. Chicago: University of Chicago Press, 2004.

Rantanen, Jason. "The Malleability of Patent Rights." Forthcoming in *Michigan State Law Review* (2015).

Rawls, John. "The Idea of Public Reason Revisited." In *The Law of Peoples: With, "The Idea of Public Reason Revisited,"* by John Rawls, 129–80. Cambridge, MA: Harvard University Press, 1999a.

A Theory of Justice. Cambridge, MA: Harvard University Press, 1999b.

Justice as Fairness: A Restatement. Cambridge, MA: Harvard University Press, 2001.

Political Liberalism. New York: Columbia University Press, 2005.

Raz, Joseph. *The Authority of Law: Essays on Law and Morality*. New York: Oxford University Press, 1979.

Reenock, Christopher, Jeffrey K. Staton, and Marcus Radean. "Legal Institutions and Democratic Survival." *Journal of Politics* 75, no. 2 (2013): 491–505.

Rhodes, P. J. *A History of the Classical Greek World*. Malden, MA: Wiley-Blackwell, 2010.

Rijpkema, Peter. "The Rule of Law beyond Thick and Thin." *Law and Philosophy* 32, no. 6 (2013): 793–816.

Riker, William H. *Liberalism against Populism: A Confrontation between the Theory of Democracy and the Theory of Social Choice*. Prospect Heights: Waveland Press, 1988.

Ringer, Thom. "Note: Development, Reform, and the Rule of Law: Some Prescriptions for a Common Understanding of the 'Rule of Law' and Its Place in Development Theory and Practice." *Yale Human Rights & Development Law Journal* 10 (2007): 178–208.

Rios-Figueroa, Julio, and Jeffrey K. Staton. "Unpacking the Rule of Law: A Review of Judicial Independence Measures." *The Committee on Concepts and Methods, International Political Science Association IPSA*, Working Paper no. 21 (2008).

Ripstein, Arthur. *Force and Freedom: Kant's Legal and Political Philosophy*. Cambridge, MA: Harvard University Press, 2009.

Roberts, Jennifer Tolbert. "Arginusae Once Again." *Classical World* 71, no. 2 (1977): 107–11.

"The Athenian Conservatives and the Impeachment Trials of the Corinthian War." *Hermes* 108, H. 1 (1980): 100–14.

Robinson, James A., Ragnar Torvik, and Thierry Verdier. "Political Foundations of the Resource Curse." *Journal of Development Economics* 79, no. 2 (2006): 447–68.

Rosivach, Vincent J. "The Tyrant in Athenian Democracy." *Quaderni Urbinati di Cultura Classica* 30, no. 3 (1988): 43–57.

Rottleuthner, Hubert. A *Treatise of Legal Philosophy and General Jurisprudence, Volume 2: Foundations of Law*. Dordrecht: Springer, 2005.

Rousseau, Jean-Jacques. *On the Social Contract*. Translated by G. D. H. Cole. New York: Dover, 2003.

Rundle, Kristen. *Forms Liberate: Reclaiming the Jurisprudence of Lon L. Fuller*. Oxford: Hart Publishing, 2012.

Ruskola, Teemu. "Legal Orientalism." *Michigan Law Review* 101, no. 1 (2002): 179–234.

Saisana, Michela, and Andrea Saltelli. "Statistical Audit." European Commission Joint Research Centre report (2012), available online at worldjusticeproject.org/sites/default/files/statistical_audit.pdf.

Sanchez-Cuenca, Ignacio. "Power, Rules and Compliance." In *Democracy and the Rule of Law*, edited by Jose Maria Maravall and Adam Przeworski, 62–93. Cambridge: Cambridge University Press, 2003.

Sangiovanni, Andrea. "Global Justice, Reciprocity, and the State." *Philosophy & Public Affairs* 35, no. 1 (2007): 3–39.

Santiso, Carlos. "Good Governance and Aid Effectiveness: The World Bank and Conditionality." *Georgetown Public Policy Review* 7, no. 1 (2001): 1–22.

"The Elusive Quest for the Rule of Law: Promoting Judicial Reform in Latin America." *Brazilian Journal of Political Economy* 23, no. 3 (2003): 112–34.

Satterthwaite, Margaret L. "Rendered Meaningless: Extraordinary Rendition and the Rule of Law." *George Washington Law Review* 75, no. 5–6 (2007): 1333–420.

Scarry, Elaine. *Rule of Law, Misrule of Men*. Cambridge, MA: MIT Press, 2010.

Schauer, Frederick. "Giving Reasons." *Stanford Law Review* 47, no. 4 (1995): 633–59.

Profiles, Probabilities and Stereotypes. Cambridge, MA: Harvard University Press, 2003.

Scheffler, Samuel. "What Is Egalitarianism?" *Philosophy & Public Affairs* 31, no. 1 (2003): 5–39.

Schlesinger, Rudolf. "Soviet Lawyers on the Problems of Their Legal System – I." *Soviet Studies* 7, no. 2 (1955): 164–82.

Schwartzberg, Melissa. "Was the *Graphe Paranomon* a Form of Judicial Review?" *Cardozo Law Review* 34, no. 3 (2013): 1049–62.

Schwartzman, Micah. "Judicial Sincerity." *Virginia Law Review* 94 (2008): 987–1027.

Scott, James C. *Seeing Like a State: How Certain Schemes to Improve the Human Condition Have Failed*. New Haven: Yale University Press, 1999.

Segev, Re'em. "Making Sense of Discrimination." *Ratio Juris* 27, no. 1 (2014): 47–78.

Sen, Amartya. "Equality of What?" *Tanner Lectures on Human Values* 1 (1980; pap. ed. 2011): 195–220. Lecture delivered at Stanford University, May 22, 1979.

Sepielli, Andrew. "The Law's 'Majestic Equality.'" *Law and Philosophy* 32, no. 6 (2013): 673–700.

Sevel, Michael. "Legal Positivism and the Rule of Law." *Australian Journal of Legal Philosophy* 34 (2009): 53–68.

Sharlet, Robert. "Soviet Legal Periodicals, 1918–1974: A Bibliography." *Soviet and Post-Soviet Review* 1, no. 1 (1974): 156.

Sharon, Assaf. "The Rule of Law: A Philosophical Investigation of Law and Liberty." *PhD diss.*, Stanford University, 2012.

Shklar, Judith N. "Political Theory and the Rule of Law." In *Political Thought and Political Thinkers*, edited by Stanley Hoffmann, 21–37. Chicago: University of Chicago Press, 1998.

Siegel, David A., and Joseph K. Young. "Simulating Terrorism: Credible Commitment, Costly Signaling, and Strategic Behavior." *PS: Political Science and Politics* 42, no. 4 (2009): 765–71.

Silva, Eduardo. "Capitalist Coalitions, the State, and Neoliberal Economic Restructuring: Chile, 1973–88." *World Politics* 45, no. 5 (1993): 526–59.

Silverman, Daniel. "The Arab Military in the Arab Spring: Agent of Continuity of Change?: A Comparative Analysis of Tunisia, Egypt, Libya, and Syria." Presentation at the American Political Science Association, New Orleans, Louisiana, August 30–September 2, 2012.

Simmonds, Nigel. *Law as a Moral Idea*. Oxford: Oxford University Press, 2007.

Simmons, A. John. *Moral Principles and Political Obligations*. Princeton: Princeton University Press, 1979.

Skaaning, Svend-Erik. "Measuring the Rule of Law." *Political Research Quarterly* 63, no. 2 (2010): 449–60.

Skinner, Quentin. *Liberty before Liberalism*. New York: Cambridge University Press, 1998.

Slobogin, Chrostopher. "Testilying: Police Perjury and What to Do about It." *University of Colorado Law Review* 67 (1996): 1037–60.

Solum, Lawrence B. "Constructing an Ideal of Public Reason." *San Diego Law Review* 30, no. 4 (1993): 729–62.

Somers, Margaret R. "Citizenship and the Place of the Public Sphere: Law, Community, and Political Culture in the Transition to Democracy." *American Sociological Review* 30, no. 5 (1993): 587–620.

Souaiaia, Ahmed E. *Anatomy of Dissent in Islamic Societies: Ibadism, Rebellion, and Legitimacy*. New York: Palgrave Macmillan, 2013.

Soule, Sarah. "Why Design Thinking Is an Effective Tool for Social Entrepreneurs." Stanford Graduate School of Business Center for Social Innovation. Last modified November 5, 2013. http://csi.gsb.stanford.edu/sarah-soule-why-design-thinking-effective-tool-social-entrepreneurs.

Stanford University Institute of Design. "Use Our Methods." Accessed March 3, 2014. http://dschool.stanford.edu/use-our-methods/.

Starr, Joseph. "The New Constitution of the Soviet Union." *American Political Science Review* 30, no. 6 (1936): 1143–52.

Stem, Rex. "The Thirty at Athens in the Summer of 404." *Phoenix* 57, no. 1–2 (2003): 18–34.

Steyn, Johan van Zyl. "Guantanamo Bay: The Legal Black Hole." *International and Comparative Law Quarterly* 53, no. 1 (2004): 1–15.

"Democracy, the Rule of Law, and the Role of Judges." *European Human Rights Law Review* 3 (2006): 243–53.

Sticht, Thomas. "The Rise of the Adult Education and Literacy System in the United States." In *Annual Review of Adult Learning and Literacy* 3, edited by John Comings, Barbara Garner, and Christine Smith. Malden, MA: John Wiley & Sons, 2002.

Stone, Lawrence. "Social Mobility in England, 1500–1700." *Past & Present* 33 (1966): 16–55.

Straat, J. Hendrik, L. Andries van der Ark, and Klaas Sijtsma. "Comparing Optimization Algorithms for Item Selection in Mokken Scale Analysis." *Journal of Classification* 30, no. 1 (2013): 75–99.

Strauss, Barry S. *Athens after the Peloponnesian War: Class, Faction and Policy, 403–386 BC*. Ithaca, NY: Cornell University Press, 1987.

Street, Sharon. "What Is Constructivism in Ethics and Metaethics." *Philosophy Compass* 5, no. 5 (2010): 363–84.

Stromseth, Jane, David Wippman, and Rosa Brooks. *Can Might Make Rights?: Building the Rule of Law after Military Interventions*. New York: Cambridge University Press, 2006.

Summers, Robert S. "A Formal Theory of the Rule of Law." *Ratio Juris* 6, no. 2 (1993): 127–42.

"Principles of the Rule of Law." *Notre Dame Law Review* 74, no. 5 (1999): 1691–712.

Tamanaha, Brian Z. *On the Rule of Law: History, Politics, Theory*. New York: Cambridge University Press, 2004.

"The Dark Side of the Relationship between the Rule of Law and Liberalism." *New York University Journal of Law & Liberty* 3 (2008): 516–47.

"The Rule of Law and Legal Pluralism in Development." *Hague Journal on the Rule of Law* 3, no. 1 (2011): 1–17.

Taylor, Martha C. "Implicating the *Demos*: A Reading of Thucydides on the Rise of the Four Hundred." *Journal of Hellenic Studies* 122 (2002): 91–108.

Teegarden, David A. "The Oath of Demophantos, Revolutionary Mobilization, and the Preservation of the Athenian Democracy." *Hesperia* 81, no. 3 (2012): 433–65.

Thomas, M. A. "What Do the Worldwide Governance Indicators Measure?" *European Journal of Development Research* 22 (2009): 31–54.

Thomas, Rosalind. "Written in Stone? Liberty, Equality, Orality and the Codification of Law." *Bulletin of the Institute of Classical Studies* 40, no. 1 (1995): 59–74.

Thompson, E. P. *Whigs and Hunters: The Origin of the Black Act*. London: Allen Lane, 1975.

Thucydides. *The Landmark Thucydides*. Edited by Robert B. Strassler. Translated by Richard Crawley. New York: Free Press, 1996.

Todd, S. C. *The Shape of Athenian Law*. New York: Oxford University Press, 1993.

Tolnay, Stewart, and E. M. Beck. "Racial Violence and Black Migration in the American South, 1910 to 1930." *American Sociological Review* 57, no. 1 (1992): 103–16.

Tuch, Steven A., and Ronald Weitzer. "Trends: Racial Differences in Attitudes toward the Police." *Public Opinion Quarterly* 61, no. 4 (1997): 642–63.
Turner, Karen. "Rule of Law Ideals in Early China?" *Journal of Chinese Law* 6, no. 1 (1992): 1–44.
United Nations Department of Peacekeeping Operations and the Office of the United Nations High Commissioner for Human Rights. *Rule of Law Indicators: Implementation Guide and Project Tools*, 2011. www.un.org/en/events/peacekeepersday/2011/publications/un_rule_of_law_indicators.pdf.
Upham, Frank. "Mythmaking in the Rule of Law Orthodoxy." *Carnegie Endowment for International Peace Rule of Law Series* (2002).
van Rooij, Benjamin. "Bringing Justice to the Poor, Bottom-Up Approaches to Legal Development Cooperation." *Hague Journal on Rule of Law* 4, no. 2 (2012): 286–318.
van Schuur, Wijbrandt H. "Mokken Scale Analysis: Between the Guttman Scale and Parametric Item Response Theory." *Political Analysis* 11, no. 2 (2003): 139–63.
Vickers, Michael. "Alcibiades at Sparta: Aristophanes' *Birds*." *Classical Quarterly* 45, no. 2 (1995): 339–54.
Visser, Margaret. "Vengeance and Pollution in Classical Athens." *Journal of the History of Ideas* 45, no. 2 (1984): 193–206.
Vlastos, Gregory. "*Isonomia*." *American Journal of Philology* 74, no. 4 (1953): 337–66.
Waldron, Jeremy. "Homelessness and Freedom." *UCLA Law Review* 39 (1991): 295–324.
"Does Law Promise Justice?" *Georgia State University Law Review* 17, no. 3 (March 1, 2001): 759–88.
"Is the Rule of Law an Essentially Contested Concept (in Florida)?" *Law and Philosophy* 21, no. 2 (March 1, 2002): 137–64.
"The Concept and the Rule of Law." *Georgia Law Review* 43, no. 1 (2008): 1–62.
"The Rule of Law and the Importance of Procedure." In *Nomos L: Getting to the Rule of Law*, edited by James E. Fleming, 3–31. New York: New York University Press, 2011a.
"Thoughtfulness and the Rule of Law." *New York University Public Law and Legal Theory*, Working Paper no. 263 (2011b).
Dignity, Rank, and Rights. Edited by Meir Dan-Cohen. New York: Oxford University Press, 2012.
Walker, Geoffrey de Q. *The Rule of Law: Foundation of Constitutional Democracy*. Melbourne: Melbourne University Press, 1988.
Wall, Steven. "Freedom, Interference and Domination." *Political Studies* 49, no. 2 (2001): 216–30.
Watt, John. *The Church in Medieval Ireland*. Dublin: University College Dublin Press, 1998.
Weeks, Jessica L. "Autocratic Audience Costs: Regime Type and Signaling Resolve." *International Organization* 62, no. 1 (2008): 35–64.
Weingast, Barry R. "The Political Foundations of Democracy and the Rule of Law." *American Political Science Review* 91, no. 2 (1997): 245–63.

West, Robin L. *Re-Imagining Justice: Progressive Interpretations of Formal Equality, Rights, and the Rule of Law*. Burlington: Ashgate, 2003.

Western, Bruce, and Becky Pettit. "Incarceration & Social Inequality." *Daedalus* 139, no. 3 (2010): 8–19.

Williamson, John. *Latin American Adjustment: How Much Has Happened?* Washington, DC: Institute for Intentional Economics, 1990.

Willms, Sarah. "'The Five Knights' Case and Debates in the Parliament of 1628: Division and Suspicion under King Charles I." *Constructing the Past* 7, no. 1 (2006): 92–100.

Wolpert, Andrew. *Remembering Defeat: Civil War and Civic Memory in Ancient Athens*. Baltimore: Johns Hopkins University Press, 2001.

Worrall, John L. "Addicted to the Drug War: The Role of Civil Asset Forfeiture as a Budgetary Necessity in Contemporary Law Enforcement." *Journal of Criminal Justice* 29, no. 3 (2001): 171–87.

Wu, Yuning, Rodney Lake, and Liqun Cao. "Race, Social Bonds, and Juvenile Attitudes toward the Police." *Justice Quarterly* (2013): 1–26. doi:10.1080/07418825.2013.778325.

Xenophon. *The Landmark Xenophon's Hellenika*. Edited by Robert B. Strassler. Translated by John Marincola. New York: Anchor Books, 2009.

Index

For EU product safety concerns, contact us at Calle de José Abascal, 56–1°, 28003 Madrid, Spain or eugpsr@cambridge.org.

www.ingramcontent.com/pod-product-compliance
Lightning Source LLC
LaVergne TN
LVHW011524200926
848484LV00001B/139

* 9 7 8 1 1 0 7 1 3 6 8 9 2 *